Teen Genre Connections

Teen Genre Connections

From Booktalking to Booklearning

Lucy Schall

LIBRARIES
UNLIMITED
A Member of the Greenwood Publishing Group

OCT – 2005

Westport, Connecticut • London

Library of Congress Cataloging-in-Publication Data

Schall, Lucy.
    Teen genre connections : from booktalking to booklearning / Lucy Schall.
      p.   cm.
    Includes bibliographical references and index.
    ISBN 1–59158–229–6 (alk. paper)
    1. Teenagers—Books and reading—United States. 2. Book talks—United
States. 3. Reading promotion—United States. 4. Best books. 5. Young adult
literature—Bibliography. 6. Fiction genres—Bibliography. I. Title.
Z1037.A1S2725   2005
028.5'5—dc22   2005014288

British Library Cataloguing in Publication Data is available.

Library of Congress Catalog Card Number: 2005014288
ISBN: 1–59158–229–6

First published in 2005

Libraries Unlimited, 88 Post Road West, Westport, CT 06881
A Member of the Greenwood Publishing Group, Inc.
www.lu.com

Printed in the United States of America

The paper used in this book complies with the
Permanent Paper Standard issued by the National
Information Standards Organization (Z39.48–1984).

10 9 8 7 6 5 4 3 2 1

To Virginia Flynn, my mother,
and Elsie Schall, my mother-in-law,
who dedicated their lives
to their families and encouraged
young people to read,
write, and learn.

Contents

Acknowledgments

I wish to thank Barbara Ittner, my editor, for her insight, encouragement, and patience; Linda Benson, from VOYA, for the generous sharing of her expertise; and Diana Tixier Herald for an excellent organizational model.

The following libraries and media centers have provided me with resources as well as staff support: St. Petersburg Public Library in St. Petersburg, Florida; The Meadville Public Library, The Meadville Middle School and High School Media Center, and the Lawrence Lee Pelletier Library in Meadville, Pennsylvania; Cochranton Public Library in Cochranton, Pennsylvania; and Rocky River Public Library in Rocky River, Ohio.

Introduction

Teen Genre Connections provides motivating titles for librarians, teachers, and families who want to keep teens reading. Professionals who talked with me about my previous books consistently complimented the theme organization but referred to the sections by genre labels. Classification by genre seems user-friendly, attractive to teens, and consistent with publishing trends. So *Teen Genre Connections* takes its cue from Diana Tixier Herald's *Teen Genreflecting: A Guide to Reading Interests, 2nd edition* (2003). The chapter titles come from her book: Issues, Contemporary Life, Adventure/Survival, Mystery/Suspense, Fantasy/Science Fiction/Paranormal, History/Period, and Multiple Cultures. These seven chapters break down into more specific divisions associated with topics and themes. Some mirror Herald's divisions, and some are my own. With excellent writing technique and universal themes, the works within these categories provide starting points for discussions about personal choices, guide students beyond their social studies textbooks, inspire lively book club programs, and keep teens in touch with books while preparing them for a better understanding and appreciation of the classics and more difficult texts.

The bibliography information for featured books and "Related Works" now includes the author name, book title, publisher and date of publication, number of pages, price and ISBN, a bracketed fiction, nonfiction, graphic novel, or reference designation, and a reading level suggestion.

CH = children
M = middle school
J = junior high
S – senior high
A = adult

I emphasize that the reading level is only a suggestion. The abbreviation "pa." indicates paperback. Hopefully, the reading guidelines for these books published between 1999 and 2004 as well as the theme/topic designations, summaries, booktalks, and related works will aid librarians, teachers, and any other professional or nonprofessional working with young people to match books, readers, and researchers.

Booktalks motivate teens to read simply by highlighting good books teens might overlook in well-developed library collections. Effective advertising for the book, library, and media center, booktalks also help teachers who use reading requirements and supplemental book lists to talk about books and coach student reading strategies instead of just making assignments. The booktalks in this volume provide ready-made presentations, or may suggest ideas on which the booktalker can build according to personal style or need. Presenter directions for some of the booktalks are in italics. The booktalks, short enough to hold a teen audience's attention, allow the booktalker to include several books from different genres in a forty-five minute school time slot or pitch an appropriate title for a class opening or conclusion. They can be adapted for a school's morning announcements or the school newspaper and are appropriate for public service segments for the local radio station, newspaper, newsletter, or Web site. Nonprofit use is permitted and encouraged. Advertise!

I have some quick advice for booktalkers:

1. Read every book you booktalk.
2. Booktalk books you respect.
3. Include books from several genres.
4. Note, in your presentation or presentation series, how a book from one genre might relate to a book from another.
5. Invite the audience to choose the books they want to hear about from the books you bring or plan to present.
6. Display the books. Their covers will hold the group's attention.
7. Keep the booktalk short.
8. Hold the book while you talk.
9. Have extra copies so that (if you're lucky) you will have a replacement for the one snatched by an eager reader.
10. Hand out an annotated list at the beginning of the program or series. The audience can refer to it when deciding which books they want to hear about and will revisit it later.
11. Involve your audience, if only with a rhetorical question, at least every five minutes.
12. Read another publication from Libraries Unlimited, *The Booktalker's Bible: How to Talk about the Books You Love to Any Audience* (2003) by Chapple Langemack.

The "Learning Opportunities" present individual and group projects based on the book and "Related Works." The opportunities include discussion topics; ideas for journals, longer papers, poems, or other creative writing; panel discussions, or presentations—visual, oral, or both. Some of the results may even provide a basis for independent studies, portfolios, or senior projects. The discussion questions will promote lively exchanges in any reading group—teenage or teen/adult—or family. All will improve reading, writing, and speaking skills. Any works mentioned in "Learning Opportunities" are listed in "Related Works."

"Related Works" include sources for expanded learning or further reading. The listings include books as well as short stories, plays, poems, articles, and Web sites. These sections will help build booktalk programs or units of study. They also will guide instructors, librarians, and parents to additional reading or information sources. The index includes authors, titles, and topics for a quick overview of a work's relationships to others mentioned in this volume.

Teen Genre Connections is the result of my reading and research guided by recommendations from professional reviews in VOYA, Booklist, School Library Journal, the ALAN Review, as well as award lists and YALSA's "best" booklists. Suggestions from friends, young and old, as well as some unexpected audience reactions also influenced the final choices. Hopefully, this volume provides positive and fruitful suggestions for you too.

Issues

These selections, which deal with physical, mental, emotional, sexual, and moral issues, fall into three divisions. In "Personal Challenges" the obstacle comes from within, and the protagonist acknowledges the challenge. In "Interpersonal Challenges" the challenge comes from dealing with other individuals—the character learns how his or her self-image meshes with the perceptions of others. "Social Challenges" includes stories of maturing or mature individuals who take strength from their experiences and help a community. In most of the selections, these processes overlap. The teen reader, who may be involved in a similar conflict or feeling overwhelmed by a smaller one, gets the message that he or she can do something positive.

Personal Challenges

Gantos, Jack. **Hole in My Life.**
New York: Farrar, Straus and Giroux, 2002. 200p. $16.00.
ISBN 0 374 39988 3. [nonfiction] JS

Themes/Topics: responsibility, crime, prison, writing

Summary/Description

Gantos tells about his willingness to sell and deliver drugs for a ten thousand dollar payoff that would ensure his college education and get him out of a dead-end job. As he describes his independent high school life, his decision to do the job, the crime, and the resulting jail sentence, he emphasizes that he did not have the ability to make good decisions in difficult times, and that his willingness to say "Count me in" almost ended any hope for a positive life. His analysis of his own behavior and his acceptance of responsibility will promote meaningful discussions. His descriptions of drinking, gang rapes, and random violence make the text more appropriate for older teens.

Booktalk

Jack Gantos has every teenager's dream life. His parents let him live on his own, and he does anything he wants. He wants to write, but drinking and drugs keep him pretty busy. Then he gets the perfect job offer—$10,000 and all the hash he can handle. This is 1971. The dream job will pay his college tuition, with change. It's a no brainer. Gantos says, "Count me in." He lines up his reading list, takes a few quick sailing lessons, and cruises right into jail. The prisoners are more interested in his body than his books, and that phrase "Count me in" gets shorter. The guard yells "Count," and the prisoner answers "In"—hour after hour and day after day. Someone always wants to know where he is even though nobody cares who he is. In this school Gantos pays attention, and learns much more than he bargained for. Read about how Gantos managed to do both the crime and the time—an "on the edge of your seat" episode he describes as the *Hole in My Life*.

Learning Opportunities

1. On pages 21 to 23, Gantos describes his journal. Re-read that section and describe your reaction. Plan your own journal, and compare it to others in the group.
2. In Chapter 4 of Part 2, Gantos describes the "I got caught story," tells why he likes them so much, and then tells his own. After reading the chapter again, identify the elements for a good "I got caught story." Now tell one of your own.
3. Gantos makes up a reading list for the sea and a reading list for prison. Choose one of the books on either list. Compare the life it describes to the life that Gantos experiences. Then discuss how reading that particular book might help or hurt Gantos.
4. Using a place, an event, or a job as your topic, make up an interesting reading list. Explain why you chose each work.
5. Above the mirror in his yellow cell, Gantos reads the words "WHAT WE HAVE HERE IS A FAILURE TO COMMUNICATE." Explain how he interprets the statement. Discuss whether or not you agree or disagree with his interpretation.
6. At the beginning of the book is a list of books by Jack Gantos. Read at least one. Discuss its purpose and how the book reflects or does not reflect the information in *Hole in My Life*.

7. In addition to the lists, Gantos alludes to several literary works in the text. Choose one of these works and explain the appropriateness of the allusion. Then compare yourself to one literary character and explain your choice.
8. Discuss the role of Gantos's father and how the father's actions affect Gantos.

Related Works

1. Burgess, Melvin. **Smack.** New York: Henry Holt and Company, 1998. 327p. $16.95. ISBN 0 8050 5801. [fiction] JS. Set in the 1980s, the novel describes the lives of teenage heroin addicts.
2. Clarke, Judith. **The Lost Day.** New York: Henry Holt and Company, 1997. 154p. $16.95. ISBN 0 8050 6152 5. [fiction] JS. Fascinated by nightclubs and Jack Kerouac, a group of teenagers lose their friend who is drugged by a stranger. They begin to question their fantasies and self-sabotaging patterns.
3. Ferris, Jean. **Bad.** New York: Farrar, Straus and Giroux, 1998. 182p. $16.00. ISBN 0374 30479 3. [fiction] JS. (See full booktalk in *Booktalks and More,* pages 137 to 139.) Sentenced to a reform school because she goes along with her friends in a robbery, Dallas finds herself learning about literature, her fellow inmates, and herself.
4. Myers, Walter Dean. **Bad Boy: A Memoir.** [nonfiction] JS. (See full booktalk in "Contemporary"/"Coming of Age" pages 54 to 56.) In this autobiography, Myers explains the choices he had to make while growing up in Harlem.
5. Paulsen, Gary. **The Beet Fields: Memories of a Sixteenth Summer.** New York: Delacorte Press, 2000. 160p. $15.95. ISBN 0 385 32647 5. [fiction] S. This autobiographical novel tells about a young man's travels in his sixteenth summer. He works as a migrant, runs from the police, joins the carnival, and experiences his sexual awakening with the carnival owner's wife.
6. Watterson, Bill. **The Days Are Just Packed.** Kansas City, MO: Andrews and McMeel, 1993. 175p. $14.95. ISBN 1 4046 5938 2. [cartoon strip collection] MJS The Calvin and Hobbes collection contains several strips involving issues related to decision-making. One that might be particularly applicable to *Hole in My Life* and its Related Works is the second strip on page 69 that begins "Paul Gauguin asked, 'Whence do we come? What are we? Where are we going?'"

ℭℨℭℨ
Going, K. L. **Fat Kid Rules the World.**
New York: G. P. Putnam's Sons, 2003. 183p. $17.99. ISBN 0 399 23990 1. [fiction] JS

Themes/Topics: self image, obesity, drug abuse, grief

Summary/Description

Seventeen-year-old Troy Billings, a little over six feet tall and 296 pounds, is so depressed about his appearance that he contemplates suicide. Small, skinny, homeless, drop out Curt MacCrae, a brilliant guitarist and high school legend, befriends Troy and asks him to be a drummer in his band. Curt's attention gives Troy personal confidence as well as status with his classmates and brother. Troy's ex-marine father gives Curt good meals and clean clothes but warns Troy that Curt is a classic drug addict. Mr. Billings realizes, however, that Curt is effecting a positive change in Troy that he is unable to achieve. He encourages Troy to appear with the band. The band finally performs, but Troy must take the critically weakened Curt to the hospital. Realizing how much Curt admires Mr. Billings, and how Curt is manipulating his medicine to stay in the safety of the hospital, Troy works an agreement between his father and Curt. Curt can live with Troy's family but must stay off drugs. In the process, Troy realizes that his father and brother are struggling with his mother's death too and need his help as much or more than he needs theirs. Language and situations that might be considered controversial require a mature audience.

Booktalk

At six foot one, 296 pounds, seventeen-year-old Troy Billings is fat. When he decides to kill himself, his little brother, so fed up with being seen with him, tells him to go ahead. Then a skinny, blond, dirty kid keeps him from jumping off the subway platform and demands that Troy buy him lunch. Curt MacCrae is a homeless high school dropout. That's the bad news. The good news is he's a genius guitar player and a high school legend. The great news is he wants Troy to play drums in his new band—their band. But Troy can't play drums, and his ex-marine father is sure that Curt is a drug addict. Right now, Troy doesn't care about either of those things. Just standing next to Curt MacCrae makes people notice him—even respect him. Troy wants the dream. But reality, drugs, and his lack of skill start to kick in. Is Troy the "Big T" that Curt sees, or just the Fat Kid staring in the mirror every morning? Is

this a case of "FAT KID HALLUCINATES ABOUT COOL FRIEND"
or *Fat Kid Rules the World*?

Learning Opportunities

1. Discuss why Curt is more successful at helping Troy than Troy's
   father is.
2. How does Curt help Troy change his perception of his father?
3. Curt is a positive influence. Is he handling his own life in a positive way?
4. Addiction to both drugs and food is a major issue in the story. Using
   your library's resources, research programs for addiction to food, drugs,
   or both. Share with the group what these programs have in common.
5. *St. Michael's Scales* (Related Work 3) and *Fat Kid Rules the World*
   both deal with size, depression, self-concept, and grief. After reading both novels, discuss which book had more impact for you.

Related Works

1. Bennett, Cherie. **Life in the Fat Lane.** New York: Delacorte
   Press, 1998. 260p. $15.95. ISBN 0 385 32274 7. (See full booktalk
   in *Booktalks Plus*, 2001, pages 1 to 3.) [fiction] MJS Lara Ardeche,
   perfect and popular, develops a condition that balloons her weight
   to over 200 pounds. She must abandon her stereotypes of fat people
   and deal with the life crises that the weight gain brings.
2. Brooks, Martha. **True Confessions of a Heartless Girl.** New York:
   Farrar, Straus and Giroux, 2003. 181p. $16.00. ISBN 0 374 37806 1.
   [fiction] JS Like Curt, the main character is an outlaw type visitor
   from an unstable home who shakes up the community yet becomes
   part of it.
3. Connelly, Neil. **St. Michael's Scales.** [fiction] JS (See full booktalk
   in "Contemporary Life"/"Sports" pages 59 to 61.) Like Troy, the
   main character plans to kill himself until joining the wrestling team
   builds his self-concept and helps him discover that he has the power
   to help another person who is also struggling with grief.
4. Holt, Kimberly Willis. **Keeper of the Night.** [fiction] JS (See full
   booktalk in "Multiple Cultures"/"World Cultures" pages 278 to
   280.) After the mother's suicide, the family members deteriorate
   until they decide to help each other.
5. Holt, Kimberly Willis. **When Zachary Beaver Came to Town.**
   New York: Henry Holt and Company, 1999. 227p. $16.95.
   ISBN 0 8050 6116 9. [fiction] MJS (See full booktalk in *Booktalks*

and More, 2003, pages 86 to 88.) The supposedly fattest boy in the world comes to a small Texas town and forces its citizens to come to grips with their own fantasies.

こ♪ こ

Hautman, Pete. **Sweetblood.**

New York: Simon & Schuster Books for Young Readers, 2003. 180p. $16.95.
ISBN 0 689 85048 4. [fiction] JS

Themes/Topics: diabetes, Goth, Internet stalking

Summary/Description

Sixteen-year-old Lucy Szabo believes her diabetes stems from rabies shots her father forced her to take at six, and that diabetics in the Middle Ages were misperceived as vampires. She abandons her schoolwork, goes Goth, and becomes involved in an Internet chat room under the identity of Sweet-blood where Draco, claiming to be a real vampire, fascinates her. Her best friend, Mark Murphy, tells her she is weird and her parents, alarmed by her behavior, ground her and take away her computer. Meanwhile, she meets Dylan Redfield, a new student and fellow Goth who connects her with a forty-year-old self-proclaimed vampire named Wayne who regularly hosts Goth teenagers in his apartment. She sneaks out of the house to attend the parties, abuses her health, and persuades Mark Murphy to help her maintain her Internet chats. The story climaxes at Wayne's Halloween party. Perceiving Wayne to be a pathetic old man pursuing young girls, Lucy leaves the party alone in an ice storm, and passes out behind Mark's house. Mark finds her in the morning, gets her to the hospital, and saves her life. She discovers her heart stopped beating for two minutes and the people who were there when she came back to life—her mother, father, and Mark—love her. She takes the black color out of her hair, develops a civil attitude toward her parents, and picks up her relationship with Mark.

Booktalk

Sixteen-year-old Lucy Szabo is a vampire. Actually, Lucy is diabetic, but she has a theory that vampires of the Middle Ages were really diabetics. The sleeping, confusion, sweet and sour smells, ravenous appetite, sweating, bloody mouth, and comas were misinterpreted as vampire traits. So Lucy decides to go with the flow of the Middle Ages. She'll dress up her disease with Goth—black hair, black clothes, and a personality to make people think she'll bite their heads off. Then someone new enters her life—a fascinating voice on the computer named Draco, a real vampire, not a poser. Trouble starts when cyberspace Draco becomes flesh, willing to invite her into his home, and very willing to drink her *Sweetblood.*

Learning Opportunities

1. Read *The Stranger* (Related Work 1) and *The Metamorphosis* (Related Work 4). Discuss why these two pieces of literature are important to Lucy.
2. Lines from Walt Whitman's poetry conclude the second chapter. After reading them, discuss how they apply or fail to apply to Lucy by the end of the novel.
3. Butterflies are a central part of the story. Cite the passages in which they appear, and then discuss their significance throughout the novel.
4. Using your library's resources, research the symptoms and treatment of diabetes. Share the information with the group. Discuss how the information you find affects your understanding of the novel.
5. The tattoo artist and Dr. Rick both give Lucy something to think about. List the messages each person gives and the effectiveness of each.
6. Lucy's name means light. Discuss how that detail impacts the story. Be sure to consider, in your discussion, some of Lucy's conclusions about her situation.
7. Throughout most of the novel, Lucy thinks her parents are stupid. Do you?

Related Works

1. Camus, Albert. **The Stranger.** New York: Vintage International Vintage Books, 1989. 123p. $9.95pa. ISBN 0 679 72020 0. [fiction] S/A A young man, on trial for murder and alienated from society, finds that he is being judged by how the jury perceives him rather than what he has actually done.
2. Dominick, Andie. **Needles.** New York: Scribner, 1998. 220p. $22.00. ISBN 0 684 84232 7. [nonfiction] S/A (See full booktalk in *Booktalks and More*, 2003, pages 175 to 177.) Andie Dominick tells about how destructive diabetes was to her life until she stopped following her older sister's abusive patterns.

3.   Huegel, Kelly. **Young People and Chronic Illness: True Stories, Help, and Hope.** Minneapolis, MN: Free Spirit, 1998. 198p. $14.95pa. ISBN 1 57542 041 4. [nonfiction] JS. Written by a person with Crohn's disease who decided to deny rather than discuss her disease, this book uses case studies and communication techniques to persuade a young person that being open about chronic illness is necessary.

4.   Kafka, Franz, and Stanley Corngold (trans. and ed.). **The Metamorphosis.** New York: Bantam Books, 1972. 201p. $5.95pa. ISBN 0 553 21369 5. [fiction] S A young man, taken advantage of by his family, wakes up one day and discovers that he has been transformed into a bug.

5.   Whitcher, Susan. **The Fool Reversed.** New York: Farrar, Straus and Giroux, 2000. 183p. $16.00. ISBN 0 374 32446 8. [fiction] S A young girl, trusting her future to tarot cards, has an affair with a twenty-nine-year-old man.

ᘓᘔ

Koja, Kathe. Straydog.

New York: Farrar, Straus and Giroux/Frances Foster Books, 2002. 106p. $16.00.
ISBN 0 374 37278 0. [fiction] JS

Themes/Topics: emotional and behavioral problems,
animal management

Summary/Description

Rachel, an individualistic and rebellious high school student, volunteers at an animal shelter where she decides to save an injured feral dog she names Grrl. Like Grrl, Rachel, hurt by neglect and abuse, lashes out at everyone around her. Reading Rachel's essay about Grrl, the English teacher encourages her to enter a writing contest. The prize will allow Rachel to work with a published author. While working with Grrl and expanding the essay, Rachel meets Griffin, a new boy in school who shares her writing interest, defends her against the in-group, and plans to build a pen for Grrl in his backyard. But before the plans are complete, the shelter authorities put the dog to sleep. Rachel's violent response to the shelter's decision tests her friendship with Griffin and ends her volunteer job at the shelter. Thinking about the reactions of those she respects and the writing she has completed, she realizes how hostile and selfish she has been.

She reconnects with Griffin and treats her mother more respectfully. Although she does not win the writing internship, she gets a paying job at Pet Depot, shares a new dog with Griffin, and begins to appreciate her supporters.

Booktalk

Rachel just endures high school—even though she is really smart. Her two favorite things are animals and writing. Everyday she goes to her dream job as a volunteer at the animal shelter and writes. In fact, she has notebooks stacked to the ceiling. But talking to and writing about animals doesn't give her much time or patience for people— especially peers and parents. Then she meets Grrl and Griffin. Grrl is a street dog that'll bite anyone who comes near. Griffin is the new kid in school, an outsider and writer like her. Rachel thinks the three will make a good team building a world filled with "happily ever after." But when fact collides with fiction, Rachel has to face the real world's story, not the feel good version—and discovers that she has more in common with that fighting, biting *Straydog* than she ever thought possible.

Learning Opportunities

1. Discuss the parents in the novel and the reliability of Rachel's descriptions of them.
2. On page 47, when Griffin asks about her work at the animal shelter, Rachel tells the starfish story. Read the story aloud in the group; discuss it in relation to the novel. Then discuss it in relation to your own lives.
3. Rachel alludes to *The Outsiders* (Related Work 3) by S. E. Hinton and the Robert Frost poem "Nothing Gold Can Stay" (Related Work 4), which is a central part of *The Outsiders*. After reading both, discuss why they are appropriate allusions for *Straydog*.
4. On pages 65 and 66, Mrs. Cruzelle talks about Rachel needing a bigger world. Discuss her observation and how it applies to Rachel and to high school in general.
5. On pages 71 to 73, Rachel and Griffin discuss the problem of being a geek. In the novel *My Heartbeat* (Related Work 2), the father identifies a geek as a person who often has "A mind with its own heartbeat." Discuss whether or not Rachel and Griffin are geeks who fit that description.
6. In Chapter 10, Rachel realizes what Grrl has taught her about herself. What does she say she has learned? Would you agree

with her? Would you add some things that you learned about Rachel also?

7. Reread the final addition to Rachel's story. Do you feel the ending is appropriate or just an attempt by Rachel to experience a happy ending?

8. Using your library's resources and visiting your local animal shelter, research the procedures and policies used to care for and help stray or abandoned animals. Prepare a presentation or display that communicates what you feel to be their most important efforts or services.

Related Works

1. Carlson, Richard. **Don't Sweat the Small Stuff for Teens: Simple Ways to Keep Your Cool in Stressful Times.** New York: Hyperion, 2000. 242p. $11.95pa. ISBN 0 7868 8597 1. [nonfiction] MJS In the essay, "Convince Yourself That One Teen Does Make a Difference," pages 10 and 11, Carlson asserts that actions, even small ones, do make a difference, and he uses an animal shelter example to support his point.

2. Freymann Weyr, Garret. **My Heartbeat.** [fiction] JS (See full booktalk under "Issues"/"Interpersonal Challenges," pages 21 to 23.) In this novel, a brother, sister, and best friend try to discover their love for each other and their sexual orientation.

3. Hinton, S. E. **The Outsiders.** New York: Penguin Putnam, Inc/ Speak, 1995. 180p. $6.99. ISBN 0 14 03572 X. [fiction] MJS This classic young adult story of the school in/out groups includes the poem "Nothing Gold Can Stay" on page 77. This edition has an interview with Hinton.

4. Lathem, Connery (ed.). **The Poetry of Robert Frost: The Collected Poems.** New York: An Owl Book/Henry Holt and Company, 1975. 607p. $18.00. ISBN 0 8050 6986 0. [poetry] S/A The poem, "Nothing Gold Can Stay" appears on pages 222–223.

5. Paulson, Gary. **My Life in Dog Years.** New York: Dell, 1998. 137p. $4.99pa. ISBN 0440 41471 7. [nonfiction] MJS Paulson writes character sketches for eight significant dogs in his life.

6. Turner, Chérie. **The Riot Grrrl Movement: The Feminism of a New Generation.** New York: The Rosen Publishing Group, Inc., 2001. 64p. (Everything You Need to Know.) $25.25. ISBN 0 8239 3400 4. [nonfiction] MJS Turner defines the movement, describes its audience and impact, and explains what is happening to it today.

ᘓ ᘔ

Lawrence, Iain. Ghost Boy.

New York: Delacorte Press, 2000. 326p. $15.95. ISBN 0 385 32739 0. [fiction] MJS

Themes/Topics: labeling, self-reliance, grief, friendship, circus, World War II setting

Summary/Description

Fourteen-year-old Harold Kline is an albino. His father was killed in World War II, and Harold has waited two years for his brother Dave, missing in action, to return. Grief transformed his mother into an overweight nagging woman dominated by Harold's cold and opinionated stepfather. The town bullies call Harold geek, freak, and ghost. Harold runs away with a traveling circus, and the freaks welcome him. Harold seeks the circus's elusive Cannibal King, also an albino, to give him answers for his life. Harold's talent with animals attracts the bareback rider, who emotionally manipulates him so that he will teach her elephants how to play baseball, her ticket to a bigger circus. Harold unifies the entire crew in an elephant baseball game. An elephant tramples one of Harold's best friends. Devastated, Harold returns home, appreciating that his mother has been suffering from loss, and that he has responsibility for defining his own character.

Booktalk

Ask if anyone in the group knows the meaning of albino.

Fourteen-year-old Harold Kline is an albino. He is the *Ghost Boy.* Somebody in town wrote a poem about him. *Read the poem in italics on page 3.* That's why Harold's only friend is his dog. Harold spends every week waiting for the train. His big brother Dave, declared missing in action during World War II never gets off. Harold never gets on. Then a circus gives Harold a place to fit in—the freak show. The main attraction—The Cannibal King—looks just like Harold, and yet he is a king—an important person. Harold wants to find out the king's secrets. So he leaves the town that hates him and the mother who nags him in order to join the circus—a world where the tiny Princess Minikin, the ugly Fossil Man, the mysterious Gypsy Magda, the beautiful Flip Pharaoh, the bearded Esther, the armless and legless Sausage Man, and the wise Thunder Wakes Him live in harmony. Or do they? In *Ghost Boy*, Harold follows a dream, and like the real world, all the nightmare consequences that come with it.

Learning Opportunities

1. Although Gypsy Magda seems to be the character that dispenses wisdom and tells the future, Harold learns from each of the characters he meets. List each character and what you think each teaches him. Use specifics from the text to support your opinion. Then compare your list with the lists of others in the group.

2. Harold leaves his small town, enters what we might consider a fantasy world, and then returns to the real world changed or transformed. Discuss the characteristics that the fantasy world shares with his own world, what he learns in that world, and how the lessons change him. Be sure to research the name "Elysium" in Chapter 44 and include in the discussion the information that you find.

3. The elephants are central to the story. Discuss their importance. Include in your discussion the trampling of Princess Minikin and the destruction of Conrad.

4. Like *Secret Heart* (Related Work 1), *Ghost Boy* uses the circus to transform the life of a bullied, physically challenged teenager. After reading the two novels, compare how the authors use the circus, the bullies, a beautiful girl, and the main character's physical challenges and talents to accomplish the story's purpose.

5. Using your library's resources, research the physical challenges that an albino person faces. Share the information with the group and discuss how those facts add to an understanding of the story.

6. On page 72 of *More Than a Label* (Related Work 4), the "Try It!" exercise suggests that a victim of labeling should write a letter to his or her labelers. Write two letters from Harold to his bullies. The first letter should be written before he runs away with the circus and the second when he returns.

Related Works

1. Almond, David. **Secret Heart.** New York: Delacorte Press, 2001. 199p. $17.99. ISBN 0 385 90065 1. [fiction] JS Bullied Joe Maloney finds a new perspective on life when a circus, which sees him as their savior, comes to town.

2. Granfield, Linda. **Circus: An Album.** New York: DK Ink, 1998. 96p. $19.95. ISBN 0 7894 2453 3. [nonfiction] MJS (See full book-talk in *Booktalks Plus*, 2001, pages 206 to 208.) *Circus: An Album* tells about the history and operation of the circus from ancient Egypt to modern international circuses.

3. Holt, Kimberly Willis. **When Zachary Beaver Came to Town.** New York: Henry Holt and Company, 1999. 227p. $16.95.

ISBN 0 8050 6116 9. [fiction] MJS (See full booktalk in *Booktalks and More,* 2003, pages 86 to 88.) Zachary Beaver, the "fattest boy in the world" makes his living as a freak, but stirs up town secrets when his trailer roles into Antler, Texas.

4. Muharrar, Aisha. **More Than a Label.** Minneapolis, MN: Free Spirit Publishing Inc., 2002. 144p. $13.95pa. ISBN 1 57542 110 0. [nonfiction] JS Muharrar distinguishes between labels and slurs and explains how each is a form of peer pressure. She provides extensive references for dealing with bullying and peer acceptance.

5. Peck, Robert Newton. **Cowboy Ghost.** New York: HarperCollins Children's Books, 1999. 200p. $15.95. ISBN 0 06 028168 5. [fiction] MJS Sixteen-year-old Titus, the family runt, proves his toughness to his distant father when he takes over the family cattle drive after Micah, Titus's brother and real father figure, is killed.

ভ৩

Nolan, Han. **Born Blue.**

New York: Harcourt, Inc., 2001. 177p. $17.00. ISBN 0 15 201916 2. [fiction] JS

Themes/Topics: foster care, drug abuse, pregnancy, talent, personal responsibility, blues

Summary/Description

Janie tells about her life from the time she is four years old when she is rescued from drowning to when she is sixteen and decides to leave her illegitimate daughter with a loving and caring family. After the near drowning accident caused by her heroin-addicted mother's neglect, Janie is placed in an abusive foster home. She bonds with seven-year-old, African-American Harmon who introduces her to the music of lady blues singers around whom she focuses her life. Finding more kindness from African-Americans than whites, Janie takes on an African-American identity—Leshaya. Her mother trades Janie to a drug dealer and his wife in exchange for a guaranteed heroin supply. She lives with the dysfunctional couple until their arrest. With stolen money, she moves in with Harmon's adopted family. Stealing, lying, experimenting with drugs and sex, she is sent to a foster home where she discovers her pregnancy. Afraid the authorities will place her baby in foster care, she runs away but leaves her child with Harmon. She uses people to pursue her music dream, but loses each one through her betrayals. Finally, she returns to her real mother who is dying of AIDS. The mother's caregiver forces them to talk. Leshaya pours out her pain in music—the blues, discovers her mother came from a wealthy and supportive family, and sees what she, herself, may become if she pursues drugs and casual sex. She plans to steal her baby back, but seeing her as part of a happy family, Janie continues her solo journey. Controversial subject matter and adult language require a mature reader.

Booktalk

Janie's mother is a heroin addict. Her mother forgets where Janie is one day, and Janie almost drowns. That's when the authorities take four-year-old Janie away. They put her in the "stink house" with Patsy and Pete who don't care if she is there or not. So Janie makes friends with seven-year-old Harmon Finch who always guards a shoebox filled with his daddy's music tapes. When Harmon plays them for her, Janie meets the ladies—Ella Fitzgerald, Odetta, Sarah Vaughan, Etta James, Billie Holiday, and Roberta Flack. She decides to join them—in their songs, their lives, and their trouble. The ladies won't leave her—ever—and throughout life's changes Janie discovers that she really wasn't born just Janie. She was *Born Blue.*

Learning Opportunities

1. On pages 4 and 211, Janie lists several jazz artists. Choose one of the artists mentioned. Using your library's resources, research the person's life and contribution to jazz. Share your information with the group or combine your information with that found by others and create a visual display or musical presentation.
2. List each person with whom Janie lives. Explain how each person affects her life.
3. Janie moves from one relationship to another and destroys it. Because of this, Mrs. Trane says Janie, like her mother, is a bridge burner. Discuss that evaluation. Before starting the discussion you might wish to refer to essays "Go the Extra Mile," and "Don't Burn Bridges" in *Don't Sweat the Small Stuff for Teens: Simple Ways to Keep Your Cool in Stressful Times* (Related Work 1).
4. As Janie describes her life, what does she reveal about herself?
5. Discuss the ending of the book. Do you agree with Nolan's choices?
6. Write an epilogue for the book. Explain what happens to each character.

Related Works

1. Carlson, Richard. **Don't Sweat the Small Stuff for Teens: Simple Ways to Keep Your Cool in Stressful Times.** New York: Hyperion, 2000. 242p. $11.95pa. ISBN 0 7868 8597 1. [nonfiction] JS "Go the Extra Mile" on pages 140 to 141 and "Don't Burn Bridges" on pages 153 to 154 talk about how life decisions affect our circumstances the rest of our lives. The group might discuss how the essays apply to several characters in the novel.

2. Elmer, Howard. **Blues: Its Birth and Growth.** New York: The Rosen Publishing Group, 1999. 64p. (The Library of African-American Arts and Culture.) $17.95. ISBN 0 8239 1853 X. [nonfiction] MJS (See full booktalk in *Booktalks Plus*, 2001, pages 201 to 203.) Elmer traces the history of blues and explains how they have been used, as Leshaya uses them, to express pain and communicate hidden messages.

3. Fleischman, Paul. **Breakout.** Chicago: Cricket Books /A Marcato Book, 2003. 124p. $15.95. ISBN 0 8126 2696 6. [fiction] JS In alternating chapters, seventeen-year-old Del speaks as she is stuck in a traffic jam after her flight from California where she has been bounced from one foster home to another, and then, eight years later, as she performs on the opening night of her one woman show about a Los Angeles traffic jam.

4. Hacker, Carlotta. **Great African Americans in Jazz.** New York: Crabtree Publishing, 1997. 64p. (Outstanding African Americans.) $8.95pa. ISBN 0 86505 818 0. [nonfiction] MJS Hacker describes the obstacles and triumphs of various jazz performers.

5. Powell, Randy. **Tribute to Another Dead Rock Star.** New York: Farrar, Straus and Giroux, 1999. 215p. $17.00. ISBN 0 374 37748 0. [fiction] JS (See full booktalk in *Booktalks and More*, 2003, pages 203 to 205.) The son of a famous rock star admits that his mother's lifestyle damaged both her and her family.

Interpersonal Challenges

෬෬

Brashares, Ann. The Sisterhood of the Traveling Pants.

New York: Delacorte Press, 2001. 294p. $8.95pa. ISBN 0 385 73058 6.
[fiction] JS

Themes/Topics: friendship, love, family, death, faith

Summary/Description

Four lifelong friends—Bridget, Lena, Carmen, and Tibby—separate during their fifteenth summer. To symbolize their commitment to each other, they circulate a pair of thrift store jeans that magically fits each of them. They compose ten rules for the pants. Their experiences and letters make up the novel. Bridget attends a camp for talented athletes where she aggressively pursues a nineteen-year-old camp counselor, and when the romance fails, she crashes emotionally. Lena and her sister travel to Greece to get acquainted with their grandparents. Lena spurns the attentions of a young man whom her grandparents love and admire and must clarify dangerous misunderstandings with both the young man and her grandparents. Carmen, invited to her father's home and wedding, recalls how the father deserted her and her mother, and she envies his closeness with his new family. She returns home and works through violent feelings until Tibby persuades her to attend his wedding. Working at a discount store, Tibby encounters Bailey, a thorny twelve-year-old with leukemia. When Bailey embraces Tibby's dream of making a documentary, Tibby discovers Bailey's insight and compassion. Their friendship teaches Tibby to look past appearances and connect with her own unconventional family. All discover their friendship is stronger because each is a stronger individual. A quotation keys each chapter.

Booktalk

Athletic Bridget, beautiful Lena, hot-tempered Carmen, and rebellious Tibby spent their summers together since before they were born. Their mothers met in an aerobics class for pregnant women and all gave birth in September. But the foursome's fifteenth summer is different. Bridget signs up for a hotshot athletic camp. Lena visits her grandparents in Greece. Carmen travels to her father's house for the first time. Only Tibby is stuck at home. She is modeling her polyester employee smock at some discount store whose name begins with a W. They know separation could mean the end of a beautiful friendship. Then Tibby decides she wants Carmen's thrift store pants as some kind of consolation prize. They probably won't fit because Carmen's rear end is way different than the other three, but Tibby insists. She tries them on. They look fantastic. The other three try them on. They look fantastic. Impossible? The foursome thinks so too. They also figure that if life handed them a magical pair of pants, they better do something about it. They do. They make up ten incredible rules (*Read the rules*) and form *The Sisterhood of the Traveling Pants*. By the end of this summer, the pants have some pretty phenomenal stories to tell.

ꗉꗊ

Brashares, Ann. **The Second Summer of the Sisterhood.**

New York: Delacorte Press, 2003. 373p. $15.95. ISBN 0 385 90852 0. [fiction] JS

Themes/Topics: friendship, love, family, death, faith

Summary/Description

In the sixteenth summer, the pants travel again. Bridget decides to anonymously visit her maternal grandmother in Burgess, Alabama. She bonds with her grandmother, learns about her emotionally unstable mother, reunites with her elementary school soccer team, and develops a love relationship with her childhood pal and soccer partner, Billy.

Tibby leaves for a film camp. She cultivates two shallow friends who encourage her to do a sarcastic movie about her mother. Brian arrives and criticizes the film. When her mother's reaction proves him right, Tibby redirects her energy to a film about Bailey. She mends her own relationships and helps everyone connected with Bailey to work through their grief. Lena works in a dress shop and dreams about Kostos. He arrives, and they renew their relationship, but when the family returns to Greece for the grandfather's funeral, Lena discovers that Kostos is married. She then meets Carmen's stepbrother and develops an immediate attraction to him. Carmen focuses on destroying her mother's dating relationship and misses the opportunity to develop her own. When her stepsister appears and acts like the Carmen she worships, Carmen realizes how divisive and offensive she is. (See summary for *Sisterhood of the Traveling Pants* for general features of both books.)

Booktalk

As you are talking, display a copy of both The Sisterhood of the Traveling Pants *and* The Second Summer of the Sisterhood.

Bridget, Tibby, Lena, and Carmen, the four members of the Sisterhood, had a wonderful summer last year searching for adventure and meeting challenges with the help of a very forgiving pair of jeans—jeans that seemed to love them all enough to fit each very different girl perfectly. Now the second summer is here. Last year's plan worked so well, they decide to try it again. But this year is different. The pants don't seem to want to be part of what each girl has become. And this year the girls' journeys are different too. Carmen's mother has a new boyfriend. Brian mysteriously appears wherever Tibby is. Lena has some big surprise visitors. The only traveler is Bridget, who digs for family secrets. It's not quite the same as last summer, but it's still funny, frightening, and fabulous. It's *The Second Summer of the Sisterhood.*

Learning Opportunities

1. In the first book, Carmen and Tibby learn more about themselves and family. Bridget and Lena learn more about themselves and romance. Compare the stories in each pair.
2. In the second book, all four girls learn more about themselves in relation to their mothers. Discuss how each relationship is the same and different. List the qualities of each girl. Then make a collage representing each girl's character.
3. In the first book, Tibby is the only one of the four who does not travel, but Bailey, her unexpected friend, provides a personal journey for her. Explain the role that Bailey takes in the story.
4. In the second book, the journey of self-discovery comes primarily through visitors. List each visitor and the lessons they bring.
5. Each summer experience involves trust or faith. Discuss what each girl learns about faith.
6. Discuss the appropriateness of the pants as a symbol. Why not a necklace, shoes, or a shirt?
7. Compare the role of the pants in the first and second book.

Related Works

1. Dessen, Sarah. **Keeping the Moon.** New York: Viking Press, 1999. 228p. $15.99. ISBN 0 670 88549 5. [fiction] JS (See full booktalk in *Booktalks and More,* 2003, pages 82 to 84.) Nicole Sparks learns about self-confidence, love, and friendship when she spends the summer with her eccentric aunt.
2. Dessen, Sarah. **Someone Like You.** New York: Viking Press, 1998. 281p. $15.99. ISBN 0 670 87778 6. [fiction] JS (See full booktalk in *Booktalks and More,* 2003, pages 219 to 221.) Halley and Scarlett form a stronger friendship during the summer that Scarlett becomes pregnant and decides to have her baby.
3. Dexter, Catherine. **Driving Lessons.** Cambridge, MA: Candlewick Press, 2000. 152p. $16.99. ISBN 0 7636 0515 8. [fiction] JS Fourteen-year-old Mattie Lewis visits her Mother's friend in South Dakota while her mother decides whether or not to marry again. Mattie acts out her anger with delinquent and manipulative acts.
4. Mosier, Elizabeth. **My Life As a Girl.** New York: Random House, 1999. 193p. $17.00. ISBN 0 679 89035 1. [fiction] S (See full booktalk

in *Booktalks Plus*, 2001, pages 121 to 123.) During her summer working at a restaurant and her freshman year at Bryn Mawr, Jaime makes decisions about achievement and romance.

5. Stern, Jerome. **Making Shapely Fiction.** New York: Dell Publishing, 1991. 283p. $6.50pa. ISBN 0 440 21221 9. [nonfiction] S/A Stern describes different types of stories. Two of these are "Journey," pages 33 to 36, and "Visitation," pages 37 to 39.

෬෪

Flinn, Alex. **Breathing Underwater.**
New York: HarperCollins Publishers, 2001. 263p. $15.95.
ISBN 0 06 029198 2. [fiction] JS

Themes/Topics: abuse, love, friendship

Summary/Description

Caitlin Alyssa McCourt takes sixteen-year-old Nick Andreas to court for beating her. The Judge issues a restraining order and sentences him to six months of family violence and anger management classes. She also requires him to write 500 words per week explaining what happened between him and Caitlin from the first time he saw her until the court appearance. Combining narrative and journal entries, Nick describes his relationship with Caitlin, his best friend Tom, his abusive father, and Mario Ortega, his anger management instructor. He tries to defy the restraining order and win Caitlin back, but eventually discovers the difference between love and possessiveness, and that his actions mirror the abuse he receives from his father. He envies Tom, a high achiever from a stable family. After Mario shares his experience as an abused abuser, Nick realizes that his relationship with Caitlin is over and decides to take the class again so that he can build healthy, stable relationships.

Booktalk

Sixteen-year-old Nick is good at *Breathing Underwater*, even though he doesn't know it. He lives in a beautiful house with his mega-rich father and drives his own expensive car. Mom left years ago. His father beat her. She was just a mistake; Nick is another mistake. But his dad is going to correct that one, even if it means beating Nick every day to do it. Nick handles it. He tells people he has the flu or that he fell down the stairs. No one really knows what Nick's life is like; how just being himself, just breathing, can set his father off. Then Nick starts coming up for air. He finds Caitlin Alyssa McCourt and falls in love. He can talk to her, but she is so pretty and nice that someone else might want to talk to her too. He won't let that happen. He'll keep her for himself. After all, he learned all about taking control from a great teacher—his father. But now he's learning something else. People who keep *Breathing Underwater* drown.

Learning Opportunities

1. Read "Teammates" on page 179. Discuss its significance in the novel. Following the assignment's directions, write your own poem.
2. Continue to research generational abuse and how the cycle might be broken. Share the information you find with the group.
3. Mr. Ortega sets classroom rules. Discuss their appropriateness for any discussion group and how they relate to Nick's father.
4. Nick distinguishes between parents and "sperm donors." Discuss the implications the distinction has for parental responsibilities.
5. On page 131, Mario asks each person in the group to write a personal Violence Policy. Follow the same directions. Write your own policy and compare it with the policy of other members.
6. Mario reminds the class of the three C's—"compromise, communication, and control." Describe a difficult situation you have experienced or observed to which those three words apply.
7. Leo's character parallels Nick's and causes him to see his own dangerous behavior. List the other characters in the novel. Explain what each character reveals about Nick.
8. Discuss the significance of the title.

Related Works

1. Dessen, Sarah. **Dreamland.** New York: Viking, 2000. 250p. $15.99. ISBN 0 670 89122 3. [fiction] JS (See full booktalk in *Booktalks and More,* 2003, pages 73 to 75.) Caitlin O'Koren is physically and psychologically abused by her boyfriend, whom she allows to control her life.
2. Klass, David. **You Don't Know Me.** New York: Farrar, Straus and Giroux/Frances Foster Books, 2001. 262p. $17.00. ISBN 0 374 38706 0. [fiction] JS (See full booktalk in *Booktalks and More,* 2003, pages 31 to 33.) A young man, abused by his mother's live-in boyfriend, mistrusts and criticizes everyone around him.
3. Lisle, Janet Taylor. **The Art of Keeping Cool.** New York: Atheneum Books for Young Readers, 2000. 207p. $17.00. ISBN 0 689 83787 9.

[fiction] MJ A young man living with his grandparents during World War II discovers that his father left home because of the boy's controlling and abusive grandfather.

4. McGraw, Jay. **Life Strategies for Teens.** (See full booktalk in "Contemporary Life"/"Coming of Age," pages 52 to 54.) This teen version of *Life Strategies* explains the ten laws of life according to Dr. Phillip C. McGraw, Jay's father. In the chapter explaining "Life Law Eight," Jay McGraw explains how behavior encourages people to react to a person in a certain way. He also distinguishes between normal and abnormal treatment.

5. Sparks, Beatrice, ed. **Annie's Baby: The Diary of Anonymous, A Pregnant Teenager.** New York: Avon Books, 1998. 245p. $4.50pa. ISBN 0 380 79141 2. [fiction] JS Fourteen-year-old Annie agrees to have sex with a popular boy who draws her into an abusive relationship that ends in pregnancy.

෪ඏ

Freymann-Weyr, Garret. My Heartbeat.

Boston, MA: Houghton Mifflin Co., 2002. 154p. $15.00.
ISBN 0 618 14181 2. [fiction] JS

Themes/Topics: friendship, sexual identity, family, social pressure

Summary/Description

Raised in an upper-class, intellectual world by yuppie parents, Ellen McConnell, the narrator, tells about the love triangle among her brother, his friend, and herself from her twelfth to fifteenth year. Ellen's parents fear that her brother, Link, and his friend, James, have a homosexual relationship. When Ellen asks her brother if he is gay, he begins dating a girl and distances himself from James. Realizing the fear and anxiety that drives the relationship, James, who has had homosexual relationships with three other men, maintains his friendship with Link in a different form and decides to date Ellen, who adores him. Through therapy, both young men learn the roots of their fears and feelings about family, achievement, and sexual identity. Fifteen-year-old Ellen, believing that James will eventually find someone else, pressures him to have sexual intercourse with her. In the end, neither James nor Link has decided if they are gay, but claim the right to be so without public judgment.

Booktalk

Link and James, two high school seniors, are inseparable. Ellen McConnell, Link's fourteen-year-old sister, thinks that's great, because more often than not, they let her make it a threesome. She loves to talk about all the books and movies the friends read and watch. But she really would do anything just to hang out with the gorgeous James. All the girls in her class want to date him. Then her girlfriends start asking an embarrassing question—Are Link and James more than just best friends? Ellen worries about that herself; so have her parents. Should she ask the question? Will knowing make a difference? Maybe not, but asking the question does, and all three must decide if the most precious thing in life is someone else's approval or "a mind with its own heartbeat."

Learning Opportunities

1. Throughout the novel, Ellen refers to *Age of Innocence* (Related Work 5) and *Jane Eyre* (Related Work 1). After reading both novels, discuss why the author alluded to them.
2. On pages 66 and 67, James and Ellen imagine the possessions and lives of complete strangers. Do the same. Then write a character sketch or poem about one stranger.
3. At the end of Chapter 11, on page 90, Ellen describes her family: "we are strangers who occasionally realize we are still living together." After reading the novel, agree or disagree with her assessment. Then, in one sentence, describe your own family. Compare your description with the descriptions of others.
4. In many situations from the novel, sex and love seem to be two very different things. Identify situations in which one seems separated from the other. Identify situations in which the two blend. Compare and contrast the circumstances.
5. Using your library's resources, research factors that may determine sexual identity. Share you information with the group.
6. Choose one character with whom you sympathize. Explain why you sympathize with the character. Then evaluate the character's judgment throughout the novel.
7. Explain the role of the parents in the novel.

Related Works

1. Bronte, Charlotte. **Jane Eyre.** New York: Signet Classics, 1997. 465p. $4.95pa. ISBN 0 451 52655 4. [fiction] JS The Introduction by Erica Jong points out that this popular 1848 novel, greatly attacked

by critics, depicts a woman as a complex human being. At that time the novel was a "pilgrimage" for women who dared to be proud.

2. Chambers, Aidan. **Postcards from No Man's Land.** New York: Dutton Books, 1999. 320p. $19.99. ISBN 0 525 46863 3. [fiction] S Seventeen-year-old Jacob Todd's trip to Amsterdam to honor his grandfather reveals family secrets, and challenges his own perceptions of sexuality.

3. Ferris, Jean. **Eight Seconds.** New York: Harcourt Brace and Company, 2000. 186p. $17.00. ISBN 0 15 202367 4. [fiction] JS (See full booktalk in *Booktalks and More,* 2003, pages 221 to 223.) A young man, frightened by the idea that he is gay, refuses to defend a gay young man and therefore loses a good friend.

4. Garden, Nancy. **The Year They Burned the Books.** New York: Farrar, Straus and Giroux, 1999. 247p. $17.00. ISBN 0 374 38667 6. [fiction] JS After the school paper suggests that the school nurse should dispense condoms, two teenagers find themselves fighting censorship and dealing with their homosexual feelings.

5. Wharton, Edith. **Age of Innocence.** New York: Quality Paperback Book Club, 1993. 353p. $5.95pa. ISBN 0 02026 478 X. [fiction] S/A Published in 1920 and a Pulitzer Prize winner in 1921, this novel explores upper-class resistance to exploring and expressing passion.

6. Yamanaka, Lois-Ann. **Name Me Nobody.** New York: Hyperion, 1999. 227p. $14.99. ISBN 0 7868 0452 1. [fiction] S Sixteen-year-old Emi-lou Kaya is socially unacceptable because she is illegitimate, overweight, Japanese, and has a lesbian friend.

❧❧

Rottman, S. L. Stetson.

New York: Viking, 2002. 192p. $16.99. ISBN 0 670 03542 4. [fiction] JS

Themes/Topics: family, independence, alcoholism, respect, death

Summary/Description

Seventeen-year-old Stetson lives with his alcoholic father in a mill town. Although he wants to be the first in his family to graduate from high school, he supplements his salary at a local scrap business by taking bribes from his classmates to disrupt classes. He uses his money for food, T-shirts, and his pet project, restoring a Honda Civic. Skipping school after an especially cruel prank, he goes home to find a sister neither his father nor he knew about. Fourteen-year-old Kayla was born shortly after his mother left them. Kayla experiments with drinking and the local boys, but wins the admiration of Jason, Stetson's boss and father figure who encourages Stetson to protect her. Kayla and Stetson discover common talents and feelings as she creates and helps him paint an eagle on his prize Civic. Then events force Stetson to salvage the good parts of his life just as he has salvaged car parts. Jason announces he is dying, their father's drinking precipitates an accident that almost kills Kayla and totals Stetson's car. Kayla persuades a cousin to allow Stetson and her to move in. Stetson concludes that the town's low expectations and his father's self-pity will destroy him and his sister. With his boss's help and encouragement, he tries a new life with Kayla.

Booktalk

Ask how many people in the group know what a salvage yard is and why it is a profitable business.

Seventeen-year-old Stetson works in a salvage yard. He loves to strip down wrecked cars, figure out what to keep, and throw the rest away. In fact, he uses some of the best scraps to build his own head-turner car. He also says he wants to graduate from high school, and he thinks he has pretty well figured out what classes to keep and throw away to do that too. But then Kayla shows up. She's his fourteen-year-old sister, born right after his social-climbing mother threw him and his father away. His father likes this surprise daughter about as much as he likes Stetson, but the boys at the local bar like her *too* much. Stetson thinks she should make her mistakes and take the consequences, but Jason, Stetson's boss, thinks it's time for Stetson to salvage some lives as well as car parts. When he gives this new life job a try, Stetson learns that a family from scraps can take a person a lot farther in life than four wheels and a motor.

Learning Opportunities

1. Rottman uses Stetson's salvage job as a powerful metaphor. Explain how keeping and throwing away is a central part of Stetson's life. Then discuss whether or not you agree or disagree with his choices.

2. Jason orders a vanity license plate for Stetson's car—FREEHND. The letters and gift can be interpreted in more than one way. Discuss what these letters might mean and what the gift reveals about the relationship between Stetson and Jason.

3. Kayla's arrival precipitates both she and Stetson leaving. Discuss how and why Kayla changes Stetson's life.
4. Compare how Rottman uses similar elements in *Stetson* and *Hero* (Related Work 6). Discuss how her use of these elements affects the results. Be sure to compare the veterans in each story.
5. Read *The Outsiders* (Related Work 3) and *Tex* (Related Work 4) by S. E. Hinton. Compare the worlds Hinton constructs to Stetson's. Discuss especially the role played by adults and institutions, such as schools, in each person's work.

Related Works

1. Bauer, Joan. **Hope Was Here.** New York: G. P. Putnam's Sons, 2000. 186p. $16.99. ISBN 0 399 23142 0. [fiction] MJS (See full booktalk in *Booktalks and More*, 2003, pages 258 to 260.) In this upbeat novel, a sixteen-year-old waitress, raised by her aunt, uses her work to define her life. She never knew her father, and her mother deserted her.
2. Brooks, Martha. **True Confessions of a Heartless Girl.** New York: Farrar, Straus and Giroux/Melanie Kroupa Books, 2003. 181p. $16.00. ISBN 0 374 37806 1. [fiction] JS Pregnant seventeen-year-old Noreen Stall steals her boyfriend's truck and money, drives to the small community of Pembina Lake, and finds a home. Her mistakes lead both Noreen and the people in town who help her to mend their own lives.
3. Hinton, S. E. **The Outsiders.** New York: Penguin Putnam, Inc./ Speak, 1995. 180p. $6.99. ISBN 0 14 03572 X. [fiction] JS Gang members try to sort through their out-group status to discover their own identity. This book was written when Hinton was sixteen.
4. Hinton, S. E. **Tex.** New York: Laurel Leaf Books, 1979. 211p. $5.50pa. ISBN 0 440 97850 5. [fiction] JS Fifteen-year-old Tex, a magnet for trouble, lives with his seventeen-year-old brother, Mason, and realizes that his home is falling apart.
5. Many, Paul. **Walk Away Home.** New York: Walker & Co., 2002. 240p. $16.95. ISBN 0 8027 8828 9. [fiction] JS Nick Doran leaves home to live with his eccentric aunt and becomes part of an unlikely family involved in a series of dysfunctional relationships.
6. Rottman, S. L. **Hero.** Atlanta, GA: Peachtree Publishers, 1997. 134p. $14.95. ISBN 1 56145 159 2. [fiction] MJS (See full booktalk in *Booktalks Plus*, 2001, pages 223 to 225.) Living with an alcoholic and abusive mother, fourteen-year-old Sean Parker finds the structure and love he needs when the court sentences him to a farm owned by a tough World War II hero.

ʗʓ ʡʒ

Wolf, Virginia Euwer. **True Believer.**

New York: Atheneum, 2001. 264p. (Make Lemonade Trilogy.) $17.00.
ISBN 0 689 82827 6. [novel in poems] JS

Themes/Topics: trust, love, family, standards,
acceptance, sexual preference

Summary/Description

In this second book of the *Make Lemonade Trilogy,* fifteen-year-old
LaVaughn struggles with trust and love. Annie and Myrtle, friends
from preschool days, want her to join the Jesus Club, which warns its
members to keep their virginity and restrict social contacts to "true"
Christians. LaVaughn pursues different interests, but romance surrounds
her. LaVaughn's mother and Jolly are dating again, and LaVaughn falls
in love with a childhood friend whom she discovers is gay. The resulting
conflicts force LaVaughn to define her personal standards. She decides to
continue her education, focus on nursing, make good friends, and keep
her old ones, even if they are not the people she would like them to be.

Booktalk

In the *Make Lemonade Trilogy*, LaVaughn knows her friend Jolly is
making the wrong choices. Cutting school and having babies will get Jolly
nowhere, and LaVaughn wants to go *somewhere* with her life. But now
LaVaughn faces some big-time choices of her own. Myrtle and Annie,
her friends from preschool, want her to join the Cross Your Legs for
Jesus Club. They think that will help them save their bodies for the "right
husband," whenever he comes along. When a gorgeous old friend, Jody,
moves back to the neighborhood, it seems that LaVaughn's Mr. Right has
come along. Her mother is still adding to that college fund, but LaVaughn
can hardly keep her mind on the books, especially when the new academic courses are so much harder, and her lab partner keeps trying to
date her. LaVaughn dreams about the future, but the dream is changing.
You decide if LaVaughn should be a *True Believer.*

Learning Opportunities

1. Read the opening poem on page 3 aloud. Discuss the appropriateness of LaVaughn's comparison at age fifteen.
2. In poem 60 on page 188, LaVaughn says that she feels "like a
   parentheses." Using the poem as a model, compare yourself to a
   grammatical structure or a piece of punctuation.

3. Myrtle and Annie, LaVaughn's mother, Jolly, Jody, and Patrick all present LaVaughn with dating choices. Discuss what LaVaughn learns from each choice.
4. Myrtle, Annie, and Patrick accuse LaVaughn of being "uppity." Discuss the perspective that Ronell and LaVaughn's mother give her about that accusation and the balance that LaVaughn achieves.
5. LaVaughn's guidance counselor helps her to keep her academic focus. Using your library's and guidance department's resources, research educational requirements for three different jobs in the same field. For example, you might choose the medical field and research the academic requirements for being a lab technician, a nurse, and a doctor. Share your information with the group.
6. LaVaughn's guidance counselor also encourages LaVaughn to meet and greet people more assertively. Using resources from your library and guidance department, find recommended techniques to present yourself memorably and positively.

Related Works

1. Atkins, Catherine. **Alt Ed.** New York: G. P. Putnam's Sons, 2003. 198p. $17.99. ISBN 0 399 23854 9. [fiction] JS Susan Callaway attends a counseling group with four other high school students and becomes close friends with an openly gay member of the group.
2. Porter, Connie. **Imani All Mine.** New York: Houghton Mifflin Co., 1999. 212p. $23.00. ISBN 0 395 83808 8. [fiction] S/A A high achieving, inner-city student, who becomes pregnant when she is raped, is overwhelmed by street life and her mother's unstable home.
3. Suskind, Ron. **A Hope in the Unseen.** New York: Broadway Books, 1998. 372p. $25.00. ISBN 0 7679 0125 8. [nonfiction] S/A (See full booktalk in *Booktalks Plus*, 2001, pages 94 to 96.) Suskind traces Cedric Jenning's life from his junior year in high school to the end of his freshman college year and describes all the financial, academic, intellectual, social, and emotional barriers that he must overcome.
4. Wolf, Virginia Euwer. **Make Lemonade.** New York: Henry Holt, 1993. 208p. (Make Lemonade Trilogy.) $15.95. ISBN 0 8050 2288 7. [novel in poems] JS In this first book of the trilogy, fourteen-year-old LaVaughn takes a babysitting job with a single mother, encourages the mother to get a GED, and decides that studying and going to college are much better choices than single motherhood.

5.   Woodson, Jacqueline. **Behind You.** New York: G. P. Putnam's Sons,
     2004. 128p. $15.99. ISBN 0 399 23988 X. [fiction, multiple percep-
     tions] JS After a talented young African-American man is killed, he
     and all those who love him must move on. His girlfriend does so
     with the help of the young man's friend who is gay.

ᘓᘔ
Woodson, Jacqueline. **Miracle's Boys.**
New York: G. P. Putnam's Sons, 2000. 131p. $15.99. ISBN 0 399 23113 7. [fiction] MJS

Themes/Topics: family, crime, grief

Summary/Description

Twelve-year-old Lafayette feels responsible for his mother's death.
He lives with his older brother Tý ree, his legal guardian, and his
fifteen-and-a-half-year-old brother Charlie. Charlie spent three years
in a correctional facility for robbery, is repeating ninth grade, and
hanging out with a gang member. Tý ree gave up an opportunity to
attend MIT so he could keep the family together. If either Charlie or
Lafayette gets into trouble, Tý ree will be judged an unfit guardian, and
the family will be split up. Charlie, angry and alienated, still blames
Lafayette for not saving their mother's life. Tý ree feels guilt about
their father's death, a drowning, and believes Charlie's anger comes
from guilt over not being there when either parent died. Charlie breaks
parole by riding in a stolen car and undergoing a gang initiation. When
Tý ree and Lafayette go to the police station to pick him up, Lafayette
decides to help Charlie. He learns that Charlie robbed the store to get
enough money to move the family back to Puerto Rico where Charlie
believes they could live a better life. In the last chapter, they are again
working as a family, sharing their memories and perceptions of the
neighborhood.

Booktalk

Twelve-year-old Lafayette lives with his brothers. Tý ree, his oldest
brother, is the guardian. Charlie, his other brother, is evil. He's back
from three years in a correctional facility for armed robbery. Now he
stares out the window or hangs out with a neighborhood thug named
Aaron. He likes to give Lafayette a hard time and tells him that it is
his fault that their mother is dead. This mean Charlie is so different
from the one who was sent away three years ago that Lafayette calls

him Newcharlie. But even though Lafayette knows that Newcharlie is evil and angry, he is also afraid that Newcharlie might be right. After all, Lafayette was the last one to see their mother. He could have tried harder. He could have thought more quickly. If he had done his part, she might be alive today. But Lafayette isn't the only one to have a guilty little secret. Each brother has one—a secret that could destroy or save every one of *Miracle's Boys*.

Learning Opportunities

1. In Chapter 15, Lafayette recalls his mother sharing a passage with him from Toni Morrison, ". . . being free means you help somebody else get free." Discuss why this quotation is central to the story.
2. Each brother carries a great deal of guilt. Discuss each brother's guilt and what that guilt reveals about him.
3. List the questions that you would like a sequel to *Miracle's Boys* to answer.
4. Aaron is an important character even though he is a minor character. Why?
5. In *Behind You* (Related Work 6), Woodson uses a series of personal essays to explain the moving on process for both the deceased person and the people left behind. After reading *Behind You* (Related Work 6) and *Miracle's Boys*, write an essay expressing what Miracle and her husband might say about dying or about the sons they left behind.
6. Research gangs and the reasons people have for joining them. You might wish to start your research by reading *Gangs: Opposing Viewpoints* (Related Work 1). Share your information with the group. Then discuss how the information you find supports the story.

Related Works

1. Egendorf, Laura. **Gangs: Opposing Viewpoints.** San Diego, CA: Greenhaven Press, 2001. 170p. (Opposing Viewpoints Series). $23.00. ISBN 0 7177 0510 8. [nonfiction] JS The articles emphasize that gangs draw teens who crave attention.
2. Franco, Betsy (ed.). **You Hear Me? Poems and Writing by Teenage Boys.** Cambridge, MA: Candlewick Press, 2000. 106p. $14.99. ISBN 0 7636 1158 1. [poetry] JS All the poems in this anthology are written by young boys. "Time Somebody Told Me," and "I'll Be Here," are closely related to the concerns in *Miracle's Boys*.
3. Frost, Helen. **Keesha's House.** New York: Farrar, Straus and Giroux/Frances Foster Books, 2003. 116p. $16.00. ISBN 0 374 34064 1. [fiction] JS Joe, accepted into this house when he was twelve by a

lady named Aunt Annie, now offers the same refuge to homeless and threatened teens. Keesha, who left her alcoholic father's home and moved in with Joe, encourages others to join her.

4.   Myers, Walter Dean. **Monster.** New York: HarperCollins Publishers, 1999. 281p. $15.95. ISBN 0 06 028077 8. [fiction, mixed format] JS (See full booktalk in *Booktalks and More,* 2003, pages 13 to 15.) Sixteen-year-old Steve Harmon, on trial for murder, structures his experience into a movie script. The script, personal journal, and comments make up the novel.

5.   Walker, Pamela. **Pray Hard.** New York: Scholastic, 2001. 176p. $15.95. ISBN 0 439 21586 2. [fiction] MJ Amelia's father died in a plane crash when Amelia was eleven. One year later she still believes that the "monster popper" toy that she put in his crop duster plane caused the crash.

6.   Woodson, Jacqueline. **Behind You.** New York: G. P. Putnam's Sons, 2004. 128p. $15.99. ISBN 0 399 23988 X. [fiction] JS A young man is killed and the people who love him express their feelings about his death and moving on.

Social Challenges

Fradin, Dennis Brindell. **Bound for the North Star: True Stories of Fugitive Slaves.**

New York: Clarion Books, 2000. 205p. $20.00. ISBN 0 395 97017 2. [nonfiction] MJS

Themes/Topics: slavery, Underground Railroad, abolition, history

Summary/Description

Outlining the horrors of slavery and the heroic efforts to escape it, Fradin uses first person accounts of Mary Prince, Eliza Harris, Henry "Box" Brown, and Harriet Tubman. In addition, he explains how entire families (the Still family), religions (Quakers), and towns (Oberlin, Ohio) dedicated themselves to the Underground Railroad. The narratives with pictures and diagrams communicate the intensity and cruelties of the slave trade as well as support for man stealing, selling free men into slavery. He emphasizes that England and Canada led the United States in the abolition of slavery and provided refuge for escaped slaves. The "Afterword" emphasizes that slavery still thrives today and includes two UN addresses that explain how a person can help combat it. The "Bibliography" and Web sites provide additional references and information. The index includes page numbers with pictures in bold print.

Booktalk

Harriet Tubman, in 1856, declared slavery to be "the next thing to hell." But slavery in the so-called New World started long before 1856. Christopher Columbus began using slaves in 1492 when his expedition forced the native population to search for treasure and grow crops. Europeans shipped in slaves from Africa. By 1776, the year of the American Revolution, the colonists held over 500,000 slaves. Who would free these people? Rarely, their owners. Not the British and Colonial armies that enlisted their help. Most of the effort had to come from the slaves themselves. One man mailed himself. Others ran to freedom across cracking ice. But to make successful escapes again and again, these fugitives had to cooperate and plan. So they built a railroad, a railroad of people, and *Bound for the North Star*, they traveled the invisible rails to freedom. These true stories of men, women, organizations, and communities tell about cruelty, greed, and the spirit to rise above them—the spirit that built an Underground Railroad to a truly New World.

Learning Opportunities

1. Continue to research the role of Quakers in the anti-slavery movement. Share the material that you find with the group. You might wish to start with *The Quakers* (Related Work 7) by Jean Kinney Williams.
2. In Chapter 3, Fradin relates the story of Eliza Harris, the inspiration for *Uncle Tom's Cabin* (Related Work 6) and Margaret Garner, the inspiration for *Beloved* (Related Work 5). After reading Fradin's descriptions, and one or both of the novels, explain the relationship of the novel to the factual account.
3. Like the citizens of Denmark in World War II (Related Work 3), the citizens of Oberlin, Ohio, banded together to protect a persecuted minority. Compare the two situations. List the traits these two communities share.
4. In the "Afterword," Fradin makes the point that slavery still exists and provides two UN addresses to contact for more information. Contact the agencies listed and share the information that you receive with the group.

5. On page 200, Fradin lists four Web sites. Explore each site. Share the information you discover and your reaction to it with the group.

Related Works

1. Cooper, Michael L. **Slave Spirituals and the Jubilee Singers.** New York: Clarion, 2001. 86p. $16.00. ISBN 0 395 97829 7. [nonfiction] MJS This history of the Jubilee Singers from Fisk University explains how central spirituals were in slave life.
2. Cox, Clinton. **Come All You Brave Soldiers.** New York: Scholastic, 1999. 182p. $5.95. ISBN 0 590 47576 2. [nonfiction] MJS (See full booktalk in *Booktalks Plus*, 2001, pages 155 to 157.) Cox explains the contradiction of a revolution that fought for basic human rights but kept African-American soldiers in slavery.
3. Levine, Ellen. **Darkness over Denmark: The Danish Resistance and the Rescue of the Jews.** New York: Holiday House, 2000. 164p. $14.95. ISBN 0 8234 1755 7. [nonfiction] MJS The narrative begins with the German invasion of Denmark, April 9, 1940. Combined with the factual description of the Nazi Occupation are the heroic stories of writers, clergy, policemen, students, doctors, and teachers who prove that individuals can make a difference in the face of overwhelming evil.
4. McKissack, Patricia, and Frederick L. McKissack. **Days of Jubilee: The End of Slavery in the United States.** New York: Scholastic Press, 2003. 144p. $18.95. ISBN 0 590 10764 X. [nonfiction] MJS McKissack's chronicle the slow realization of, and resistance to, freedom for the slaves.
5. Morrison, Toni. **Beloved.** New York: Alfred A. Knopf, 1990. 273p. $24.95. ISBN 0 394 53597 9. [fiction] S/A The main character, Sethe, is haunted by the memory of the child she killed in the form of Beloved. She tries to live in the present even though Beloved is slowly taking possession of it.
6. Stowe, Harriet Beecher. **Uncle Tom's Cabin or Life Among the Lowly.** Pleasantville, NY: The Reader's Digest Association, Inc., 1991. 416p. $20.00. ISBN 0 89577 367 8. [fiction] S/A This nation shaping novel describes the many aspects of slavery and illustrates why even the most positive slave/owner relationships are evil. Many of the stories, like that of Eliza Harris, parallel the narratives in *Bound for the North Star*. Written in 1852 and published again in the 1960s during the Civil Rights movement, it presents the good and evil in slaves and slaveholders as well as conditions that teens will associate with concentration camps. The "Afterword" by Alfred Kazin points out

that many negative stereotypes about the book come from post-Civil War dramatizations rather than from the book itself.

7. Williams, Jean Kinney. **The Quakers.** Danbury, CT: Franklin Watts, 1998. 110p. $22.00. ISBN 0 531 11377 9. [nonfiction] MJS (See full booktalk in *Booktalks Plus,* pages 248 to 249.) Kinney explains the origins of the religion, the perceptions it encouraged, and the national policies that it influenced.

ᘓᘓ

Goobie, Beth. **The Lottery.**

Victoria, BC: Orca, 2002. 272p. $16.95. ISBN 1 55143 161 0. [fiction] MJS

Themes/Topics: peer pressure, family, friendship, outsiders, grief, personal responsibility, fate

Summary/Description

Fifteen-year-old Sally Hanson, haunted by the automobile accident that killed her father, is chosen to be "the victim" in the Saskatoon Collegiate lottery. Shadow Council, a secret society made up of school leaders, each year chooses one student whom they isolate from the rest of the student body and use as a messenger to carry out harassment against students or faculty who offend, defy, or ignore them. Intimidated into carrying out their missions, she realizes that she can't hurt classmates already wounded by their own personal problems. She learns that her selection is special—a revenge directed toward her brother who fought the council. With the surreptitious support of the Shadow Council president, she overcomes a planned intimidation that involves the mock hanging of her best friend. Discovering that she did not cause her father's accident, that her brother depends on her for emotional support, and that her best friend decides to stay loyal to her despite physical threat, she finds the strength to refuse her role as victim. Her example encourages other students to defy the council rule.

Booktalk

Hold up a lottery ticket. Ask the group what they associate with it.

Once we buy a lottery ticket we know that we have a chance to win. We may even become millionaires overnight just by paying a dollar and picking a few numbers. Saskatoon Collegiate has *The Lottery* too. But at Saskatoon, the winner is the loser—the victim, and the victim doesn't have any choice about whether or not his or her name is drawn. Listen to how it is done. *Read the first paragraph of Chapter 1.* The victim has to do whatever the secret Shadow Council says for a year. No one else in the school can talk to the victim. If they do, they could be Shadow Council's next target. This year's lucky winner is Sal Hanson. She thought she was invisible, but fate found her. Now she's trapped, just like she was trapped in the accident that killed her father, just like she's trapped her family into taking care of all her problems. Fate seems to keep Sal and everyone she loves in the loser box. But maybe now Sal needs to start thinking outside of that box; lives, including her own, could depend on it.

Learning Opportunities

1. Fate versus choice is a dominant theme. Identify how each character carries out the theme.
2. At some points in the novel, Sal gets positive feelings about being part of the Shadow Council plans. Discuss why you feel she has both the positive and negative feelings about her activities.
3. Although Sal is almost destroyed by the victim experience, she comes out of it a better and stronger person. Some of that change is due to Willis Cass. Discuss how he affects her life. Consider her rejection of him.
4. Discuss the following question: Should Sal tell the school administration or any other adult about the Shadow Council?
5. Choose two of the characters mentioned in the story. Project what they will be doing and what kind of people they will be in fifteen years.
6. Discuss how Linda Paboni functions in the novel and whether or not her character is believable.
7. Chris Busatto refuses the task because he says that he does not have to give into peer pressure, yet he is the character who attempts suicide when confronted with harassment. Research techniques or behaviors that Chris or anyone else confronting harassment or severe peer pressure might use to combat it.
8. Obesity and autism are both issues in the novel. Choose one and research it. Then share with the group what you find.
9. Read the essay "Root for the Underdog," (Related Work 1). Then discuss how this essay might have helped the students at Saskatoon Collegiate.

Related Works

1. Carlson, Richard. **Don't Sweat the Small Stuff for Teens: Simple Ways to Keep Your Cool in Stressful Times.** New York: Hyperion, 2000. 242p. $11.95pa. ISBN 0 7868 8597 1. [nonfiction, essays] MJS In "Root for the Underdog" on pages 50 to 52, Carlson points out the power of reaching out to the less popular crowd.

2. Cormier, Robert. **The Chocolate War.** New York: Dell Laurel Leaf, 1974. 263p. $5.50pa. ISBN 0 440 94459 7. [fiction] MJS A young man, who recently lost his mother, finds himself confronting overwhelming peer pressure because of his refusal to sell chocolates for his school.
3. Eliot, George. **Silas Marner.** New York: Signet Classic, 1999. 186p. $3.95pa. ISBN 0 451 52721 6. [fiction] S/A Marner, a falsely accused outcast, learns to give and receive love.
4. Golding, William. **Lord of the Flies.** New York: Perigee/Penguin Putnam, Inc., 1954.208p. $6.95 pa. ISBN 0 399 50148 7. [fiction] JS Marooned on an island by a plane crash, young boys embrace tribal life and try to destroy each other.
5. Jackson, Shirley. **The Lottery and Other Stories.** New York: Farrar, Straus and Giroux, 1977. 305p. $14.00. ISBN 0 374 51681 2. [fiction] S/A In this short story collection, "The Lottery," a classic story about a traditional stoning, appears on pages 291 to 302.
6. Knowles, John. **A Separate Peace.** New York: Scribner, 1987. 204p. $8.00. ISBN 0 7432 5397 3. [fiction] JS Two young men are drawn into peer group competition and jealousy in their boarding school.

ℭℑℭ

Gray, Dianne E. Together Apart.

New York: Houghton Mifflin Co., 2002. 193p. $16.00. ISBN 0 618 18721 9. [fiction] MJ

Themes/Topics: women's rights, friendship, love, independence, grief, family, historical setting of late nineteenth century

Summary/Description

The story, following the winter of the deadly Nebraska blizzard, begins in early May of 1888 and ends in the fall of 1888. Fourteen-year-old Hannah Barnett and fifteen-year-old Isaac Richards tell the story in alternating segments. Hannah answers a help wanted advertisement posted by Eliza Moore, a progressive thinking widow who owns a large home she supports with dwindling resources. Eliza already hired Isaac to help print her publication, the *Women's Gazette*. She challenges Hannah to think of another way to use the house to make money. Hannah suggests opening a resting room supported by goodwill donations from farmwomen. The room develops into a women's community support group, exchange, and market.

Hannah and Isaac, during the blizzard, kept each other alive in a haystack by holding each other. False rumors claim Isaac violated her. Hannah feels guilt because she enjoyed being with Isaac, and she thinks that her father blames her for the death of her two brothers who died in the storm. Working, she discovers some of her talents and concludes that her father should share the guilt, if any, for her brothers' deaths. Isaac flees his abusive stepfather and persuades his mother to do the same. Eliza and Hannah help them. The story concludes with letters exchanged between Eliza and Isaac that reveal the feelings that some day will bring them together.

Booktalk

Fourteen-year-old Hannah Bartlett and fifteen-year-old Isaac Richards both survived the Nebraska blizzard of 1888. They survived by holding each other tight in a haystack. The rumors are flying about both of them. Now they have something else in common. They both work for the most controversial woman in town—the Widow Moore. The Widow prints progressive ideas about women's rights. Isaac helps keep the press running. Hannah has some suggestions to keep the Widow's house running too. Hannah plans a "resting room" for women who come to town and have to wait for their husbands. They pay for their stay with donations. But no one knows Isaac and Hannah are working together for the Widow. Isaac is on the run from his abusive stepfather; Hannah's father thinks Isaac is no good for lots of reasons. During the storm, Isaac and Hannah liked being together. Working at the Widow's doesn't change their minds, but will they ever have a chance to live any other way but—*Together Apart*?

Learning Opportunities

1. Eliza Moore starts a revolution. Is it simply a revolution for women?
2. The Widow Moore's house is luxurious for its day. Specifically, the story cites the necessary room and the washing machine. Using your library's resources, find descriptions and pictures of appliances used in the 1880s. Share the pictures with the group.
3. Using your library's resources, research the women's movement in the late 1800s and early 1900s. Be sure to include the part that working girls played in this movement.
4. Discuss the role of Mr. Tinka in the story. Be sure to consider him in relation to Mr. Barnett and Mr. Richards.
5. Discuss the roles that Dru and Eliza play in the novel.
6. The story definitely leaves the reader wondering about the future. Either describe the sequel to *Together Apart* that you would like to read or write an epilogue that describes the characters' lives in ten years.

Related Works

1. Bartoletti, Susan Campbell. **Kids on Strike.** Boston, MA: Houghton Mifflin, 1999. 208p. $20.00. ISBN 0 395 88892 1. [nonfiction] MJS Bartoletti explains the growing awareness of a much exploited labor force. In the first chapter, she explains how the factory girls dedicated themselves to self-improvement.

2. Donnelly, Jennifer. **A Northern Light.** New York: Harcourt, Inc., 2003. 389p. $17.00. ISBN 0 15 216705 6. [fiction] JS (See full booktalk in "History/Period"/"Choices in Change," pages 220 to 223.) Mathilda Gokey, caring for her family and working at the Glenmore Hotel, becomes involved in a murder mystery that inspires her to develop her talents.

3. Janeczko, Paul B. (col.). **Blushing: Expressions of Love in Poems and Letters.** New York: Orchard Books, 2004. 112p. $15.95. ISBN 0 439 53056 3. [poetry] MJS Including Shakespeare, Browning, Angelou, and Ogden Nash, the poetry collection explores the many faces of love in both closeness and separation.

4. Murphy, Jim. **Blizzard!** [nonfiction] MJS (See full booktalk in "Adventure/Survival"/"Land," pages 97 to 99.) Through human-interest stories, Murphy describes why the 1888 storm was so surprising, violent, and devastating.

5. Naylor, Phyllis Reynolds. **Blizzard's Wake.** New York: Atheneum Books for Young Readers, 2002. 212p. $16.95. ISBN 0 689 85220 7. [fiction] MJS In the March 1941 blizzard in North Dakota, a young girl finds herself helping the man who killed her mother.

❦

Hiaasen, Carl. Hoot.

New York: Alfred A. Knopf, 2002. 292p. $15.95. ISBN 0 375 82181 3. [fiction] MJ

Themes/Topics: environment, bullies (including peers, parents, and companies), outsiders, friendship

Summary/Description

Roy Eberhardt, a new student in Trace Middle School, wants to find out why a barefoot boy, running parallel to the school bus, never gets on the bus. Roy's curiosity draws him into an environmental fight to save burrowing owls threatened by the construction of a new restaurant. Napoleon Bridger Leep, the mysterious boy, is a nature genius, who cannot live at home because of his parents' fighting and his mother's abuse. His stepsister, Beatrice Leep, tough and athletic, helps him survive in a junkyard. She also becomes friends with Roy and defends him against the school bully, Dana Matherson. Napoleon (a.k.a. Mullet Fingers) spends each night sabotaging the construction site by pulling out the stakes, taking apart the equipment, or planting alligators and poisonous snakes. Roy, Napoleon, and Beatrice, with the help of Roy's father, foil the company and save the owls. The book explores how kids can take on all kinds of bullies: the biggest, meanest boy in the class; abusive parents; or greedy companies.

Booktalk

Roy Eberhardt is a new student in Trace Middle School, Florida. He has played the new kid role six times already in his school career. So when Dana Matherson, the school bully, mushes Roy's face against the bus window, Roy doesn't take it personally, but he doesn't just take it either. He decides to stand his ground. That decision makes his life both complicated and dangerous. But Dana Matherson's mush against the window accomplishes something. It makes Roy notice a strange boy running along the sidewalk. The boy is dirty and barefoot. He seems focused and anxious, but he isn't worried about catching the bus. In fact he runs right by. That makes Roy pretty curious, so he follows the boy. The path that he finds himself on is exciting and scary—full of snakes, alligators, attack dogs, owls and some pretty unusual pancakes. But what Roy discovers is that the running boy is not really so strange. He, like Roy, and lots of other people, just gives a *Hoot*.

Learning Opportunities

1. Using your library's resources, research the burrowing owl. Answer the questions—who, what, when, where, why, and how. Share the information with the group either in a bulletin board or oral presentation.
2. Examine each prank. Discuss how they characterize Mullet Fingers.
3. Discuss the realism of each of the characters and how their presentation affects the story.
4. In Chapter 8, Roy compares himself to the osprey. Explain his comparison. Choose an animal to which you might compare yourself. Explain your choice and similarities.
5. On page 160, Roy's mother explains that decisions often mean choosing between conflicting messages of the head and the heart. Explain how you feel about the discussion. Then discuss how Roy, Mullet Fingers, and Beatrice apply that thinking to their own lives.

6. Discuss more than one way that the title *Hoot* could apply to the story.
7. Law enforcement is a thread that runs throughout the story. List the instances in which the law and its officers are issues. Then discuss any relationships or patterns that you might find.
8. Because Roy's family moves so frequently, Hiaasen could use the framework of the "new kid" to build a series of stories involving Roy. What location would you suggest for the next book? Explain your answer.

Related Works

1. Bloor, Edward. **Tangerine.** New York: Scholastic, 1997. 294p. (An Apple Signature Edition). $4.99pa. ISBN 0 590 43277 X. [fiction] MJ (See full booktalk in *Booktalks Plus*, 2001, pages 16 to 19.) A new middle school student in Tangerine County, Florida, finds himself in the middle of family and environmental conflict.
2. Burgess, Melvin. **Kite.** New York: Farrar, Straus and Giroux, 2000. 182p. $16.00. ISBN 0 374 34228 8. [fiction] MJ Taylor Mase lives on Hale Magna, an English estate where his father works as a gamekeeper in the 1960s. After trying to rob a kite nest, he commits himself to saving one surviving kite in spite of the landowner's pressure to kill the bird. His father's resolve to kill predators that threaten the estate's pheasants, his friend's bragging, and his own fear of losing the family's home and livelihood play out in the book.
3. Myers, Anna. **Flying Blind.** New York: Walker & Company, 2003. 192p. $16.95. ISBN 0 8027 8879 3. [fiction] MJ Murphy, a seer macaw, inspires thirteen-year-old Ben and his adopted father, Professor Elisha Riley to reroute their Shakespearean medicine show to Flamingo, Florida, so that Ben might embrace his destiny of saving wild birds.
4. Sweeney, Joyce. **The Spirit Window.** New York: Delacorte Press, 1998. 243p. $15.95. ISBN 0 385 32510 X. [fiction] MJS (See full booktalk in *Booktalks Plus*, 2001, pages 19 to 21.) When Miranda and her family travel to Florida to visit her sick grandmother, Miranda discovers that each person has a responsibility to preserve family and nature.
5. Vaupel, Robin. **My Contract with Henry.** New York: Holiday House, 2003. 244p. $16.95. ISBN 0 8234 1701 8. [fiction] MJ In a hastily conceived Henry David Thoreau English assignment with three other out-group classmates, thirteen-year-old Beth Gardner finds herself in conflict with her mother's boyfriend over the use of the local Wayburn Woods for a housing project.

Cʃʋ

Lawlor, Laurie. Helen Keller: Rebellious Spirit.

New York: Holiday House, 2001. 168p. $22.95. ISBN 0 8234 1588 0. [nonfiction] MJS

Themes/Topics: sight, hearing, history

Summary/Description

Lawlor describes the Keller household, its post-Reconstruction Southern context, and the period's prevailing prejudice against "defectives." She also explores Annie Sullivan's pauper life and why her work with Helen might have been tied to self-interest, influenced by the striving, self-improvement mentality of Sullivan's time and social class. Throughout Helen's education culminating at Radcliffe, Annie's bouts with depression and marriage to Helen's editor, John Macy, as well as Helen's own short-lived romance, Helen remains the driving force who supports herself, those around her, and social movements such as child welfare, equal rights, and socialism. A chronology, source notes, extensive suggestions for further reading and viewing, as well as a name and subject index, make this book reader friendly and motivating for further research.

Booktalk

Ask how many in the group have ever heard of Helen Keller. Ask them how and where they first heard about her.

Usually people know that Helen Keller was blind and deaf. They also know that Anne Sullivan, her teacher, gave her the gift of language. What they don't know much about is Helen Keller, the student, activist, and adult. Keller finished a college education at Radcliffe with honors, supported the rights of the downtrodden, and fell in love. This woman, seen in her time as a "defective," became one of the most important figures of the twentieth century. No goal was out of reach. No challenge was too great. Helen Keller never played the needy, helpless, or saintly role that many tried to give her. She was, instead, a hardheaded individual who did what she thought was right. She was *Helen Keller: Rebellious Spirit*.

Learning Opportunities

1. At the end of her book, Lawlor presents an extensive list of books and films. Choose one book or film. Share your information with the group, and explain the insight it gives you into Helen Keller's life and times.

2. Alexander Graham Bell was a lifelong friend to Helen Keller. Using your library's resources, research the contributions he made to the deaf. Share them with the group in an oral or visual presentation.
3. Using your library's resources, research the Gilded Age. Discuss why a high number of strikes occurred during that period. You might wish to start by reading *Kids on Strike!* (Related Work 1).
4. Study signing. Try to communicate a message to another person by using it. Then describe your experience.
5. Contact the American Federation of the Blind. You might want to start with their Web site listed on page 163. Ask the Federation to send information about their services. Set up a display or information center in your local school or library.

Related Works

1. Bartoletti, Susan Campbell. **Kids on Strike!** Boston: Houghton Mifflin Company, 1999. 208p. $20.00. ISBN 0 395 88892 1. [nonfiction] MJS Bartoletti traces the American labor movement, which heavily involved children. Chapter 7 describes and explains the significance of The Lawrence Strike.
2. Broyles, Janell. **The Triangle Shirtwaist Factory Fire of 1911.** New York: Rosen Central, 2004. 48p. (Tragic Fires Throughout History.) $23.95. ISBN 0 8239 4489 1. [nonfiction] MJS Broyles describes the context of the tragedy, the protests preceding it, the actual incident, and the legislation it produced.
3. Dash, Joan. **The World at Her Fingertips: The Story of Helen Keller.** New York: Scholastic Press, 2001. 256p. $15.95. ISBN 0 590 90715 8. [nonfiction] MJS Dash describes the childhoods of both Anne Sullivan and Helen Keller to explain their complicated relationship.
4. Denenberg, Barry. **Mirror, Mirror on the Wall: The Diary of Bess Brennan.** New York: Scholastic Inc., 2002. 144p. (Dear America.) $10.95. ISBN 0 439 19446 6. [fiction] MJ After losing her sight in a sledding accident, a twin attends the Perkins School for the Blind to learn how to live an independent life.
5. Fradin, Dennis Brindell, and Judith Bloom Fradin. **Ida B. Wells: Mother of the Civil Rights Movement.** New York: Clarion Books, 2000. 178p. $18.00. ISBN 0 395 89898 6. [nonfiction] MJS (See full booktalk in *Booktalks and More*, 2003, pages 249 to 252.) Born a slave in 1862 and coming of age during the Reconstruction, Ida B. Wells became one of the first African-American investigative reporters. Like Helen Keller, she maintained her social activism in spite of pressures against her.

6. Freedman, Russell. **Eleanor Roosevelt: A Life of Discovery.**
    New York: Clarion Books, 1993. $17.95. ISBN 0 89919 862 7.
    [nonfiction] MJS Living in the same time period as Helen Keller,
    Eleanor Roosevelt fought for many of the same controversial
    causes. A picture of Eleanor Roosevelt and Helen Keller appears
    on page 188.

✿✿

Nelson, Marilyn. Carver: A Life in Poems.

Asheville, NC: Front Street, 2001. 103p. $16.95. ISBN 1 886910 53 7.

[biography in poems] MJS

Themes/Topics: ecology, responsibility, faith, generosity,
African-American history

Summary/Description

Beginning with baby Carver, his mother, and his brother being bush-whacked, this series of poems concludes with the dying religious
Professor Carver ruminating on the shame of war pilots training on his
beloved Tuskegee Campus. Nelson also includes portrayals of Carver's
foster parents. He emphasizes Carver's dedication to nature and education, outstanding mental ability, artistic talent, religious faith, work
ethic, love of nature, and humbling generosity. A time line of events and
pictures from Carver's life and period clarify the purpose of each poem
and the significance of its speaker.

Booktalk

*Hold up a peanut, a bag of peanuts or a Planter's Peanut can that shows
the dancing peanut. Ask the group what or whom they associate with it.
Then ask what they would expect of someone called "The Peanut Man."
Probably both questions will draw humorous responses.*

We think of peanuts, and we think of parties, circuses, nicknames,
and ballgames—maybe even jokes. But the original Peanut Man and
the peanut itself are serious business. (*Read "Araclis Hypogaea" on
page 28.*) George Washington Carver, the Peanut Man, a former slave,
saw the humble peanut as a gift from God. Carver thought his job was
to open the package. When he did, he found—(*Read list on page 84
beginning with "his peanut axle grease."*) A man humble enough to learn
from nature and share what he found, Carver allowed both the poorest
farmer and the wealthiest industrialist to prosper. Read about his life,
his work, and the world he loved in *Carver: A Life in Poems.*

Learning Opportunities

1. Research the uses of the peanut today. Prepare a presentation, with visual aids, to explain peanut growing, harvesting, and production.
2. Booker T. Washington was also a famous figure in African-American history. Research his life, contributions, and mission. Share your information with the group.
3. Research African-American education during Reconstruction. Share your information with the group. Explain how that period of history relates to African-American education today.
4. Using the Carver poems as an example, choose a person from history or a family member. Write ten poems about the person's life. Join the poems with a picture and a time line.
5. Read a Carver poem each day. Explain or write what you feel the poem reveals about Carver.
6. Find a prose account of Carver's life. You might wish to read an encyclopedia entry. List the information that both the prose and poetry present. Discuss how each form affects your reaction to the information.
7. Contact the Negro College Fund. Create a display of materials from African-American institutions of higher learning. Note the history of each and how the mission statement has changed or remained the same.

Related Works

1. Cooper, Michael L. **Slave Spirituals and the Jubilee Singers.** New York: Clarion, 2001. 86p. $16.00. ISBN 0 395 97829 7. [nonfiction] MJS This history of the Jubilee Singers from Fisk University also reveals the post-Civil War efforts in African-American education.
2. Ellis, Dr. Rex M. **With a Banjo on My Knee: A Musical Journey from Slavery to Freedom.** New York: Franklin Watts Publishers, 2001. 160p. $20.00. ISBN 0 531 11747 2. [nonfiction] MJS Ellis explains how the banjo became linked to prejudice in the post-Civil War era.
3. Fradin, Dennis Brindell, and Judith Bloom Fradin. **Fight On! Mary Church Terrell's Battle for Integration.** New York: Clarion Books, 2003. 181p. $17.00. ISBN 0 618 13349 6. [nonfiction] MJS Terrell, born the daughter of slaves in 1865, helped found the NAACP and integrate public facilities in Washington, D.C. Her greatest civil rights challenge came when she was ninety.
4. Fradin, Dennis Brindell, and Judith Bloom Fradin. **Ida B. Wells: Mother of the Civil Rights Movement.** New York: Clarion, 2000.

178p. $18.00. ISBN 0 395 89898 6. [nonfiction] MJS This biography explains the importance of Wells in the civil rights movement.

5. Litwin, Laura Baskes. **Benjamin Banneker: Astronomer and Mathematician** Berkeley Heights, NJ: Enslow Publishers, Inc., 1999. 112p. (African-American Biographies.) $20.95. ISBN 0 7660 1208 5. [nonfiction] MJS Another African-American genius of the post-Civil War era, Banneker lived in relative isolation because of racial prejudice.

Contemporary Life

Contemporary novels reflect the now, but without the level of angst seen in Issues novels. Life is hard, but maybe not as tough as people think. In these stories, teens grapple with teen problems—those things that many of us encounter as we grow up. In "Coming of Age" works, modern life directly affects the characters' maturation and sometimes intrudes on or challenges old attitudes. For many, "Sports," athletics and athletic competition, have a central part in that coming of age. "Humor" books remind readers how important it is to laugh in the struggle to enter a new and often frightening adult world.

Coming of Age

ঞ্চ

Cooncy, Caroline B. **Tune in Anytime.**
New York: Delacorte Press, 1999. 186p. $8.95. ISBN 0 385 32649 1. [fiction] MJS

Themes/Topics: family relationships, love, divorce

Summary/Description

Sixteen-year-old Sophie Olivette tries to save her family with love and responsibility. Her forty-five-year-old father is going to marry her sister's twenty-year-old college roommate, a trophy wife, and refuses to award Sophie's mother half of their worth. Avoiding a fight with him even though his plan will harm their daughters, she focuses instead on her latest passion, stones. Her interest leads her to Ted Larkman, Sophie's schoolmate, and his family, who own the local gravel pit. She convinces them to help her organize a winter solstice celebration, coinciding with the Larkmans's thirtieth wedding anniversary. In the planning, Ted and Sophie fall in love. To show his love, Ted decides to park a bulldozer in the Olivette's front yard as a threat to Sophie's father and his new wife. As Sophie's mother drives it toward the house, Sophie's father agrees to a fair settlement. Sophie lets her family take more responsibility for their actions, and she and Ted begin to build their own independent relationship.

Booktalk

Sixteen-year-old Sophie Olivette's life is a soap opera. Her father is going to marry her sister's college roommate after knowing her only two months. Her sister is busy looking for rich husband material in case daddy cuts off her funds. And her mother is talking to rocks—great big Stonehenge types whose magic is supposed to connect people's energies. The rock passion rolls Sophie's mother into the path of Ted Larkman, a boy Sophie is kind of interested in. The Larkmans are like their rock quarry—solid and stable. Sophie worries that the Larkmans, especially Ted, might discover that Sophie's family is a mixture of broke and nuts. If he pays attention, it won't take him long. After all, her family isn't quiet or private, and Sophie knows that the Larkmans, or anyone else, can *Tune in Anytime* to watch the action.

Learning Opportunities

1. Using your library's resources, research Stonehenge. Explain how the information relates to the story. You may wish to start with *The Illustrated History of the World: From the Big Bang to the Third Millennium* (Related Work 4).
2. On pages 144 to 147, Mr. Larkman and Sophie talk about life in rock and bulldozer terms. Read that section aloud. Discuss the passage and each character's perception of life.
3. Divorce is a very serious topic, but Cooney includes a great deal of humor in her story. Identify a humorous character, line, or incident. Then explain why it seems humorous to you.
4. Sophie demands Ted deliver the bulldozer even though she knows that he will probably get in trouble. Discuss why she makes the demand. Is it fair?
5. True love is a major theme in the story. Discuss how it is defined by the couples Cooney includes in her story.

Related Works

1. Aydt, Rachel. **Why Me?: A Teen Guide to Divorce and Your Feelings.** New York: The Rosen Publishing Group, 2000. 64p. (The Divorce Resource Series.) $19.95. ISBN 0 8239 3113 7. [nonfiction] MJS The Divorce Resource Series uses stories, definitions, and examples to explain how to cope with the many aspects of divorce including feelings, property, the law, and independence. The information is for teenage children in the first stages of the divorce. The reader may pursue further information through Web sites and toll-free numbers presented at the end of each book. This volume emphasizes the positive side of divorce; assures the children that they are not the cause; reminds them that they can help emotionally, physically, and financially; and clarifies that they are now relating to their parents individually rather than as a couple.

2. Creech, Sharon. **Bloomability.** New York: Harper Trophy/Joanna Cotler Books, 1998. 273p. $5.95. ISBN 0 06 440823 X. [fiction] MJ When thirteen-year-old Dinnie is placed in an international boarding school by her aunt and uncle, she discovers that rich kids have dysfunctional families too, and that she must pursue her own wishes and talents in spite of family problems.

3. McNeal, Laura, and Tom McNeal. **Crooked.** New York: Alfred A. Knopf, 1999. 246p. $16.95. ISBN 0 679 89300 8. [fiction] MJ (See full booktalk in *Booktalks and More,* 2003, pages 3 to 5.) Fourteen-year-old Clara Wilson and Amos Mackenzie find friendship and maybe love when Clara's parents divorce and Amos's father dies.

4. Morris, Neil et al., and Paola Ravaglia et al. (illus.). **The Illustrated History of the World: From the Big Bang to the Third Millennium**. New York: Enchanted Lion Books, 2004. 288p. $29.95. ISBN 1 59270 019 5. [nonfiction] MJS. Organized chronologically and then geographically within time periods, this illustrated global history of the world, on pages 30 and 31, provides a context for the Stonehenge allusion.

5. Powell, Randy. **Run If You Dare.** New York: Farrar, Straus and Giroux, 2001. 185p. $16.00. ISBN 0 374 39981 6. [fiction] JS (See full booktalk in *Booktalks and More,* 2003, pages 24 to 26.) In this coming of age novel, fourteen-year-old Gardner Dickinson decides he won't emulate his father but will get a specific direction in life.

CYED

Hobbs, Valerie. Tender.

New York: Farrar, Straus and Giroux/Francis Foster Books,
2001. 256p. $18.00. ISBN 0 374 37397 3. [fiction] MJS

Themes/Topics: family, cancer, responsibility, love

Summary/Description

Fifteen-year-old Liv Trager lives in New York with her grandmother.
Her mother died in childbirth, and her father communicates from
California with sporadic support checks. When her grandmother dies,
Liv moves to California to live with her father. Indulged and loved
unconditionally all her life, Liv confronts a man who works hard, hides
his feelings, and wants Liv to do the same. When Liv spends all the
money from the household box, she finds herself working on her father's
boat as the tender to pay back the money. Sam, her father's girlfriend,
who mediates the father/daughter relationship, discovers she has cancer.
Both Liv and her father struggle with how to love a person they might
lose. A boating accident that almost kills Liv clarifies their conflicts and
emotions. The story ends with Liv's father finally marrying Sam even
though her cancer may return, and Liv assessing the difference between
love and infatuation.

Booktalk

Fifteen-year-old Liv Trager never met her father, and her mother is
dead, but she loves her life. Her grandmother supports whatever she
wants. Her offbeat friends and alternative lifestyle make her a standout
even in a big city like New York. Then her grandmother dies, and Liv
is sent to California to live with her father. What a disappointment!
Her father works all day, falls asleep in his chair, and rarely gets beyond
"Huh?". Liv figures that she'll avoid him, and talk to Sam, his girlfriend.
Liv likes Sam better anyway. But suddenly, Daddy is paying attention to
his daughter. He discovers that Liv spent all the money in the household moneybox, and he wants it paid back. She'll work for him. They
spend hours together on his diving boat. She is his tender, the person
who guards his lifeline. Then Sam, the woman to whom Liv can tell all
her troubles, discovers she has cancer. Suddenly Liv, grandma's little
girl, is a major caregiver. With hard work, tough words, big risks, and
lots of love, Liv, the *Tender,* discovers what commitment and family are
all about.

Learning Opportunities

1. Liv's father dives for abalone. Using your library's resources, try to find pictures of abalone, the equipment needed to catch them, and their use.
2. Discuss the title. How many ways can it apply to the novel? Be sure to consider how the job of a tender can serve as a metaphor.
3. Compare Liv's life with her grandmother and her life with her father. What elements make her transition difficult, easy?
4. Using the characters presented in the novel, try to write a definition of love. Be sure to include Sam and Spinuchi.
5. Death is a major element in Liv's life as well as her father's. List the deaths mentioned in the novel. Discuss the impact of each.

Related Works

1. Bagdasarian, Adam. **First French Kiss and Other Traumas.** (See full booktalk in the section "Contemporary Life"/"Humor," pages 73 to 74.) JS A young man recalls all the traumas of growing up, but remembers most how his father insisted on self-discipline and responsibility.
2. Bauer, Joan. **Hope Was Here.** New York: G. P. Putnam's Sons, 2000. 186p. $16.99. ISBN 0 399 23142 0. [fiction] MJS (See full booktalk in *Booktalks and More,* 2003, pages 258 to 260.) When sixteen-year-old Hope and her aunt Addie take jobs at the Welcome Stairways Diner, Hope discovers the satisfaction of hard work and the joy of love and sadness of loss with the father she always wanted.
3. Going, K. L. **Fat Kid Rules the World.** (See full booktalk in "Issues"/"Personal Challenges," pages 4 to 6.) Never recovering from his mother's death, a young man contemplates suicide, is rescued by a local homeless teenage legend, and discovers that building a family is his responsibility as well as his father's.
4. Haddix, Margaret Peterson. **Takeoffs and Landings.** New York: Simon & Schuster Books for Young Readers, 2001. 201p. $16.00. ISBN 0 689 83299 0. [fiction] MJ Living with their grandparents after their father's death, two teenagers accompany their motivational speaker mother on one of her tours. All three rediscover their relationship and themselves.
5. Lamm, Drew. **Bittersweet.** New York: Clarion Books, 2003. 213p. $15.00. ISBN 0 618 16443 X. [fiction] JS High school junior, Taylor Rose, loses her celebrating and supportive grandmother through a stroke and then death. She struggles to relate to a quiet father she never really knew and friends, whom she misunderstood, as she searches for her own creative energy.

Cฦℭ

Lawrence, Iain. The Lightkeeper's Daughter.

New York: Delacorte Press, 2002. 246p. $16.95.
ISBN 0 385 72925 1. [fiction] JS

Themes/Topics: independence, family,
change, fear, freedom, control

Summary/Description

Seventeen-year-old Elizabeth McCrae (Squid) returns to Lizzie Island, a remote lighthouse station where she grew up, bringing her three-year-old daughter, Tatiana, with her. Squid's brother, Alastair, drowned four years ago. During the visit, the family explores the relationship between Alastair's death and Squid's pregnancy.

Schooled in the island's ecology by their father, the lightkeeper, Alastair developed into a brilliant scholar who, in his teenage years, wished to leave the island and study whale language. Squid is the risk taker. A year and a day apart in age, the brother and sister move into a small house built for the junior keeper, a position left empty because no one can meet their father's standards. Alastair moves first and names the house Gomorrah. Because of her children's closeness, their isolation, their curiosity about sex, and Tatiana's similarity to Alastair, Hannah, their mother, fears that Alastair is Tatiana's father, and that Squid's pregnancy drove him to suicide. Alastair's journals, discovered by Squid, reveal that the father's possessiveness and rigidity suffocated Alastair and verify that a drifter landed on the island and impregnated Squid. Alastair despaired that he could not, like the drifter, consummate his relationship with Squid, the only person who understood him. Mother and daughter bury the journals. Squid decides to leave the island and join her fiancé before her planned departure, but she leaves Tatiana for the remainder of the month to bond with her grandparents. Squid regrets leaving the island, a place her father still sees as a safe paradise, but realizes that separation is her road to adulthood.

Booktalk

Seventeen-year-old Elizabeth McCrae and her three year old daughter, Tatiana, are coming to Lizzie Island for a visit. Elizabeth hasn't been on the island for more than three years. She wants Tatiana to see where her mother grew up, meet her grandparents, and listen to the music of the whales—the whales her brother Alastair tried so hard to talk with before he died.

Hannah and Murray McCrae want to see their daughter and granddaughter. But they have some fears. They wonder why Elizabeth, the girl they nicknamed Squid, stayed away so long. They wonder if her leaving was tied to her brother's death. And they fear that her homecoming will open horrible secrets about two very important people: their son Alastair, whose voice Hannah hears in the night; and their granddaughter's father, a man they never saw. When the center of all their secrets, fears, hopes, and mysteries—*The Lightkeeper's Daughter*—returns, what and who will be changed forever?

Learning Opportunities

1. Discuss the characters of Murray and Hannah McCrae. What makes them good parents? What makes them bad parents? How do they work with both freedom and control?
2. Tatiana is a central character even though she says little. Note each time she is mentioned and the effect she has upon the scene or situation.
3. List the similarities and differences between Squid and Alastair. Then discuss why they are so close.
4. The setting of Lizzie Island dominates the story. Discuss how it is used and why we learn so little of Squid's life off the island.
5. Further research the language of whales. You might wish to start by consulting the addresses of whale conservation and research organizations listed in *Gone A-Whaling: The Lure of the Sea and the Hunt for the Great Whale* (Related Work 2). Share your information with the group.
6. Using your library's resources, research the name Gomorrah. Discuss why the information that you find is significant to the novel.
7. Chapter 16 contains Alastair's poems about the whales. Read them aloud and discuss their significance.
8. Certain phrases are central to the McCrae family—"It's the men against the girls," "Gather round," "The natives are restless." Discuss the significance of each. Then make a list of phrases your family or group might use often. Explain the function or significance of each.

Related Works

1. Juby, Susan. **Alice I Think.** New York: Harper Tempest, 2003. 290p. $16.89. ISBN 0 06 051544 9. [fiction] JS Sheltered and home-schooled by eccentric parents, a teenager humorously chronicles the difficulties of making the transition into regular high school.
2. Murphy, Jim. **Gone A-Whaling: The Lure of the Sea and the Hunt for the Great Whale.** New York: Clarion, 1998. 208p. $18.00. ISBN 0 395 69847 2. [nonfiction] MJS (See full booktalk in *Booktalks Plus*, 2001, pages 108 to 110.) Murphy explains how

man's attitude toward the whale has changed over the history of whaling. Formerly, whaling referred to hunting the whale. Now it refers to observing and learning from it.

3.   Napoli, Donna Jo. **Zel.** New York: Dutton Children's Books, 1996. 227p. $15.99. ISBN 0 525 45612 0. Based on the fairy tale *Rapunzel,* the story tells about a teenage girl who finds love even though an overprotective mother tries to imprison her in a tower.

4.   Pullman, Philip. **His Dark Materials Trilogy.** New York: Alfred A. Knopf. [fiction] MJS (See full booktalks in *Booktalks and More,* 2003, pages 161 to 166.)

The Golden Compass. 1995. 399p. $20.00. ISBN 0 679 8794 2. Lyra, an orphan, discovers the identity of her parents and, as the lone reader of *The Golden Compass,* finds herself in a struggle between good and evil.

The Subtle Knife. 1997. 362p. $20.00. ISBN 0 679 87925 0. Will, seeking his father, enters an alternative reality and meets Lyra. Together they find Will's father and Will's role in the universe as the keeper of *The Subtle Knife.*

The Amber Spyglass. 2000. 518p. $19.95. ISBN 0 679 87926 9. As the new Adam and Eve, Lyra and Will use their powers to keep their two worlds separate.

℃℥℥

McGraw, Jay. Life Strategies for Teens.

New York: Fireside Press, 2000. 236p. $14.00.
ISBN 0 7432 1546 X. [nonfiction] JS

Themes/Topics: identity, independence, decision-making, self-respect

Summary/Description

Adapted from Phillip C. McGraw's *Life Strategies, Life Strategies for Teens* presents "The Ten Laws of Life" with experiences from Jay McGraw's own life as well as the lives of other teens. Each chapter includes short exercises inviting reader response and concludes with "Lightbulbs," listing the chapter's main ideas. Assessment checklists or sample action plans are bolded, indented, and starred within the text. Chapter 8: "We Teach People How to Treat Us" distinguishes between normal and abnormal behavior and lists contact numbers for teens dealing with rape, abuse and neglect, violence, and suicide.

Booktalk

Ask how many people watch Dr. Phil or have seen him on Oprah. Ask for their responses.

Dr. Phil McGraw had so much success with his book *Life Strategies* that he decided to write a teen version. His son, Jay McGraw, read that book. But he had to tell his dad that when it came to teenagers, Dr. Phil McGraw just didn't get it. It took Jay six years to figure out what his dad was trying to say. Jay knew that most teenagers, since they weren't living with the author, wouldn't have that kind of patience or time. So his dad gave him a challenge.—You write the book, and Jay did.

Do you feel you are stuck in a rut? Afraid of what tomorrow will bring? Seeing other people succeed when you can't seem to? Fighting instead of working with parents and teachers? Overwhelmed by a whole new world? Read *Life Strategies for Teens*. Jay McGraw has been there and done that—just recently. He gets it and writes down his experiences so that you can get it too.

Learning Opportunities

1. Read the entire book and complete the exercises. Then start a *Life Strategies* journal. Each week, focus on one of the ten strategies. In your journal, explain how you have applied the strategy and how the application has made a difference in your life.
2. Observe others in your daily life. Identify situations that relate to the ten strategies. Explain how the strategy was used or how using it might have helped the situation. Include these observations in your journal also.
3. In a discussion group, share some of your information and experiences with others who have also completed Learning Opportunity 1 or 2. Note your agreements and disagreements.
4. McGraw lists no other self-help books or Web sites. Research self-help literature for teens. Prepare an annotated bibliography of self-help books that you recommend.
5. After researching and reading self-help literature, note the common messages that these books deliver. Prepare your own pamphlet, oral presentation, or visual display that highlights these messages.
6. Using the information gathered in Learning Opportunities 1 through 5, work with a guidance counselor, teacher, librarian, or school administrator to prepare a student Successful Life program.
7. Prepare a *Life Strategies* presentation for an audience younger than yourself.

Related Works

1. Carlson, Richard. **Don't Sweat the Small Stuff for Teens: Simple Ways to Keep your Cool in Stressful Times.** New York: Hyperion, 2000. 242p. $11.95pa. ISBN 0 7868 8597 1. [nonfiction] JS Like the adult version, these insightful essays help teens think about behavior and life choices.

2. Cohen, Michael. **Identifying, Understanding and Solutions to Stress.** London, England: Caxton Editions, 2001. 95p. $24.95. ISBN 1 84067 288 9. [nonfiction] JS/A Although this book is not written specifically for teens, its clear explanations of controlling and directing stress are appropriate for a teen audience.

3. Covey, Sean. **The 7 Habits of Highly Effective Teens: The Ultimate Teenage Success Guide.** New York: Fireside, 1998. 268p. $14.00. ISBN 0 684 85609 3. [nonfiction] JS (See full booktalk in *Booktalks and More,* 2003, pages 264 to 266.) In this teen version of *7 Habits of Highly Effective People,* Sean Covey explains his father's principles for the teen reader.

4. Graham, Stedman. **Teens Can Make It Happen: Nine Steps to Success.** New York: Scholastic, Inc., 2000. 250p. $6.95pa. ISBN 0 439 40498 3. [nonfiction] JS This teen adaptation of the adult *You Can Make It Happen: A Nine Step Plan for Success* focuses on "active optimism" and three "success circles"—Career, Personal Development, and Relationships.

5. Zielin, Lara. **The Key to Networking for Teens.** Montreal, Canada: Lobster Press, 2003. 107p. $9.95pa. ISBN 1 894222 43 1. [nonfiction] JS Zielin defines networking as learning about oneself in relation to the world of school and work.

❧❧

Myers, Walter Dean. **Bad Boy: A Memoir.**
New York: Harper Tempest, 2001. 206p. $6.95pa.
ISBN 0 06 447288 4. [nonfiction] JS

Themes/Topics: heritage, family, prejudice, identity, choices

Summary/Description

In this autobiography, Myers tells about his early life. "Roots" explains the relationships of his parents and grandparents and how he came to live in Harlem. Subsequent chapters describe his elementary and high school education as well as his dysfunctional but loving home life.

He includes incidents of his unruly behavior, his passion for reading and writing, descriptions of adults who helped him succeed, the effects of society's discouraging unspoken stereotypes, and his own poor and sometimes dangerous teenage choices.

Booktalk

Ask how many people in the group know Harlem's location and something about its reputation and history. Ask how many people have read books by Walter Dean Myers, and ask them to briefly describe them.

Walter Dean Myers grew up in Harlem. He joined his son in producing a book about it (*Show the book* Harlem *and some of the pictures*) (Related Work 2). He wrote many other books also including *Monster* (*Hold up the book*) (Related Work 3), the first young adult book to win the Printz Award for young adult literature. In this autobiography, *Bad Boy,* he tells how he survived school, his family, and the Harlem streets, and how all of those things helped him and sometimes discouraged him from writing. If you have read any of Myers's books, you will enjoy reading about his path to success. If this is the first Myers's book you've read, it won't be the last. He makes no apologies or excuses. He just describes in his prizewinning style what life was like for someone who could be a very *Bad Boy.*

Learning Opportunities

1. Chart the relationships in Myers family. Also mark or draw a map to show where they lived.
2. Myers refers to Harlem as a "magical place." Continue to research the history of Harlem and share your information with the group. You might wish to start with *Harlem* (Related Work 2) by Myers and his son.
3. Myers talks about the adults in his life and how they influenced him. List the adults he discusses. Then list what you feel each contributed, good and bad, to his life.
4. Myers talks about how stereotyping affected his life. Define stereotyping and prejudice. Then discuss how, according to Myers's account, stereotyping operated both in and out of the African-American community.
5. War and Myers's perceptions of war influence his actions. Cite the references he makes to war.
6. Myers talks about his separation from black writers, and in the chapter "God and Dylan Thomas," describes his fascination with Dylan Thomas and his ignorance of Langston Hughes. Read works by both writers. Compare their themes and styles (Related Works 1 and 4).

Related Works

1. Berry, S.L. (text). **Langston Hughes.** Mankato, MN: Creative Education, 1993. 45p. (Voices in Poetry.) $27.10. ISBN 0 88682 616 0. [poetry] MJS Using biographical narrative, Hughes's poems, and pictures depicting Hughes's life and times, this thin, oversize volume communicates much about Hughes and the world in which he lived.

2. Myers, Walter Dean (poem), and Christopher Myers (illus.). **Harlem.** New York: Scholastic Press, 1997. 30p. $16.95. ISBN 0 590 54340 7. [poetry] JS (See full booktalk in *Booktalks Plus*, 2001, pages 241 to 243.) The poem lists the people, places, beliefs, pastimes, and feelings of Harlem in the language and rhythms of the community. The listing provides a reference for further research. The pictures are a motivating background.

3. Myers, Walter Dean. **Monster.** New York: HarperCollins Publishers, 1999. 281p. $15.95. ISBN 0 06 028077 8. [fiction] JS (See full booktalk in *Booktalks and More*, 2003, pages 13 to 15.) Sixteen-year-old Steve Harmon, on trial for murder, creates a play about the trial and his experiences before the trial. The tone that Myers creates is similar to the tone of Camus's *The Stranger*, he alludes to in the chapter, "The Stranger" of *Bad Boy.*

4. Poets.org. Available: http://poets.org (Accessed June 2005.) The Web site allows the user to access information about the poets, their work, and individual poems.

5. Wright, Richard. **Black Boy: A Record of Childhood and Youth.** New York: Perennial Classics, 1998. 419p. $13.00pa. ISBN 0 06 092978 2. [nonfiction] S/A Written in 1944, the autobiography records Wright's growing up in the Jim Crow South. This edition includes a chronology and notes.

ぱ

Zusak, Markus. Getting the Girl.
New York: Arthur A. Levine, 2003. 272p. $16.95.
ISBN 0 439 38949 6. [fiction] S

Themes/Topics: family, love, sex, identity

Summary/Description

As in *Fighting Ruben Wolfe*, Cameron tries to define himself in relation to his physically and emotionally tougher brothers Ruben and

Stephen. Cameron falls in love with one of Ruben's cast-off girlfriends. Discovering the relationship, Ruben beats Cameron up. Both the girl and Cameron's sister tell Cameron that he must stand up for himself if he doesn't want to be the loser in the family, as Stephen calls him. Cameron decides that his words, not his fists define him. He confronts his older brother Stephen about the loser label. Stephen apologizes. Cameron confronts Ruben about the beating, and Ruben admits that he feared that the girl would prefer Cameron. Then when Ruben is badly beaten by a gang defending another one of his cast-off girlfriends, Cameron carries him home. By the end of the novel, Cameron has the girl and the respect of his sister and two older brothers. Each chapter ends with journal pages in which Cameron reflects on events and his feelings. The language and subject matter make this a selection for more mature teens.

Booktalk

(Note: This booktalk assumes the audience has read the previous book.)

You probably all remember Cameron and Ruben Wolfe, Markus Zusak's fighting Australian brothers and the rest of the pack—brother Steve, sister Sarah, Mrs. Wolfe, and the now employed—easier to get along with—"old man." (*While reminding the audience, you might want to hold up a copy of* Fighting Ruben Wolfe.) Well, the Wolfe pack from *Fighting Ruben Wolfe* is back. This time the Wolfes aren't using boxing gloves—just their bare fists. But Cameron isn't so sure that fists are the way to go, especially when he'll be the one with the bruises. He wants his brother Ruben's girl, the beautiful Octavia. The whole idea seems dangerous, but after all, Ruben is so handsome and popular that his girlfriends are practically disposable. Maybe if Cameron waits until the new one shows up he can get Octavia by default. Then again, maybe Ruben will kill him. Now Cameron, the runt of the Wolfe pack, has to decide how much he is willing to risk for *Getting the Girl*.

Learning Opportunities

1. At the end of each chapter, Cameron writes a reflection. Reread just those ending passages. Then describe Cameron. Discuss both his strengths and weaknesses.
2. In Chapter 2, Cameron compares himself to Stephen. Choose one person in your family. Describe yourself by comparing yourself to that person.

3. In Chapter 14, Sarah shows him her drawings. He discovers that she expresses herself through pictures as he expresses himself through words. Pair up with another person in the group who communicates perceptions in a way different from you. The expression might include words, songs, pictures, film, or sculpture. Then focus on a mutual experience, person, or object. Each person should express his or her impressions through the medium of choice.

4. Both Sarah and Octavia push Cameron to stand up for himself. Discuss their demands and why they make them.

5. Cameron constantly worries about where he fits in relation to his older brothers. Using library resources and the Internet, research how birth order might effect each child in a family.

Related Works

1. Chambers, Aidan. **Postcards from No Man's Land.** New York: Dutton Books, 1999. 320p. $19.99. ISBN 0 525 46863 3. [fiction] S A young man who intends to honor his grandfather's war efforts finds family secrets and his own sexual awakening.

2. Frank, Hillary. **Better than Running at Night.** Boston, MA: Houghton Mifflin Co., 2002. 263p. $17.00. ISBN 0 618 10439 9. [fiction] S A college freshman tries to figure out her art talent, her exploitive boyfriend, and her desire to be part of something.

3. Mosier, Elizabeth. **My Life As a Girl.** New York: Random House, 1999. 193p. $17.00. ISBN 0 679 89035 1. [fiction] S (See full booktalk in *Booktalks Plus,* 2001, pages 121 to 123.) Jamie Cody, a freshman at Bryn Mawr, must decide if she will succumb to the charms of a charming, lazy boyfriend or build her own career and life.

4. Peck, Robert Newton. **Cowboy Ghost.** New York: HarperCollins Children's Books, 1999. 200p. $15.95. ISBN 0 06 028168 5. [fiction] MJS (See full booktalk in *Booktalks Plus,* 2001, pages 15 to 16.) Titus MacRobertson, considered the runt of the family, worries that he will never be as big or as important as his older brother until his brother dies. Titus discovers that his brother was a sensitive writer afraid to reveal his feelings.

5. Zusak, Markus. **Fighting Ruben Wolfe.** (See full booktalk in "Contemporary Life"/"Sports," pages 70 to 72.) Offered opportunities to fight professionally, two brothers begin fighting each other and themselves.

Sports

ℭℨℨℭ

Connelly, Neil. St. Michael's Scales.
New York: Arthur A. Levine Books, 2002. 320p. $16.95.
ISBN 0 439 19445 8. [fiction] MJS

Themes/Topics: wrestling,
responsibility, suicide, sixties setting

Summary/Description

Fifteen-year-old Keegan Flannery is the oldest and smallest ninth grader at the almost bankrupt Our Lady of Perpetual Help High School in Allentown, Pennsylvania during the sixties. Keegan's twin brother, Michael, died at birth. Keegan thinks the wrong twin died, because his mother, in a mental hospital for six years, dwells on the dead brother. He blames himself for the brother's death, his mother's illness, his father's emotional distance, and his oldest brother's running away. He decides that killing himself in two weeks—on his sixteenth birthday—will solve his family's problems. Each chapter brings the reader closer to the suicide decision date. In high school, because of his size and physical limitations, he has been in the extreme out-group. He eats lunch everyday with Nathan Looby, another outcast, a boy with one arm and a hearing aid. But at eighty-four and three-quarter pounds, Keegan is the only student eligible to wrestle in the 95-pound weight class. In wrestling, he finds another world of pain, punishment, and friendship with its own commandments. Then, Nathan commits suicide. Keegan fails to stop him—another event proving that he isn't fit to live. Preparing to carry out his own death, Keegan discovers a suicide note from Nathan and realizes that trying hard in spite of pain, reaching out to others, and taking responsibility can make good things happen.

Booktalk

Ask how many people in the group know about making weight for school wrestling.

Keegan Flannery doesn't worry about making weight. He is always eighty-four and three-quarter pounds. His coach calls him Three-Quarters. The only team Keegan ever thinks he'll be on is at the Rockdale Juvenile Detention Center. Regular teams don't want a guy who killed his twin brother, made his mother crazy, drove his older brother out of the house, and is so lame in gym that he has to play dead to get extra credit. But Our Lady of Perpetual Help High School is a kind of the misfit's paradise. Even their low budget statue of Christ, with the heart on the wrong side, is a mistake. The team has to fill the ninety-five pound slot or forfeit. Keegan is the only "Warm Body" at Our Lady's small enough to do it. He says OK. After all, in two weeks he'll just be a cold body—dead on his sixteenth birthday. He can use the wrestling pain to get into heaven. That's how the saints and martyrs make it, isn't it? They suffer, die, and go to heaven. His suffering and suicide will save his family. All those bad things he did—the ones too horrible to confess—will finally balance out at heaven's gate on *St. Michael's Scales.*

Learning Opportunities

1. Using your library's resources, research the history and process of sainthood. Share your information with the group.
2. List each member of the Flannery family. Describe the effect each has on Keegan.
3. Connelly chooses the story settings carefully. List each setting. Describe it. Then explain how each is necessary to the novel as a whole.
4. St. Michael is the patron saint of the sick and of battle—an appropriate combination for Keegan. Why does Connelly choose to name Keegan's twin brother Michael also?
5. Nathan Looby is a central figure in the novel. Discuss his importance. In the discussion, be sure to include his suicide note.
6. Compare the world that Keegan usually lives in and the world of wrestling. Then discuss how the world of wrestling transforms him.
7. Keegan believes that the statue of Christ with the heart on the wrong side is an appropriate symbol for Our Lady of Perpetual Help High School. Discuss whether or not you agree or disagree. Then select what you feel to be an appropriate symbol for Keegan.

Related Works

1. Cobain, Bev. **When Nothing Matters Anymore: A Survival Guide for Depressed Teens.** Minneapolis, MN: Free Spirit Publishing Inc., 1998. 164p. $13.95. ISBN 1 57542 036 8. [nonfiction] JS Bev Cobain, cousin of Kurt Cobain, explains why suicide, as a permanent solution to a temporary problem, is a bad choice.
2. Collins, Pat Lowery. **Signs and Wonders.** New York: Houghton Mifflin, 1999. 176p. $15.00. ISBN 0 395 97119 5. [fiction] MJS

Feeling rejected by her family and living in a Catholic boarding school, fourteen-year-old Taswell fantasizes that she has been chosen to give birth (virgin birth) to the prophet for the new millennium.

3. Griffin, Adele. **The Other Shepards.** New York: Hyperion Books for Children, 1998. 218p. $14.95. ISBN 0 7868 0423 8. [fiction] MJ (See full booktalk in *Booktalks and More,* pages 67 to 69.) Sisters, born after the death of their older siblings, find it impossible to live up to their dead sibling's perfect lives until a stranger who is very much like their dead sister appears and helps them move on.

4. Klass, David. **You Don't Know Me.** New York: Farrar, Straus and Giroux/Francis Foster Books, 2001. 262p. $17.00. ISBN 0 374 38706 0. [fiction] JS (See full booktalk in *Booktalks and More,* 2003, pages 31 to 33.) Believing that his mother does not know or love him, a young man endures the abuse from her live-in boyfriend. Like Keegan, he discovers that the parent he thinks rejects him really loves him.

5. Lawrence, Iain. **The Lightkeeper's Daughter.** New York: Delacorte Press, 2002. 246p. $16.95. ISBN 0 385 72925 1. [fiction] S (See full booktalk in "Contemporary Life"/"Coming of Age," pages 50 to 52.) Overwhelmed by his father's rigid standards and isolated from the rest of the world, a young teenager kills himself. When his sister returns to the island where they grew up, she tries to sort out the reasons for his choice.

6. Many, Paul. **Walk Away Home.** New York: Walker & Co., 2002. 240p. $16.95. ISBN 0 8027 8828 9. [fiction] S Nick Doran, alienated from his parents since his brother's death several years ago, leaves home and discovers a new life with his eccentric aunt and an unusual in-group/out-group challenge.

☙❧

Jeter, Derek with Jack Curry. **The Life You Imagine: Life Lessons for Achieving Your Dreams.**

New York: Scholastic Inc., 2000. 279p. $4.99pa.
ISBN 0 439 35601 6. [nonfiction] JS

Themes/Topics: baseball, skill,
character, goals, choices, family

Summary/Description

D erek Jeeter describes himself as an ordinary guy with extraordinary dreams. He talks about setting high goals, dealing with setbacks, choosing role models, keeping a balance between focus and fun, being a team leader, thinking before acting, and greeting each day as a new challenge. He uses experiences from his biracial family, strong work ethic, supportive friends, exploitive acquaintances, and leader/follower roles to illustrate his beliefs, and he emphasizes that he maintained high academic performance in case his athletic dreams did not materialize. Pictures illustrate the highlights of his family and career. Inserts explain how other players perceive him.

Booktalk

Ask if anyone in the room knows who Derek Jeter is.

Derek Jeter always wanted to be a Yankee. He not only became a Yankee, but also a multi-million-dollar baseball man. How did he do it? It took more than talent. He set and met his goals to go along with his dream. He learned to ignore the stares and rude comments directed toward him and his biracial family. In his first season, so homesick and afraid he wouldn't make it to the majors (56 errors in his first season), he cried himself to sleep every night. That was after he called his parents and cried on the phone. Some of his teammates, jealous of the attention he was getting, tried to make him quit. But Derek stayed. A Yankee uniform hung on the wall of his room when he was growing up. Now he was going to have a chance to wear it. He will tell you how he did it. Paying attention may mean that you too can have *The Life You Imagine*.

Learning Opportunities

1. Derek Jeter illustrates his principles to live by in ten chapters, but he uses more than ten principles to direct his life. Using complete sentences, write the principles you feel Derek Jeter uses to shape his life.
2. Drawing on the sentences that you have composed, find examples in real life that illustrate or contradict Jeter's beliefs. Then explain the results of those examples.
3. Using complete sentences, write the principles that you use to shape your life.
4. Illustrate how each principle helps you to succeed.
5. List other principles that you might incorporate. Explain your reasons for doing so.
6. Derek Jeter talks quite a bit about living up to the Yankee ideal. Using your library's resources, research the history of the New York Yankees. Share your information with the group in an oral or a visual display.

Related Works

1. Conroy, Pat. **My Losing Season.** New York: Doubleday, 2002. 402p. $27.95. ISBN 0 385 48912 9. [nonfiction] S/A The author of *The Prince of Tides* explains how his brutal Citadel basketball experience was tied to his abusive home life. The language requires a mature audience. The passage beginning on page 3 with "The lessons I learned while playing basketball . . . " and ending on page 4 with the words " . . . sweet, swift game" makes a good strong read aloud indicating the relationship between sports and self-discovery.

2. Hamm, Mia, with Aaron Heifetz. **Go for the Goal: A Champion's Guide to Winning in Soccer and Life.** New York: HarperCollins Publishers, 1999. 222p. $21.00. ISBN 0 06 019342 5. [nonfiction] JS (See full booktalk in *Booktalks and More*, 2003, pages 132 to 134.) Part 1 talks about preparing to achieve one's goal. Part 2 explains specific soccer skills. Part 3 emphasizes personal qualities that define a true champion.

3. Johnson, Scott. **Safe at Second.** New York: Philomel Books, 1999. 254p. $17.99. ISBN 0 399 23365 2. [fiction] MJS (See full booktalk in *Booktalks Plus*, 2001, pages 101 to 103.) Like Derek Jeter, Todd Bannister is a baseball standout. Unlike Jeter, he does not have a backup when his dream of becoming a professional ballplayer is destroyed in an accident. His friend, Paulie Roy Lockwood, lives through Todd.

4. Peck, Robert Newton. **Extra Innings.** New York: Harper Trophy, 2001. 215p. $5.99pa. ISBN 0 06 447229 9. [fiction] MJS After sixteen-year-old Tate Stonemason is injured in a plane crash that kills his sister, parents, and grandparents, he moves in with his eighty-two-year-old great grandfather and his seventy-year-old adopted African-American aunt. Each of the three books is one of the characters' perceptions of the situation and their lives.

5. Robinson, Sharon. **Jackie's Nine: Jackie Robinson's Values to Live By.** New York: Scholastic Incorporated, 2001. 192p. $15.95. ISBN 0 439 23764 5. [nonfiction] MJS (See full booktalk in *Booktalks and More*, 2003, pages 123 to 125.) Sharon Robinson illustrates the nine principles she feels guided her father's life—courage, determination, teamwork, persistence, integrity, citizenship, justice, commitment, and excellence. You might wish to use this book in conjunction with *The Life You Imagine* to compare both the attitudes expressed and the formats used.

ᘓᘔ

Klass, David. Home of the Braves.

New York: Farrar, Straus and Giroux/Francis Foster Books,
2002. 312p. $18.00. ISBN 0 374 39963 8. [fiction] JS

Themes/Topics: wrestling,
soccer, love, competition, bullies

Summary/Description

Eighteen-year-old Joe Brickman is a senior at Lawndale High School
in Northern New Jersey. He captains the wrestling team and
losing soccer team, and is comfortable with his life of athletics, mediocre
academics, a small circle of close friends that includes Kris—the girl
who lives across the street—and washing cars at his father's car wash.
Three events change his life. The arrogant, rich, and talented Antonio
Silva transfers into the school from Brazil, joins the soccer team, and
starts to date Kris. The school bullies target Antonio who disables two
of them, both football stars, and causes the football team to lose the
championship while bringing wins and attention to the soccer team.
They also target Mouse, Joe's nerdy computer friend, who decides to
fight them, and eventually, with his father's support, leaves the school.
Consequently, Joe reconsiders his feelings for Kris, the student code
of silence, and his own future. He finally refuses to be drawn into the
town's cycle of violence and decides to develop, with Kris's help, an academic record that can take him to a promising future.

Booktalk

Joe Brickman is looking forward to his senior year at Lawndale High
even though getting along with some of the football bullies is like
walking through a minefield. Joe is no football player. He captains the
Lawndale Braves's soccer and wrestling teams. It doesn't matter that
it's a losing soccer team. All his friends are on it, and they have a good
time—practice or game, win or lose. The big change in his life is Kris,
who lives across the street. These days he thinks about her more as a
date than a buddy, and maybe he'll ask her out—sometime. But then
Antonio Silva, a Brazilian import, shows up. He's rich, handsome, and
moves down a soccer field as fast as he takes over Joe's "could have
been" girlfriend. But the really bad news is that the Brazilian bombshell
blows up the football team's starring role. The football bullies unleash a
reign of terror that targets Joe's best friend—the nerdy, computer whiz,

Mouse. Joe's world, his own comfortable home, has never been perfect, but at least he knew how to survive in it. Suddenly it's all disappearing, and if he is going to build a new *Home of the Braves,* he has to decide what he can still use and what he has to throw away.

Learning Opportunities

1. At the end of Chapter 4, Joe says "… I was keenly aware of a reality that is as true in other areas of life as it is in soccer: If you can only play defense, you're setting yourself up for disappointment." Discuss that statement. Use examples or illustrations to support your opinions.
2. In Chapter 5, on pages 45 and 46, Joe describes his room. In Chapter 17, on page 260 he tells about clearing shelves and packing his old trunk. Discuss what each scene reveals about Joe.
3. Both Mouse and Antonio leave Lawndale High School because of harassment. Compare the two departures and the two characters. Then describe what qualities allow Joe Brickman to stay. In your discussion, consider Joe's name.
4. Discuss the father/son relationships in the story. What does each relationship have to say about moving on?
5. Using your library's resources, gather information on how to deal with bullies. Share your information with the group (Related Work 2).
6. Both Kris and Dianne are formidable characters in the novel. Discuss the role each plays.

Related Works

1. Atkins, Catherine. **Alt Ed.** New York: G. P. Putnam's Sons, 2003. 198p. $17.99. ISBN 0 399 23854 9. [fiction] JS After shocking her father, the head football coach, with an act of vandalism, sophomore Susan Callaway is forced to join a counseling group where she learns to become more sensitive to both the bullied and the bullies in her school.
2. Bott, C. J. **The Bully in the Book and in the Classroom.** Lanham, MD: The Scarecrow Press, Inc., 2004. 185p. $30.00pa. ISBN 0 8108 5048 6. [professional reference] In her analysis and discussion of bullying, Bott features *Home of the Braves, Alt ED* (Related Work 1) and *Give a Boy a Gun* (Related Work 6). It is primarily a teacher and librarian text, but students researching reports or conducting discussion groups may find the extensive bibliographies and suggestions useful as well.

3. Lubar, David. **Dunk.** New York: Clarion, 2002. 249p. $15.00. ISBN 0 618 19455 X. [fiction] JS (See full booktalk in "Contemporary Life"/"Humor," pages 79 to 81.) Chad Turner lives with the fear that he will be like the father who deserted him and his mother, but slowly learns to appreciate his own abilities and builds a life for himself.

4. Powell, Randy. **Run If You Dare.** New York: Farrar, Straus and Giroux, 2001. 185p. $16.00. ISBN 0 374 39981 6. (See full booktalk in *Booktalks and More*, 2003, pages 24 to 26.) The main character sees that he shares some of the habits and attitudes of his unsuccessful father and decides to work hard and become a different person.

5. Rottman, S. L. **Stetson.** (See full booktalk in "Issues"/"Interpersonal Challenges," pages 23 to 25.) A young man who works on rebuilding cars must decide what he will do to salvage his own life and family.

6. Strasser, Todd. **Give a Boy a Gun.** New York: Simon and Schuster, 2000. 146p. $16.00. ISBN 0 689 81112 8. (See full booktalk in *Booktalks and More*, 2003, pages 116 to 118.) Brendan and Gary, bullied by the school athletes, decide to retaliate Columbine style.

ℭℨℨ

Murphy, Claire Rudolf. **Free Radical.**
New York: Clarion Books, 2002. 198p. $15.00.
ISBN 0 618 11134 4. [fiction] MJ

Themes/Topics: baseball, Vietnam protest, crime, restitution, family, choices

Summary/Description

Fifteen-year-old Luke Henry lives with his mother and his stepfather in Alaska. A drunk driver killed his real father before Luke was born. As Luke focuses on qualifying for baseball All Stars, his mother reveals that she helped set a pipe bomb that killed a college student when, at Berkley, she was protesting the Vietnam War. She wants to turn herself in, serve her prison time, and reunite with her family. When Luke's team qualifies for regionals, both baseball and the trial bring Luke and his mother to California. Luke, who has resisted his mother's efforts to confess, decides to support her, attends her trial, witnesses her sentencing, and suggests a meeting between her and the victim's family. Even though his mother must serve prison time, her confession and meeting begin a healing process that impresses on Luke and his friends how foolish actions bring lifelong consequences.

Booktalk

Luke McHenry, at fifteen, has his first chance to be a baseball All Star. If he makes the team and gets them to work together, they are on their way to California and the big time. Amy, a beautiful girl with her own car, loves being around him. But there is one big problem—his mother. Suddenly, she wants to know where he is every minute. She starts going to church. People whisper about her past, and then she drops the big secret. The FBI wants her for murder. Fairbanks, Alaska, is more than their home. It's her hideout. Just when Luke is finally getting a life, he stumbles over hers and its unbreakable connections with the Vietnam War. How can he stop his mother, this *Free Radical,* from blowing up his world too?

Learning Opportunities

1. On page 23, Chapter 4, Luke describes victim offender mediation. In Chapter 20, Peter Rodriquez explains restorative justice. As a group, use your library and community resources to research these concepts and their place in the penal system. Then debate the merits for both the victim and offender.
2. Although baseball and reparation seem an incongruous mix, Luke is a key part of both. Discuss how the skills he develops in baseball allow him to help his mother.
3. Sid and Amy have small but important roles in the novel. Discuss their impact.
4. Neither Luke's final game nor his mother's confession has a completely happy ending. Discuss the problems in each conclusion and why the author chose to include problems.
5. On page 27, Chapter 4, Kathleen explains free radicals. After reading the passage, discuss why *Free Radical* is both an appropriate and ironic title.
6. *Free Radical* mentions several issues about the period of the Vietnam War. Research that period as a group. Divide your research into several sections such as religious, political, economic, academic, and lifestyle choices.
7. Chapter 24, the concluding chapter, contains several elements that relate the novel's events to nature's patterns. Discuss those relationships and why they are appropriate or inappropriate for the conclusion.
8. On pages 193 and 194 in Chapter 23, Luke's friend introduces the idea of writing poetry by using the phone book. Following their example, choose phrases and apply them to yourself, family, and friends.

Related Works

1. Hobbs, Valerie. **Sonny's War.** New York: Farrar, Straus and Giroux/ Frances Foster Books, 2002. 215p. $16.00. ISBN 0 374 37136 9. [fiction] JS A sister watches her brother and family change after their father's death, her brother's tour of duty in Vietnam, and her mother's feeling of independence.
2. Lynch, Chris. **Gold Dust.** New York: HarperCollins Publishers, 2000. 196p. $15.95. ISBN 0 06 028174 X. [fiction] MJ Like Luke, the main character prefers baseball's certitude of rules and scoring to the social problems of racism that surrounds him.
3. Mazer, Norma Fox. "Carmella, Adelina, and Florry." In **Help Wanted: Short Stories about Young People Working**, compiled by Anita Silvey. New York: Little, Brown, and Co., 1997. 174p. $15.95. ISBN 0 316 79148 2. [fiction] JS A mother tells her daughter about being influenced by a union organizer who used her to further his own social agenda.
4. McDonald, Joyce. **Swallowing Stones.** New York: Laurel Leaf Books, 1997. 245p. $4.50pa. ISBN 0 440 22672 4. [fiction] JS (See full booktalk in *Booktalks and More*, 2003, pages 97 to 99.) Michael MacKenzie fires his new rifle and kills a man he has never met. Trying to hide and deny his mistake, he finally decides to take responsibility for his actions and confess to the victim's daughter.
5. Mikaelsen, Ben. **Touching Spirit Bear.** New York: HarperCollins Publishers, 2001. 241p. $15.95. ISBN 0 380 97744 3. [fiction] MJ (See full booktalk in *Booktalks and More,* pages 80 to 82.) This story about a radical approach to juvenile rehabilitation includes victim offender mediation.

ᘓᘔ

Swanson, Julie A. **Going for the Record.**

Grand Rapids, MI: Eerdmans Books for Young Readers,
2004. 217p. $8.00pa. ISBN 0 8028 5273 4. [fiction] JS

Themes/Topics: soccer, family,
death, hospice, love, life balance

Summary/Description

Seventeen-year-old Leah Weiczynkowski, a soccer star, qualifies for her first step to the World Cup and Olympic teams at the same time that her father and biggest fan announces that he has terminal cancer. He chooses hospice. As she helps her mother care for him, she, like her dying father, battles denial and withdraws from life. She rejects her long time friend, Luke, who loves her, and although she qualifies for the next step toward her soccer dream and multiple college scholarships, quits soccer. After her father dies, she realizes that she loves Luke, but sees soccer as "just a game" that robbed her of family time. She seeks a more significant way to direct her life—working in her father's restaurant or volunteering at hospice—but her family and friends know that she needs to return to her passion. They manipulate a pickup game that resurrects her joy of competition and skill. It promises to help her re-focus her life, but with the deep spiritual experience of her father's death, a more balanced one.

Booktalk

Leah Weiczynkowski is only seventeen, but she is part of the big time. This summer she qualified for the Olympic soccer team, a lifelong dream she shares with her biggest fan, her father. She can't wait to tell him. But Leah's father has a new dream of his own right now, a nightmare. He has just been diagnosed with terminal cancer. And the man who has always taught her to fight and compete is going to just let it happen. He isn't going to try any experimental treatments. When he tells her the bad news, he is already signed up with hospice. Suddenly, life is just a blur for Leah. She is scheduling her summer around good days, bad days, visits from endless family and friends, and death. What will happen to the scholarships, the interested coaches, and the Olympic dream—her whole life? Life changes. So does Leah. Her biggest fan becomes her best teacher. Maybe life has many games to offer, and choosing which ones to play and how to play them has a whole lot to do with *Going for the Record.*

Learning Opportunities

1. *Going for the Record* has several meanings in relation to the novel. Discuss the many ways that it might apply. Refer to the text and share your conclusions with the group.
2. Should Leah pursue her soccer dream or limit the soccer in her life to casual pickup games?
3. After her father dies, Leah tries to find activities that make a difference. Discuss how you perceive her choices.
4. Was Leah's father right in refusing experimental treatment?
5. Using your library and community resources, research the role that hospice plays in life and death. You might wish to invite a hospice representative to talk to your group.
6. List each character in the novel. Then explain the effect that you feel each character has on Leah and on the purpose of the novel.

7. The spiritual side of death is very important in the novel. List the events and reread the passages that speak to belief and faith. Explain your selections. Compare your choices with the selections of others in the group. Then discuss them in relation to your own beliefs.

Related Works

1. Abelove, Joan. **Saying It Out Loud.** New York: DK Publishing, Inc./Richard Jackson, 1999. 136p. $15.95. ISBN 0 7894 2609 9. [fiction] JS A selfish, perfectionist father refuses to talk with his daughter about her mother's terminal cancer.
2. Bauer, Joan. **Hope Was Here.** New York: G. P. Putnam's Sons, 2000. 186p. $16.99. ISBN 0 399 23142 0. [fiction] MJS (See full booktalk in *Booktalks and More*, 2003, pages, 258 to 260.) An upbeat, confident young woman from a dysfunctional home situation finds the stable stepfather she has always hoped for. Then he dies of cancer.
3. Peck, Robert Newton. **Extra Innings.** New York: Harper Trophy, 2001. 215p. $5.99pa. ISBN 0 06 447229 9. [fiction] MJS Seventeen-year-old Tate Stonemason, a talented pitcher looking forward to a professional career, survives a plane crash that kills his sister, parents, and grandparents. His injuries effectively end his hopes for being a star athlete. His great grandfather and aunt help him redirect his life.
4. Pennebaker, Ruth. **Both Sides Now.** New York: Henry Holt and Company, 2000. 202p. $16.95. ISBN 0 8050 6105 3. [fiction] JS (See full booktalk in *Booktalks and More*, 2003, pages 199 to 201.) Liza, a hardworking, high achieving sophomore, deals with her mother's terminal cancer and her father's insistence that it can be cured.
5. Woodson, Jacqueline. **Miracle's Boys.** (See full booktalk in "Issues"/"Interpersonal Challenges," pages 28 to 30.) [fiction] MJS A family of three boys works through the guilt and grief that result from the sudden deaths of both parents.

✂✂

Zusak, Markus. **Fighting Ruben Wolfe.**
New York, Arthur A. Levine Books, 2000. 224p. $15.95.
ISBN 0 439 24188 X. [fiction] S

Themes/Topics: boxing, survival, identity, family

Summary/Description

The Wolfes are a family of survivors. Seriously injured, Mr. Wolfe refuses the dole and goes door to door to find work. Mrs. Wolfe cleans houses.

Stephen, the oldest son, works for an education and a good job. Sarah Wolfe, the only daughter, is straightening herself out after experimenting with drinking and promiscuity. Cameron and Ruben Wolfe, the younger brothers, are seeking a place in this family and the world. Defending his sister's name, Ruben attracts the attention of a fight promoter. Both boys decide to box for money. Fighting shapes their identities. Ruben, a winning machine, fears losing. Cameron loses and struggles to prove he is a winner. Ruben tells the story. A dialogue with himself or his brother ends each chapter. The climax centers on a match between Cameron and Ruben. Ruben defeats him but will not finish him off when the promoter tells him to. Their brotherhood is more important than money or the crowd's cheers. The language requires a mature audience.

Booktalk

Cameron and Ruben are Wolfes. In nature, wolves survive by sticking together, but the Wolf family seems to be falling apart. Mr. Wolf can't find work. Mrs. Wolfe has to clean more houses to make ends meet. Older brother Steve plans to move out, and older sister Sarah is coming home drunk every night. Cameron and Ruben wonder if any Wolfe can hope for more than trouble. But when Ruben throws a punch defending his sister's honor, the brothers find out that handling trouble pays off. Perry Cole, a local fight promoter, offers them a chance to fight for money. They accept. But Ruben changes, becoming a stranger to his brother, a winning machine that pleases the crowd and the girls. Cameron takes the punches in fight after fight. Ruben has the fame, but Cameron has the guts to keep coming back. Both brothers have to make big decisions when they find themselves *Fighting Ruben Wolfe*.

Learning Opportunities

1. Read aloud the passage in Chapter 10 that begins with the sentence "I notice a deliberate change in my brother." and ends with the sentence "Each hope." Here fighting becomes a metaphor for what is going on inside Ruben Wolfe. Discuss what Cameron is trying to figure out about his brother and what he reveals about himself in the process.
2. After completing Learning Opportunity 1, discuss the many ways that the title might be interpreted in addition to how it might be interpreted in that chapter.
3. At the end of Chapter 12, Ruben says to Cameron, "I think I like your money better than mine." Discuss what he means by that remark.

4. Read again the passage at the end of Chapter 14 that begins "Rube speaks." Read to the end of the chapter. Discuss the distinction made between a winner and a fighter and what Ruben's concern reveals about him.

5. List each family member. Note actions, descriptions, or statements you feel best characterize each member. Then discuss what each character adds to the novel.

6. Each chapter ends with a short conversation. Read just the conversations aloud. Discuss what they contribute to the novel.

7. Using the library's resources, research boxing and its promotion. From that research, list everything that the characters are risking in addition to their relationship.

Related Works

1. Bacho, Peter. **Boxing in Black and White.** New York: Henry Holt and Co., 1999. 122p. $18.95. ISBN 0 8050 5779 X. [nonfiction] JS This historical account explains why boxing was seen as the poor, dark skinned man's opportunity to prove his bravery and dominance.

2. Karr, Kathleen. **The Boxer.** New York: Farrar, Straus and Giroux, 2000. 169p. $16.00. ISBN 0 374 30921 3. [fiction] MJ (See full booktalk in *Booktalks and More,* pages 128 to 130.) Fifteen-year-old John Aloysius Xavier Woods lives in New York's East Side in the late nineteenth century. He pulls his family out of poverty through boxing, but eventually decides to use his brain rather his fists.

3. Myers, Walter Dean. **145th Street: Short Stories.** New York: Delacorte Press, 2000. 151p. $15.95. ISBN 0 385 32137 6. [fiction] JS (See full booktalk in *Booktalks and More,* 2003, pages 91 to 93.) In ten short stories about residents of Harlem's 145th Street, Myers portrays tragedy, frustration, achievement, and compassion. In the short story "Fighter" on pages 27 to 38, a man is dying because he trusts his fists rather that his brain to earn money for his family.

4. Myers, Walter Dean. **The Greatest: Muhammad Ali.** New York: Scholastic Press, 2000. 192p. $16.95. ISBN 0 590 54342 3. [nonfiction] MJS (See full booktalk in *Booktalks and \More,* 2003, pages 125 to 128.) The biography explains how boxing defined Muhammad Ali and how Muhammad Ali defined boxing.

5. Zusak, Markus. **Getting the Girl.** (See full booktalk in "Contemporary Life"/"Coming of Age," pages 56 to 58.) In this sequel to *Fighting Ruben Wolfe,* Cameron, falling in love with a former girl of Ruben's, decides that his words, not his fists define him.

Humor

Bagdasarian, Adam.
First French Kiss and Other Traumas.

New York: Farrar, Straus and Giroux/Melanie Kroupa Books,
2002. 134p. $16.00. ISBN 0 374 32338 0. [fiction] JS

Themes/Topics: family, peer pressure, love, coming of age

Summary/Description

In five groups of essays, a fictional character tells his traumatic and sometimes humorous life experiences in becoming a man. He recalls his family relationships, the struggle to become popular, young love, fighting, earning money, gifts, and his father's death. The essays, which chronicle his life from five to twenty years old, are arranged randomly rather than chronologically, and form an entire coming of age story, but each essay can stand on its own. The opening letter invites the reader to enjoy reading about the journey as much as the character did living it. The epilogue relates another memorable experience with his father, painting a pump, which is a reminder to finish each job, no matter how difficult or intimidating.

Booktalk

Read the opening letter that begins on ix and concludes on x.

These stories tell about experiences that are both familiar and unfamiliar. Some of these events happen to everyone. But the way they happen to Will, the hero, is just a little different. For him, the little league is the big league; the first girlfriend is a complicated romance; a bump on the head is a malignant tumor; a laxative is a ticking bomb; summer camp is a marine's nightmare. And that first French kiss? Well, read about it!

Learning Opportunities

1. Several of the stories involve Will's father. Describe him. Explain why you think he was so important to Will.
2. The *life and times* pages introduce each section of essays. Read these pages in order. Then explain how you feel Will develops through the novel, even though he says that he tells the stories randomly.
3. In the last life and times, Will's father comments on filmmakers who depend too heavily on a single image used symbolically. Read the

image he uses. Then make a list of at least five images that you feel could be used symbolically and explain their meanings.

4. Will frames his essays with "the French kiss" and the "epilogue." Discuss the significance of their placement.

5. Write one essay that describes an important event in your life.

6. Bagdasarian is Armenian. Research other Armenian writers and their work. Choose one other Armenian writer from your research. Compare his or her works to Bagdasarian's.

Related Works

1. Bagdasarian, Adam. **Forgotten Fire: A Novel.** New York: DK INK, 2000. 273p. $17.95. ISBN 0 7894 2627 7. [fiction] MJS (See full booktalk in *Booktalks and More,* 2003, pages 49 to 54.) A young man tells how he survives the 1915 Turkish purge of the Armenians. It is Bagdasarian's first book.

2. Carlson, Richard. **Don't Sweat the Small Stuff for Teens: Simple Ways to Keep Your Cool in Stressful Times.** New York: Hyperion, 2000. 242p. $11.95pa. ISBN 0 7868 8597 1. [nonfiction] MJS With specific examples, wisdom, and wit, Carlson helps teens gain perspective on daily coming of age challenges.

3. Sones, Sonya. **What My Mother Doesn't Know.** New York: Simon Pulse, 2003. 259p. $6.99pa. ISBN 0 689 85553 2. [fiction] JS In a series of poems, fourteen-year-old Sophie relates her love journeys in the midst of her cold father's and manipulative mother's marital conflict. She finally discovers that she has more in common with Murphy, the boy in her art class who is labeled a reject.

4. Vizzini, Ned. **Teen Angst? Naaah . . . : A Quasi Autobiography.** Minneapolis, MN: Free Spirit Publishing Inc., 2000. 232p. $12.95. ISBN 1 57542 084 8. Vizzini, changing the names to protect the innocent—namely him, recalls the anxious high school life of a high achieving teenager.

5. Weiss, M. Jerry, and Helen S. Weiss, (ed.). **From One Experience to Another.** New York: A Forge Book, 1997. 224p. $4.99pa. ISBN 0 812 56173 2. [fiction] MJS This collection of short stories deals with a series of teen experiences, some amusing and some serious.

6. Wolf, Virginia Euwer. **True Believer.** (See full booktalk in "Issues"/ "Interpersonal Challenges," pages 26 to 28.) In this second book of the *Make Lemonade Trilogy,* fifteen-year-old LaVaughn struggles with trust, love, and personal standards. Many of her decisions are influenced by the strong bond she has with her mother.

CRO

Earls, Nick. 48 Shades of Brown.

New York: Houghton Mifflin, 1999, 2004. 288p. $6.99pa.
ISBN 0 618 45295 8. [fiction] S

Themes/Topics: coming of age, sexual identity

Summary/Description

Sixteen-year-old, sheltered, and intellectual Dan, the narrator, decides to stay with his twenty something Aunt Jacq in Australia and finish high school while his parents spend the year in Geneva, Switzerland. His aunt and her attractive, flighty housemate, Naomi, unlike his parents, expect him to share household responsibilities and invite him to drink beer. Naomi who has the room next to his, invites her boyfriend over regularly. In his new situation, Dan experiences his own sexual awakening. He develops a crush on Naomi, and tries to use his intellectual abilities to win her. After a wild university party, he discovers that his aunt is also attracted to her. When Naomi chooses a new male lover, Dan and his aunt both pursue people they met at the party. The subject matter could be considered controversial and requires a mature audience.

Booktalk

Sixteen-year-old Dan has lived all his life in Australia. Then in his last year of school, his mother and father decide to move to Geneva, Switzerland, for a year. He prefers to stay down under and finish school, so his Aunt Jacq invites him to live with her. A great idea? It makes him throw up. Sure, he will be in Australia, but his aunt is twenty-one years younger than Dan's mother. Jacq just graduated from university, and she isn't the most understanding woman on the planet. She thinks that everyone should just solve his or her own problems. And her beautiful blond housemate expects Dan to talk to her. Since he goes to an all boys' school, he hasn't had much practice. The whole idea is pretty intimidating at first. But Dan is an intelligent person; he has something to say. Naomi seems to like nature, and she could be interested in birds. He'll study them and share what he learns, and later, maybe some other things with her. But this house doesn't run textbook perfect, like school. Dan thinks he might have taken on a bit more than he can handle when he begins his own independent study of his feathered and not so feathered friends. He is trying to sort out everyone's true colors in *48 Shades of Brown.*

Learning Opportunities

1. Throwing up is a central image in the story. Discuss why you think it is important.
2. Discuss what you feel the setting contributes to the story.
3. Writing postcards to his parents becomes an almost impossible job for Dan. Discuss why.
4. Choose what you think is the funniest scene in the novel. Explain your choice.
5. The party is central to the story. Discuss the build up and the ramifications.
6. Discuss the title's significance.
7. After talking to a friend or relative, discover a topic that interests the person, but about which you know very little. Using your library's resources, research that topic. Then try to work your newfound information into the conversation. Write about the results.

Related Works

1. Dunton Downer, Leslie Riding, and Alan Riding. **Essential Shakespeare Handbook.** New York: DK Publishing, Inc., 2004. 480p. $25.00 pa. ISBN 0 7894 9333 0. [reference] JS This user-friendly Shakespeare reference includes plot summaries and interpretative material on all thirty-nine plays and an analysis of the poetry. It also has essays on Shakespeare's life and times as well as his impact on world culture. Pages 304 to 313 deal with *Romeo and Juliet*. "Beyond the Play" within that section refers to the focus of Dan's assignment, Baz Luhrmann's *Romeo + Juliet*, set in fictional, gang-filled Californian "Verona Beach." "Beyond the Play" alludes to several other productions, which might be useful for comparison.
2. Rennison, Louise. **Angus, Thongs, and Full Frontal Snogging: Confessions of Georgia Nicolson.** New York: HarperCollins, 2000. 247p. $15.95. ISBN 0 06 028814 0. [fiction] S In this first book of the series, fourteen-year-old Georgia Nicolson worries about being a lesbian, getting a boyfriend, and embarrassing herself if she has a boyfriend.
3. Wallace, Rich. **Playing Without the Ball.** New York: Alfred A. Knopf, 2000. 213p. ISBN 0 679 98672 3. [fiction] S Seventeen-year-old Jay McLeod, deserted by his mother and father, lives in a single room above Shorty's Bar. With Shorty as a kind of guardian, Jay tries to build some stability in his life through basketball and girlfriends. The story is not a comedy.

4. Vizzini, Ned. **Teen Angst? Naaah ... : A Quasi Autobiography.**
   Minneapolis, MN: Free Spirit Publishing Inc., 2000. 232p. $12.95.
   ISBN 1 57542 084 8. [nonfiction] S Vizzini, changing the names to
   protect the innocent—namely him, recalls the anxious high school life
   of a high achieving teenager and some of the mistakes involved in it.
5. Zusak, Markus. **Getting the Girl.** New York: Arthur A. Levine,
   2003. 272p. $16.95. ISBN 0 439 38949 6. [fiction] S (See full book-
   talk in "Contemporary Life"/"Coming of Age," pages 56 to 58.)
   When the intellectual Cameron falls in love with one of Ruben's
   cast-off girlfriends, he begins to define his personality through his
   sexual coming of age.

☙❧

Hite, Sid. The King of Slippery Falls.

New York: Scholastic Press, 2004. 217p. $15.95. ISBN 0 439 34257 0. [fiction] MJS

Themes/Topics: adoption, identity,
coming of age, friendship, family, faith

Summary/Description

On Lewis Hinton's sixteenth birthday, he discovers that he is adopted.
That year he also spots a monster trout living in back of Slippery
Falls that he vows to catch. On his seventeenth birthday, his mother
gives him the note left by his biological mother. It reveals that his name
is French, Louis Poisson. Poisson means fish. His friends, who include
eighty-eight-year old Maple Baderhoovenlisterah and his would-be girlfriend, Amanda Dot, encourage him to inquire about his birth. Maple
even suggests that he is of French royal blood. The rumors about royalty
grow, as well as Lewis's fascination with the fish and falls. When Lewis
finds the hidden lagoon, the trout's home, he injures himself trying to
catch it, but the trout carries him to safety. As he recovers, the entire
town realizes how important Lewis and his story are to them. They are
inspired to pursue their own dreams and stories, and, after his recovery,
help him pay his way to France to connect with his heritage.

Booktalk

*Ask if anyone in the group goes trout fishing. Ask them to explain why
trout fishing requires so much skill.*

Lewis Hinton is fishing for a giant trout in Slippery Falls, Idaho. He
spends most of his time trying his luck in Little Lost River, the river that

feeds the falls. He always fishes from the steep cliffs. He is the only one in town surefooted enough to risk the climb. Fishing gives him time to think. On his sixteenth birthday, his parents told him that he was adopted, and now he is trying to figure out just who he is. His seventeenth birthday is coming up. He is going to receive a secret letter from his birth mother. The letter will tie him to a royal birth. The giant trout will bring him a near death experience. Where will all that lead? Well, where it leads any trout fisherman, to an unexpected romance. A story that's a little too crazy to believe? Life can be too. Ask the unsuspecting *King of Slippery Falls*.

Learning Opportunities

1. Using your library's resources, research the history of your family name. Share the information with others in the group, who have completed a similar project. Discuss how the information affects you.
2. On pages 32 to 34, Maple Baderhoovenlisterah shares her philosophy of life with Lewis. Begin with the words "*Who* you are ..." and end with "... plot-twisters." Read the passage aloud. Discuss with the rest of the group her idea of a person's life story.
3. Although other people in the town affect Lewis, he also influences them. Discuss the changes he effects.
4. Reread the opening chapter. You may wish to read it aloud. What details tell you that Lewis is distinctive.
5. The novel suggests that attitude and perceptions may be even bigger parts in shaping one's life than the events themselves. List three attitudes expressed in the book that are important in shaping a character's life.

Related Works

1. Cabot, Meg. **The Princess Diaries.** New York: HarperCollins Publishers, 2000. 238p. $15.95. ISBN 0 380 97848 2. [fiction] MJS In this first book of the series, fourteen-year-old Mia Thermopolis discovers that the father who visits her from overseas is the prince of Genovia and that she must then deal seriously, and not so seriously, with her new identity.
2. Carlson, Richard. **Don't Sweat the Small Stuff for Teens: Simple Ways to Keep Your Cool in Stressful Times.** New York: Hyperion, 2000. 242p. $11.95pa. ISBN 0 7868 8597 1. [nonfiction] MJS Several essays in this collection deal with attitude. One of the most relevant is "Become a Teenage Warrior" on pages 67 to 69. Carlson maintains that "... circumstances don't make a person—they *reveal* her or him!"

3. Hardman, Ric Lynden. **Sunshine Rider: The First Vegetarian Western.** New York: Laurel Leaf Books, 1998. 343p. $4.99pa. ISBN 0 440 22812 3. [fiction] JS Wylie Jackson discovers that John Boardman, the trail boss whom he has always admired, is his real father.

4. Hite, Sid. **Stick and Whittle.** New York: Scholastic Press, 2000. 208p. $16.95. ISBN 0 439 09828 9. [fiction] MJS This Western journey of two good friends combines the humor, excitement, paranormal events, and a journey to truth and love that characterize *The King of Slippery Falls.*

5. Holt, Kimberly Willis. **When Zachary Beaver Came to Town.** New York: Henry Holt and Company, 1999. 227p. $16.95. ISBN 0 8050 6116 9. [fiction] MJS (See full booktalk in *Booktalks and More,* 2003, pages 86 to 88.) When Zachary Beaver arrives in Antler, Texas, the citizens discover how each person's perception of an event can change attitudes and lives.

ⓒ⅋

Lubar, David. **Dunk.**

New York: Clarion, 2002. 249p. $15.00. ISBN 0 618 19455 X. [fiction] JS

Themes/Topics: clowns, family, friendship, employment, health, love

Summary/Description

Fifteen-year-old Chad Turner lives on the Jersey shore, and every summer he earns money by doing favors for the boardwalk game proprietors. But his ambition is to be the Bozo, whose job is to make a "mark" or "vic" so angry that he or she will buy endless chances (3 balls for two dollars) to dunk the Bozo in the tank. The Bozo he admires and who coincidentally rents a small apartment from Chad's single mother is Malcolm Vale, who lost his family in a car accident that maimed him and destroyed his career. At first the two conflict, but as Vale helps and challenges Chad through sick friends and girl problems, Chad begins to appreciate Vale. Vale teaches him how to become a Bozo—an acting job that takes much more talent and training than Chad ever imagined. The story involves father/son, mother/son, audience/actor, humor/health, teacher/student, employer/employee, and peer relationships.

Booktalk

Some kids want to be doctors, lawyers, firefighters, teachers, or storekeepers, but fifteen-year-old Chad Turner wants to be a Bozo. He and his mother live on the Jersey boardwalk and every summer he watches the Bozo, the guy everybody loves to dunk in the tank, drive the tourists wild. The Bozo is the teacher who embarrasses them, the friend who stabs them in the back, and the cop who gives them a hard time. Before they know it, the Bozo has all their cash—because marks, especially angry marks, are really bad shots. So for Chad, the Bozo job has big pay offs—big bucks, license to insult, and control. Chad figures that pushing people's buttons is easy. People push his all the time. But when a super Bozo moves into Chad's house and starts taking over his life, he discovers that the only easy job in life is *getting* pushed. A Bozo has to work a lot harder to get the *Dunk*.

Learning Opportunities

1. Every Bozo wears clown make-up. On page 4, Chad comments, "Like most clowns, he was scary as hell." Discuss why the Bozo wears make-up and why Chad, or anyone else, might perceive clowns as scary. Using the library's resources and the Internet, research clown make-up. Demonstrate to the group by pictures, by inviting a professional clown to class, or by applying your own clown make-up, the reasons for make-up choices.
2. Malcolm Vale is a Bozo, an actor, and a father figure. Discuss the relationship among those roles.
3. In Chapter 7, on pages 32 to 34, Chad discusses the odds of winning a prize in a carnival game. Using your library's resources, continue to research games of chance. Find the odds of winning in each game that you research. Make a chart that shows your findings.
4. In Chapter 17, on pages 103 to 104, Chad and Jason discuss tattoos. Chad comments that tattoo dots are like life choices. Discuss this comparison and whether or not you could apply the comparison to your own life.
5. *Of Mice and Men* (Related Work 4) and "Araby" from *Dubliners* (Related Work 2) are two of Gwen's favorites. After reading these works, discuss what they reveal about Gwen and what she might have in common with Chad.
6. Chapters 28, 29, and 32 include the names of several movies and books that Malcolm suggests to study humor and healing. Using some of the materials listed and your library's resources, research either the necessary elements of humor or the power of humor to heal. Share your findings with the group.
7. Two major pieces of advice in the story are "Identify the leader" and "Get off the couch." Discuss how these two statements apply to life.

Related Works

1. Duncan, Lois (ed.). **Trapped! Cages of Mind and Body.** New York: Simon & Schuster Books for Young Readers, 1998. 228p. $16.00. ISBN 0 689 81335 X. [fiction] JS In this collection, Duncan explores the many ways teens can be trapped by the pressures of others and their own thinking. The stories would be interesting to discuss in relation to the image of the Bozo cage.

2. Joyce, James. **Dubliners.** New York: Signet Classic, 1991. 240p. $4.95pa. ISBN 0 451 52543 4. This short story collection is a picture of Dublin at the turn of the century. It was first published in 1914. The 1991 volume reprints the 1968 revised edition of the 1958 Viking Compass edition prepared by Robert Scholes and published by Penguin Books. "Araby" tells the story of a young many who promises to buy a gift for the girl to whom he is attracted but cannot reach the bazaar in time to keep his promise.

3. Klass, David. **You Don't Know Me.** New York: Farrar, Straus and Giroux/Frances Foster Books, 2001. 262p. $17.00. ISBN 0 374 38706 0. [fiction] JS (See full booktalk in *Booktalks and More,* 2003, pages 31 to 33.) Klass combines humor and pain in this story of abuse and angst suffered by a young man whose mother allows her boyfriend to move into their house.

4. Steinbeck, John. **Of Mice and Men.** New York: Penguin Books, 1993. 107p. $8.00pa. ISBN 0 14 017739 6. [fiction] JS/A Written in 1937, *Of Mice and Men* relates the sad story of two best friends, itinerant workers, who find themselves caught in a web of poverty, bullies, and death.

5. Vorhaus, John. **The Comic Toolbox: How to Be Funny Even If You're Not.** Los Angeles, CA: Silman James Press, 1994. $14.95pa. ISBN 1 879505 21 5. Vorhaus uses a series of explanations, examples, and exercises to illustrate how to develop jokes. The chapter most relevant to *Dunk* is Chapter 1, "Comedy Is Truth and Pain."

ය⅋ව

Moriarty, Jaclyn. **The Year of Secret Assignments.**

New York: Arthur A. Levine Books, 2004. 352p. $16.95.
ISBN 0 439 49881 3. [fiction] JS

Themes/Topics: friendship, grief,
students' rights, stereotypes

Summary/Description

Lydia, Emily, and Cassie, three high school friends, acquire pen pals through their high school English class. The girls attend a private girls' school, stereotyped as a rich snob school, and will write to students at Brookfield High School, stereotyped as a juvenile delinquent haven. Lydia and Emily discover boys, from less affluent backgrounds, who are rougher but actually more responsible and mature than themselves. Cassie, whose father died a year ago, is victimized by a hostile, destructive pen pal to whom she persists in writing. Her friends and their pen pals cooperate to protect Cassie and block her correspondent from getting them expelled as well. By the end of the novel, Cassie and her mother are on their way to healing, the two schools are planning a cooperative performance, and Lydia and Emily are beginning strong friendships and perhaps budding romances. Letters, e-mails, bulletins, diary entries, and a school court record make up this Australian novel. The secret assignments (some school disrupting) and occasionally strong language require mature readers and may be considered quite controversial by some audiences.

Booktalk

Lydia, Emily, and Cassie attend Ashbury High School in Australia. It's a very exclusive school. Their English teacher has a bright idea—the Ashbury Brookfield Pen Pal Project. Pen Pals aren't unusual, but Brookfield, in comparison with Ashbury, is. Are the Ashbury students upset? (*Read the protest on the first Ashbury High Notice Board. It begins "Protest in Mr. Botherit's English Class today."*) Mr. Botherit acknowledges that Brookfield students are involved in tattoos and prison time, but sticks with his assignment anyway. Will these three tenth grade girls be victims of Mr. Botherit and his band of idealized juvenile delinquents? Well the girls have made up their own secret assignments for years to handle their bothersome parents, and they certainly have their own school running the way they want it to. Maybe the Brookfield students are the ones who need the protection. But, in any case, the girls, boys, families, and schools are never the same when the Ashbury Brookfield Pen Pal Project brings together white-collar crime and blue-collar life in *The Year of Secret Assignments*.

Learning Opportunities

1. Using your library's resources, research the organization of Australian education. Compare it to your own. Share your information with the group.

2. Throughout the year, each girl changes. Identify what you feel are the most significant changes. Explain the reasons for your answer.
3. Read *The Sisterhood of the Traveling Pants* and *The Second Summer of the Sisterhood.* Explain the similarities and differences between *The Year of Secret Assignments* and the *Sisterhood* books.
4. Describe the sequel to *The Year of Secret Assignments* that you would like to read.
5. Describe each of the parents mentioned. How does each influence the story?
6. *The Year of Secret Assignments* is an interesting mix of lawyers, laws, law breaking, and personal standards. Describe the combination and how it affects the story.
7. Describe Charlie, Seb, and Paul. Explain what each character adds to the story.

Related Works

1. Brashares, Ann. **The Sisterhood of the Traveling Pants.** (See full booktalk in "Issues"/"Interpersonal Challenges," pages 15 to 16.) Four lifelong friends, separated for their fifteenth summer, communicate through letters and the magical pair of thrift store jeans that they share.
2. Brashares, Ann. **The Second Summer of the Sisterhood.** (See full booktalk in "Issues"/"Interpersonal Challenges," pages 17 to 18.) The pants travel again, but this time they are not as forgiving in relation to the girls' decisions and attitudes.
3. Danziger, Paula, and Ann M. Martin. **P.S. Longer Letter Later.** New York: Scholastic, Apple Paperbacks, 1998. 234p. $4.99pa. ISBN 0 590 21311 3. [fiction] MJ (See full booktalk in *Booktalks Plus*, 2001, pages 172 to 176.) In this epistolary novel, seventh graders, separated by an out of town move, work out their life problems through letters.
4. Danziger, Paula, and Ann M. Martin. **Snail Mail No More.** New York: Scholastic, 2000. 336p. $16.95. ISBN 0 439 06335 3. [fiction] MJ (See full booktalk in *Booktalks Plus*, pages 173 to 176.) In this eighth grade version, the girls continue to mature, but discover that e-mail may allow a person to communicate before thinking about what is being said.
5. Juby, Susan. **Alice I Think.** New York: Harper Tempest, 2003, 290p. $16.89. ISBN 0 06 051544 9. [fiction] JS Alice, home-schooled by her eccentric parents, decides to enter high school to please her therapist. Her diary is a satirical and insightful look at combining these worlds and adult advice given to her in the process.

ය්‍ය

Rylant, Cynthia. God Went to Beauty School.

New York: Harper Tempest, 2003. 56p. $15.89.
ISBN 0 06 009434 6. [poetry] JS

Themes/Topics: God's relationship to humanity

Summary/Description

In twenty-three poems, Rylant characterizes God as an almighty being who puts the world in motion and then discovers, when getting involved, the pain and beauty in His creation. He goes to beauty school, the doctor, the movies, India, and work. He gets a dog, sails in a boat, buys a couch from Pottery Barn, makes spaghetti, gets arrested, drinks coffee, takes a bath, tries rollerblading, catches a cold, writes a book ("not *that* one"), gets cable, finds God, climbs a mountain, wants to be a guy but knows he is also a girl, has a cousin Lucifer, gets a desk job, tries to make a batch of fudge, writes a fan letter, and decides to die. Through all these experiences, he finally becomes "All Knowing." His experiences in the world teach him to appreciate the simple things in life and the profound meaning that common events may have for humans.

Booktalk

Read the title poem, "God Went to Beauty School."

This poem, and twenty-two others, describe a trip God takes to the world. He does human things, like writing a fan letter, climbing a mountain, trying to figure out his identity, signing up for cable, and attempting to straighten out some family members. But when God does things, they turn out a little differently. He is the Creator, not just somebody who is dropped in with no choice or warning. If you would like to see His reactions to the things we do every day, keep reading. You might be pleasantly and unpleasantly surprised.

Learning Opportunities

1. Choose one more experience that you think God might want to explore. Write your own poem about it. You may want to consult *How to Write Poetry* (Related Work 3).
2. Organize a choral reading with two or three other people. Perform the reading for a group.
3. After reading *God Went to Beauty School*, describe God's character according to Rylant.

4. Ask two or three religious leaders to read the book also. Then discuss with them Rylant's perception of God. Ask them to suggest some other books that might give you insight into religious topics. Share your discussions and book list with your reading group.

5. Read *God Went to Beauty School* and *The Heavenly Village* (Related Work 5). Discuss Rylant's view of the relationship between the spiritual and physical worlds. Then, in an oral or written explanation, agree or disagree with her.

Related Works

1. Fraustino, Lisa Rowe (ed.). **Soul Searching: Thirteen Stories about Faith and Belief.** New York: Simon & Schuster Books for Young Readers, 2002. 267p. $17.95. ISBN 0 689 83484 5. [fiction] MJS The stories talk about the great faith required in all cultures to face life's problems and responsibilities.

2. Ikeda, Daisaku. **The Way of Youth: Buddhist Common Sense for Handling Life's Questions.** Santa Monica, CA: Middleway Press, 2000. 188p. $14.95. ISBN 0 9674697 0 8. [nonfiction] JS Ikeda gives advice about parents, friendship, learning, work, and compassion. In Rylant's book, God takes some advice from Buddha.

3. Janeczko, Paul B. **How to Write Poetry.** New York: Scholastic, 1999. 117p. (Scholastic Guides.) $12.95. ISBN 0 590 10077 7. [nonfiction] MJS (See full booktalk in *Booktalks Plus*, 2001, pages 215 to 217.) Janeczko provides a step-by-step approach to writing poetry.

4. Nolan, Han. **When We Were Saints.** New York: Harcourt, Inc., 2003. 291p. $17.00. ISBN 0 15 216371 9. [fiction] JS. A young man, whose grandfather declares that he is a saint, is persuaded to leave home with a girl, who believes she too is a saint, but he finally realizes that perhaps her sainthood is a mental illness.

5. Rylant, Cynthia. **The Heavenly Village.** New York: The Blue Sky Press, 1999. 95p. $15.95. ISBN 0 439 04096 5. [fiction] MJS (See full booktalk in *Booktalks Plus*, 2001, pages 52 to 54.) In a series of short characterizations, Rylant tells about people who died with unfinished business on earth.

6. Singer, Marilyn (ed.). **I Believe in Water: Twelve Brushes with Religion.** New York: HarperCollins, 2000. 280p. $24.89. ISBN 0 06 028398 X. [fiction] Twelve short stories examine how real life and spiritual beliefs can both complement and collide.

Adventure/Survival

Humans often measure their strengths by encounters with Mother Nature—which usually lead to great adventure. These action-packed tales appeal to teens, who are generally experiencing physical changes and increases in strength. The stories are often fast-paced and filled with suspense and drama. The "Land" adventures focus on challenges from nature, but other humans, and the characters themselves are part of nature too. The "Sea" adventures include all those things plus the romance of this independent and romantic world. Although *The Wreckers*, by Iain Lawrence actually takes place on land, it is included in the sea stories because it is the first book in Lawrence's trilogy related to the sea.

Land

の

Allende, Isabel. Margaret Sayers Peden (trans.).
City of the Beasts.

New York: HarperCollins, 2002. 406p. $21.89. ISBN 0 06 050917 1. [fiction] MJ

Themes/Topics: Amazon, coming of age, ethnic cleansing, rain forest

Summary/Description

Fifteen-year-old Alex Cold visits his eccentric paternal grandmother while his mother undergoes chemotherapy. The grandmother has an assignment from *International Geographic* to do an article about the Beast, the Amazon version of the Abominable Snowman, and takes the reluctant Alex with her. He meets Nadia Santos, the guide's twelve- or thirteen-year-old daughter. Alex and Nadia learn that Captain Ariosto, commander of the local barracks, and Mauro Carías, a wealthy local entrepreneur, want to eliminate a native tribe, "The People of the Mist." The tribe kidnaps Alex and Nadia because Walimai, the shaman, knows that the teenagers can save them. Walimai takes Alex and Nadia to the native village where Alex undergoes a ceremonial rite of passage. Both Alex and Nadia become subordinate chiefs. Journeying to "The Sacred Mountain," they meet the Beasts, sloth-like creatures that the tribe considers gods entrusted with tribal history. Nadia requests " The Crystal Eggs" to save the tribe, and Alex requests "The Water of Health" to save his mother's life. Each completes the quest alone and surrenders a prized possession. Nadia leaves the amulet that guarantees her safety, and Alex sacrifices his grandfather's flute that provides him with the universal language of music, but both gain personal strength. Returning to the expedition, they discover that the expedition doctor, working with Ariosto and Carías, intends to poison the natives. Alex and Nadia, aided by two Beasts, save the day.

Booktalk

Fifteen-year-old Alex Cold lives in California with his father, mother, two younger sisters, and his dog Poncho. Life is great until his mother gets sick, so sick that his father must take her to Texas for special treatments. That means his sisters will stay with one grandmother, and he will stay with the other. Except Grandma doesn't like Alex to call her grandmother. Just Kate is fine with her. And she doesn't like to stay at home either. She has a special assignment for *International Geographic* magazine. The magazine wants her to go to the Amazon and investigate sightings of the Beast, a South American version of the Abominable Snowman. Alex is going too, whether he wants to go or not. Looking for this "Abominable Jungleman" in a land of deadly snakes and bloodsucking insects, Alex discovers an ancient tribe called "The People of the Mist." Their shaman has visions of a hero who will save their people. They believe that hero is Alex. Then Alex has some visions of his own and is swept up in a mystical world—a combination of beauty and ugliness; peace and war; loyalty and treachery; life and death—the unbelievable world of the *City of the Beasts*.

Learning Opportunities

1. Using your library's resources, find a map of the Amazon River. Try to locate the areas described in the novel.
2. Continuing your research, find information about at least one animal thriving in the Amazon region (Related Works 2 and 5). Share the information with the group. Ask other members of the

group to do the same. Then discuss how those animals might help or complicate the expedition.

3. Using the library's resources, investigate the characteristics of the sloth. Use that information to draw a picture. Develop a character description of a Beast.

4. Using the library's resources, investigate one aspect of the tropical rain forest that has been lost or will be lost because of commercial land development or mining (Related Works 2 and 5).

5. Research the legend of El Dorado. Share the information that you find with the rest of the group. You may also want to read *Sir Walter Ralegh and the Quest for Eldorado* (Related Work 1).

6. Chapters 15 and 16 describe Nadia's quest for the crystal eggs and Alex's quest for the water of health. Trace each quest. Identify what the events in each quest teach the characters and reveal about them.

7. Names are emphasized in the novel. Kate influences the choice of Alex's birth name, and when Nadia and Alex are in their quest, they take on the names Jaguar and Eagle. Discuss why names are so important in the novel.

8. Chapters 13 through 16 include spectacular and mystical descriptions. Try to present the scenes described with visual techniques.

Related Works

1. Aronson, Marc. **Sir Walter Ralegh and the Quest for El Dorado.** New York: Clarion Books, 2000. 22p. $20.00. ISBN 0 395 84827 X. [nonfiction] MJS (See full booktalk in *Booktalks and More*, 2003, pages 232 to 235.) This biography of Sir Walter Ralegh explains Ralegh's fascination with the promise of El Dorado.

2. Dicks, Brian. **Brazil.** New York: Facts on File, 2003. 61p. (Countries of the World.) $30.00. ISBN 0 8160 5382 0. [nonfiction] MJS This geographical description of Brazil explains the tension between commercial development and the rain forest.

3. Divakaruni, Chitra Banerjee. **The Conch Bearer.** Brookfield, CT: Roaring Book Press/A Neal Porter Book, 2003. 263p. ISBN 0 7613 2793 2. [fiction] MJ Twelve-year-old Anand and a girl street sweeper named Nisha fight evil forces to secure a sacred conch that will keep the world safe and heal his family physically and emotionally.

4. Hollander, Malika. **Brazil: The Culture.** New York: Crabtree Publishing Company/A Bobbie Kalman Book, 2003. 32p. (The Lands, Peoples, and Cultures Series.) $16.95. ISBN 0 7787 9340 0. [nonfiction] MJ This volume explains the many beliefs, traditions, art, literature, and music of Brazil. It also includes a Brazilian nature myth.

5. Hollander, Malika. **Brazil: The Land.** New York: Crabtree
    Publishing Company/A Bobbie Kalman Book, 2003. 32p. (The
    Lands, Peoples, and Cultures Series.) $16.95. ISBN 0 7787 9338 9.
    [nonfiction] MJ This volume describes the geography, animals, and
    the vanishing rain forest.

ぐうひ

Cindrich, Lisa. **In the Shadow of the Pali: A Story of the Hawaiian Leper Colony.**

New York: G. P. Putnam's Sons, 2002. 245p. $18.99. ISBN 0 399 23855 7. [fiction] MJS

Themes/Topics: leprosy, family, friendship, identity,
nineteenth-century history

Summary/Description

In the late nineteenth century, twelve-year-old Liliha, a leper, is sent to
the newly formed, lawless Hawaiian Leper Colony. She contracted leprosy from her abusive grandmother she cared for. Her mother, accepting
Liliha's abuse, refuses to go to the island with Liliha. Kalani, the colony
bully, terrorizes Liliha and anyone who helps her in a world where citizens
survive by fighting for, making, stealing, or begging for their food and
supplies. Liliha makes friends with Ahia, another leper; Hana, Ahia's wife;
and Manukekua, the superintendent's half-cast servant. Hana and her
husband find refuge with a Christian friend. Hana encourages Liliha to be
peaceful and forgiving, but does not offer her shelter or protection. Liliha
refuses to be intimidated. Manukekua and Liliha travel to another village
to trade for food, supplies, and money. Kalani then steals from Liliha,
blocks her efforts to contact family, and attacks her hut. Attempting to kill
Liliha, Kalani falls from the f cliff (pali) and sustains fatal injuries. At the
end of the story, Liliha and Manukekua support each other completely,
and Liliha welcomes a newly arrived ten-year-old leper. Liliha accepts her
disease and resolves to make the colony her home. Maps of the Hawaiian
Islands, Molokai, and the area where Liliha lives provide a clear context
for the story. The glossary clarifies the meanings of terms and places.

Booktalk

Twelve-year-old Liliha lives in Hawaii. But she is being sent to a leper
colony. Supposedly she will have a hospital, food, and shelter, but in the
second half of the nineteenth century, the colony has no law, no shelter,
and very little food. In Kalawao, only the strong survive. Since she can
never leave, Liliha knows that the place is a prison, a cage, not a colony.

The fierce and bitter Kalani, one of the first residents on the island, hates Liliha. Kalani withholds rations and terrifies everyone on the island. She can kill Liliha before the disease ever has a chance. Will Liliha build any life at all or quickly die in her new home *In the Shadow of the Pali*?

Learning Opportunities

1. Using the Internet and your library's resources, research the history of the leper colonies in Hawaii. Share the information with the group.
2. Using the Internet and your library's resources, research leprosy. Be sure to include pictures of those infected with the disease. Share the information with the group.
3. The pali is central in the story. Cite the places where it appears. Discuss what you think it contributes to the story.
4. Hana preaches forgiveness and peace to Liliha, struggling with Kalani's hatred. Discuss Hana's perception and advice.
5. Manukekua is a central character in Liliha's life. Discuss how they help each other and what they teach each other.
6. The island's superintendent, Liliha's mother, uncle, and grand-mother have very small roles in the novel, but affect Liliha's life tremendously. Discuss each adult's behavior and what it teaches you about living your own life.
7. Re-read the last chapter. Then write an epilogue for the novel.

Related Works

1. Donnelly, Karen. **Leprosy.** New York: The Rosen Publishing Group, Inc., 2002. 64p. (Epidemics: Deadly Diseases Throughout History.) $19.95. ISBN 0 8239 3498 5. [nonfiction] MJS Donnelly defines leprosy, traces its history, and discusses its modern status. On pages 26 and 27, in the insert "Father Damien: Missionary of Kalaupapa," Donnelly outlines the conditions of Kalaupapa Leper Settlement.
2. Duncan, Lois (ed.). **Trapped! Cages of Mind and Body.** New York: Simon & Schuster Books for Young Readers, 1998. 228p. $16.00. ISBN 0 689 81335 X. [fiction] JS In this short story collection, the main characters must decide to accept or rebel against the barriers life gives them and those they give themselves.
3. Gormley, Beatrice. **Adara.** Grand Rapids, MI: Eerdmans Books for Young Readers, 2002. 151p. ISBN 0 8028 5216 5. [fiction] MJ Adara, a young slave girl from Israel, tells Naaman, afflicted with leprosy, to seek out Elisha. Abandoned by her own family, she earns respect in Naaman's house for her integrity and beliefs.
4. Mathes, Ben, with Laura Raines. **Lessons from the Forest.** Lincoln, NE: Writers Club Press, 2002. 115p. $10.95. ISBN 0 595 23436 4. [nonfiction] MJS/A In this collection of essays, Dr. Ben Mathes shares

his experience as head of Rivers of the World, an international exploration and development agency that ministers to people in remote areas of the world. "Learning to See" on pages 71 to 74 tells about a band of lepers who form a harmonica choir and donate their earnings to a Korean orphanage.

5.   Yolen, Jane, and Robert J. Harris. **Girl in a Cage.** New York: Philomel Books, 2002. 234p. $18.99. ISBN 0 399 236279 9. [fiction] MJ Eleven-year-old Marjorie Bruce, imprisoned in a public cage by Edward Longshanks when her father, Robert Bruce, rebels, finds her role as a princess and turns public opinion against Longshanks.

ぴ む

Hobbs, Will. **Wild Man Island.**

New York: HarperCollins Publishers, 2002. 184p. $15.95.
ISBN 0 688 17473 6. [fiction] MJ

Themes/Topics: archaeology, dog, ecology, Alaska

Summary/Description

Fourteen-year-old Andy Galloway, the youngest member of an Adventure Alaska program, leaves the group to search for where his father Alex Galloway—archaeologist, paleontologist, and flintknapper—died. A treacherous storm drives Andy to Admiralty Island of Alaska's ABC islands. Suffering from hypothermia, he must find shelter and food. After five days, he discovers an abandoned building and encounters a wild man. The man disappears but leaves him a spear and a stone blade knife. A stray Newfoundland dog saves Andy's life and guides him to the hermit's cave. The man, David Atkins, living in the ancient way, is investigating ancient peoples. Afraid of being killed, Andy escapes the camp and encounters the Wildlife Service helicopter. They are tracking the Atkins and his Newfoundland. He hunts on the island illegally, and they fear that the dog may mate with the island's newly arrived wolves and interfere with the environment. Andy returns to warn the Atkins, an archaeologist, that he is being tracked. They all escape to another island. The two become friends. Atkins returns to the island and continues his research. Andy takes the Newfoundland home. They continue their correspondence, which confirms the theories of Andy's father, via computer.

Booktalk

Will Hobbs knows that Action + Suspense = A Great Story. *Wild Man Island* is no exception. In this Hobbs adventure, fourteen-year-old Andy

Galloway—the youngest member of the Adventure Alaska program—makes a dangerous decision. He leaves the group to find the place where his archaeologist father died. He knows the terrain. He is sure he can find his way. Nature has another idea. A sudden storm throws Andy off course and into cold, dangerous waters. An unknown island is his only chance—an island filled with grizzly bears, wolves, and a wild man. If Andy can get shelter, water, and food to stay alive, he can deal with the wolves and the bears—but the wild man? Armed with spears, knives, and a cunning mind, the man is a more formidable and life threatening opponent than any other animal.

Related Activities

1. Using the library's resources and the Internet, research hypothermia. Report to the group when it occurs, how it manifests itself, and what can be done to prevent it.
2. Hobbs sets his story on Alaska's ABC Islands. Find out more about them through the Internet and library resources. Use the information to construct a visual display.
3. Continue to research the theories of how humans first arrived in North America. Share the information you find with the group. Be sure to include the Clovis people.
4. Research the art of flintknapping. Describe the art to the group. Show pictures of or create tools that flintknapping might include.
5. Describe what you think Andy and David Atkins each might be doing in ten years.

Related Works

1. Helbig, Alethea K., and Agnes Regan Perkins. **Dictionary of American Young Adult Fiction, 1997–2001: Books of Recognized Merit.** Westport, CT: Greenwood Press, 2004. 558p. $75.00. ISBN 0 313 32430 1. [professional reference] A This reference of young adult authors, titles, and characters includes three entries related to Will Hobbs. "Hobbs, Will(iam Carl)" appears on page 147 and lists seven of his eighteen survival books. Summaries of *Far North* and *The Maze* appear on pages 101 and 217 respectively.
2. Hobbs, Will. "On the Trail with Jack London: My Journey to *Jason's Gold* and *Down the Yukon*." *The ALAN Review*. (Winter, 2004): 60–65. Hobbs explains how he came to write *Jason's Gold* and its sequel. An interview from the 2003 ALAN Workshop follows the Hobbs article. The interview deals with his general research and development.
3. Mikaelsen, Ben. **Touching Spirit Bear.** New York: HarperCollins Publishers, 2001. 241p. $15.95. ISBN 0 380 97744 3. [fiction] MJS

(See full booktalk in *Booktalks and More,* 2003, pages 80 to 82.)
Fifteen-year-old Cole Mathews learns about himself and the ramifications of his crime when he is sentenced to an isolated Alaskan
island for a year.

4. Paulsen, Gary. **Brian's Winter.** New York: Delacorte Press, 1996.
    133p. $15.95. ISBN 0 385 32198 8. [fiction] MJS This "what if"
    sequel to *Hatchet* extends Brian's stay to the winter months. Brian
    finds a Cree family to rescue him and begins to think that life in the
    wilderness might be his way of life.

5. Sullivan, Paul. **Maata's Journal.** New York: Atheneum Books for
    Young Readers, 2003. 240p. $16.95. ISBN 0 689 83463 2. [fiction]
    JS Seventeen-year-old Maata, an Inuit, records her survival in an
    Arctic expedition from April to July of 1924. Maata uses her journal
    to reflect on two situations—the resettlement of the Inuits by the
    Canadian government and the expedition itself which intends to
    map and measure nature rather than listen to it. Many of the situa-
    tions target an older female audience.

ऌॐऌ

Mikaelsen, Ben. Tree Girl.

New York: HarperCollins Children's Books, 2004. 240p. $16.99.

ISBN 0 06 009004 9. [fiction] JS

Themes/Topics: family, guerrillas, Guatemala,
refugees, sharing, history

Summary/Description

Fifteen-year-old Gabriela Flores lives in a Guatemalan village with
her mother, father, and six brothers and sisters. Although she cel-
ebrates the traditional entry into womanhood, her parents and teacher
tell her that she must learn about other cultures and the unrest that now
grips her own country. When U.S. trained government troops begin a
systematic Indian massacre, Gabriela loses her teacher, classmates, and
most of her family. Escaping two raids, she flees with one little sister and
a baby she helped birth. Gabriela enters a pueblo for food, but soldiers
invade it. She climbs a tree for protection and witnesses the torture,
murder, and rape of the townspeople. Now alone, she joins the other
refugees on a trek north, crosses the Mexican border, enters a refugee
camp, and eventually is reunited with her sister and the baby. She builds
a new family from refugees and begins to share her teaching talents with

the camp's children. When her fellow teacher decides to join the guerillas in Guatemala, Gabriela tries to take her sister and leave also, but she discovers her ties and responsibilities to this new life are deep and important. The book is dedicated to a real *Tree Girl* whose experiences inspired the novel.

Booktalk

Fifteen-year-old Gabriela Flores lives in Guatemala. (*You may need to show a map of Central America and point out Guatemala.*) She is a dreamer who finds a place to think at the top of the tall trees she climbs so quickly. Her parents respect her dreams, and even though she is a girl, they send her, rather than her older brother, to school. There she learns Spanish, the language that can take her away from the forest. The old ways are dying with the Indians. Government troops and guerillas just use them as pawns in war. From her tree top perch, Gabriela cannot see the blood, tears, and death on her horizon. But she does know health and strength come from deep roots planted in family, land, and country. Gabriela, out of respect for those roots, climbs higher and higher. Her knowledge, her race, her friendships may mean death. But she dares to reach for the new and weaker branches. She faces the hostile elements. Can a *Tree Girl* hang on to those branches to pull herself above the crowd, or like so many other Guatemalans, will she fall and be ground into the dust?

Learning Opportunities

1. Using the library's resources, research the relationship between the United States and Guatemala. Be sure to discuss how that relationship involved or involves guerrilla warfare. Share your information with the group. You may wish to start your research by consulting *The Book of Rule: How the World Is Governed* (Related Work 3).
2. At the end of Chapter 2, Gabriela compares herself to a child watching the smooth surface of a great river. Reread that comparison out loud. Explain her point in your own words. Then discuss why Mikaelsen placed this passage at the end of a chapter describing Gabriela's entry into the status of womanhood.
3. Spanish is referred to as the country's lingua franca. Find the meaning of the term. Then discuss why learning a lingua franca is so important.
4. Identify the lingua franca of your own country. Then discuss how knowing it or not knowing it could affect your life.
5. In Chapter 4, Papí prays. Read the prayers out loud. Discuss what they reveal about him and his culture.

6. Gabriella's definition of a tree girl in the last chapter reveals what Gabriella has learned about herself and courage. Read the passage out loud. Ask each of the listeners to choose one part of her definition that seems most important. Then ask each person to explain the choice.

Related Works

1. Armstrong, Jennifer (ed.). **Shattered: Stories of Children and War.** New York: Alfred A. Knopf, 2002. 166p. $15.95. ISBN 0 375 9112 X. [fiction] JS This short story collection includes the struggles of children caught in wars all over the world.
2. Bagdasarian, Adam. **Forgotten Fire.** New York: DK Publishing, Inc., 2000. 273p. $17.95. ISBN 0 7894 2627 7. [fiction] JS (See full booktalk in *Booktalks and More*, 2003, pages 49 to 51.) Based on fact, this novel tells the story of Vahan Kenderian, an Armenian boy who, between 1915 to 1918, suffered under the persecution of the Armenian holocaust.
3. Cain, Timothy (ed.). **The Book of Rule: How the World Is Governed.** New York: DK Publishing, Inc., 2004. 320p. $30.00. ISBN 0 7894 9354 3. [reference] MJS This reference for world government explains governments of 193 countries. The analysis of Guatemala appears on page 248.
4. Cameron, Sara in conjunction with UNICEF. **Out of War: True Stories from the Front Lines of the Children's Movement for Peace in Colombia.** New York: Scholastic Press, 2001. 224p. $15.95. ISBN 0 439 29721 4. [nonfiction] JS (See full booktalk in *Booktalks and More*, 2003, pages 58 to 61.) Nine teenagers, ages fifteen to nineteen, tell about their attempts to seek peace in the Colombian civil conflicts through the Children's Movement for Peace in Colombia.
5. Mathes, Ben, with Laura Raines. **Lessons from the Forests.** New York: Writers Club Press, 2002. 115p. $10.95pa. ISBN 0 59523436 4. [nonfiction] JS This series of essays describes the experiences of Christian workers providing aid to people plagued by disease, war, and natural disasters. "Soldiering in El Salvador," pages 51 to 54, describes a Special Forces soldier who is working to help children in the country and then is maligned in death by an American newspaper commentator.
6. Ung, Loung. **First They Killed My Father: A Daughter of Cambodia Remembers.** New York: HarperCollins Publishers, 2000. 239p. $23.00. ISBN 0 06 019332 8. [nonfiction] JS (See full booktalk in *Booktalks and More*, 2003, pages 54 to 56.) Loung describes the destruction of her family under the Khmer Rouge. She now works for Campaign for a Landmine Free World.

$C\mathcal{F}\mathcal{D}$

Murphy, Jim. **Blizzard!**

New York: Scholastic Press, 2000. 136p. $18.95. ISBN 0 590 67309 2. [nonfiction] MJS

Themes/Topics: storms, social class,
late nineteenth-century history

Summary/Description

Describing why the 1888 storm was so surprising, violent, and devastating, Murphy depicts the quiet before the storm, and traces the blizzard's destruction, duration, and results through human interest stories of its participants and victims—both powerful and humble. He includes the quiet heroes, the exploited immigrants, the forgotten poor, and the arrogant rich in his documentation, and points out that the storm's aftereffects include the installation of underground electric wiring, street maintenance, antilittering laws, subway systems, the transfer of weather monitoring from the Signal Corps to the Weather Bureau, and the realization that technology cannot protect humans from the elements. In fact, a reliance on technology might make them more vulnerable. Sketches, maps, and photographs complement the high interest text. "Notes on Sources and Related Reading Material" provide a personal anecdote and descriptions of Murphy's many sources. A name and topic index provides easy access to information.

Booktalk

Ask each person in the group to write down the criteria required for a storm to be labeled a blizzard. Ask each person to quickly read his or her response. Then read the second paragraph of Chapter 3 in which Murphy defines a blizzard and compares that definition to the conditions of the Blizzard of 1888.

According to those statistics, the Blizzard of 1888 was at least twice as bad as the most extreme snowstorm defined by man. Thinking it was just another snowfall, many walked into it and died. Why? Because no one thought that white fluffy stuff could be that bad, and like the people aboard the fated Titanic, they believed that their inventions would protect them from whatever nature could produce. Wrong! Digging out those buried alive, watching their friends carried out to sea on chunks of ice, losing limbs from exposure, the entire population from Virginia to Maine learned to respect the *Blizzard!*

Learning Opportunities

1. Using the Internet and your library's resources, find other weather or storm definitions. Make a visual display that lists the terms, the definitions, and an example for each.
2. Invite a weatherperson to your group. Ask him or her to explain how storms are identified and tracked.
3. In "Notes on Sources and Related Reading Material," Murphy recounts his own intimidating encounter with nature. Write an essay about your own natural crisis (actual or based on the facts of your weather research). Then share the experience with the group.
4. Murphy notes that before the Blizzard of 1888, many saw themselves as well protected by technological advances. Research the Titanic disaster. Draw as many parallels as you can between the two events. You might wish to start by reading *The Tragedy of the Titanic* (Related Work 2).
5. After reading the factual information in *Blizzard,* write a poem that might express the tone of the storm and its aftermath. You might wish to refer to *How to Write Poetry* (Related Work 1) to complete the task.

Related Works

1. Janeczko, Paul B. **How to Write Poetry.** New York: Scholastic, 1999. 117p. (Scholastic Guides.) $12.95. ISBN 0 590 10077 7. [nonfiction] MJS (See full booktalk in *Booktalks Plus,* 2001, pages 215 to 217.) Janeczko provides step-by-step advice about the poetry writing process, from gathering words and ideas to polishing the finished product.
2. Kupperberg, Paul. **The Tragedy of the Titanic.** New York: Rosen Publishing Group, 2003. 48p. (When Disaster Strikes!) $17.95. ISBN 0 8239 3679 1. [nonfiction] MJS This description of the disaster places the Titanic in the context of the Gilded Age and mechanical progress. An extensive bibliography, suggestions for further reading, and a list of Web sites provide material for continued research.
3. Naylor, Phyllis Reynolds. **Blizzard's Wake.** New York: Atheneum Books for Young Readers, 2002. 212p. $16.95. ISBN 0 689 85220 7. [fiction] MJS In March 1941, fifteen-year-old Katie Sterling saves her mother's killer during a blizzard and then finds herself having to shelter him in her home.
4. Sullivan, Paul. **Maata's Journal.** New York: Atheneum Books for Young Readers, 2003. 240p. $16.95. ISBN 0 689 83463 2. [fiction] JS Seventeen-year-old Maata, an Inuit, records her survival in an Arctic expedition from April to July of 1924. In addition to the fellowship

and dangers she and her fellow explorer share, Maata uses her journal to reflect on two situations that brought her here—the resettlement of the Inuits by the Canadian government and the expedition
itself that intends to measure nature rather that listen to it.

5. Weber, Paige. **New York.** New York: Enchanted Lion Books, 2003.
   44p. (Great Cities Through the Ages.) $18.95. ISBN 1 59270 003 9.
   [nonfiction] MJS A flashy combination of photographs, drawings, sketches, maps, and charts, this description of New York—
   historical and present day—includes other significant events and
   people that shape New York's character. "Bright Lights, Big City"
   includes the Great Blizzard in the timeline section with the first
   "ticker tape parade."

☙❧

Paulsen, Gary. **Brian's Hunt.**

New York: Wendy Lamb Books, 2003. 103p. $14.95. ISBN 0 385 74647 4. [fiction] MJS

Themes/Topics: bears, death, relationship
of man and nature

Summary/Description

Sixteen-year-old Brian is thinking about Susan Smallhorn, the daughter
of his Cree trapping family, as he heads north to visit them. When he
makes camp, a wounded dog calls to him for help and becomes his companion. As they near the Cree camp, the dog growls. Brian discovers that
a rogue bear killed the Cree couple and most of their dogs, driving Susan
back to the lake. Brian finds Susan, brings her to camp, leaves her with
authorities, and decides to hunt the bear. But the bear is also hunting him.
In the final confrontation, Brian almost dies. Killing the bear gives him no
sense of victory. He heals his and his dog's wounds as he prepares to use as
much of the bear parts as possible. The "Afterword" explains why Paulsen
resurrected Brian and why he chose the bear as the focus of the hunt.

Booktalk

Gary Paulsen said that *Brian's Return* was the last Brian book, but hundreds of letters a day from readers made him change his mind. Now
sixteen-year-old Brian of Paulsen's *Hatchet* series returns in *Brian's
Hunt.* His story continues and what a story! Brian is no longer new to
the woods. He can read the noise and the silence equally well, and he is
thinking about Susan Smallhorn, his Cree friend's daughter. He's never
met Susan, just saw her picture. Yet something draws him to her and her

northern home. When Brian makes camp one night, he hears a strange crying sound. He finds a wounded dog, a dog that seems to call just to him. Together they continue the journey, a trip that now takes on a mysterious urgency. As his new friend pulls him to their destination, not even Brian can anticipate the horrors and challenges that await them.

Learning Opportunities

1. Using your library's resources, research the lives and habits of bears. Share the information that you find with the group.
2. After reading the other books in the series, discuss what new aspect of Brian this book reveals and the old qualities upon which it builds.
3. Brain now sees learning in an entirely new way. Read aloud the passage in Chapter 2 beginning with the words "He had returned to his world, the wilderness ..." on page 9 and ends with the words, "He *knew*." on page 11. After listening to the passage, discuss his new attitude toward learning and compare it with your own.
4. "The Hunt," the last chapter, is relatively short and separated from the rest of the book with a special title. Reread the chapter. Then discuss how Paulsen prepares the reader for it.
5. Discuss the titles *Brian's Hunt* and the chapter title "The Hunt." Consider the double or multiple meanings that each title might carry.
6. In the "Afterword," Paulsen reveals that readers sent him hundreds of letters a day to continue writing about Brian. Write the author a letter of your own and in it, outline what you expect to see in the next Brian book.

Related Works

1. Goodson, Lori Atkins. "Singlehanding: An Interview with Gary Paulsen." *The ALAN Review.* (Winter, 2004): 53–59. This interview was conducted at the 2003 ALAN Workshop in San Francisco. Paulsen talks "about his dogs, his boat, his writing, and his own many adventures."
2. Paulsen, Gary. **Brian's Return.** New York: Delacorte Press, 1999. 117p. $13.50. ISBN 0 385 32500 2. [fiction] JS (See full booktalk in *Booktalks and More,* 2003, pages 40 to 42.) In this supposedly concluding volume of the Brian series, Brian discovers that he is no longer comfortable in civilization and returns to the wilderness to discover himself in relation to nature.
3. Paulsen, Gary. **Brian's Winter.** New York: Delacorte Press, 1996. 133p. $15.95. ISBN 0 385 32198 8. [fiction] MJS This "what if" sequel to *Hatchet* extends Brian's stay to the winter months. In this

volume, the Smallhorns rescue him, and he begins to realize that life in the wilderness might be his way of life.

4. Paulsen, Gary. **Hatchet.** New York: Puffin Books, 1987. 195p. $4.95pa. ISBN 0 14 032724 X. [fiction] MJS This first novel in the series includes the plane wreck, survival test, and rescue that teach Brian to be a man.

5. Paulsen, Gary. **The River.** New York: Delacorte Press, 1991. 132p. $15.00. ISBN 0 385 30388 2. [fiction] MJS In this *Hatchet* sequel, a government psychologist asks Brian to return to the wilderness so that they can record for others the things that helped Brian survive. Brian saves himself and the psychologist.

6. Vanasse, Deb. **Out of the Wilderness.** New York: Clarion Books, 1999. 165p. $15.00. ISBN 0 395 91421 3. [fiction] JS This story about two brothers who live in the wilderness is framed by two bear encounters. The first separates the brothers because the younger tries to shoot a charging bear. The second illustrates that the older brother's dedication to nature has grown into a mental illness that will cause his death.

C3 CO

Tolan, Stephanie. **Flight of the Raven.**
New York: HarperCollins Publishers, 2001, 294p. $15.89.
ISBN 0 06 029620 8. [fiction] MJ

Themes/Topics: psionic powers, terrorism, friendship, family, Native-American beliefs

Summary/Description

When nine-year-old African-American Elijah (Raven) runs away from a mental hospital where he was part of an experimental group called the Ark (Related Work 5), he is found by a group of environmental terrorists. He joins twelve-year-old Amber Landis, her ten-year-old brother Kenny, and their stepmother Cassie in hiding and fleeing from FBI agents. Besides super intelligence, Elijah has telepathic powers that allow him to communicate with animals and humans. Cassie, half Indian, sees his talent and persuades her husband and the group leader, Charles Landis, to keep Elijah. Amber discovers her own telepathic powers and bonds with Elijah, who becomes a valuable group member. Kenny, jealous and violent, bullies Elijah and tries to kill him. Landis moves to international terrorism with biological weapons, but Cassie and his second in command resist. Landis tries to lethally inject the rebellious officer, but Elijah turns the poison on Landis and Amber.

Landis dies, but Elijah saves Amber. Cassie leaves the group and takes Amber and Elijah. Although Kenny discovers their escape and tries to kill them, a bear, one of Elijah's animal friends, frightens him off.

Booktalk

Eight-year-old Elijah (a.k.a. Raven) lives in a mental hospital. When he runs away, the hospital asks people to look for an African-American autistic child, but their description is not true.

Twelve-year-old Amber lives in her father's environmental terrorist camp. When he kills people, blows up buildings, and runs from the FBI, he tells her not to listen to the media lies about him. But Amber is beginning to wonder who is telling the truth.

The terrorist group finds Elijah in the woods, almost dead. Thinking he'll make a good hostage, they bring him back for Amber to watch and keep alive—not her favorite job. Amber begins to get strange messages and has unexplained feelings. She thinks silent Elijah is sending them. Elijah can join his mind with animals. They teach him survival. But can Amber survive when she joins her lonely, terrified existence with the *Flight of the Raven*?

Learning Opportunities

1. Read the story of Noah and the Ark in a bible of your choice. Research how the story is interpreted in Christian thinking. Share your research with the group. You might wish to start with the *Student Bible* (Related Work 5).
2. Survival is key in the story. Discuss how it is carried out by each of the characters. Be sure to include the story of Noah and the Ark in your discussion.
3. Tolan uses a remote camp and the winter season for her setting. Discuss how these choices enhance her story.
4. Cassie sees Elijah as a shaman. Research the role of the shaman. Share your information with the group. How does that information enhance your reaction to the story?
5. The wolf is the symbol for the terrorist group. Research the life and habits of wolves, and then discuss the appropriateness of the symbol.
6. The novel uses the words "flight," "journey," and "quest." Define each word. Consider the connotation of each, and discuss how each applies to the novel.
7. In the animal fantasy *Fire Bringer* (Related Work 2), meeting the wolf and raven are part of the main character's journey. Compare the wolf and raven in both *Fire Bringer* and *Flight of the Raven*.

8. After reading both *Welcome to the Ark* (Related Work 5) and *Flight of the Raven,* discuss the relationship of the two books and the appropriateness of other sequels. In your discussion, consider the ideas of connectedness and networking used in the two novels.

Related Works

1. Cameron, Sara in conjunction with UNICEF. **Out of War: True Stories from the Front Lines of the Children's Movement for Peace in Colombia.** New York: Scholastic Press, 2001. 224p. $15.95. ISBN 0 439 29721 4. [nonfiction] JS (See full booktalk in *Booktalks and More,* 2003, pages 58 to 61.) Like the characters in *Welcome to the Ark* and *Flight of the Raven,* these young people use their talents and experiences to build peace in their families, communities, and the world.

2. Clement-Davies, David. **Fire Bringer.** New York: Firebird, 1999. 498p. $6.99pa. ISBN 0 14 230060 8. [fiction] JS The main character, a stag born to save the herd, can speak to animals other than deer. Because of his kindness, the raven and wolf are central to the herd's survival.

3. Lubar, David. **Hidden Talents.** New York: Tom Doherty Associates, 1999. 213p. $16.95. ISBN 0 312 86646 1. [fiction] MJ (See full booktalk in *Booktalks and More,* 2003, pages 63 to 65.) Thirteen-year-old Martin Anderson is assigned to an alternative school where he discovers that his problems are actually paranormal assets when channeled positively.

4. Philbrick, Rodman. **The Last Book in the Universe.** New York: The Blue Sky Press, 2000. 224p. $16.95. ISBN 0 439 08758 9. [fiction] JS (See full booktalk in *Booktalks and More,* 2003, pages 146 to 148.) This novel depicts the Ark's ultimate fear, a world ruled by gangs and void of thought.

5. **Student Bible: New International Version.** Philip Yancey and Tim Stafford (notes). Grand Rapids, MI: Zondervan, 2002. 1440p. $32.99. ISBN 0 310 92784 6. This user-friendly version includes "Insights" (background information), "Guided Tour" (essays providing "bird's eye view"), and "100 People You Should Get to Know." Four of these short essays clarify the story of Noah on pages 10 to 14.

6. Tolan, Stephanie S. **Welcome to the Ark.** New York: Morrow Junior Books, 1996. 250p. $12.50. ISBN 0 688 13724 5. [fiction] MJ In this first book, Elijah is one of four geniuses whose intelligence and paranormal powers join them as a family in an experimental program called the Ark. At the end of the novel, Elijah is the only

character not accounted for. For more information about these two books and Tolan's other works, go to Tolan's Web site at http://www.stephanietolan.com/.

ᏨᎤ

Wadsworth, Ginger. **Words West: Voices of Young Pioneers.**

New York: Clarion Books, 2003. 191p. $18.00. ISBN 0 618 23475 6. [nonfiction] MJS

Themes/Topics: opening of the West, preparation, hazards of travel, history

Summary/Description

Fourteen chapters use the words of children and young adults to describe the opening of the West, preparations for leaving home, the dangerous travel conditions, work, entertainment, and the fulfillment of the promise. Pictures, sketches, and maps give a vivid picture of the people, times, and travel challenges. Inserts explaining specific details: "James K. Polk's Presidency," "Some Necessities for the Journey West," "The Santa Fe Trail," "Steady or Stubborn," (mule vs. oxen), "Fort Laramie," "The Mormon Trail," "Mansion of Happiness," "Buffalo," "Rachel Pattison" (most famous grave), "Photographing the West," "The Platte River," "The Kidnapping of Olive Oatman," "The Whitman Masacre," and "Number of Travelers Who Migrated West by Wagon Train," amplify the general narrative. "Epilogue and Sources" gives as much detail as possible about the people mentioned in the text and suggest further reading. A "Chronology" lists relevant events from the Louisiana Purchase to New Mexican statehood. "For Further Reading and Research" provides sources for "Special Interest," adults, and juveniles. An index with bolded pages designating illustrations provides easy access to information.

Booktalk

Read the passage opening the "Author's Note" on page xi. It begins "Cook beans . . ." and ends "No way!"

And that's not the half of it. The passage doesn't even mention the disease, blistering and freezing temperatures, rustlers, rattlesnakes, amputations, and deaths. So why did people head West in wagons, push carts, and even on just their two feet? They were poor, hungry, discouraged, enslaved, or restless—and there it was—more space, more land, and a chance to start over. Plus the salesmen were good. Here is a sample sales pitch. (*Read the passage on page 44 that starts "They do* say ..." and ends "... whenever you are hungry.") For the most part, the people making the decisions about leaving and where to go were adults. Their children usually didn't have much to say. Now the children have a chance to tell their side of the story—the piece of history they often found themselves dragged into, through their journals in *Words West: Voices of Young Pioneers*.

Learning Opportunities

1. Using your local library, research the history of settlement in your own town. In your research, try to locate some primary sources or speakers.
2. Using the material from Learning Opportunity 1, produce a dramatic reading or scene that would educate others about your town's or city's beginnings.
3. Choose one person from the research in Learning Opportunity 1 who seems to have an interesting personal story. Using the facts as a base, write a fictional journal entry relating what that person might have experienced. You might first wish to read some lengthier fictional journals related to moving West and listed below (Related Works 1, 3, 5, 6).
4. Select one of the sources listed in "For Further Reading and Research" of *Words West: Voices of Young Pioneers*. Read it and share its information with the rest of the group.
5. Using words of the young pioneers, produce a reading or a short dramatic scene.

Related Works

1. Bruchac, Joseph. **The Journal of Jesse Smoke.** New York: Scholastic Inc, 2001. 203p. (Dear America/My Name is America.) $10.95. ISBN 0 439 12197 3. [fiction] MJ Sixteen-year-old Cherokee Jesse Smoke lives in Tennessee in 1837, the year before the Trail of Tears. Educated at Mission schools and successfully assimilated into the white man's culture, he is still perceived as a savage. The journal emphasizes how much the Cherokee, embracing the world of the white man, were betrayed and driven to the West.
2. Calabro, Marian. **The Perilous Journey of the Donner Party.** New York: Clarion Books, 1999. 192p. $20.00. ISBN 0 395 86610 3. [nonfiction] MJS (See full booktalk in *Booktalks and More*, 2003, pages 37 to 39.) In contrast to most of the travelers West, the Donner Party left prosperous lives. Their reliance on one source of written information and their refusal to listen to those who went before them shaped their tragedy.

3. Gregory, Kristianna. **Seeds of Hope: The Gold Rush Diary of Susanna Fairchild.** New York: Scholastic, 2001. 180p. (Dear America.) $10.95. ISBN 0 590 51157 2. [fiction] MJ Fourteen-year-old Susanna Fairchild finds herself in the middle of the California gold rush when her family, traveling to Oregon City to open her father's new medical practice, faces a reverse of fortune.

4. Schmidt, Thomas, and Jeremy Schmidt. **The Saga of Lewis and Clark: Into the Uncharted West.** New York: DK Publishing, Inc., 1999. 210p. (A Tehabi Book). $35.00. ISBN 0 7894 4638 3. [nonfiction] MJS (See full booktalk in *Booktalks and More*, 2003, pages 235 to 237.) This multi-layered volume combines the text with extensive maps, photographs, paintings, and sketches to tell the story of Lewis Clark, the two explorers who mapped the American West and reinforced the concept of Manifest Destiny.

5. Levine, Ellen. **The Journal of Jedediah Barstow: An Emigrant on the Oregon Trail.** New York: Scholastic Inc., 2002. 176p. (Dear America/My Name is America.) $10.95.ISBN 0 439 06310 8. [fiction] MJ Losing his entire family early in the journey to Oregon, fourteen-year-old Jedediah escapes several other near fatal events and becomes part of a family formed from the survivors of the wagon train.

6. McDonald, Megan. **All Stars in the Sky: The Santa Fe Trail Diary of Florris Mack Ryder.** New York: Scholastic, Inc, 2003. 192p. (Dear America.) $10.95. ISBN 0 439 16963 1. [fiction] MJ When Florrie's mother marries Mr. Ryder, part owner of a general store in Santa Fe, the family heads for Santa Fe. The journey teaches Florrie that family is defined by more than a blood relationship.

Sea

୯ଽୱ

Creech, Sharon. The Wanderer.
New York: HarperCollins/Joanna Cotler, 2000. 305p. $15.95.
ISBN 0 06 027730 0. [fiction] MJS

Themes/Topics: quest, adoption, identity, family, perception

Summary/Description

Sophie, adopted after living in a series of foster homes, embarks with her cousins and uncles on a journey to see her new grandfather,

Bompie. The story is told in alternating points of view. First Sophie and then her cousin Cody, both thirteen, record their reactions to the same people and situations. Sophie has blended her own history with that of her new family's. Cody, as he grows closer to Sophie, his father, cousin Brian, and uncles Stew and Dock, learns that his insight helps him manage the six personalities on the long and sometimes dangerous journey. Each uncle finds part of the dream he left behind in his youth. Bompie, the grandfather, about whom Sophie continually tells stories, reaffirms his commitment to include everyone born or adopted into his family.

Booktalk

Sophie is going to sail the seas this summer. She has many reasons not to make the trip. She will be the only girl. Something about the water scares her to death, and—Oh yes!—she is the only adopted family member.

Cody, her new cousin, really shouldn't go either. According to his father, he can never do anything right. According to his Uncle Stu, he'll never be as smart as his cousin Brian. But Uncle Dock takes a chance on both of them, and Uncle Dock has been willing to take lots of chances in life—more than his two uptight brothers.

If everyone can all get along, they will eventually see Bompie, their grandfather who decided to move back to England. If everyone is patient, they will finally get to know the mysterious Sophie, the girl she used to be, the girl she never wants to talk about. If everyone lets go a little, each will discover that to reach a destination, each person, for a little while, must be willing to be *The Wanderer.*

Learning Opportunities

1. The names of the characters are closely related to their personalities. Research each character's name and explain its relationship to the character's role in the novel.
2. The journals of Sophie and Cody make up the book. Choose one incident that they both describe and that involves another character. Then write a chapter from that character's point of view.
3. As Sophie and Cody journey to see their grandfather, they also see themselves more clearly. List the things that they find out about themselves. Then list what they find out about each other. In two paragraphs, one about each character, explain how you perceive each of them.
4. Sophie, Brian, and Cody all become closer because of the trip they make to see their grandfather. Write the description of the trip that one of them might one day write for their grandchildren.

5. In "Gifts," Chapter 76, Uncle Mo expresses himself in pictures. Discuss what each picture reveals about him. Then write the letters that Cody and his father might exchange if they expressed themselves in writing.
6. Discuss the function of Rosalie in the novel. Be sure to include in your discussion your opinion about whether Dock will ever persuade Rosalie to marry him.
7. Discuss how the title applies to all the characters in the novel.

Related Works

1. Collins, Pat Lowery. **Signs and Wonders.** New York: Houghton Mifflin, 1999. 176p. $15.00. ISBN 0 395 97119 5. [fiction] MJS Neglected, fourteen-year-old Taswell is sent to a convent school. She focuses her loneliness and hurt into the fantasy that she is selected to give birth (virgin birth) to the prophet for the new millennium. She gives up the fantasy when her new, pregnant stepmother assures Taswell that she is part of the family.
2. Giff, Patricia Reilly. **All the Way Home.** New York: Dell Yearling, 2001. 169p. $5.99pa. ISBN 0 440 41182 3. [fiction] MJ Eleven-year-old Mariel lives in Brooklyn, a few blocks from Ebbets Field with her "almost mother" Loretta. Mariel fantasizes about how wonderful life would be with her real mother, runs away to find her, and discovers a new friend and her deep love for Loretta.
3. Haddix, Margaret Peterson. **Takeoffs and Landings.** New York: Simon & Schuster Books for Young Readers, 2001. 201p. $16.00. ISBN 0 689 83299 0. [fiction] MJ Fourteen-year-old Lori—a perfectionist—and fifteen-year-old Chuck—an overweight misfit—leave their rural town and accompany their single mother, a motivational speaker on one of her big city speaking tours. Told primarily in alternating chapters from the teen siblings' point of view, the story reveals the anger and fear the brother and sister have about their lives, each other, and their mother as well as their eventual understanding and bonding.
4. Helbig, Alethea K. and Agnes Regan Perkins. **Dictionary of American Young Adult Fiction, 1997–2001: Books of Recognized Merit.** Westport, CT: Greenwood Press, 2004. 558p. $75.00. ISBN 0 313 32430 1. [reference] Dealing with books already recognized by selection committees, the authors include biographical information, summaries, and character descriptions. Biographical information about Creech appears on page 64. Detailed summaries of *Chasing Redbird* and *The Wanderer* appear on pages 54 and 380 to 381 respectively.

5. Myers, Walter Dean. **The Dream Bearer.** New York: Harper
    Collins, 2003. 181p. $16.89. ISBN 0 06 029522 8. [fiction] JS.
    Twelve-year-old David Curry lives on 145th Street in Harlem.
    A homeless man calling himself the dream bearer claims he is over
    300 years old and relates to David's dreams about slavery and lynch-
    ing. David doubts the man but realizes that everyone may fall into
    the trap of false dreams. Moving on, the dream bearer warns David
    that old men rely on dreams but must move aside for young men
    with the vision to build their own dreams.
6. Nolan, Han. **Born Blue.** (See full booktalk in "Issues"/ "Personal
    Challenges," pages 13 to 15.) Growing up in destructive foster situ-
    ations and dreaming about a singing career, sixteen-year-old Janie
    decides to leave her own illegitimate daughter with a loving and
    caring family.

Fama, Elizabeth. Overboard.

Chicago, IL: Cricket Books, 2002. 158. $15.95. ISBN 0 8126 2652 4. [fiction] MJS

Themes/Topics: Indonesia, Muslims, world health
service, coming of age, trust

Summary/Description

Fourteen-year-old Emily lives in Indonesia with her physician parents who run a clinic. Feeling ignored, out of place, and burdened
by clinic work, Emily wants to return to the states. After a confrontation with her parents, she decides to visit her uncle who is vacationing
nearby. She boards a boat filled with Muslim pilgrims. The boat sinks.
She spends the next seventeen hours struggling for survival, reflecting on
her priorities, and bonding with a nine-year-old Muslim boy, Isman, who
accepts Allah's will. Both she and Isman risk their own lives to save each
other. When rescued, they clearly are committed to staying with each
other. The book opens with maps of Thailand, Malaysia, and Sumatra.
The author's note explains the inspiration and factual base for the story.

Booktalk

Fourteen-year-old Emily lives in Indonesia—a twenty-four hour steam
bath. And since Emily is blond, everyone stares at her and talks about her.
Everyone, except her parents. They are so busy working in their clinic and
giving her orders that Emily feels transparent. She would prefer living in

the United States, without them. Then she could have real friends, a real house, and maybe even some real fun. Finally, she just tells them off, but they don't care. In fact, her father accuses her of going "overboard." So Emily decides to take a trip of her own She plans on hopping a boat, and joining her uncle who happens to be visiting close by. Her parents won't even notice that she is gone. But her simple plan rapidly unravels. The boat is old and crowded with Muslim pilgrims. It sinks. Now Emily is really *Overboard* in a dark ocean off Sumatra. She has no life jacket or life raft. No one really knows her. She is exhausted. Any of the other survivors will take her life if it means saving theirs. And those dolphins the other foreigners think they see? Well, they aren't dolphins. They're sharks. Emily may die here—soon. And no one, not even her parents will know it.

Learning Opportunities

1. Discuss how Emily and Isman combine their strengths.
2. Emily labels the moment that she breaks out of the locker as her rebirth. Discuss why?
3. Using your library's resources, continue to research the meaning and practices of Ramadan. Share the information that you find with the class.
4. List all the characters besides Emily and Isman. Explain what each contributes to the journey.
5. Isman says that Emily is a grown up because when she sees something that is necessary, she does it. Discuss the implications of his definition. Does he also fit that definition?
6. Divide Emily's journey into challenges. List each challenge. Describe it. Then explain what it reveals about Emily. Do the same for Isman's journey, which joins Emily's. Then discuss how the two are alike and different.
7. Write an epilogue for the story.

Related Works

1. Carmi, Daniella. **Samir and Yonatan.** New York: Arthur A. Levine Books, 2000. 192p. $15.95. ISBN 0 439 13504 4. [fiction] MJ Samir, a Palestinian, and Yonatan, a Jew, supposedly enemies, bond while in a Jewish hospital. Only in an imaginary world created by Yonatan do they feel that they can live in peace.
2. Mathes, Ben, with Laura Raines. **Lessons from the Forests.** New York: Writers Club Press, 2002. 114p. $10.95pa. ISBN 0 595 23436 4. [nonfiction] JS An explorer, minister, and world health advocate, Dr. Ben Mathes, in a series of narratives, tells about his encounters around the world that have taught him about the power of faith.

3. Napoli, Donna Jo. **Stones in Water.** New York: Dutton Children's
    Books, 1997. 209p. $15.99. ISBN 0 525 45842 5. [fiction] MJS (See
    full booktalk in *Booktalks and More,* 2003, pages 189 to 192.) In this
    World War II coming of age survival novel set in Italy after the attack
    on Pearl Harbor, thirteen-year-old Roberto is sent to a German
    work camp where he finds his life and survival tied to the secret that
    another boy is Jewish. After the boy dies, Roberto escapes and finds
    his way home by remembering the boy's stories and faith.
4. Philbrick, Rodman. **The Young Man and the Sea.** New York: The
    Blue Sky Press, 2004. 192p. $16.95. ISBN 0 439 36829 4. [fiction]
    MJ A young man frustrated with his father's depression and alco-
    holism following the mother's death, decides to earn money to fix
    their boat. He embarks on a secret attempt to catch a blue fin tuna.
    Finding himself in a life-threatening situation, he thinks through his
    priorities, survives, and rediscovers his father.
5. Schuerger, Tina, and Michele Schuerger. **Gutsy Girls: Young
    Women Who Dare.** Edited by Elizabeth Verdick. Minneapolis,
    MN: Free Spirit Publishing Inc., 1999. 261p. $15.95. ISBN
    1 57542 059 7. [nonfiction] JS Part 1 includes essays by girls who
    have undertaken tasks requiring physical, mental, and emotional
    challenges. Part 2 gives suggestions and activities for building self-
    esteem, being positive, developing confidence, setting goals, visual-
    izing success, showing courage, and overcoming obstacles.

High Seas Trilogy

ርჽ℩ჽ

Lawrence, Iain. The Wreckers.

New York: Delacorte Press, 1998. 196p. $15.95. ISBN 0 385 32535 5. [fiction] MJ

Themes/Topics: crime, faith, friendship, late eighteenth,
early nineteenth-century historical novel

Summary/Description

Although his father takes him to sea to illustrate how boring it is, a
fourteen-year-old John Spencer falls in love with the sea's mystery
and danger. *The Isle of Skye* crashes on The Tombstones, a natural rock
formation. The guiding lights of *The Wreckers* leads ships to the rocks to
collect the salvage. John's crew dies, and John flees to the nearby town,
Pendennis. A legless beggar shows John a ring belonging to John's father

and implies that John must cooperate or the father will die. When other Wreckers attempt to kill John, Simon Mawgan comes to his rescue. Simon Mawgan and his niece, Mary, keep John at Galilee, Mawgan's estate. Mary befriends John, but John mistrusts Simon—kind one minute and violent the next. John also mistrusts Parson Tweed, to whom Mary and Simon appeal for help. A mysterious widow predicts when the ships will crash, and the tongueless Eli, Mary's uncle, sends cryptic warnings. While sorting the characters' mysterious relationships, John discovers that the Wreckers will not release his father until they find out about the cargo. Parson Tweed masterminds the Wreckers. Simon Mawgan warns boats away from the coast. John rescues his father and discovers the cargo is only sawdust. The author's note explains the strange profession that profited from others' misfortune and how greed fueled its violence. An introductory map shows Pendennis in the County of Cornwall.

Booktalk

You are all alone on a stormy, rocky sea. Lights promise to guide you to shore. Suddenly, the land comes, too fast and hard. The crash is a confusion of broken bodies and smashed cargo. You wake on a beach to your crew's moans and empty, staring eyes. Strangers pass you. They drown a man they find alive. You gather enough strength to run away. This "safe" place proves even stranger. A man with no legs says he holds your father prisoner. A man with no tongue tries to tell you stories. A stranger from the beach attempts to slit your throat, and you don't know if you can trust the man who drives him away. You have entered the world of *The Wreckers,* a world of greed, destruction, and death. At fourteen, John Spencer must find the truth. His life and his father's life depend on it.

Lawrence, Iain. **The Smugglers.**
New York: Delacorte Press, 1999. 183p. $15.95. ISBN 0 385 32663 7. [fiction] MJ

Themes/Topics: crime, trust, superstition, late eighteenth, early nineteenth-century historical novel

Summary/Description

John and his father are on their way to purchase a new ship, *The Dragon.* A highwayman robs the stagecoach and stuns the father. When the coach stops at the Baskerville Inn, Mr. Larson, their fellow traveler, refuses to enter the Inn and warns the Spencers against buying the Dragon. When the Spencers enter, however, they meet Captain

Turner Crowe, who is eager to captain the ship. The originally contracted captain is killed. Mr. Spencer hires Crowe who produces an instant crew. John travels on the ship to supervise the cargo. When Mr. Larson's dead body turns up, John discovers a map, letter, and ledger detailing the crimes of the Burton gang, notorious smugglers. John realizes that he is traveling with the gang and that the highwayman is one of his shipmates. The novel ends at the Baskerville Inn, the center of the smuggling ring, and John saves the day, the ship, and the cargo.

Booktalk

John just has to supervise the cargo. His father buys the ship, *The Dragon*, and hires the trustworthy Captain Turner Crowe. So Mr. Spencer leaves his son with confidence and peace of mind. That was a mistake. Captain Crowe loses his temper easily and carries a knife. One of Crowe's sailors wears a cork vest because he's afraid of drowning, and they just found a man with his head smashed in. John can watch the cargo, but he can't seem to control where it's going. *The Smugglers* are in control. More than one person has warned them that the ship carries a curse, and John realizes that he could lose the cargo, the ship, and his life. Danger lurks in the mouth of *The Dragon*.

⚜

Lawrence, Iain. The Buccaneers.

New York: Delacorte Press, 2001. 242p. $15.95. ISBN 0 385 32736 6. [fiction] MJ

Themes/Topics: friendship, treachery, superstition, late eighteenth, early nineteenth-century historical novel

Summary/Description

Seventeen-year-old John Spencer is sailing the Caribbean with Captain Stanley Butterfield, his father's partner on *The Dragon*. When they rescue Horn, a man in a lifeboat, the gunner claims Horn is a Jonah. Horn tells about the diabolical and disfigured Bartholomew Grace, one of the captains of Horn's many sunken ships. When Grace appears on his ship, *The Apostle*, Horn is certain that the ship is doomed. In the subsequent struggles through battles, storms, and disease, Spencer, with the help of the infamous Dashing Tommy Dusker and Horn, foils Grace's attempts to secure the Captain Kidd treasure and destroy *The Dragon*. In the final conflict, Horn gives his own life to save the ship from Grace. Although John fears that the luck left the ship when Horn went overboard, he manages to sail the boat to land, the scene of *The*

Wreckers, where he reunites with Simon and Mary. John loves Mary but realizes that she is planted on the land while his heart is with the sea. A map of the West Indies introduces the novel.

Booktalk

Ask how many people know what a Jonah is on the sea.

John Spencer is now seventeen, and he is about to meet a Jonah. He is sailing on *The Dragon* with his father's business partner. They discover a man in a lifeboat. They rescue him. The man is likable enough, maybe too likable. He is strong and able, but the gunner sees something else. He sees a man whose sea chest holds bits of boats, all the ships he has sunk. He sees a man who tells too many stories, too hard to believe. The shipmates call him Spinner. One of his stories is about the evil Bartholomew Grace, the pirate captain of *The Apostle,* who cuts off arms and legs, or takes lives on the authority of "The Black Book." When the notorious Grace appears, he will give no quarter. He will destroy everything he can. How will John fight him? Will he take the advice of the gunner, hired to defend the ship? Or will he learn from the stories of the charming man plucked out of the sea? A man who was one of *The Buccaneers.*

Learning Opportunities

1. On page 31, Simon Mawgan and Parson Tweed of *The Wreckers* compare the Wreckers group to a barrel hoop and the staves. He suggests that without the hoop, the barrel can hold nothing. Discuss how this comparison is central to the story. Using a metaphor, describe a group to which you belong.

2. Compare the qualities of John Spencer, the trilogy's main character, and Tamo, one of the main characters in *The Pirate's Son* (Related Work 3). Both young men face difficult choices between good and evil. How do their circumstances and personal qualities aid them?

3. Dasher is a significant, although minor, and sometimes comic character. After reading all three books in the trilogy, try to describe him in relation to the other characters presented.

4. Outline the plot of each novel. Describe the ingredients that Lawrence uses to construct his adventures. Using some of those same elements, outline an adventure of your own.

5. Even though *The Wreckers* takes place on land, it's plot and characters are tied to the sea. After reading the entire trilogy, make up a code of honor that applies on both land and sea.

6. What do the three novels have to say about the importance and dangers of inferences and judgments?

7. Using your library's resources, find information about one of the following: wreckers, smugglers (late eighteenth and early nineteenth centuries), or buccaneers. You may wish to start with *Pirate* (Related Work 4).

Related Works

1. Blackwood, Gary. **The Year of the Hangman.** (See full book-talk in "Mystery/Suspense"/"History/Period," pages 142 to 144.) In this revision of history, the British, not the colonies, win the Revolutionary War, and, at one point, the main character and his uncle are at the mercy of colonial privateers.
2. Jaques, Brian, and David Elliot (illus.). **The Angel's Command: A Tale from the Castaways of the Flying Dutchman.** New York: Philomel Books, 2003. 374p. $23.99. ISBN 0 399 23999 5. [fiction] MJ Set in 1628, this story sees Ben and Ned confronting pirates, privateers, and gypsy bandits in two action filled adventures.
3. McCaughrean, Geraldine. **The Pirate's Son.** New York: Scholastic, 1998, American ed. 294p. $16.95. ISBN 0 590 20344 4. [fiction] MJ (See full booktalk in *Booktalks Plus,* 2001, pages 74 to 77.) Three eighteenth-century teenagers join forces to defeat the prejudices of civilization as well as the pirates and superstitions of the sea.
4. Platt, Richard. **Pirate.** New York: Alfred A. Knopf, 1994. 63p. (Eyewitness Books.) $19.99. 63p. ISBN 0 679 97255 2. [nonfiction] MJS Platt distinguishes among privateers, buccaneers, and corsairs—all falling under the general umbrella of pirate. He traces their long history in many countries and explains why the pirate operations, so falsely romanticized in literature and movies, diminished in the late nineteenth century.
5. Stevenson, Robert Louis. **Treasure Island.** New York: Signet Classic, 1998. 203p. $3.95pa. ISBN 0 451 52704 6. [fiction] MJS Published in 1883, this sea adventure about young Jim Hawkins working to outsmart Long John Silver and his crew has many of the plot and character elements of the Lawrence trilogy.

☙❧

Martin, Nora. **Flight of the Fisherbird.**
New York: Bloomsbury USA Children's Books, 2003. 150p. $15.95. ISBN 1 58234 814 6. [fiction] MJ

Themes/Topics: family, friends, crime, marriage, Scott Act, prejudice, nineteenth century

Summary/Description

Thirteen-year-old Clem Granger, a tomboy, lives with her mother and father on Granger Island off the Northwest Coast. Fifteen-year-old Sarah Hersey, better educated and more sophisticated, will live with the Grangers until spring. Sarah plans to marry Clem's uncle, Doran Granger. Sarah's father who just died and Clem's uncle, Doran Granger, were business partners. Sailing her boat, the Fisherbird, Clem sees three bundles thrown off her uncle's boat. She fishes one out of the water and finds Tong Ling, a Chinese man. In violation of the Scott Act, Tong Ling, is reentering the country. She suspects that her uncle is a smuggler and now a killer, Clem hides Tong Ling. Then she and her new friend, Jed, decide to take him to Whatcom to get work. Sarah follows Clem and, inadvertently, becomes part of the escape. Uncle Doran and Ray Chung, the Chinese man to whom Doran has gambled away his boat, ambush and try to kill them. Sarah alerts the authorities, Tong Ling escapes, and Clem and Sarah decide they are sisters.

Booktalk

Find a map of the San Juan Islands. Show it to the group.

In 1889, thirteen-year-old Clem Granger lives off the northwest coast of the United States. Her family owns all of Granger Island, and her handsome uncle owns the Doran Bull, a supply ship selling goods to the San Juan Islands inhabitants. Life seems perfect. Then Paul Hersey, her uncle's business partner accidentally dies. His prissy orphaned daughter, Sarah Hersey, decides to stay with the Grangers all winter. Clem can't stand her, but Clem's parents wonder why she can't be more ladylike, like Sarah. And—oh yes, Clem fishes a man out of the ocean—a Chinese man thrown from her uncle's boat in a brown bag. Should she tell her uncle she found him? No. Should she help a man who dares to break the law? Yes. The *Flight of the Fisherbird* begins a journey to freedom in which Clem finds herself battling nature, prejudice, evil—and herself.

Learning Opportunities

1. Using your library's resources, research the legislation passed in the United States between 1882 and 1910 that restricted the rights of Chinese immigrants and United States citizens of Chinese descent. Share the information with the group through either a timeline or an oral presentation.

2. On page 63, Tong Ling says, "We all wear many different faces." Discuss how that statement applies to each of the characters.

3. Tong Ling calls Clem's lists "poetry" and Jed calls them "recipes for living." Discuss the appropriateness of each label. Decide if you would use either of these words to describe the lists or if you would choose a different one. Explain your answer.
4. Write your own list poems. You may wish to refer to *How to Write Poetry* (Related Work 2).
5. At the end of the novel, a blank book arrives from Tong Ling. Fill the first page. Share your responses with the other members of the group.
6. Discuss Jed's place in the story. Is his character important?
7. Write an epilogue to the story.

Related Works

1. DeFelice, Cynthia. **Under the Same Sky.** New York: Farrar, Straus and Giroux, 2003. 215p. $16.00. ISBN 0 374 38032 5. [fiction] MJS When fourteen-year-old Joe Pedersen decides to work on his father's farm to earn a new motorbike, he earns the respect of his family and crew and commits himself to defending the migrant workers from his friends' prejudice and the immigration authorities.
2. Janeczko, Paul B. **How to Write Poetry.** New York: Scholastic, 1999. 117p. $12.95. ISBN 0 590 10077 7. MJS (See full booktalk in *Booktalks Plus*, 2001, pages 215 to 217.) In this guide to writing poetry, the explanation for writing list poems appears on pages 44 to 55.
3. McCaughrean, Geraldine. **The Pirate's Son.** New York: Scholastic, 1998, American ed. 294p. $16.95. ISBN 0 590 20344 4. [fiction] MJ (See full booktalk in *Booktalks Plus*, 2001, pages 74 to 77.) Three eighteenth-century teenagers, joining forces against pirates, nature, superstition, and the establishment, define themselves.
4. Miklowitz, Gloria D. **Secrets in the House of Delgado.** Grand Rapids, MI: Eerdmans Books for Young Readers, 2001. 182p. $16.00. ISBN 0 8028 5206 8. [fiction] MJ (See full booktalk in *Booktalks and More*, 2003, pages 185 to 187.) Orphaned fourteen-year-old Maria Sanchez seeks refuge from the church and is sent to be a servant/spy in Conversos household of the Delgado family. Although pressured to betray them to the Inquisition, she learns to see them as friends whom she must protect. In her journey, she also discovers love and the resolve to improve herself.
5. Napoli, Donna Jo. **Stones in Water.** New York: Dutton Children's Books, 1997. 209p. $15.99. ISBN 0 525 45842 5. [fiction] MJ (See full booktalk in *Booktalks and More*, 2003, pages 189 to 192.) In this

coming of age survival novel, thirteen-year-old Roberto protects a young Jewish boy from the Germans and then saves himself.

6.   Yep, Laurence. **The Journal of Wong Ming Chung: A Chinese Miner.** New York: Scholastic Inc., 2000. 224p. (Dear America/My Name is America.) $10.95pa. ISBN 0 590 38607 7. Set in 1851, this gold mining story tells about Bright Intelligence and his no luck uncle working together to outsmart the Americans, who rob and bully the Chinese, and then finding their home in America.

ᏨᏗ

Meyer, L. A. Bloody Jack: Being an Account of the Curious Adventures of Mary "Jacky" Faber, Ship's Boy.

New York: Harcourt, Inc., 2002. 278p. $17.00. ISBN 0 15 216721 5. [fiction] JS

Topics/Themes: orphans, plague, sexual identity, women's roles, pirates, Royal Navy life, eighteenth-century history

Summary/Description

Mary (Jacky) Faber is orphaned in 1797 and joins child street gangs to survive. When her gang leader is killed, she takes his clothes, selects the name Jack, and masquerades as a ship's boy—"The Deception." Her reading skills get her a job on a ship, but her quick mind, musical skill, and charisma cause division on the ship. She kills a pedophile stalking her and encourages a young officer to fight the ship's bully. Thought to be gay and having more difficulty hiding her identity, she isolates herself and eventually shares her secret with another ship's boy she loves. When the ship is disabled in a fight with pirates, the crew finds temporary refuge on a deserted island and attaches Jacky to a kite so that she might spy a more permanent haven. The kite detaches and takes her to a much larger island. She sends signal fires seen by both the ship's crew and the pirates. The Royal Navy defeats the pirates, saves Jacky's life, and discovers her identity. Instrumental in securing treasure beyond the Captain's wildest dreams, she is held in custody for her protection and sent, with warm wishes and her part of the treasure, to a Boston girls' school. Her sea journey takes place between her thirteenth and fifteenth years, and her dream is to someday reunite with the ship's boy she loves. A fully labeled drawing of the HMS Dolphin introduces the novel.

Booktalk

Mary Faber lives in London with her mother, father, and sister. The year is 1797—the year of pestilence. All the Fabers, except Mary, die. When the men come to pick up the bodies, the man named Muck takes Mary out to the curb and promises that he will be back in a week to pick her up in the death wagon. That ride sounds fine to Mary. She prays "for Jesus to come take [her] in his lovin' arms." But Jesus doesn't come, and Mary survives on the streets. It doesn't take her long to figure out that being a boy has a lot more to offer than being a girl. Nobody tries to snatch a boy for the "workhouses, or worse." The dumbest boy will get picked for a job ahead of the brightest girl. And boys take care of just themselves. So Mary Faber decides to become Jack Faber. She signs on as a "ship's boy." She gets food, shelter, clothes, mates, money, and a chance to fight pirates and capture riches. When battle tests her, she becomes *Bloody Jack*. Her shipmates notice and talk about her. Some dangerous ideas come with the looks and talk, ideas that could end both "The Deception" and her life.

Learning Opportunities

1. *Oliver Twist* (Related Work 2) explores street life in nineteenth-century London. Oliver belongs to a theft ring. Compare Oliver's street life with Mary Faber's.
2. Using your library's resources, research the life of children and women in nineteenth-century England. Share the information with the group.
3. Read the passage that begins "It's easier bein' a boy ..." on page 32 and ends on page 33. Rewrite the passage by drawing on your own experience.
4. The professor's vocabulary reflects the book's issues. Find the definitions for each of the words and explain how each applies to the events in the novel.

    Chapter 13: buggery, sodomy, pederasty
    Chapter 15: insidious, surreptitious, disingenuous
    Chapter 18: debauchery, dissipation, wantonness
    Chapter 19: billowing, burgeoning, blossoming

5. After defining the words and discussing their definitions, discuss Tilden's reluctance to conduct sex education.
6. In Chapter 33, the new words are monologue, dialogue, and soliloquy. Define each. Write a monologue, dialogue, or soliloquy for one or two of the characters. Perform it for the group. You might want to use it as a booktalk that would encourage others to read *Bloody Jack*.

7.   Bravery is a major theme in the novel. Define bravery by using examples from the novel. In the definition, be sure to use examples of what bravery is not as well as what bravery is.

8.   Each part of the novel is introduced by a brief passage keying the events and tone. Write similar passages for each of the characters in the novel. Discuss what you have written with the rest of the group or compare your writing with passages others in the group may have also written.

Related Works

1.   Dunton Downer, Leslie, and Alan Riding. **Essential Shakespeare Handbook.** New York: DK Publishing, Inc., 2004. 480p. $25.00. ISBN 0 7894 9333 0. [reference] MJS This user-friendly reference includes plot summaries and interpretative material on all thirty-nine plays and an analysis of the poetry. It also includes essays on Shakespeare's life, times, and impact on world culture. Pages 304 to 313 deal with *Romeo and Juliet.* Pages 324 to 335 discuss *Hamlet,* both related to Mary Faber's perception of female roles.

2.   Dickens, Charles. Don Freeman (illus.). **Oliver Twist.** New York: William Morrow and Company, 1994. 442p. $20.00. ISBN 0 688 12911 0. [fiction] MJS/A Published in the middle of the nineteenth century, this novel about a street urchin points up the unfair labor and penal practices of the time.

3.   McCaughrean, Geraldine. **The Kite Rider.** New York: HarperCollins, 2001. 272p. $15.95. ISBN 0 06 623874 9. [fiction] MJS Twelve-year-old Haoyou supports his family through his ability to make and transport himself with giant kites.

4.   McCaughrean, Geraldine. **The Pirate's Son.** New York: Scholastic, 1998, American ed. 294p. $16.95. ISBN 0 590 20344 4. [fiction] MJ Three teenagers survive the perils of eighteenth-century life that include death, prejudice, cultural clash, storms, sickness, and pirate attacks.

5.   Meyer, L. A. **Curse of the Blue Tattoo: Being an Account of the Misadventures of Jacky Faber, Midshipman and Fine Lady.** New York: Harcourt, Inc., 2004. 488p. $17.00. ISBN 0 15 205115 5. [fiction] JS In the sequel, Jacky Faber continues her adventures when she leaves the Navy ship and enrolls in the Lawson Peabody School for Young Girls where she will learn to be a lady.

6.   Platt, Richard. **Pirate.** New York: Alfred A. Knopf, 1994. 63p. (Eyewitness Books.) $19.99. ISBN 0 679 97255 2. [nonfiction] MJS Platt explains the different classifications of pirates, the role of female pirates, and the myths and divisions of pirate treasure.

7. Yolen, Jane, and David Shannon (illus.). **The Ballad of the Pirate Queens.** New York: Harcourt Brace & Company, 1995. 28p. $15.00. ISBN 0 15 200710 5. [poetry] CH MJS Although this might be considered a children's book, its characterization of Anne Bonney and Mary Reade, two famous women pirates, who dressed like men, fought off an attack while their shipmates drank and hid, and cheated the hangman through pregnancy, presents a thought-provoking story relevant to Mary Faber's choices.

(ʃ)(ʆ)

Smith, Sherri L. **Lucy the Giant.**

New York: Delacorte Press, 2002. 217p. $15.95. ISBN 0 385 72940 5. [fiction] MJS

Themes/Topics: alcoholism, identity, self-concept, fishing

Summary/Description

Fifteen-year-old Lucy Otswego lives in Sitka, Alaska with her alcoholic father. Her mother left when Lucy was seven. Over six feet tall and regularly carrying her father home from drunken binges, Lucy is the town misfit, pitied by adults and mocked by peers. When a stray dog follows her home, she finds hope in her life. The dog gets sick, the father refuses to help her, and the dog dies. Grief stricken and angry, Lucy signs up for a crabbing expedition under a false name. The crew becomes her family as she proves herself physically, mentally, and emotionally fit. After her identity and age are revealed, she must return to her father but decides that she will let him take responsibility for his own decisions, and she will build a future for herself.

Booktalk

Lucy the Giant—that's what the kids in Sitka, Alaska, call her. And they're probably right. Not many fifteen-year-old girls are big enough and strong enough to pick up a man every night, throw him over her shoulder, and carry him home.—That man is Lucy's father. He drinks for a living. Mom got fed up and ran away when Lucy was seven. Size and circumstances make Lucy the town freak. So when Lucy gets the chance to leave town, she takes it—big time. She signs up for a King crab expedition on the Bering Sea. Now her name is Barbara. Barbara travels far, makes some friends, and earns more money than her father would ever imagine. But most important, as she fights the treacherous sea, she finds out if she is *Lucy the Giant,* Barbara the Adult, or someone else—someone she never met before.

Learning Opportunities

1. Lucy in *Lucy the Giant* and Jenna Boller in *Rules of the Road* (Related Work 1) have alcoholic fathers, are self conscious about their size, and leave home with jobs that allow them to discover themselves. Discuss how each author uses these elements to accomplish the story's purpose.
2. On page 12, the English teacher assigns a paper about "My Biggest Fish." Discuss how that assignment might be interpreted literally and metaphorically. Then respond to the assignment yourself.
3. Using your library's resources, research the Bering Sea and the industries it supports. Share the information with the group.
4. Alcoholism is a central part of the novel. Research the disease, its treatment, and the support groups available for both the alcoholics and their families.
5. Lucy reads *The Old Man and the Sea* (Related Work 2). After reading the book, describe how Lucy might react to it after her brief fishing career. You might want to write a dialogue in which she discusses the book with her English teacher.
6. Discuss the significance of the survival suit. Consider its literal and figurative function.
7. On pages 98 to 102 and pages 191 to 196, Lucy describes the storm. Read these descriptions again. Then discuss their relationship to each other and the rest of the novel.
8. The story suggests several possible endings. React to the ending Smith chose. If you agree that it was the right choice, explain why on the basis of what you know about the character. If you disagree, write your own ending and justify it.

Related Works

1. Bauer, Joan. **Rules of the Road.** New York: G. P. Putnam's Sons, 1998. 201p. $15.99. ISBN 0 399 23140 4. [fiction] MJS (See full booktalk in *Booktalks Plus,* 2001, pages 114 to 116.) Taking a summer job so that she can get away from her alcoholic father, Jenna Boller discovers new friends and new abilities.
2. Hemingway, Ernest. **Old Man and the Sea.** New York: Scribner, 2003. 127p. $10.00pa. ISBN 0 684 80122 1. [fiction] JS/A Written in 1952, this story involves bravery and persistence in the face of defeat, as an old man battles a giant marlin in the Gulf Stream.

3. Hobbs, Valerie. **Tender.** (See full booktalk in "Contemporary Life"/"Coming of Age," pages 48 to 49.) A pampered teenager goes to live with a father she has never seen and learns about her own abilities when she works on his boat.

4. Logue, Mary. **Dancing with an Alien.** New York: HarperCollins, 2000. 134p. $14.95. ISBN 0 06 028318 1. [fiction] JS Seventeen-year-old Tonia, six feet tall and solidly built, falls in love with and makes love to an alien who sees her strong muscular body as beautiful.

5. Rottman, S. L. **Stetson.** New York: Viking/Penguin Putnam. 192p. $16.99. ISBN 0 670 03542 4. (See full booktalk in "Issues"/"Interpersonal Challenges," pages 23 to 25.) Stetson, who lives in an abusive home and disrupts school, works for a Vietnam veteran who serves as a father figure, and with his sister, eventually decides to build another life for himself.

෯ ෯

Vance, Susanna. **Deep.**
New York: Delacorte Press, 2003. 272p. $15.95. ISBN 0 385 73057 8. [fiction] MJS

Themes/Topics: Caribbean, family, family dysfunction, identity, independence

Summary/Description

Indulged, sarcastic, and fragile thirteen-year-old Birdie Sidwell lives a safe, normally stressed life in rain soaked Oregon where her "best friend" dominates and manipulates her. Birdie's mother, superintendent of schools, and Birdie's father, a famous scientist, decide to spend a year in the Caribbean and include Birdie. Birdie longs to discover horrendous adventures to write about. She gets her wish. In St. Maarten, she is kidnapped in broad daylight by a serial killer.

Emotionally deprived, brutally realistic, and hardy child of the sea, seventeen-year-old Morgan experiences the gruesome—her siblings' death, her parents' alcoholism, and social isolation. She parents the family, but eventually leaves the adults in port because she knows their behavior will kill them all, just as it killed her sister. After taking the boat, she sets out to secure papers to fool the authorities. Unknowingly, she contacts Birdie's kidnapper, a well-known forger. In alternating chapters, Birdie and Morgan describe the journeys that find them fighting for their lives on the criminal's island. Working together, they free themselves and lead authorities to the killer. They realize that each person is responsible for their own actions and must develop mental as well as physical strength to deal with consequences.

Booktalk

Read aloud the first two chapters—"One Girl," and "Another Girl."

No two girls could be more different. For Birdie, the Caribbean is an exciting vacation with protective parents. For Morgan, it is home with parents who might kill her. Yet the two will share one very significant experience—being kidnapped by a serial killer. Why does he choose such different victims? Can anyone find this master of disguise who seizes his prey and then melts into the islands without a trace? The outside world doesn't know he exists. They think many men commit his crimes—not just one. Their confusion gives him time. And with time, the search will end. The *Deep,* after all, buries its victims and keeps its secrets. Only Birdie and Morgan can reveal the horrors. But they are well hidden—and working together may mean they just die sooner.

Learning Opportunities

1. Birdie opens the novel with the claim that she is deep. Discuss the number of ways that the title, *Deep,* applies to the novel.
2. Discuss why the Nu Way school and Birdie's friendship with Kirin is introduced into the novel.
3. Birdie's father, Morgan's father, and Nicholas all make money from the misfortune of others. Discuss how this similarity affects you as a reader.
4. "Bound to happen" is used in connection with Kirin and Oona. Discuss how that phrase applies to others in the novel.
5. Morgan and Birdie are extremely different. Discuss what makes them friends.
6. Discuss what the character Bajo adds to the story.
7. Morgan's mother, Birdie's mother, and Kirin's mother present three different independent women. Discuss how each character affects her daughter.

Related Works

1. Cormier, Robert. **Tenderness.** New York: Bantam Doubleday Dell, 1997. 229p. $16.95. ISBN 0 385 32286 0. [fiction] MJS In this ironic thriller, a runaway girl joins up with a serial killer. Eluding prosecutions for the crimes that he did commit, the killer is arrested for her accidental death.

2. Desetta, Al, and Sybil Wolin (ed.). **The Struggle to Be Strong.** Minneapolis, MN: Free Spirit Publishing, 2000. 179p. $14.95. ISBN 1 57542 079 1. [nonfiction] JS This work defines, discusses, and illustrates the elements of resilience—Independence, Relationships, Initiative, Creativity, Humor, and Morality. Both Morgan and Birdie illustrate these qualities.

3. Nolan, Han. **Born Blue.** (See full booktalk in "Issues"/"Personal Challenges," pages 13 to 15.) A young girl tells her survival story as she experiences abuse and neglect. Like the characters in *Deep*, she must decide how she will build her own life in spite of adults.

4. Ryan, Pam Muñoz. **Becoming Naomi León.** New York: Scholastic Press, 2004. 256p. $16.95. ISBN 0 239 26969 5. [fiction] MJ When the mother who deserted her shows up and plans to take her away to exploit her, eleven-year-old Naomi learns the truth about her family, asserts herself, and becomes responsible for her life.

5. Thompson, Julian F. **Terry and the Pirates.** New York: Atheneum, 2000. 262p. $17.00. ISBN 0 689 83076 9. [fiction] MJS At the end of her junior year, Teresa Fremont Talley learns that her divorced parents think that she needs to choose a boarding school for her senior year. Instead, she stows away on a ship with a fifteen-year-old boy struggling for his father's attention. They join forces to save themselves when pirates seize the ship.

Mystery/Suspense

Mystery and Suspense often combine. Both challenge readers to "figure out" what happened, and both keep readers on the edge of their seats. "Contemporary" books focus on modern, realistic situations. "History"/ "Period" selections use a particular time period as a backdrop or a necessary part of the story. "Paranormal" stories add ghosts and supernatural abilities to the mix. All contain thrills and chills. (Note: Although Haddix's *Escape from Memory* appears in the "History"/"Period" section of this chapter, it could just as easily fit in "Paranormal" section.)

Contemporary

⟡⟡

Cooney, Caroline B. Fatality.

New York: Scholastic, 2001. 198p. $4.99pa. ISBN 0 439 13524 9. [family] MJS

Themes/Topics: murder, family secrets, family unity, identity

Summary/Description

When a four-year-old murder case reopens, fifteen-year-old Rose Lymond, who is believed to have witnessed the murder, once again becomes a police focus. She steals a police car so she can run away and destroy her diary, which tells about her discovering that she was born after her mother's love affair. Rose decides to protect the family by not saying anything about what she did or saw that weekend. Her best junior high friend and her junior high crush decide to protect her from a stalker trying to kill her. They assume it is the wealthy and powerful man, who is accused of the crime or his daughter. When the man's daughter asks Rose to leave school with her, Rose's friends follow them and discover that Rose left with her brother's former friend, not the daughter. The young man believes that Rose saw him commit the crime, but is protecting him because she loves him. He fears that she will be pressured into confessing and plans to kill her. The friends alert the police who intercept the couple at a roadblock. The friends and police know her secret and encourage her to confront her parents. Her father knew about the affair all along and feared only that her biological father would take her away from him. They decide to confront the mother together but resolve to leave the secret behind and maintain their family unit.

Booktalk

Fifteen-year-old Rose Lymond is an honor student, a field hockey star, a soprano, a camp counselor, a baby sitter, and a fugitive from the law. That fugitive from the law role doesn't last long, however. She steals the police car just long enough to destroy the diary that her mother handed to the police. The diary that might give them a clue for solving a four-year-old murder. The diary containing a secret that could destroy their family. Someone else seems very interested in what Rose has to say too—someone who is trying to run Rose off the road with a big, dark SUV. Someone who is very willing to make Rose Lymond the next *Fatality*.

Learning Opportunities

1. Describe Aunt Sheila and the role that she plays in the novel.
2. Using your library's resources, research the definition and punishment for hit and run. Share your information with the group.
3. Describe Anjelica Lofft. Discuss the role that she plays in the novel.
4. How does Clooney use false leads in her novel? Give some examples of the false leads. Explain how they affected you as a reader.
5. Write one more chapter. In it describe the mother's reaction. Tie the conclusion to the details from the novel. List and explain those details.
6. Silence is a major factor in the novel. List the instances when silence, rather than words or action, impact the novel.

Related Works

1. Anderson, Laurie Halse. **Speak.** New York: Farrar, Straus and Giroux, 1999. 198p. $16.00. ISBN 0 374 37152 0. [fiction] JS (See full booktalk in *Booktalks and More*, 2003, pages 75 to 77.) After Melinda Sordino is raped, she withdraws until a teacher and two

students draw her out by advice and example. When she finally tells, her life changes positively.

2. Fraustino, Lisa Rowe. **Dirty Laundry: Stories about Family Secrets.** New York: Viking, 1998. 181p. $16.99. ISBN 0 670 87911 8. [fiction] MJS Dealing with sex change, abortion, suicide, mental illness, the occult, abuse, unwed pregnancy, and divorce, these stories tell about most of the situations families wish they could avoid but often must face.

3. Hardman, Ric Lynden. **Sunshine Rider: The First Vegetarian Western.** New York: Laurel Leaf Books, 1998. 343p. $4.99pa. ISBN 0 440 22812 3. [fiction] MJS Wylie Jackson discovers that John Boardman, the trail boss whom he has always admired, is his real father and that the "aunt" who raised him is really his mother.

4. Tomey, Ingrid. **Nobody Else Has to Know.** New York: Delacorte Press, 1999. 229p. $15.95. ISBN 0 385 32624 6. [fiction] MJS Fifteen-year-old Webb Freegy finally decides to break his silence and admit that he is responsible for the hit and run for which his grandfather is willing to take the blame.

5. Van Steenwyk, Elizabeth. **Maggie in the Morning.** Grand Rapids, MI: Eerdmans Books for Young Readers, 2001. 128p. $16.00. ISBN 0 8028 5222 X. [fiction] MJ When Maggie is ten, she spends a summer with her aunt, whom Maggie discovers is really her mother.

❧❧

Cormier, Robert. The Rag and Bone Shop.
New York: Delacorte Press, 2001. 154p. $15.95. ISBN 0 385 72962 6. [fiction] MJS

Themes/Topics: murder, interrogation, identity, evil

Summary/Description

Twelve-year-old Jason is accused of murdering a seven-year-old girl. Trent, an expert interrogator, intimidates Jason into confessing even though Trent's training tells him that Jason is innocent. Trent sees this confession as a step up in his career. As Jason confesses, the victim's brother admits to the crime. Trent loses his reputation. Jason, haunted by the interview and the possibility that he has the capacity to kill, sets out to stab the school bully with whom he has previously fought.

Booktalk

Twelve-year-old Jason is kind of a loner, or maybe just one of a kind. He gets angry with bullies—even beats one up. But mostly he hangs around seven- and eight-year-old girls—friends of his sister Emily. Trent is a top interrogator. He can get a confession from the best and baddest. He waits for the accused to make a mistake and then he goes in for the kill.

Suddenly there is a murder. The town wants to know who did it. Jason is the last one to see the victim—an eight-year-old girl. Trent comes to town to get a confession. He begins to work over the obvious suspect, Jason, but in *The Rag and Bone Shop* of the heart, evil isn't always so obvious or easy to find. Maybe the worst killer of all is hiding is the last place anyone would expect to look.

Learning Opportunities

1. In the poem, "The Circus Animals' Desertion" (Related Work 5), Yeats talks about the relationship among words, experience, and death. From that poem, Cormier uses the last stanza and chooses the title for his novel. Read the entire poem and then discuss its appropriateness as an allusion for the novel.
2. In *Monster* (Related Work 4), *Silent to the Bone* (Related Work 3), and *The Rag and Bone Shop* young men are characterized as evil. After reading the three books, discuss how the characterization relates to guilt and evidence.
3. The words "specific" and "context" haunt Jason. Define these words and then explain why they present such significant blocks for him.
4. The sentence "You are what you do" is a significant statement in the novel. Explain the importance. Then discuss whether you agree or disagree with the statement.
5. In both *Tenderness* (Related Work 2) and *The Rag and Bone Shop,* Cormier uses an ironic conclusion. Describe each conclusion and explain how each affects the rest of the novel.

Related Works

1. Cormier, Robert. **Heroes.** New York: Delacorte Press, 1998. 135p. $15.95. ISBN 0 385 32590 8. [fiction] JS (See full booktalk in *Booktalks and More,* 2003, pages 118 to 120.) Two winners of the Silver Star confront each other over not so heroic secrets. Again, Cormier explores the relationship between good and evil.
2. Cormier, Robert. **Tenderness.** New York: Bantam Doubleday Dell, 1997. 229p. $16.95. ISBN 0 385 32286 0. [fiction] JS (See full booktalk in *Booktalks Plus,* 2001, pages 64 to 66.) A young man guilty of one crime is accused of another crime that he did not commit.
3. Konigsburg, E. L. **Silent to the Bone.** New York: Atheneum Books, 2000. 261p. $16.00. ISBN 0 689 83601 5. [fiction] MJS (See full booktalk in *Booktalks and More,* 2003, pages 151 to 152.) An

extremely intelligent teenager, accused of hurting his baby sister, is unable to defend himself because he has lost the power to speak.

4. Myers, Walter Dean. **Monster.** New York: HarperCollins Publishers, 1999. 281p. $15.95. ISBN 0 06 028077 8. [fiction] JS (See full booktalk in *Booktalks and More,* 2003, pages 13 to 15.) The reader never knows if a young man accused of a crime is really guilty or innocent.

5. Yeats, William Butler. "The Circus Animals' Desertion." In **W. B. Yeats: The Poems, a New Edition** edited by Richard J. Finneran. New York: Macmillan Publishing Company, 1983. 747p. $14.29. ISBN 0 02 632940 9. [poetry] A The speaker ponders whether words or writing can create an actual experience. The poem appears on pages 346 to 348, and a full discussion appears on pages 242 to 244 in *Yeats* by Douglas Archibald, New York: Syracuse University Press, 1983. 280p. $23.78. ISBN 0 8156 2263 5.

༒༇

Cross, Gillian. **Phoning a Dead Man.**

New York: Holiday House, 2002. 252p. $16.95. ISBN 0 8234 1685 2. [fiction] MJS

Themes/Topics: Russia, family, responsibility, love

Summary/Description

Hayley and her family learn that John, Hayley's brother, ten years her senior, died in a detonation accident. Annie Glasgow, his wheelchair-bound girlfriend, and Hayley travel to Russia to investigate. The chapters divide mainly among Annie and Hayley trying to find John and a recovering John trying to remember who he is. In Russia, Annie and Hayley see where he supposedly died, but don't believe the story. Annie traces his cell phone to a remote village where John recuperated from tick fever with the help of Frosya, a mentally challenged middle-aged woman. The Russian Mafia accompanies them to the village but leaves them there when Hayley suggests John's possible whereabouts.

On his journey, John steals a bike. He enters a town and is hidden, fed, and put on a train by a teacher's family. In the city, a taxi driver and his brother risk their lives to help him. To save the taxi driver's brother, John gives himself up. The Mafia returns him to the village where he discovers his detonation is key in a power struggle between two Mafia brothers. Frosya dies attempting to save John. The police arrest the brother planning the detonation. John decides to stay in Russia for a while with Annie to make restitution for his decisions.

Booktalk

Hayley Cox has an older brother John. John just died in a detonation accident in Russia. The family tries to wipe John from their memories. They won't talk about him. They burn all his things. But Annie Glasgow, John's girlfriend, won't accept his death that easily. John was a detonation expert—a very slow and careful one. She calls Hayley and proposes a plan. They will travel to Russia and see where John supposedly died—even though Annie is in a wheelchair. But their trip gets more complicated when the Russian Mafia volunteer to be their tour guides. And then things get even more complicated when Annie decides to pick up her trusty cell phone and start *Phoning a Dead Man.*

Learning Opportunities

1.   The theme of being in control, or taking charge is carried through with several characters. List the characters that feel they have some way to control their own lives or the lives of others. Describe what each desires to control and his or her level of success.
2.   Discuss the part religion plays in the story.
3.   Construct a journey for John in which he returns to each person he encountered and gives explanation or makes restitution.
4.   Using your library's resources, research Russian organized crime. You may wish to start with *Organized Crime: An Inside Guide to the World's Most Successful Industry* (Related Work 4). Share your findings with the class and explain how your information supports the story.
5.   Cross employs a rather complicated structure for her story. Describe the structure. Then explain how the parts contribute to the whole.
6.   Read *Tightrope* (Related Work 2) and *Phoning a Dead Man,* both by Cross. Compare their structures and themes.

Related Works

1.   Cooney, Caroline B. **Wanted!** New York: Scholastic, 1997. 230p. $4.99. ISBN 0 590 98849 2. [fiction] MJS (See full booktalk in *Booktalks Plus,* 2001, pages 117 to 119.) Accused of being her father's murderer, Alice flees the police and discovers the murderer is her mother's boyfriend.
2.   Cross, Gillian. **Tightrope.** New York: Holiday House, 1999. 216p. $16.95. ISBN 0 8234 1512 0. [fiction] MJS (See full booktalk in *Booktalks and More,* 2003, pages 130 to 132.) Fourteen-year-old Ashley Putnam and her invalid mother receive help from a local gang leader and find the price he demands in return might destroy their lives.

3. Levitin, Sonia. **The Singing Mountain.** New York: Simon & Schuster Books for Young Readers, 1998. 261p. $17.00. ISBN 0 689 80809 7. [fiction] MJS. (See full booktalk in *Booktalks Plus*, 2001, pages 86 to 89.) Although not a mystery, this novel involves twin journeys. Fearing that Mitch Green has been captured by a cult, his mother and cousin travel to Israel where they find Mitch has decided to stay at the Yeshiva and continue his study of Orthodox Judaism. The two female travelers also have spiritual revelations of their own in the process.

4. Lunde, Paul. **Organized Crime: An Inside Guide to the World's Most Successful Industry.** New York: DK Publishing, 2004. 192p. $30.00. ISBN 0 7894 9648 8. [nonfiction] JS Using full color photographs, maps, and charts, the oversized volume deals with the history, development, and current statues of organized crime groups all over the world. "The Russian Mafiya" appears on pages 85 to 91.

5. Stevenson, James. **The Unprotected Witness.** New York: Laurel Leaf Library, 1997. 170p. $4.50pa. ISBN 0 440 22820 4. [fiction] MJS Pete and his father become part of the witness protection program. After his father is killed, Pete finds himself targeted by the mob, and is finally saved by the help of his misfit friend.

ርፇ፝ፎ

Halliday, John. **Shooting Monarchs.**
New York: Margaret K. McElderry Books, 2003. 135p. $15.95.
ISBN 0 689 84338 0. [fiction] MJS

Themes/Topics: crime, abuse, physical handicap, out-group

Summary/Description

Eighteen-year-old Macy, born during the Macy's Thanksgiving parade, is the victim of physical and emotional abuse and becomes a career criminal by the time he is a teenager. Sixteen-year-old Danny Driscoll, a brilliant teenager, suffers from congenital scoliosis, comes from a poor but loving home, and suffers bullying from the boyfriend of the girl he loves from afar, Leah Hoffman, who is targeted as Macy's fourth murder victim. Leah's younger sister Sally constantly encourages Danny to tell Leah he loves her. Shooting pictures in the woods where Macy is hiding the kidnapped Leah, Danny finds and saves Leah. Macy fatally shoots Danny, but Danny tells Leah his feelings before he dies. At Danny's memorial service and Macy's murder trial, the town is finally forced to focus on Danny's wonderful character and spirit.

Booktalk

Ask the group if they know what a monarch butterfly is. You might want to show them a picture of one.

Eighteen-year-old Macy lives by the gun. He is a killer. Sixteen-year-old Danny is physically disabled, poor, and a loner. He loves to shoot too, but he uses a camera. He takes as many pictures as he can—especially pictures of butterflies. Macy and Danny have never met. Even though she never intended to, a girl in Danny's class, the beautiful, intelligent Leah Hoffman will bring them together. One of the three will die. Which one? The answer is anything but logical, but it has everything to do with *Shooting Monarchs*.

Learning Opportunities

1. The title can be interpreted in different ways. Explain several ways it might apply to the story.
2. On page 135, Halliday supplies the reader with the Web site for the National Center for Missing and Exploited Children (NCMEC): www.ncmec.org. Investigate the Web site and share the information that you find and the impressions that you have with the group.
3. Compare Macy and Danny. Discuss how they are the same and different.
4. Danny's grandmother tells Danny "Handsome is just a matter of inches." Discuss your reactions to her statement.
5. Although Chapter 10 focuses on Danny and Chapter 11 focuses on Macy, each chapter involves both young men. Discuss how each applies to both and what each reveals about their environments.
6. Chad Peterson and Sally Hoffman are minor characters. Discuss what they contribute to the novel.
7. The court house in which Macy is tried has an inscription from the Bible, "He makes the sun rise on the evil and on the good, and sends rain on the just and on the unjust." Discuss the inscription's relationship to the novel.

Related Works

1. Cormier, Robert. **Tenderness.** New York: Bantam Doubleday Dell, 1997. 229p. $16.95. ISBN 0 385 32286 0. [fiction] MJS (See full booktalk in *Booktalks Plus*, 2001, pages 64 to 66.) This thriller describes the partnership of a teenage serial killer and his groupie girlfriend.
2. Cross, Gillian. **Tightrope.** New York: Holiday House, 1999. 216p. $16.95. ISBN 0 8234 1512 0. [fiction] MJS (See full booktalk in *Booktalks and More*, 2003, pages 130 to 132.) Fourteen-year-old

Ashley Putnam, caught in the web of the gang world, is saved with the help of a wheelchair-bound admirer.
3. Flinn, Alex. **Breathing Underwater.** (See full booktalk in "Issues"/ "Interpersonal Challenges," pages 19 to 21.) Brutally abused by his father, sixteen-year-old Nick Andreas must learn how to control his own tendency toward violence.
4. Hartnett, Sonya. **What the Birds See.** Cambridge, MA: Candlewick Press, 2002. 196p. $15.99. ISBN 0 7636 2092 0. [fiction] MJS In 1977, nine-year-old Adrian, whose mother is mentally unstable and whose father left him with a distant and abusive maternal grandmother, is bullied at school and turns to his neighbor Nicole, a social isolate, who leads them both to their deaths when she persuades him that they can become heroes.
5. Walker, Virginia (text), and Katrina Roechelein (graphics). **Making Up Megaboy.** New York: DK Ink/Richard Jackson, 1998. 63p. $16.95. ISBN 0 7894 2488 6. (See full booktalk in *Booktalks Plus*, 2001, pages 82 to 84.) [fiction] MJS Thirteen-year-old abused Robbie Jones, identifying with Megaboy, a cartoon hero he and his best friend create, commits murder because he has a crush on a popular girl who comments on the victim's rudeness.

Harrison, Michael. Facing the Dark.
New York: Holiday House, 2000. 128p. $15.95.
ISBN 0 8234 1491 4. [fiction] MJS

Themes/Topics: murder, friendship, gangsters

Summary/Description

In this murder mystery, the accused murderer's son, Simon, and the victim's daughter, Charley, give their perceptions of the crime and its solution in alternating chapters. Devastated by his father's arrest, Simon decides he will become a juvenile Hercule Poirot. When Charley hears her father's murder attributed to road rage, she suspects foul play and decides to investigate. They discover each other and a mutual suspicion of Charley's Uncle John, a family friend who now wants to buy the taxi business from Charley's mother. Charley reasons that Uncle John will also purchase Simon's family taxi business, have the biggest company, and wipe out all competition. They start to follow John, and discover that gangsters are coercing him and trying to take over all the area's taxi business. Both he and Simon's father were used unwittingly in the plot to kill Charley's father. The three flush out the killers who, at the end of a high-speed chase, grab Charley and threaten to kill her. John calls the police, but Simon proves the hero as he knocks the knife out of the killer's hand. All are cleared, and the three taxi companies merge.

Booktalk

One day, Charley's father takes a routine taxi call and winds up dead. Simon's father is taken away in handcuffs. Simon and his mother know it's a mistake, but the police seem satisfied that they have a murderer. The police talk about road rage and a seatbelt that wasn't fastened, but Charley thinks that good old Uncle John, the long time family friend, murdered her father to get the family business. Both Simon and Charley have something to prove and a lot to lose—like their lives. They decide to team up and find the real murderer, but the real murderer decides to find them. Tabloid ghouls and gangster goons surround them as they gather evidence the police can't find, but discovery and delivery are two different things, and suddenly they are alone and scared *Facing the Dark*.

Learning Opportunities

1. Simon is inspired by the character of Hercule Poirot in Agatha Christie's *Murder on the Nile*. Research the character of Poirot, and then discuss the appropriateness of the comparison (Related Work 1).

2. Both Simon and Charley imagine information sources that might apply to their lives—newspaper articles, field guides, and recipes. Using their writing as models, write about your own life by using information sources. You might consider want ads, garage sale descriptions, or directions in addition to the forms that Simon and Charley have chosen.

3. In both *Silent to the Bone* (Related Work 4) and *Facing the Dark*, teenagers become detectives so that they might help the people they care about. In the search, they also improve themselves. After reading each novel, explain how the problem comes to each sleuth and what the path to the solution contributes to their lives.

4. The paragraph on page 32 distinguishes between worried and frightened. Choose two other closely related words such as happy and joyful or smart and intelligent. Write a paragraph that explains the difference.

5. The Simon and Charley chapters sometimes describe the same events. On pages 96 and 97, John describes the events as he sees them and ends with "All this is just my word. I have no evidence."

After a school play, pep rally, or simple observation, ask three or four people who participated to write a description of what they saw and did. You might even want them to include the why. Then ask each person to read the description. Compare the similarities and differences. Discuss how those differences might be helpful and harmful in an investigation.

Related Works

1. Christie, Agatha. **The Under Dog and Other Stories: A Hercule Poirot Collection.** New York: Berkley Books, 1984. 201p. $5.99pa. ISBN 0 425 06808 0. [fiction] JS/A Agatha Christie's detective stories illustrate the remarkable Poirot's deductive abilities.
2. Dahl, Roald. **Skin and Other Stories.** New York: Viking, 2000. 212p. 15.99. ISBN 0 670 89184 3. [fiction] JS In the story "Lamb to the Slaughter" on pages 22 to 34, Mary Malony kills her husband with a frozen leg of lamb and then feeds the murder weapon to the detectives.
3. Duncan, Lois (ed.). **On the Edge: Stories at the Brink.** New York: Simon & Schuster Books for Young Readers, 2000. 211p. $17.00. ISBN 0 689 82251 0. [fiction] MJ The short story "Unbalanced" by William Sleator, on pages 129 to 139 describes how two dancers manage to break the neck of a third and get away with it.
4. Konigsburg, E. L. **Silent to the Bone.** New York: Atheneum Books, 2000. 261p. $16.00. ISBN 0 689 83601 5. [fiction] MJS (See full booktalk in *Booktalks and More,* 2003, pages 151 to 152.) A teenage sleuth constructs a language so that he and his friend can work together and save the friend from child abuse charges.
5. Weiss, M. Jerry, and Helen S. Weiss (eds.). **From One Experience to Another.** New York: A Forge Book, 1997. 224p. $4.99pa. ISBN 0 812 56173 2. [fiction] MJS In the short story "No Matter What" by Joan Lowery Nixon, ten-year-old Danny and his older sister Megan discover a hit man masquerading as a nurse, follow him, and sedate him until the police can come.

ɷɷ

Miklowitz, Gloria D. The Enemy Has a Face.

Grand Rapids, MI: Eerdmans Books for Young Readers, 2003. 139p. $16.00. ISBN 0 8028 5243 2. [fiction] MJ

Themes/Topics: terrorism, Jewish/Palestinian conflict, street crime, stereotyping

Summary/Description

When seventeen-year-old Adam disappears, the Hofmans, a Jewish family from Israel, now living in Los Angeles, suspect foul play. They believe Palestinian terrorists kidnapped or killed Adam, but eventually discover three American boys from good homes shot him in a random thrill killing. The police find Adam's body in a car fallen over an embankment. The body of a Palestinian girl he has been talking with on the Internet is also in the car. Before Adam is found, Adam's sister Netta, a middle school student, pursues every lead. A new Palestinian boy in her class, living with a Muslim family, helps her enter a Palestinian, anti-Jewish chat room. They argue constantly, but become friends in spite of their differences. A girl she meets in temple provides emotional support and introduces Netta and her parents to her own parents, a happy Jewish/Irish Catholic couple. By the time the police find Adam's body, the Hofmans have a diverse circle of supportive American friends and judge individuals rather than groups.

Booktalk

Netta Hofman is a new middle school student in Los Angeles. Her father is a scientist doing important work for the United States. The Hofman's are from Israel—a dangerous home. In America, they hope they have left behind those dangers. *Show a picture of hooded Palestinian terrorists.* Then, one night, seventeen-year-old Adam Hofman, Netta's brother, disappears. Where is he? Why doesn't he call? The Palestinian students at Adam's high school don't like Adam and his outspoken views on Israeli/Palestinian conflicts. A new Palestinian boy in Netta's class is strangely friendly to her. Are these people like the faceless and cowardly killers she has learned to fear? Or are there others who would harm the Hofmans—others who know how important her father's work is to U.S. security? Who are they? Where are they? Netta is determined to find out. She is convinced *The Enemy Has a Face,* and she will find it, even if the search means risking her own life.

Learning Opportunities

1. Immediately Netta connects Laith Al Salaam with the Arab underground. Research Arab terrorist groups. Make a chart that describes each group and any relationships that you find. Explain the chart in an oral or written presentation. You may wish to start your research with *Hamas: Palestinian Terrorists* (Related Work 5).

2. In chapter 13, on page 109, Netta alludes to Masada. Research this historical event and explain why her reference is ironic. You may wish to read Miklowitz's historical novel *Masada: The Last Fortress* (Related Work 4).

3. In *The Enemy Has a Face* and *The Terrorist* (Related Work 2), teenagers' experiences shape the way they trust and perceive the world. In each book, the main character loses a brother to violence. Compare and contrast the two novels. Discuss which story, if either, has a significant effect on your thinking.

4. *The Enemy Has a Face* speaks about a very timely situation. Discuss whether or not the problems the story explores limit the novel's universal appeal.

5. As the Hofmans fear, Adam is dead. Discuss how the identity and description of his killers affect the novel.

Related Works

1. Byers, Ann. **Lebanon's Hezbollah.** New York: The Rosen Publishing Group, Inc., 2003. 64p. (Infamous Terrorist Organizations.) $26.50. ISBN 0 8239 3821 2. [nonfiction] MJS Byers explains the conflicts between Israel and Palestine that created Hezbollah and its goals as well as its connections to Iran's fundamentalist movement and terrorist organizations.

2. Cooney, Caroline B. **The Terrorist.** New York: Scholastic, 1997. 198p. $15.95. ISBN 0 590 22853 6. [nonfiction] MJS (See full book-talk in *Booktalks Plus*, 2001, pages 135 to 138.) In trying to find the terrorist who killed her brother, Laura unknowingly is helping the murderer escape.

3. Margulies, Phillip. **Al Qaeda: Osama bin Laden's Army of Terrorists.** New York: The Rosen Publishing Group, Inc., 2003. 64p. (Infamous Terrorist Organizations.) $26.50. ISBN 0 8239 3817 4. [nonfiction] MJS Margulies explains Osama bin Laden's position in Arab terrorism and his connection with Palestinian terrorist groups.

4. Miklowitz, Gloria D. **Masada: The Last Fortress.** Grand Rapids, MI: Eerdmans Books, 1998. 188p. $16.00. ISBN 0 8028 5165 7. [fiction] MJS (See full booktalk in *Booktalks Plus*, 2001, pages 162 to 164.) This historical novel tells the story of Masada through the two perceptions of Simon, the seventeen-year-old son of Zealot leader Eleazar ben Yá ir and the materialistic Flavius Sila, commander in chief of the Roman Tenth Legion.

5. Rosaler, Maxine. **Hamas: Palestinian Terrorists.** New York: The Rosen Publishing Group, Inc., 2003. 64p. (Infamous Terrorist

Organizations.) $26.50. ISBN 0 8239 3820 4. [nonfiction] MJS
Rosaler explains the background of the Israeli/Palestinian conflict and
the rise of Hamas. The "For More Information" section provides a
Rosen Web site that updates Internet sources on the topic of terrorism.

Oates, Joyce Carol. **Freaky Green Eyes.**

New York: Harper Tempest, 2003. 341p. $17.89. ISBN 0 06 623757 2. [fiction] MJS

Theme/Topic: abuse, murder, family, celebrity

Summary/Description

Fourteen-year-old Franky (Francesca) Pierson is the daughter of
famous sports announcer, Reid Pierson, who dominates his family.
Friction grows between Franky's parents as her mother cultivates her
artistic talent and develops an independent life. Her mother spends
more and more time away from home in her family's cabin. The father
turns the children against her. When he allows the two girls to visit their
mother, he cuts the visit short in a violent rage. Franky suspects that
her father physically abuses their mother, but blames her mother for
provoking a man they all know as volatile and violent. When her mother
and her mother's friend are missing, the father is a suspect. The father
and his lawyer choreograph the children's testimony, but Franky remembers her mother's cryptic message to her before she disappeared, and finds
her mother's diary, which convicts the father. The girls move in with their
mother's sister. Their stepbrother vows to seek revenge against the aunt
whom his father accuses of turning the girls against him.

Booktalk

Fifteen-year-old Franky Pierson has it made. Her mother is beautiful and
talented. Her father is a famous sports announcer and an ex-professional
football player. Being Reid Pierson's daughter opens lot of doors. But
being Reid Pierson's wife might not be such a good deal. Another
person inside Franky, a person called *Freaky Green Eyes,* hears and
sees things that Franky would like to ignore—the sounds of fighting and
crying, the scarves and long sleeved blouses that cover up her mother's
bruises. Franky can't understand why her mother provokes her father.
Everybody in the family knows that his word is law. Everybody knows
that breaking the law brings consequences. But no matter how she tries,
she can't silence *Freaky Green Eyes,* and what this strong and independent Freaky has to say could change their lives forever.

Learning Opportunities

1. Part 1 is titled "Crossing Over." Define the term. Then identify an instance from real life to illustrate the definition.
2. Describe how Reid Pierson abuses each person in his family.
3. In "the celebration: April 18," Franky defines heart. Apply the definition to Franky's character.
4. Describe the possible sequel to this novel.
5. Franky's father believes that people will forgive anything if they love you enough. Do you agree or disagree? Use examples from the novel and real life to support your opinion.
6. Discuss the appropriateness of the title.
7. Using your library's resources, define domestic violence and develop a profile of an abuser and his or her family. Share your findings with the group and discuss how the information supports the story.

Related Works

1. Anderson, Laurie Halse. **Speak.** New York: Farrar, Straus and Giroux, 1999. 198p. $16.00. ISBN 0 374 37152 0. [fiction] JS (See full booktalk in *Booktalks and More*, 2003, pages 75 to 77.) Like Franky, Melinda Sardino goes to a party with older teenagers, but Melinda, unable to fight off her attacker, a star high school athlete, is raped. The novel deals with her learning how to deal with the incident and fight off her attacker a second time.
2. Bloor, Edward. **Crusader.** New York: Harcourt Brace and Company, 1999. 390p. $17.00. ISBN 0 15 201944 8. [fiction] MJS (See full booktalk in *Booktalks and More*, 2003, pages 139 to 141.) Fifteen-year-old Roberta Ritter finds the power to assert herself and discovers that her father engineered a plot that killed her mother.
3. Brooks, Kevin. **Martyn Pig.** New York: The Chicken House, 2002. 240p. $10.95. ISBN 0 439 29595 5. [fiction] JS Martyn's abusive father dies while trying to hit him. Martyn figures out a way to hide the body and becomes involved with an older neighborhood girl who pretends to help him but really betrays him.
4. Conroy, Pat. **My Losing Season.** New York: Doubleday, 2002. 402p. $27.05. ISBN 0 385 48912 9. [nonfiction] S/A The author of *The Prince of Tides* describes his challenging experience at the Citadel and how it related to the treatment he received from his abusive father who envied and tried to undercut Conroy's athletic achievement.
5. Johnston, Tim. **Never So Green.** New York: Farrar, Straus and Giroux, 2002. 228p. $18.00. ISBN 0 374 35509 6. [fiction] JS Twelve-year-old Davy Donleavy learns to deal with his deformed right hand

when he takes baseball lessons from his new stepfather and then learns that his idol sexually abuses his own daughter, Davy's stepsister.

History/Period

ᘓᘔᘓ

Blackwood, Gary. **The Year of the Hangman.**
New York: Dutton Books, 2002. 261p. $16.99. ISBN 0 525 46921 4. [fiction] MJS

Themes/Topics: Revolutionary War, family, loyalty, patriotism, historical novel

Summary/Description

Set in 1777, the alternate history (uchronia) novel speculates what America would have been like if the British had prevailed. A delinquent British teenager, Creighton Brown, is forcibly sent to America and placed in the custody of his uncle, Colonel Hugh Gower. Traveling to West Florida where Gower will serve as Lieutenant Governor, their ship is captured by pirates led by Benedict Arnold. Gower instructs Creighton to pose as his indentured servant, spy on the Americans, and give Gower the intelligence. Creighton agrees in return for information about the death of his father, Major Harry Brown. Creighton travels with the pirates to New Orleans where he meets Benjamin Franklin and two independent teenagers—the witty aggressive Sophie Ducet, and the strong, intelligent, but countrified Peter. He carries out his promise to Gower by facilitating his escape and revealing that Franklin publishes a seditious newspaper. The British burn Franklin's print shop where Franklin dies. Creighton realizes his responsibility for killing a man he admired. Creighton learns that his father was sentenced to hang for warning an American settlement of an Indian attack. Losing respect for the British, Creighton helps Sophie continue the print shop. He joins Arnold and Peter in an American spy operation to give Gower misinformation. Gower suspects the plot, challenges Arnold, and dies in a duel. Before his death, Gower directs Creighton to a cell imprisoning Creighton's father. Arnold, Peter, and Creighton rescue him. With all his experiences, Creighton decides that any war becomes mired in greed and power.

In a brief introduction, Blackwood clarifies what really happened in the American Revolution. The "Author's Note" explains the facts Blackwood incorporated and changed, defines alternate history (uchronia), and provides a Web site address (www.uchronia.net).

Booktalk

The rebels won the Revolutionary War. George Washington is the father of our country and the first president. We all live in a democracy. Right? But what if history didn't come out that way? What if the British captured Washington, put down the rebellion, and held the territory? It is 1777, and British fifteen-year-old Creighton Brown is about to enter that other world, the world of the British conquerors. His uncle, Colonel Gower controls a big part of it. His father Major Harry Brown died defending it. But Creighton discovers that even though the British declared victory, the war isn't over. Pirates sail the seas. Spy webs cover the colonies, and Spain and France are ready to join the Americans against the English. Creighton doesn't think any of this should involve him. He wants to return to England and have fun with his buddies. Up until now, war and politics just provided money for his good times and gambling. But in this new world the stakes are life and death. Benedict Arnold and Benjamin Franklin are major players. And every loser pays. Like it or not, Creighton is part of a dangerous game played quietly and earnestly in *The Year of the Hangman.*

Learning Opportunities

1. At the end of the "Author's Note," Blackwood refers the reader to www.uchronia.net to further research the concept of alternative history. Review the Web site and share the information with the group.
2. Pages 3, 4, and 5 explain the title of the *Year of the Hangman* in terms of penalties and games. Discuss how that unusual combination sets the stage for the rest of the novel.
3. Benjamin Franklin is a central figure in Creighton's life. Further research Franklin's life and writings. Share your information with the class. You may wish to start with *B. Franklin Printer* (Related Work 1).
4. After reading and discussing Franklin's life, design a self-improvement project. Follow it for at least six months. Record your progress each day. Then share your results and recommendations.
5. Creighton concludes that war muddles principles. Trace how he comes to that conclusion.
6. On pages 176 and 177 in Chapter 16, Arnold and Creighton discuss the meaning of courage. After their discussion, Creighton asks the question, "With no one to guide you, how can you know which path is the right one?" Discuss in a group the sources one might use to answer his question.
7. List each character. Discuss the function of each in the novel's overall purpose.

Related Works

1. Adler, David A. **B. Franklin, Printer.** (See full booktalk in "History"/"Period"/"Leaders and Defining Events," pages 243 to 245.) In fifteen chapters, Adler describes the life and times of the brilliant and eccentric Benjamin Franklin, who saw himself primarily as a printer throughout his life.
2. Cox, Clinton. **Come All You Brave Soldiers.** New York: Scholastic, 1999. 182p. $15.95. ISBN 0 590 47576 2. [nonfiction] JS (See full booktalk in *Booktalks Plus,* 2001, pages 155 to 157.) Cox describes the contributions that black soldiers made to both sides of the Revolutionary War as fighters, spies, and guides as they tried to figure out which side would grant them freedom.
3. Denenberg, Barry. **The Journal of William Thomas Emerson: A Revolutionary War Patriot.** New York: Scholastic, 1998. 152p. (Dear America: My Name is America.) $10.95. ISBN 0 590 31350 9. [fiction] MJ (See full booktalk in *Booktalks Plus,* 2001, pages 12 to 14.) Orphaned twelve-year-old Will acts as a spy for the patriots throughout the Revolutionary War.
4. Rinaldi, Ann. **Cast Two Shadows.** New York: Gulliver Books, 1998. 276p. $16.00. ISBN 0 15 200881 0. [fiction] MJ (See full booktalk in *Booktalks Plus,* 2001, pages 46 to 48.) Caroline Whitaker takes a journey with two purposes: to save her white Loyalist brother from the "tender mercies" of the British and to rediscover her true family roots with her black slave grandmother.
5. Sterman, Betsy. **Saratoga Secret.** New York: Dial Books for Young Readers, 1998. 249p. $16.99. ISBN 0 8037 2332 6. [fiction] MJS (See full booktalk in *Booktalks Plus,* 2001, pages 21 to 23.) In this coming of age novel, sixteen-year-old Amity Spencer must notify Benedict Arnold of Burgoyne's attack.

ℭℑℨ

Haddix, Margaret Peterson. **Escape from Memory.**
New York: Simon & Schuster Books for Young Readers, 2003. 220p. $16.95.
ISBN 0 689 85421 8. [fiction] MJS

Themes/Topics: Chernobyl, paranormal, responsibility, memory, history related

Summary/Description

At a sleepover, fifteen-year-old Kira, under hypnosis, shares a strange memory from another country. Her girlfriends speculate about its origin, and her mother, both horrified and angry, mysteriously disappears. A strange woman, identifying herself as Aunt Memory, arrives and tells her that Sophia, the woman Kira calls mother is actually someone who kidnapped her. Now Sophia is kidnapped, and Kira must save her. They fly, in a private plane, to Crythe, California. Crythe, an ancient civilization of people who remember everything, was evacuated from the Soviet Union and relocated in California after Chernobyl. Kira is kept under guard in a castle-like compound and discovers that Lynne, her best friend, is stowed away in the suitcase. Aunt Memory is really Rona Cummins, an American woman who, because she wanted the advanced computers Kira's parents developed, turned a materialistic faction against them, and caused their death. She wants Kira to unite the fragmented community. Kira refuses to cooperate. Rona imprisons her with Sophia and Lynne. Sophia convinces Rona that the necessary technical information is in Ohio. Lynne and Kira will accompany Rona and give her the information. If they fail, Sophia will die. Lynne and Kira, with the help of the townspeople, foil Rona. Kira discovers, through an implanted memory, that Sophia really is her mother living with the implanted memory of Kira's aunt. The novel ends with Sophia in a mental ward. Kira is going to confront her about accepting the identity of being her mother, the woman whose decisions may have produced the war in Crythe, or hiding in the memory and identity of her aunt Sophia, the more passive, dependent, and protected sister.

Booktalk

Fifteen-year-old Kira knows her mother is a little different. Her mother doesn't want anything to do with televisions, cars, and computers. She doesn't socialize. In fact she doesn't talk much, even to Kira. Her favorite thing is sitting and staring. But that's all right because their hometown, Willistown, Ohio accepts her mother and Kira just as they are. Then Kira goes to a sleepover. The girls play games, and someone decides to hypnotize Kira. Suddenly, she is a small girl, almost a baby, running with her mother. Thunder and lightning are booming all around them. Her mother is speaking Russian. Kira understands. Then she wakes up. Her friends start to ask about Kira's life before she came to Willistown. Kira can't give them the answers. When she asks her mother, her mother is angry, frightened, and desperate, and she disappears. She leaves an overturned chair, a key on the floor, and a note telling Kira to get out of the house. But before Kira can leave, a woman who calls herself Aunt Memory arrives. She tells Kira that her mother is in danger. Only the two of them can save her. What she can remember may keep her mother alive and yet the only hope for both of them to survive might be Kira's ability to *Escape from Memory*.

Learning Opportunities

1. Research the meanings of the following words: recall, identification, application, analysis, and synthesis. Discuss how each word applies to the thinking that takes place in the book.
2. Responsibility is a main idea in the novel. Discuss how the author views responsibility.
3. Discuss the statement in Chapter 18, "Life is best lived many times."
4. Identify and discuss how the past, present, and future successfully work together in an individual's life.
5. Discuss whether or not this novel is a story about a war between good and evil.

Related Works

1. Allende, Isabel, and Margaret Sayers Peden (trans.). **City of the Beasts.** (See full booktalk in "Adventure/Survival"/"Land," pages 87 to 90.) In this survival adventure, The People of the Mist entrust their tribal history to sloth-like creatures called the Beasts.
2. Fleischman, Paul. **Mind's Eye.** New York: Henry Holt and Company, 1999. 108p. $15.95. ISBN 0 8050 6314 5. [fiction] JS (See full booktalk in *Booktalks and More*, pages 173 to 175.) An eighty-eight-year old convalescent home resident teaches a teenager how both memorization and fantasy can help her cope in her now restricted life.
3. Haddix, Margaret Peterson. **Turnabout.** New York: Simon and Schuster, 2000. 223p. $17.00. ISBN 0 689 82187 5. [fiction] MJS After participating in a DNA experiment, Melly and Anny Beth live two lifetimes, and now must find someone to take care of them as they return to infancy.
4. Helbig, Alethea K., and Agnes Regan Perkins. **Dictionary of American Young Adult Fiction, 1997–2001: Books of Recognized Merit.** Westport, CT: Greenwood Press, 2004. 558p. $75.00. ISBN 0 313 32430 1. [reference] In this dictionary of recognized authors, works, and characters, the author entry provides biographical information and refers the reader to five other entries explaining Haddix's works.
5. Philbrick, Rodman. **The Last Book in the Universe.** New York: The Blue Sky Press, 2000. 224p. $16.95. ISBN 0 439 08758 9. [fiction] MJS (See full booktalk in *Booktalks and More*, 2003, pages 146 to 148.) In a world dependent on brain probes and gang protection, a young epileptic realizes that his memories and deeds may make up the last book.

6. Roberts, Katherine. **Spellfall.** England: The Chicken House, 2000. New York: Scholastic, 2001. 256p. $15.95. ISBN 0 439 29653 6. [fiction] MJ (See full booktalk in *Booktalks and More*, 2003, pages 157 to 159.) Natural, supernatural, and technical worlds combine in the war between good and evil.

ᏨᎦᏸ

Kirkpatrick, Katherine. **Voyage of the Continental.**
New York: Holiday House, 2002. 297p. $16.95.
ISBN 0 8234 1580 5. [fiction, mixed format] JS

Themes/Topics: romance, coming of age, ocean adventure, pioneer life, historical novel

Summary/Description

Beginning in March 1865, and concluding in June 1866, the historical mystery traces the journey of orphaned seventeen-year-old Emeline from her mill job in Lowell, Massachusetts, to her eventual marriage in Seattle, Washington, to Roger ("Rod") Conant, a young journalist and lawyer. Emeline decides to leave the mill drudgery and signs on with Asa Mercer, who is looking for 500 women to relocate in Seattle, Washington. Fifty-year-old Ruby Shaw, who is a stutterer like Emeline, befriends her, pays for her voyage, and confides that her husband is trying to kill her. The Captain and second mate stage Ruby's death and funeral to make the murderer think that he has been successful. Then Emeline begins to suspect someone is also targeting her. After several lucky escapes, a few romantic attractions, and the eventual sorting out of Ruby's death and property, Emeline finds both the would-be murderer and true love. The author includes a map tracing "The Voyage of the Continental," "Historical and Research Notes," that distinguish fact from fiction, and an extensive article, "As a Mercer and The Mercer Expeditions" that explains Mr. Mercer's place in pioneer history.

Booktalk

Seventeen-year-old Emeline McCullough comes from a hardworking family. Her parents left Scotland to build a new life. But Emeline's mother died of diphtheria, and both her brother and father were lost in the great Civil War of the United States. Now she works in the Merrimack Woolen Mill in Lowell, Massachusetts to support herself and lives in Boardinghouse number two. The company is her family now. Emeline would like to find a new one. When Asa Mercer offers her the chance to sail safely, with 499 other girls to Seattle, Washington, she decides to try her luck. In Seattle, men outnumber women nine to one. Since she attended high school, she is promised a teaching job even though she stutters. It all sounds too good to be true. Unfortunately, a great deal of it is. Being a Mercer Girl, or a MG, isn't exactly what Mr. Mercer promised because he forgot to pay for quite a bit of what he promised. And safety? There's a murderer aboard targeting Emeline's best friend—and Emeline!. If she is to survive, Emeline must learn quickly to deal with a new world filled with mystery, love, and treachery when she commits herself to *The Voyage of the Continental.*

Learning Opportunities

1. Using your library's resources, research the lives of working girls in the nineteenth century.
2. Describe Emeline's character. In your description, be sure to consider her stuttering.
3. How does Emeline come to her decision to marry Roger Conant? What makes her decision a good one?
4. Is Pom a necessary character? Discuss her role in the novel.
5. Discuss what the setting contributes to the novel.

Related Works

1. Bartoletti, Susan Campbell. **A Coal Miner's Bride: The Diary of Anetka Kaminska.** New York: Scholastic Inc., 2000. 219p. (Dear America.) $10.95. ISBN 0 439 05386 2. In 1896, Anetka is married to an American miner who agrees to pay her family's passage from Poland to America. In her marriage and after her husband's death, she works to build her home and family in this new country.
2. Bartoletti, Susan Campbell. **Kids on Strike.** Boston, MA: Houghton Mifflin, 1999. 208p. $20.00. ISBN 0 395 88892 1. [nonfiction] MJS Bartoletti explains the growing awareness of a much exploited labor force. In the first chapter, she explains how the factory girls dedicated themselves to self-improvement.
3. Jordan, Sherryl. **The Raging Quiet.** New York: Simon & Schuster, 1999. 266p. $17.00. ISBN 0 689 82140 9. [fiction] JS (See full book-talk in *Booktalks and More,* 2003, pages 15 to 17.) Sixteen-year-old Marnie agrees to marry Isake Isherwood, son of the lord of the manor, so her family can keep their home. She finds herself wed to an abusive man and chooses a love mate after he dies.
4. Karr, Kathleen. **The Boxer.** New York: Farrar, Straus and Giroux, 2000. 169p. $16.00. ISBN 0 374 30921 3. [fiction] MJ (See full book-talk in *Booktalks and More,* 2003, pages 128 to 130.) Fifteen-year-old

John Aloysius Xavier Woods works in a sweatshop in New York's Lower East Side during the late nineteenth century and turns to illegal boxing to support his family.

5. Rinaldi, Ann. **Mine Eyes Have Seen.** New York: Scholastic Press, 1998. 275p. $16.95. ISBN 0 590 54318 0. [fiction] MJS (See full booktalk in *Booktalks Plus*, 2001, pages 243 to 245.) Annie Brown, John Brown's fifteen-year-old daughter lives on her father's Maryland farm in the summer of 1859 and is the lookout as Brown gathers his sons and supporters to raid Harper's Ferry. Although he fights to free the slaves, he has a very low regard for his daughter's talents.

ꙮ

Rinaldi, Ann. **Girl in Blue.**

New York: Scholastic, Inc., 2001. 320p. $15.95. ISBN 0 439 07336 7. [fiction] MJ

Themes/Topics: Civil War, Pinkerton spies, nineteenth-century life, identity, independence, historical novel

Summary/Description

Inspired by a book about a girl who takes on a man's role on the sea, fifteen-year-old Sarah Louisa runs away from her abusive father and the crude man he wants her to marry, and joins the Union Army. Masquerading as Neddy Compton, she becomes a respected soldier and skilled nurse. When the army discovers her gender, Sarah Louisa is offered a job as a Pinkerton detective rather than face prosecution. Disguised as a personal maid, she spies on Rose Greenhow, a spy who has smuggled critical information to the rebels. Sarah breaks Greenhow's message system and avoids a romantic entanglement that could compromise her assignment. Overtaken by exhaustion and fever, Sarah is nursed back to health and told to take time off to recover her strength. Disguised as a man, she returns home to find her father dead, and her sister willing to marry the man Sarah rejected. Only her brother knows she visited, and Sarah returns to the independent life that she loves. An "Author's Note" explains the factual basis of the story.

Booktalk

If fifteen-year-old Sarah Louisa disobeys her father, she must kneel and watch him eat his supper while she is allowed none. When he decides that she should marry a man who will enjoy beating her and working her to death, Sarah knows she must run away. She can outwork any man, and with the help of her faithful gun "Fanny," she can outshoot most.

Since she knows what it is to live like a slave, she decides to help free some. She disguises herself as a man and joins the Union Army. As a *Girl in Blue*, Sarah Louisa, soldier, nurse, and spy, saves her own life and the lives of hundreds of boys in blue as well.

Learning Opportunities

1. Rinaldi provides a bibliography that yields more information about the role of women and girls in the Civil War. Continue to research the role of women in the war and share your findings with the group. You may wish to start with *Women Civil War Spies of the Union* (Related Work 8) and *Women Civil War Spies of the Confederacy* (Related Work 4).
2. Reconstruction saw an even greater expansion of women's rights. Find out as much as you can about that era. Share the information with the group. You might want to start your research by reading *Ida B. Wells: Mother of the Civil Rights Movement* (Related Work 3).
3. List the male characters. Describe the role that each plays.
4. List the female characters. Describe the role that each plays.
5. Discuss how gender stereotypes affect each character.
6. Discuss how Sarah changes and grows in her roles as both soldier and spy.

Related Works

1. Bartoletti, Susan. **No Man's Land: A Young Soldier's Story.** New York: The Blue Sky Press, 1999. $15.95. 169p. ISBN 0 0590 38371 X. [fiction] MJ (See full booktalk in *Booktalks Plus*, 2001, pages 37 to 39.) Fourteen-year-old Thrasher Magee enlists in the Southern Army and eventually discovers that the best soldier in his unit is really a woman.
2. Fradin, Dennis Brindell. **Bound for the North Star: True Stories of Fugitive Slaves.** ("Issues"/"Social Challenges," pages 30 to 33.) Fradin tells the stories of slaves struggling for freedom. Chapter 12 describes Harriet Tubman's activity as a Civil War spy.
3. Fradin, Dennis Brindell, and Judith Bloom Fradin. **Ida B. Wells: Mother of the Civil Rights Movement.** New York: Clarion, 2000. 178p. $18.00. ISBN 0 395 89898 6. [nonfiction] MJS (See full booktalk in *Booktalks and More*, 2003, pages 249 to 252.) Born a slave in 1862, Ida B. Wells fought for equal rights and helped found organizations to support livelihood, education, and political activism for women and African-Americans.
4. Phillips, Larissa. **Women Civil War Spies of the Confederacy.** New York: The Rosen Publishing Group, Inc., 2004. 112p.

(American Women at War.) $29.95. ISBN 0 8239 4451 4. [nonfiction] MJS This account of six female spies includes Rose O'Neal Greenhow, a based on fact character in *Girl in Blue*, and Mary Surratt, alluded to in *An Acquaintance with Darkness* (Related Work 6).

5. Rinaldi, Ann. **Amelia's War.** New York: Scholastic Press, 1999. 272p. $15.95. ISBN 0 590 11744 0. [fiction] MJ (See full booktalk in *Booktalks and More,* 2003, pages 47 to 49.) Living in a state split by the war, Amelia tries not to become involved, but must make a heroic decision to save her family and community.

6. Rinaldi, Ann. **An Acquaintance with Darkness.** New York: Harcourt Brace and Co., 1997. 294p. $16.00. ISBN 0 15 201294 X. [fiction] MJS Emily Bransby Pigbush finds herself overwhelmed by intrigue when the Surratts, her best friend's family, are the center of the investigation surrounding Lincoln's assassination.

7. Rinaldi, Ann. **Mine Eyes Have Seen.** New York: Scholastic Press, 1998. 275p. $16.95. ISBN 0 590 54318 0. [fiction] MJS (See full booktalk in *Booktalks and More,* 2003, pages 243 to 245.) Annie Brown, John Brown's fifteen-year-old daughter, is the unappreciated lookout for her father's famous raid. Her father charges her to tell the story. Her character integrates several historical accounts of John Brown and his mission.

8. Sakany, Lois. **Women Civil War Spies of the Union.** New York: The Rosen Publishing Group, Inc., 2004. 112p. (American Women at War.) $29.95. ISBN 0 8239 4450 6. [nonfiction] MJS The seven chapters recounting the exploits of Union spies include Sarah Emma Edmonds, the spy upon whose life Sarah Wheelock is based.

ॶॺ

Zindel, Paul. The Gadget.

New York: HarperCollins Publishers, 2001. 184p. $15.99.
ISBN 0 06 028255 X. [fiction] MJ

Themes/Topics: World War II, Cold War, family, atom bomb, spies, historical novel

Summary/Description

Stephen Orr spends his thirteenth year in Los Alamos where his father works with other scientists to build the atom bomb. Frustrated by his father's distance and secrecy, Stephen, in spite of their housekeeper's warnings, befriends an older Russian boy who shares his curiosity. Together, they question a scientist injured in a radioactive accident, look for the addresses rumored to be connected to the project, and ultimately witness an atom bomb test. When Stephen and his friend are discovered at the test, Stephen's father forbids Stephen to leave the house until the project is finished. Stephen runs to his friend's home, discovers the family to be Russian spies, and flees when they see and try to kill him. The Russian boy, not Stephen, dies in the pursuit. Zindel includes "A Chronology of Important Events of World War II and The Making of the Atomic Bomb" a list of "Some of the Important People of the Bomb," and a list of sources consulted in writing the story. Within the story, the father explains why he, as a scientist, agreed to work on the bomb, and why he believes that it must be used against the Japanese.

Booktalk

Ask if anyone knows a significant event that happened in 1945.

In 1945, President Harry S. Truman made the decision to drop an atom bomb on Japan. He hoped that such a horrible weapon would force the Japanese to surrender. He was right. This is the story of one boy whose father helped develop that bomb.

When Stephen Orr is twelve years old, he is on a rooftop in London. He sees his cousin killed in a German air raid. When he is thirteen, he is in the United States. He lives in a town named Los Alamos, a town that doesn't even appear on a map. His father is known by the code name Olaf. He works long hours, but he won't discuss his work. Stephen has just one person he can really talk to—fifteen-year-old Alexei. Alexei has the same questions as Stephen. And Alexei seems to know how to get some answers. Together they will find out why everyone gets mail from a post office box in another town and why 109 Palace Avenue has so many scientists in for tea. But most important, they will find out why a wounded scientist was wrapped in an aluminum body bag and why, as he died, he so frantically wanted to tell the story of *The Gadget*.

Learning Opportunities

1. A major theme of the story is trust. Discuss how the story carries out that theme in both personal and international relationships.
2. Discuss how the setting, both time and place, contributes to Zindel's purpose.
3. Stephen's father asserts that the war with Germany and the war with Japan are two separate issues. Using your library's resources, research when and how the United States entered the war with Germany and Japan. Then ask them to share the information with the group.
4. Read Hersey's *Hiroshima* (Related Work 2). Discuss how the book affects your attitude toward the atom bomb.

5. Using your library's resources, research the power of explosives being used by the United States today. Compare their power to the power of the bomb dropped on Hiroshima and Nagasaki.

6. Using your library's resources, research how Russia became allies with England and the United States and what the post-war relationship was between Russia and the United States. Then discuss how that information adds to your appreciation of the story.

Related Works

1. Granfield, Linda. **I Remember Korea: Veterans Tell Their Stories of the Korean War, 1950–53.** New York: Clarion Books, 2003. 136p. $16.00. ISBN 0 618 17740 X. [nonfiction] MJS This collection of stories from thirty-two men and women who served in the U.S. and Canadian forces in Korea, tells the personal conflicts and tragedies in the historical and geographical backdrop. "Special Missions," pages 58 to 62 mentions the confusion that many of the Japanese had about the bombs the Americans dropped to end World War II.

2. Hersey, John. **Hiroshima.** New York: Vintage Books, 1985. 152p. $6.50pa. ISBN 0 679 72103 7. [nonfiction] JS/A Written in 1946, this journalistic account of the atom bomb compiles memories of the survivors. In the final chapter, written four decades after the original, Hersey tries to revisit the people he originally interviewed.

3. Janeczko, Paul B. **Top Secret: A Handbook of Codes, Ciphers, and Secret Writing.** Cambridge, MA: Candlewick Press, 2004. 144p. $16.99. ISBN 0 7636 0971 4. [nonfiction] MJ This how to guide and history of spy communication leads the user through codes, ciphers, and secret language. A short exercise follows each system presented.

4. Lisle, Janet Taylor. **The Art of Keeping Cool.** New York: A Richard Jackson Book/Atheneum Books for Young Readers, 2000. 207p. $17.00. ISBN 0 689 83787 9. [fiction] MJS Living with their grandparents in Sachem's Head during 1942, thirteen-year-old cousins, Robert and Elliot discover that neighbors and families can contain threats as dangerous as any foreign power. The town attacks Elliot's friend, a German artist they think is a spy. Robert learns that his father will never return to the house because Robert's grandfather once shot him.

5. Morris, Neil, et al. (text), and Paola Ravaglia et al. (illus.). **The Illustrated History of the World: From the Big Bang to the Third Millennium.** New York: Enchanted Lion Books, 2000. 288p. $29.95. ISBN 1 59270 019 5. [nonfiction] MJS In this chronologically and geographically organized history, short descriptions and extensive illustrations clearly show the relationships of events happening

sequentially and simultaneously. Pages 230 and 231 explain "The War in Europe." Pages 232 and 233 explain "The War in the Pacific." Pages 244 and 245 explain "The Cold War."

Paranormal

ॐ

Funke, Cornelia. **The Thief Lord.**
New York: The Chicken House, 2001. 352p. ISBN 0 439 40437 1. [fiction] MJ

Themes/Topics: family, orphans, disguise, crime

Summary/Description

A detective, hired by a disagreeable couple to find their two runaway orphaned nephews, discovers them with a group of child thieves living in an abandoned theater. Their leader, *The Thief Lord,* is the son of wealthy but indifferent and demanding parents. Building his reputation on items he steals from his own home, the Thief Lord takes a job from a mysterious old man to steal a wooden wing. In the group's bungled theft, the owner, a lady photographer, explains that the wing will restore supernatural power to a carousel that controls youth and old age. As the thieves try to deliver the wing, avoid capture, and protect each other, the detective and photographer become attracted to each other and attached to the children. Discovering the carousel's secret, the Thief Lord increases his age and becomes an assistant detective. The dishonest fence for stolen goods decreases his age and becomes an unmanageable child adopted by the disagreeable couple. Two of the thieves remain thieves, and three, including the two nephews, find a home with the photographer who is an orphan.

Booktalk

Victor Getz, a private detective, finds things other people lose. But he has never been asked to find two lost boys before. Where will he look in Venice's winding streets and dark alleys? Small people and objects have many places to hide. He decides to choose one of his many disguises and let them run into him. But when they do, he finds himself tied, tricked, and troubled—not by just two children, but by six. Is this a job he really needs? Then he begins to fall in love with a very brave lady who has a few disguises of her own and knows about a magical carousel that can change everyone's life forever. Will the "just the facts" man Victor Getz stick to his facts or enter a world of what if that may join him forever with *The Thief Lord*?

Learning Opportunities

1. Draw a picture of the Thief Lord.
2. Much of the story centers on mask, disguise, and acting. Even the children's home is a theater. Point out as many instances as possible of the use of masks and disguise. Discuss how each aids the author's purpose.
3. If you had the opportunity to ride the carousel and change your age, would you do so? Explain your reasons.
4. Describe what you perceive to be the perfect age. Then describe your life at that age.
5. Both *The Thief Lord* and *Turnabout* (Related Work 3) discuss the ability to choose one's age. Discuss the problems that each book associates with the choice.
6. Scipio chooses to change his age. Prosper does not. Are their choices consistent with their characters?
7. Does *The Thief Lord* have a happy ending?
8. Discuss the sequel that you might construct for *The Thief Lord*.
9. *The Thief Lord* presents the theme of young people's rights. Using your library's resources, research children's rights in the United States today. List the rights that you feel the author would support. Then identify the character and situation that led you to that conclusion.

Related Works

1. Dickens, Charles, and Don Freeman (illus.). **Oliver Twist.** New York: William Morrow and Company, 1994. 442p. $20.00. ISBN 0 688 12911 0. [fiction] MJS/A This story of a young orphan describes homeless children living together and stealing to survive. Published in the middle of the nineteenth century, it was a commentary on the social problems of the day.
2. Funke, Cornelia. **Inkheart.** New York: The Chicken House, 2003. 544p. $19.95. ISBN 0 439 53164 0. [fiction] MJ Twelve-year-old Meggie lives in both real and fictional worlds as she tries to help save her father from evil characters in a novel that he has "read" into existence.
3. Haddix, Margaret Peterson. **Turnabout.** New York: Simon and Schuster, 2000. 223p. $17.00. ISBN 0 689 82187 5. [fiction] MJS Participating in an age reversal experiment, two women find themselves growing young with no one to care for them.
4. McCaughrean, Geraldine. **The Pirate's Son.** New York: Scholastic, 1998, American ed. 294p. $16.95. ISBN 0 590 20344 4. [fiction] MJ

(See full booktalk in *Booktallks Plus*, 2001, pages 74 to 77.) Three eighteenth-century, fatherless, English children join forces to survive as they deal with death of loved ones, prejudices, culture clash, storms, sickness, and pirate attacks.

5.   Quarles, Heather. **A Door Near Here.** New York: Delacorte Press, 1998. 231p. $13.95. ISBN 0 385 32595 9. [fiction] MJ In this realistic story, fifteen-year-old Katherine copes with her mother's alcoholism, her father's emotional distance, her little sister's reliance on the imaginary world of Narnia, and her own web of lies and fantasies.

 barf

Bunting, Eve. The Presence: A Ghost Story.
New York: Clarion Books, 2003. 195p. $15.00. ISBN 0 618 26919 3. [nonfiction] JS

Themes/Topics: ghosts, afterlife, serial killer, friendship

Summary/Description

Noah Vanderhost died 120 years ago at the age of seventeen. He calls himself a Presence rather than a ghost and haunts the church where he commits murders. He is waiting for seventeen-year-old Catherine, who is visiting her grandmother after experiencing a traumatic automobile accident that killed a good friend. Catherine feels responsible for the accident because both girls were drinking. Noah makes himself visible and promises Catherine that he will help her talk to her dead friend. Old Miss Lottie Lovelace warns Catherine to stay away from the church. As Catherine works through Noah's promises and the secret diary Lottie gives her, she realizes that she resembles other girls connected with the church, who have mysteriously disappeared while recovering from a trauma. She goes to the church to save the most recent victim, but Noah finds her. Since Noah is now in human form, he dies in the fire, which Catherine accidentally sets. Four bodies are found in the church basement. Lottie still fears that Noah lives. Catherine is building a romantic relationship, which her grandmother has encouraged, with the minister's son.

Booktalk

Ghosts and serial killers, both are pretty scary. The combination is almost too much to believe. Seventeen-year-old Catherine never imagined that she would meet either one. But Noah Vanderhost is a ghost who has been killing Catherine look-alikes for over 100 years. Each girl feels guilty about a death. Each girl looks to Noah for comfort. All the girls, except one, disappear. Now that one girl may come back to haunt Noah. Will her return cause or prevent more deaths? Catherine finds out when she herself engages in a life and death struggle with *The Presence.*

Learning Opportunities

1. Discuss whether or not Noah is finally dead.
2. What details does Bunting use outside Catherine's experiences to give credibility to the ghost? How do these details affect the story?
3. Describe Noah's character. Be sure to consider the idea of hope as presented on page 152.
4. How do the church and Christmas settings affect the story?
5. Using your library's resources, research other ghost stories or stories of the supernatural. Try retelling some of the stories that you find to the group. You may wish to start your search by reading some of the stories in either *Irish Fairy Tales* (Related Work 4) or *Ozark Ghost Stories* (Related Work 6).

Related Works

1. Beagle, Peter S. **Tamsin.** New York: ROC, 1999. 275p. $21.95. ISBN 0 451 45763 3. [fiction] JS/A Nineteen-year-old Jennifer Gluckstein moves into a haunted estate and decides to help Tamsin, a ghost from the time of the Bloody Assizes, reunite with her lover.
2. Cabot, Meg. **Haunted: A Tale of the Mediator.** New York: HarperCollins, 2003. 246p. $15.99. ISBN 0 06 029471 X. [fiction] JS Susannah Simon, a mediator, falls in love with Jesse, the ghost who lives in her room, but is tempted to increase her powers and expand her love life through Paul Slater, another mediator, who decided to stalk her.
3. Cabot, Meg. **Twilight: The Mediator.** New York: HarperCollins Children's Books, 2005. 256p. $16.89. ISBN 0 06 072467 6. [fiction] JS In this episode, book six, Susannah and Paul bring Jesse to life and the twentieth century through time travel.
4. Curtin, Jeremiah. **Irish Fairy Tales.** New York: Dorset Press, 1992. 198p. $5.95. ISBN 0 880 29814 6. [nonfiction] JS/A This collection communicates that there is almost no barrier between living and dead. The challenge to the user will be fleshing out the story to make it interesting and gripping for a teen audience.
5. Rice, Bebe Faas. **The Place at the Edge of the Earth.** New York: Clarion Books, 2002. 186p. $15.00. ISBN 0 618 15978 9. [fiction] MJ Jenny Muldoon, unhappy about moving to historic Fort Sayers after her mother's marriage, discovers a ghost, Jonah Flying Cloud, who needs help in moving to the afterlife.

6. Young, Richard, and Judy Dockrey Young (comp. and ed.). **Ozark Ghost Stories.** Little Rock, AR: August House Publisher, Inc., 1995. 187p. (American Storytelling.) $10.95. ISBN 0 87483 410 4. [nonfiction] JS/A Divided into seven categories, these stories could be memorized and recited. "Mary Calhoun" on pages 62 to 66 is almost identical to "The Blood Drawing Ghost" on pages 180 to 191 of *Irish Fairy Tales* (Related Work 4).

ℭℨℭℨ

McAllister, Margaret. **The Octave of Angels.**

Grand Rapids, MI: Eerdmans Books for Young Readers, 2001. 119p. $16.00.
ISBN 0 8028 5245 9. [fiction] MJ

Themes/Topics: extended family, friendship, responsibility,
English history

Summary/Description

Calum Lowry and his family move into his great aunt's house in Beckerton, England. His mother and father work at White Fox Farm owned by Drew and Peggy Fisher. Calum befriends their son, Mark Fisher, and Bernice Carter, an unusual girl who loves animals. The story centers on the Octave of Angels, a moneymaking festival that recalls the community's failure to help an ill child. As Calum learns the town's secrets, he focuses on a theft involving an abandoned baby girl named Myrrh and Aunt Dorcas's grandfather, an abusive husband and notorious poacher. Calum moves through the preparations, festival, and a harrowing rescue of Bernice, who falls into the quarry while trying to rescue her dog. His experiences lead him to conclude that Myrrh was taking a special gift to the new son of the town's most prominent family and that Calum's disreputable ancestor chased her into the quarry where she died. Calum's conclusions imbue the town with an openness that represents the true Octave of Angels spirit.

Booktalk

Ask if anyone in the group looks forward to a particular celebration in their town or family. Ask them to briefly explain why. Then ask if anyone experienced a holiday that has a dark or difficult side. Again, ask them to briefly explain why they feel that way.

Calum is moving to a new house in a new town. Actually, the town and house are new to Calum, but really quite old. Since his father lost his job, they decided to accept his great aunt's invitation to move in.

Her home is in Beckerton, England, a town with strong traditions and prejudices, some directed against an ancestor of Calum's—a notorious poacher, others against a gypsy girl who died one night in the quarry. What do those people have to do with Calum? Why should he care? When *The Octave of Angels,* an old Beckerton tradition begins, Calum, with the rest of the town, joins in its ghostly blend of sin and celebration. As rumors build, Calum finds himself tangled in that ancient mystery. It once again might take a life, and this time the life might be his.

Learning Opportunities

1. Calum and his family move from a city to a small village. List the differences in the two settings and how those differences might affect the people's attitudes.
2. The novel blends three different time periods: the original Octave of Angels, the short life of Myrrh, and the present day. Discuss how each time period contributes to the novel.
3. From the ending of Chapter 2, Calum tries to describe Beckerton in a postcard. Try to do the same thing with the town or city in which you live. Ask others to do the same and compare your postcards. Then discuss what you learned about your perception of your town or city in comparison with the perceptions of others in the group.
4. Generosity is a major theme in the story. Discuss the many instances of generosity or lack of generosity in the story and the results. Don't confine yourself to generosity involving money or gifts.
5. Visions on the moors propel this story. Describe the visions included in the story and how real you think they are.

Related Works

1. Almond, David. **Kit's Wilderness.** New York: Delacorte Press, 2000. 229p. $15.95. ISBN 0 385 32665 3. [fiction] MJS (See full booktalk in *Booktalks and More,* 2003, pages 209 to 211.) Thirteen-year-old Kit Watson and his parents move to Stoneygate, a coal-mining town filled with legends and family histories. Here, like Calum, he finds his own identity as he makes friends and explores the town's mystical history.
2. Beagle, Peter S. **Tamsin.** New York: ROC, 1999. 275p. $21.95. ISBN 0 451 45763 3. [fiction] JS (See full booktalk in *Booktalks and More,* 2003, pages 61 to 63.) This ghostly/coming of age novel focuses on nineteen-year-old Jennifer Gluckstein, who moves to a haunted estate managed by her stepfather. Here she encounters Tamsin Willoughby, a ghost from three hundred years ago, whom she must save from Lord Chief Justice Jeffreys. But first she must

confront her own hostile feelings toward her mother, father, step-family, and peers.

3. Fraustino, Lisa Rowe (ed.). **Soul Searching: Thirteen Stories about Faith and Belief.** New York: Simon & Schuster Books for Young Readers, 2002. 267p. $17.95. ISBN 0 689 83484 5. [fiction] MJS Each story centers on a clarifying spiritual experience that may or may not have a supernatural base.

4. Jacques, Brian. **Castaways of the Flying Dutchman.** New York: Philomel Books, 2001. 327p. $22.95. ISBN 0 399 23601 5. [fiction] MJ When, in 1620, the evil Captain Vanderdecken of the Flying Dutchman brings the curse of the Lord on his ship, an angel charges a mute cabin boy and his dog to "roam this world, /and wherever need is great, /bring confidence and sympathy, /help others to change their fate." Their first task is in Chapelvale, England, 1896, where they dispel superstition and help the main target of the town bullies save the town from unscrupulous businessmen.

5. Rinaldi, Ann. **The Staircase.** New York: Harcourt, Inc., 2000. 230p. $16.00. ISBN 15 202430 1. [fiction] MJ Thirteen-year-old Lizzy Enders is left at a convent school after her mother's death, and through her support of a mysterious itinerant carpenter who builds a seemingly miraculous circular stairway for the convent, reconciles with her father and learns to risk a leap of faith.

ርጓ፝

McDonald, Joyce. Shades of Simon Gray.

New York: Delacorte Press, 2001. 245p. $15.95. ISBN 0 385 32659 9. [fiction] MJS

Themes/Topics: time travel, cheating, suicide, rebirth, friendship

Summary/Description

When sixteen-year-old Simon Gray of Bellehaven, New Jersey, slips into a coma after an automobile crash, he is joined in time with Jessup Wildemere, a young man hanged without trial for the stabbing death of a local resident. The victim's daughter was to run away with Jessup but framed him after stabbing her father. Simon sees Jessup's foolish acceptance of death and decides to fight for life. The town thinks that the car crash is an accident. Simon intentionally crashed because he fears a computer hacking project he facilitates will be discovered. Devin, a senior girl benefiting from stolen test answers, discovers she cares for Simon and leaves the group that manipulated her and Simon into cheating. His younger sister Courtney realizes her perfect brother is vulnerable. Simon's best friend Liz experiences an inspiration for a class report on Jessup and has dreams that parallel Simon's condition. When Simon becomes conscious, he finds that the computer science teacher compromised the school system by allowing football players to download pornography. Many students could have accessed critical information but Simon realizes that living with his secret will be difficult. He rights part of Jessup's unjust conviction by placing a plaque on the Hanging Tree.

Booktalk

On April Fools Day in Bellehaven, New Jersey, the temperature is an unseasonable eighty-five degrees. So many frogs explode out of nature that their squashed bodies cover the roads, and thousands of crows appear to eat them. On this eerie night, sixteen-year-old Simon Gray smashes his Honda Civic into the Liberty Tree, leaving him in a coma. The roads are slippery; the frogs distracting. It was an accident, right? Perfect Simon has the brightest future in town. But the crash joins Simon's life with a notorious criminal and town legend—Jessup Wildemere, hanged in 1798. Why does Simon find himself in this limbo with a murderer? Do they have anything in common? And most important—Will they be trapped forever in the *Shades of Simon Gray*?

Learning Opportunities

1. Choose one person in your area of historical significance. Using the resources of your library and historical society, research the person's life. Share the information with the group in either an oral report or a display.
2. Devin, Liz, and Courtney are three very different girls. Each has a close relationship with Simon. Describe how each girl perceives Simon and how each perception is important.
3. The Shakespearean play, *Macbeth* (Related Work 5) is a significant reference in the novel. After reading *Macbeth* or viewing a production of the play, identify as many parallels as you can to *Shades of Simon Gray*.
4. Several times Bellahaven is described as a town that doesn't change. Why is such a place appropriate for the novel?
5. In both *Swallowing Stones* (Related Work 3) and *Shades of Simon Gray*, McDonald uses secret guilt as a central theme and a tree as a vehicle to communicate that theme. The endings of the novels, however, show a sharp contrast. After reading both, discuss the difference and how each ending affects each story.

Related Works

1. Beagle, Peter S. **Tamsin.** New York: ROC, 1999. 275p. $21.95. ISBN 0 451 45763 3. [fiction] JS (See full booktalk in *Booktalks and More*, 2003, pages 61 to 63.) As nineteen-year-old Jennifer Gluckstein helps Tamsin Willoughby, a three-hundred-year-old ghost, escape the evil Lord Chief Justice Jeffreys, the judge of the Assizes, she rids herself of her own mistakes and insecurities.

2. Dunton Downer and Alan Riding. **Essential Shakespeare Handbook.** New York: DK Publishing, 2004. 480p. $25.00. ISBN 0 7894 9333 0. [reference] JS This handbook includes overviews of the categories and plays, short character descriptions, various reading approaches, highlights of the play's performance history, and a discussion of its significance. The *Macbeth* material appears between pages 358 to 367.

3. McDonald, Joyce. **Swallowing Stones.** New York: Laurel Leaf Books, 1997. 245p. $4.50. ISBN 0 440 22672 4. [fiction] JS (See full booktalk in *Booktalks and More*, 2003, pages 97 to 99.) As seventeen-year-old Michael MacKenzie deals with his guilt in an accidental shooting, he and the victim's daughter are drawn to The Ghost Tree, a Native American sacred place where one talks with ancestors.

4. Rice, Bebe Faas. **The Place at the Edge of the Earth.** New York: Clarion Books, 2002. 186p. $15.00. ISBN 0 618 15978 9. [fiction] MJ Eighth grader, Jenny Muldoon, helps Jonah Flying Cloud, the one-hundred-twenty-three-year-old ghost she finds in her room, join the spirit world. In this way, she helps make up for the injustice he suffered in the Indian school.

5. Shakespeare, William, and John Crowther (ed.). **Macbeth.** New York: Spark Notes, 2003. 219p. (No Fear Shakespeare.) $4.95pa. ISBN 1 58663 846 7. [drama] S/A This edition of *Macbeth*, first written and performed in the early seventeenth century, includes the complete text, a line by line translation, a character list, and a commentary.

ແ໑

Nixon, Joan Lowery. **Nightmare.**

New York: Delacorte Press, 2003. 166p. $15.95. ISBN 0 385 90151 8. [fiction] MJS

Themes: self-esteem, perceptions

Summary/Description

For eight years, seventeen-year-old Emily Wood has experienced a repeating dream that includes a dead body and someone trying to pursue her. She deals with the subsequent anxiety by underachieving so that people won't notice her. Her parents, who have two other high achieving daughters, send her to Camp Excel. Haley Griffin, her camp roommate, draws Emily into reading and interpreting runes. When the runes consistently predict danger, Haley persuades Emily to go to a folk healer, who tells her that she must heal herself and gives her a small potion filled bottle for protection. A camp staff member, recognizing Emily as the girl who witnessed the murder of the Institute's cofounder, realizes that the surroundings may bring back her full memory. When she tries to murder Emily too, Emily saves herself by throwing the healer's oil into her face.

Booktalk

Read the opening paragraph of Chapter 1.

Seventeen-year-old Emily Wood has lived this dream again and again for eight years. She won't talk about it, not even to her parents. She just wants to hide from it and the world. Emily's parents see hiding as a problem. They want her to stand out and enroll her in Camp Excel, where they believe she can tap into her full potential. But the camp taps into her worst fears, not her potential. The nightmare comes to life, but this time Emily will be the dead body—not the one dreaming about it. A murderer is on the loose. Emily is the targeted victim. For reasons even she doesn't understand, Emily, not her parents, is right. For Emily, standing out could be a *Nightmare,* a fatal one.

Learning Opportunities

1. Joan Lowery Nixon gives the reader many clues. List the clues. Then explain how many of them throw the reader off.
2. Are Emily's parents wrong to send her to Camp Excel?
3. Hair and clothes are discussed throughout the novel. How do they relate to the overall story?
4. Discuss the role that the supernatural, if any, plays in the story.
5. Using your library's resources, find self-help books on setting goals. Read at least three. List the common advice they give for achievement. Then discuss how that advice applies to Emily and her friends. You might want to use the books listed in related works.

Related Works

1. Cameron, Ann. **Colibrí.** (See full booktalk in "Multiple Cultures"/ "World Cultures," pages 269 to 271.) Kidnapped and victimized, Colibrí, with the help of a magically empowered Day-Keeper, asserts herself, recalls her past, and frees herself from her abuser.

2. Heneghan, James. **The Grave.** New York: Farrar, Straus and Giroux/Frances Foster Books, 2000. 245p. $17.00. ISBN 0 374 32765 3. [fiction] JS (See full booktalk in *Booktalks and More,* 2003, pages 65 to 67.) In this time travel mystery, Tom Mullen, abandoned in a toy department as a baby, is reunited with his true father.

3. McGraw, Jay. **Life Strategies for Teens.** (See full booktalk in "Contemporary Life"/"Coming of Age," pages 52 to 54.) This teen-age version of *Life Strategies* by Dr. Phillip C. McGraw presents "The Ten Laws of Life" with teen examples. Related Works in this entry include additional life directing sources for teenagers.

4. Nixon Joan Lowery. **Who Are You?** New York: Delacorte Press, 1999. 184p. $15.95. ISBN 0 385 32566 5. [fiction] MJS Horrified to find that a shooting victim has kept a record of her life, sixteen-year-old Kristin Evans discovers his identity, confirms her own, and uncovers an art forgery ring.

5. Ryan, Pam Muñoz. **Becoming Naomi León.** New York: Scholastic Press, 2004. 256p. $16.95. ISBN 0 439 26969 5. [fiction] MJ Naomi Soledad León, once abused by her mother and now living with her great-grandmother, becomes more assertive to protect herself from her newly returned selfish mother and her boyfriend who wish to gain custody of Naomi for welfare benefits.

ɔ͡ʃɔ

Plum-Ucci, Carol. **The She.**

New York: Harcourt, Inc., 2003. 280p. $17.00. ISBN 0 15 216819 2. [fiction] JS

Themes/Topics: brothers, relationships, sea stories

Summary/Description

Eight years ago, Evan and his brother Emmett learned their parents were lost at sea. Now, at seventeen, Evan decides to revisit the scene and discover what really happened. One theory is that a jealous sea monster, *The She,* sucked the parents down. The other theory is that the parents agreed to run drugs, were being pursued by the authorities, and decided to fake their deaths. Evan, who thinks he hears *The She* before she strikes, believes the mystical theory. He is joined in his belief by a girlfriend/classmate, Grey Shailey, who is in a mental hospital after having had a similar sea experience and is dealing with being sexually exploited by her underworld-connected lawyer father. Emmett, who is now twenty-five and dedicated to the academic world, believes the criminal theory.

Edwin Church, a Vietnam POW, a highly educated mystic, and a family friend, acts as an arbitrator between the brothers as the "evidence" for both theories evolves. In the climax, the two brothers and the girlfriend experience the sea phenomenon that caused the parents' accident. The experience redirects their lives. Evan gains confidence in his own instincts and abilities. Emmett becomes less cerebral. Grey testifies against her father and enters the witness protection program.

The language used may be considered controversial and requires a mature audience.

Booktalk

Seventeen-year-old Evan lost his parents in an accident at sea eight years ago. The day they died he heard the terrible shriek of a sea monster. Legends have it that the monster swallows sailors who don't follow her rules. Evan returns to West Hook, their seaside home, to learn the truth, but he has to deal with another rumor. This one comes from his twenty-five-year-old brother Emmett. Emmett's memories of the accident center on the Drug Enforcement Administration officials, who questioned him. How and why did their parents die? Did they die at all? And if that isn't upsetting enough, Grey Shailey, one of his meanest and most beautiful classmates, asks him to visit her in a mental hospital. She heard the shrieks too, during another sea accident she caused. As Evan tries to sort it all out, he begins to question his own sanity. Would it be best to hide from both the truth and *The She* that holds them all?

Learning Opportunities

1. Discuss what the affluent setting adds to the story.
2. Using your library resources, find other sea legends. Share them with the group. You might wish to start by reading *The Fish Prince and Other Stories: Mermen Folk Tales* (Related Work 5).
3. Edwin Church has a central role in the story. Why?
4. Discuss how the brothers' relationship changes as the story develops. Describe them ten years from now.
5. Grey Shailey adds another dimension to the story. Discuss the function of her character in the story.
6. Discuss what this story suggests to you about different types of intelligence.

Related Works

1. Jaques, Brian. **Castaways of the Flying Dutchman.** New York: Philomel Books, 2001. 327p. $22.95. ISBN 0 399 23601 5. [fiction]

MJS In 1620, Captain Vanderdecken of the legendary Flying Dutchman brings the curse of the Lord on his ship. According to legend, the captain and his ghost crew are doomed to sail eternally, but an angel charges the young mute Neb and his dog Den—the innocents on the ship—to roam the world and help others.

2. Many, Paul. **Walk Away Home.** New York: Walker & Co., 2002. 240p. $16.95. ISBN 0 8027 8828 9. [fiction] JS Nick Doran decides to move in with his eccentric middle-aged aunt, who lives in a hippie colony, and finds he is falling in love with and taking responsibility for a girl from an affluent family whose father is molesting her.

3. Myers, Walter Dean. **The Dream Bearer.** New York: HarperCollins, 2003. 181p. $16.89. ISBN 0 06 029522 8. [fiction] MJS Twelve-year-old David Curry, who lives in Harlem, meets Moses Littlejohn, a homeless man who claims to be over 300 years old. David suspects that Moses is living in an unreal world, but sees some truth in the dreams the homeless man bears.

4. Nolan, Han. **When We Were Saints.** New York: Harcourt Inc., 2003. 291. $17.00. ISBN 0 15 216371 9. [fiction] JS When fourteen-year-old Archibald Lee Caswell's grandfather tells him that he is a saint and sixteen-year-old Clare Simpson, the daughter of a local fortuneteller encourages him to pursue that sainthood, Archibald must decipher the real from the supernatural.

5. Yolen, Jane, Shulamith Oppenheim, and Paul Hoffman (illus.). **The Fish Prince and Other Stories: Mermen Folk Tales.** New York: Interlink, 2001. 160p. $29.95. ISBN 1 56656 389 5. [nonfiction] JS In the introduction, the authors define a mermen, provide its history, and then explain the female focus of sea myths. The mermen stories and anecdotes include the Northern Waters, Russia and Slavic Countries, British Isles, Southern Europe, Asia, Middle East, Africa, Pacific Islands, and the New World.

The Ruse Series

☙❧

Waid, Mark. **Enter the Detective.**
Oldsmar, FL: CrossGeneration Comics, 2003. 132p. (Ruse). $9.95.
ISBN 1 59314 012 6. [graphic] JS/A

Themes/Topics: Victorian period, city crime, good versus evil, solving mysteries by deduction, period setting

Summary/Description

In chapters 1 through 6 from the ongoing series *Ruse*, Simon Archard, master detective and favorite son, and Emma Bishop, his assistant, who possesses paranormal or supernatural powers, cannot stop a city-wide crime spree. The Baroness Miranda Cross and her huge manservant, Antaeus, seem to be behind the crimes. The Baroness absorbs the power of others through touch, and has paranormal powers equal to Emma's. Policemen and social pillars come under her control through her distribution of mind drugs, and she kills one of Simon's operatives, Otto Pressmonk. Simon's murder investigation points to Miranda, but she frames him for the murder of the distinguished Lady Wainscott. Simon and Emma go to Miranda's house where hypnotized men try to kill Simon, and Miranda attempts to destroy Emma. Their confrontation causes Miranda's anger to escalate a fire that destroys the men's electromagnetic hypnosis. Simon mysteriously enters the fire to retrieve clippings. Miranda disappears. Simon is gone for eight days and Miranda's control over city leaders is broken, when Emma, accompanied by Peter Grimes, another Simon operative, decides to solve the murders of several prostitutes. Emma ultimately discovers that David Kingsley, the detective heading the investigation, is the murderer, and that Simon and operatives have been watching over her. Reunited, Emma and Simon attend a magic show where the magician, really the infamous Lightbourne and Simon's former partner, murders a detective. Simon prevents the murder of the detective's partner, and when Simon decides to reconstruct the crime scene, Emma prevents Lightbourne, now impersonating the stage manager, from killing Simon and suspects that the clippings Simon retrieved from Miranda's home related to Lightbourne.

Booktalk

Smuggling of a mysterious narcotic, theft, and homicide control the once quiet city of Partington. Coincidentally, the crime wave arrives with the intoxicatingly beautiful Miranda Cross, the Baroness of Kharibast and her gigantic manservant, Antaeus. This is the nineteenth century, and there are no computer networks for crime fighting, or advanced labs for analysis—just the raw brain power of master detectives and, in some cases, a little magical power—sometimes called luck—to go with it. The frantic and confused Partington citizens turn to their own master detective and favorite son, the much-celebrated Simon Archard. He is the brainpower. Where is his luck? It's the beautiful Emma Bishop, his assistant. The stage is set. The plot begins with complication and turmoil. What next? *Enter the Detective.*

ℭℨℰℨ

Waid, Mark. **The Silent Partner.**

Oldsmar, FL: CrossGeneration Comics, 2002–2003. 132p. $15.95.
ISBN 1 931484 48 1. [graphic] JS

Themes/Topics: Victorian period, crime, deduction, good versus evil

Summary/Description

Pursuing Lightbourne, Simon and Emma travel to the supposedly haunted town of Telestroud. The invisible citizens suffer from a "severe photosynthetic dermal condition" that causes them to come out only at night. The men hope to protect future generations by breeding with captive gypsy women. Simon frees the ladies. The grateful gypsies give them safe passage and reveal that Lightbourne, who has gypsy heritage, visited them and shared two obsessions: his hatred for Simon and his desire to possess the "Enigmatic Prism."

When Simon and Emma return to Partington, one of Simon's agents reports the sudden death of Lionel Oxford Collins, who owns the most land in Partington. The will is gone. Simon concludes that a bugle poisoned by the Collins daughters killed Collins at the beginning of a foxhunt, and that Lightbourne masterminded the crime. When Simon and Emma find Lightbourne, they walk into a trap. He will flood the city unless Simon humbles himself and returns the "Enigmatic Prism." A flashback tells about their partnership and the prism, a "jewel of nefarious power." To get information, Malcolm beats anyone he suspects has knowledge of the stone. When he begins beating Emma, Simon frees himself, and Emma snatches the prism ironically concealed in Lightbourne's cane head. Lightbourne escapes through the water, but when he reaches a waiting boat, the ruthless Baroness Miranda Cross pushes him under.

This edition also includes drawings of the Archard residence, "Archard's Agents," "Gargoyles," and "Miranda's Henchmen."

Booktalk

Continuing to follow the trail of his diabolical mentor and former partner, Malcolm Lightbourne, Simon takes Emma to Telestroud, a ghost town. The detectives *don't* find Lightbourne, but *do* find more questions. Is Telestroud really a ghost town or something more sinister? Is Lightbourne running away from them or bringing them to him? What does Lightbourne want from Simon? If he gets it, can the world ever be safe again? Simon knows the man. But does he know him well enough to defeat him? Perhaps not. Maybe this time the mastermind detective will need the help of a very *Silent Partner.*

Learning Opportunities

1. Using your library's resources, find the meaning of "ruse." Be sure to distinguish it from its many synonyms. Then decide if you would have chosen it as a title for the series.
2. The series employs two teams of good and evil. List each character on each team. Then discuss each team's power and weakness.
3. Describe the next sequel you would like to see in the ongoing series.
4. Discuss what the setting contributes to the story? In the discussion, consider how a change of setting would alter the characters and possibly the plots.
5. The plots are complicated and often difficult to follow. Construct a plot diagram that shows the relationship of subplots to the main plot.
6. Choose five of your favorite frames in the series. Share and explain your choices.
7. Deductive reasoning is a major tool in solving the crimes. Using your library's resources, define deduction and find other examples of its use. You may wish to read selections featuring Agatha Christie's Hercule Poirot (Related Work 1) or Sir Arthur Conan Doyle's Sherlock Holmes (Related Work 2).

Related Works

1. Christie, Agatha. **The Under Dog and Other Stories: A Hercule Poirot Collection.** New York: Berkley Books, 1984. 201p. $5.99pa. ISBN 0 425 06808 0. [fiction] JS/A Like Simon, Hercule Poirot exhibits incredible deductive powers.
2. Doyle, Sir Arthur Conan Doyle, and Peter Haining (col.). **The Final Adventures of Sherlock Holmes.** New York: Barnes & Noble, 1995. 208p. $29.99. ISBN 1 56619 X. [fiction] JS/A In this collection of short stories, essays, poems, and plays, Haining presents work never known to exist. In "The Field Bazaar," pages 80 to 82, and "A Gaudy Death," pages 188 to 193, Doyle illustrates and explains the source of Holmes's famous process.
3. Hayakawa, S.I., and Eugene Ehrlich (rev. ed.). **Choose the Right Word: A Contemporary Guide to Selecting the Precise Word for Every Situation, 2nd ed.** New York: HarperCollins Publishers, 1994. 532p. $20.00pa. ISBN 0062731319. [reference] MJS/A This source lists and explains synonyms in relation to each other.

4. Rowling, J. K. **Harry Potter and the Sorcerer's Stone.** New York: 1997. 509p. $17.95. ISBN 0 590 35340 3. [fiction] MJS Harry Potter establishes himself as the good soldier in the battle between good and evil as he discovers his powers and is forced to fight the evil Voldemort.

5. Updale, Eleanor. **Montmorency: Thief, Liar, Gentleman?** New York: Orchard Books, 2003. 240p. $16.95. ISBN 0 439 58035 8. [fiction] MJS Montmorency, a Victorian criminal, lives a double life as a common and rich man and eventually, through his good choices and love of learning, improves himself and becomes a spy for England.

Fantasy/Science Fiction/
Paranormal

All these selections can be classified as "speculative fiction"—they ask the question "what if?" "Legends and Stories" use old favorites to inspire new perspectives on oral tradition fantasy and mythology. "Magical Coming of Age," kind of a combination of fantasy and paranormal, reminds us all that the new supernatural powers of these characters might be similar to our own natural ones. "The Unexplained" deals with those unnerving, seemingly impossible, but possibly paranormal, incidents that every life contains. "Futuristic," an aspect of science fiction, proposes what the future might look like based on what we know about technology and human nature. These larger than life characters and plots that often include clear conflict resolutions allow readers to take a little vacation from the pressures of the real world and yet find a bit of wisdom or advice to bring home.

Legends and Stories

Napoli, Donna Jo. **Beast.**

New York: Atheneum Books for Young Readers, 2000. 260p. $17.00.
ISBN 0 689 83589 2. [fiction] JS

Themes/Topics: Beauty and the Beast, love, suffering

Summary/Description

Orasmyn, a young Persian prince, selects an imperfect camel for sacrifice, an animal that has suffered. Punishing spirits change Orasmyn into a lion, an animal banished from the kingdom. He will learn, like the camel, about suffering. Only a woman's love can break the curse. Living the lion's life and seeking a return to humanity, he discovers a traveler in an empty house. The Beast orders the man to bring his daughter back or the Beast will kill the entire family. The daughter is a woman, not a little girl, whom he can raise to love him. He controls his bestial instincts, and they become close. He allows her to leave to visit her sick father. Returning voluntarily, she demonstrates her love for him, and he becomes human.

Booktalk

Once upon a time, there was a *Beast*. Not the Walt Disney version surrounded by dancing dishes and pastel colors. He was the rip from limb to limb, real-life predator—half man, half lion. As king of the jungle, life wasn't that bad. What did he do? Learn to be the biggest, meanest leader of the pack or find his way back to humanity and a human kingdom? Is there a happy ending? Maybe. But a happy ending depends on what you think the difference is between being human and being a *Beast*.

Learning Opportunities

1. Orasmyn must deal with living the life of a beast. Discuss if, as the pari (fairy) wishes, he learns about the suffering of animals.
2. Identify real-life parallels in the story. Explain your choices.
3. Is this a story about the forces of good and evil? Explain your answer.
4. Orasmyn is a devout follower of Islam. In Chapter 2, he cites the fourth article of faith. Further research the beliefs of Islam and discuss how Orasmyn follows, or fails to follow, those beliefs (Related Work 2).
5. Discuss Napoli's choice not to have the beauty of the story be of the Islam faith.
6. In Chapter 17, Orasmyn compares his first encounter with the girl to the story of Persophone. Read the story of Persophone and explain the similarities (Related Work 3).
7. Find as many versions of "Beauty and the Beast" as possible. Watch the Walt Disney version of the story. List the constants that you find among the versions. Then list the other details that have been added. Explain which details you would wish to keep and why (Related Work 6).

Related Works

1. Coville, Bruce (comp. and ed.). **Half-Human.** New York: Scholastic Press, 2001. 224p. $15.95. ISBN 0 590 95944 1. [fiction] JS (See full booktalk in *Booktalks and More*, 2003, pages 101 to 103.) This collection of stories questions what makes a human being. "How to Make a Human," a poem by Lawrence Schimel appearing on pages 94 and 95, presents a negative view of man forgetful of his ties to nature.

2. Jomier, Jacques. **How to Understand Islam.** New York: Crossroad, 1989. 168p. $14.95pa. ISBN 0 8245 0981 1. [nonfiction] JS/A Jacques explains the emergence and expansion of Islam, its beliefs, law, and practice, and its relationship to Christianity and the modern world. The discussion of the five pillars of belief appears on pages 53 to 72.

3. Jordan, Michael. **Encyclopedia of Gods: Over 2,500 Deities of the World.** New York: Facts on File, Inc., 1993. 337p. $40.00. ISBN 0 8160 2909 1. [reference] The entries not only explain the function of each god, but also talk about their relation to gods in other cultures. Persophone appears on page 204.

4. Napoli, Donna Jo. **The Great God Pan.** New York: Wendy Lamb Books, 2003. 149p. PLB $17.99. ISBN 0 385 90120 8. [fiction] JS Napoli joins the stories of Pan and Iphigenia to form a love story in which mutual love once again breaks a spell.

5. Napoli, Donna Jo. **Sirena.** New York: Scholastic, 1998. 210p. $15.95. ISBN 0 590 38388 4. [fiction] JS (See full booktalk in *Booktalks Plus,* 2001, pages 91 to 93.) In this mythical tale based on the Trojan War, Sirena, a siren, falls in love with a Greek warrior. Like Belle, she challenges the concept of heroism.

6. Zipes, Jack (trans.). **Beauty and the Beast and Other Classic French Fairy Tales.** New York: Signet Classic, 1997. 430p. $5.95pa. ISBN 0 451 52648 1. [fiction] MJS The fairy tale focuses on Beauty more than on the Beast, and will promote discussion as a comparison with the *Beast*.

〰〰

Napoli, Donna Jo. Breath.
New York: Atheneum Books for Young Readers, 2003. 260p. $16.95.
ISBN 0 689 86174 5. [fiction] JS

Themes/Topics: Pied Piper of Hamelin, cystic fibrosis, witches, family

Summary/Description

Twelve-year-old Salz (salt) suffers from cystic fibrosis. His symptoms—gasping for breath, salty skin, and severe gut pain—and his membership in his grandmother's coven cause the 1284 village of Hamelin to distrust him. A mysterious disease, caused by a killer fungus called ergot, produces dementia and gangrene in both animals and citizens. Salz and Ava, the little girl his grandmother adopts, are the only members of the family remaining disease-free because they do not drink beer made with infected grain. Trying to attack Salz, his older brother kills their grandmother. When Salz is called to testify at the brother's trial, the brother accuses Salz of being a warlock and claims St. Michael told him to kill Salz. The grandmother accidentally was in the brother's way. Salz blames the rats overrunning the area for the disease and persuades the town to hire a piper to lead the rats out of town. They hire the piper for an exorbitant fee. He completes the job, and during the town celebration, he discovers the town's people are cheating him. In revenge, he leads the children into the mountains. Salz, like others still infected with the fungus, is too sick to keep pace. He leaves his dying family, abandons the coven, and resolves to find his two sisters, whom his family sold after their mother died, and Ava. He wants them to form a new family together. Some erotic and graphic content may be considered controversial and requires a mature reader.

Booktalk

Twelve-year-old Salz should not be living. His lungs fill with mucus almost everyday. At any time, he can double over with gut pain. In order to keep him alive, his grandmother makes him part of her coven where he learns the healing arts and how to break the devil's spells. It is 1284, and common people don't trust coven members. So, when a strange disease strikes the town, suspicions run rampant. First the animals stagger; later their limbs turn black and fall off. Next, people show the same symptoms. Are rats bringing the disease? Is the coven unable to break a terrible spell, or is someone in the coven itself casting a spell? Is that someone the boy with salty skin? The boy, who in order to stay alive himself, is willing to take everyone else's *Breath*?

Learning Opportunities

1. On page 16, Salz spells his name and tells the meaning of each letter. Assign a meaning to each letter of your own name.
2. "Burial" describes the coven and its activities in detail. Discuss your impressions.
3. The Crusades and Arab contributions to German culture are mentioned several times throughout the novel. Using your library's resources, research how the Crusades influenced Western life.
4. Explain how religion and superstition intertwine in Hamelin.
5. At the end of the novel, Salz rejects the coven. Discuss why he makes that choice.
6. Find a version of the Pied Piper. Read it. Discuss how the original relates to the story.
7. Using your library's resources, research cystic fibrosis and share your findings with the group.

Related Works

1. *Folklore and Mythology Electronic Texts.* Available: http://www.pitt. edu/~dash/folktexts.html (Accessed September, 2004). The Web site, edited and translated by D. L. Ashliman, gives many versions of the Pied Piper story as well as other folk stories and mythologies.
2. Hautman, Pete. **Sweetblood.** (See full booktalk in "Issues"/"Personal Challenges," pages 6 to 8.) A teen diabetic assumes a Goth persona when she imagines herself living in the Middle Ages, where villagers perceive her as a vampire.
3. Jordan, Sherryl. **The Raging Quiet.** New York: Simon & Schuster, 1999. 266p. $17.00. ISBN 0 689 82140 9. [fiction] JS (See full booktalk in *Booktalks and More,* 2003, pages 15 to 17.) Living in a cursed house inherited from her husband and able to communicate with a deaf man, Marnie is perceived to be a witch and is forced to undergo a witchcraft trial.
4. Lee, Justin. **Everything You Need to Know about Cystic Fibrosis.** New York: The Rosen Publishing Group, Inc., 2001. 63p. (The Need to Know Library.) $25.95. ISBN 0 8239 3321 0. [nonfiction] MJS Lee defines and describes the disease, explains its treatment, discusses its implications for the patient's life, and provides extensive addresses, books, and Web sites for further research.
5. Levitin, Sonia. **The Cure.** New York: Harcourt Brace and Company, 1999. 184p. $16.00. ISBN 0 15 201827 1. [fiction] JS When Sixteen-year-old Gemm time travels to the Middle Ages, he discovers how the Jews are used as scapegoats for the Black Death.
6. Meltzer, Milton. **Witches and Witch Hunts: A History of Persecution.** New York: The Blue Sky Press, 1998. 128p. $16.95. ISBN 0 590 48517 2. [nonfiction] MJS (See full booktalk in *Booktalks and More,* 2003, pages 187 to 189.) Meltzer explains the psychology of witch hunts and cites several examples throughout the ages.

CℲ℔

Schmidt, Gary D. Straw into Gold.

New York: Clarion Books, 2001. 172p. $15.00. ISBN 0 618 05601 7. [fiction] MJS

Themes/Topics: Rumpelstiltskin, relationships, greed

Summary/Description

Rumpelstiltskin takes Tousel, his foster son, to the king's celebration. The king and his knights crushed a rebellion against Lord Beryl.

Innes, a blind boy, is one of the rebels paraded to be hanged. When the queen and Tousel speak for the rebels, the king promises to spare them if Tousel can bring back the answer to a riddle. In his search, Tousel is accompanied by Innes. Eventually they seek the answer from the queen and discover that Innes is the lost prince whom Lord Beryn wishes to kill because he is an heir. Tousel, Innes, and the queen join forces to defeat Lord Beryn. In the journey, Tousel discovers he has the gift of giving himself, and all discover that relationships are more important than gold.

Booktalk

Ask how many people have heard of Rumpelstiltskin. If they can't remember him, remind them that he is the nasty little man who spun straw into gold for a miller's daughter and then demanded her first born.

The story's central question is—"Why does he want the daughter's son?" Spinning gold all day, the little man with the long beard and bulging eyes can buy anything he wants, including a baby. Why does he want *this* baby? In fact, why does he even want to get involved with the miller's daughter? Maybe this spinner of *Straw into Gold* sees something more valuable than gold. But changing another's life often means changing your own—changes that even a magic man can't always control as the threads twist, turn, and weave a human as well as magical tapestry.

Learning Opportunities

1. Discuss the role played by the King's Grip and the nurse. How do these characters enable Schmidt to accomplish his purpose?
2. The statement "Nothing is quite by chance" is a refrain in the novel. Is Rumpelstiltskin a facilitator of a plan or interference in a plan?
3. Identify the clues that tell the reader that Innes is royal.
4. Each character in the novel has a gift. Da identifies Tousel's gift on page 166 as "the gift of giving himself." Identify a gift of personality that you or a friend has. Explain why it is important to that person and to others.
5. Discuss how Innes's blindness affects the story. Be sure to include the paragraph on page 168, which describes the king realizing what things are, rather than what they are worth.
6. Many would classify *Straw into Gold* as a story about greed. Discuss the other themes that the story suggests.
7. Research the story of Rumpelstiltskin. Share with the group its roots and as many variations as possible.

Related Works

1. Hettinga, Donald R. **The Brothers Grimm: Two Lives, One Legacy.** New York: Clarion Books, 2001. 180p. $22.00. ISBN 0 618 05599 1. [nonfiction] JS Within this story of two close and scholarly brothers, Hettinga lists all the brothers' publications and the tales they gathered.

2. Napoli, Donna Jo. **Crazy Jack.** New York: Delacorte Press, 1999. 134p. $15.95. ISBN 0 385 32627 0. [fiction] MJS (See full booktalk in *Booktalks and More,* 2003, pages 107 to 109.) Jack is a visionary who lives by the advice his father forgot. The important parts of life are "to have food on the table and a roof over our heads, but most of all, to have each other."

3. Napoli, Donna Jo, and Richard Tchen. **Spinners.** New York: Puffin Books, 1999. 197p. $5.99pa. ISBN 0 14 131110 X. [fiction] JS In this version of the tale, Rumpelstiltskin's daughter, a gifted spinner, grows up thinking her father is the drunken miller. In a much different way than *Straw into Gold,* the novel incorporates the elements of love, pride, morality, and greed.

4. November, Sharyn (ed.). **Firebirds: An Anthology of Original Fantasy and Science Fiction.** New York: Firebird/Penguin, 2003. 420p. $19.99. ISBN 0 14 250142 5. [fiction] MJS This anthology uses many original variations on familiar stories and themes. "The Baby in the Night Deposit Box," on pages 42 to 67 explores, like *Straw Into Gold,* the importance of finding a safe and nurturing environment for children to learn wisdom and compassion.

5. Vande Velde. **The Rumpelstiltskin Problem.** New York: Houghton Mifflin Company, 2000. 116p. $15.00. ISBN 0 618 05523 1. [fiction] JS (See full booktalk in *Booktalks and More,* 2003, pages 213 to 215.) Vande Velde analyzes the Rumpelstiltskin story and retells it six different ways. One of the versions is titled "Straw into Gold."

ॐॐ

Spinner, Stephanie. Quiver.
New York: Alfred A. Knopf, 2002. 176p. $15.95. ISBN 0 375 81489 2. [fiction] JS

Themes/Topics: Atlanta and Hippomenes, love,
Trojans, abuse

Summary/Description

Combining the boar hunt, the race with the golden apples, and the transformation of Atlanta and her husband Hippomanes into lions,

Spinner explains the why behind Atlanta's cruel marriage conditions and her resulting capitulation to the suitor who enlisted Aphrodite's aid. Abandoned at birth by her father, bullied, ignored, or mocked by the Trojan heroes, Atlanta sets a marriage standard that she believes no one will challenge. When suitors enter the death race she proposes, Atlanta gives them poison, a merciful death, and wins. Wounded by Eros, she is attracted to Hippomanes. She loves him because he truly loves and accepts her. She chooses to lose the race and marry Hippomanes in spite of her promise to Artemis. When Zeus changes them into lions for violating sacred ground, they thrive, and Atlanta passes her independent spirit to their female cubs.

The gods discuss Atlanta's struggles and their own rivalries in dialogues separate from the story. The "Author's Note" emphasizes that *Quiver* combines several versions and explains the historical context. "About the Gods" briefly explains the deities and their relationships.

Booktalk

Atlanta's father throws her out of the house when she is born. Greek kings wanted sons, not daughters. He leaves her in the wilderness to die, but the goddess Artemis sends a she bear to nurse her. Atlanta thinks a distant mother is better than none at all, and he dedicates her life to her immortal stepmother. In the forest, Atlanta learns to run and shoot like a man. In fact, she is bigger and better than many of the Trojan heroes who want her out of their way—and she knows it. Her father, never having any heirs, wants Atlanta back to produce one before he dies. Two problems exist. One, Atlanta promised Artemis she would never marry. Two, learning more about her father and getting to know the local heroes, she isn't too interested in marriage. She has a plan. If a suitor can win a foot race against her, she'll marry him; if he loses, he dies. It seems discouraging enough. So when the contestants line up, Atlanta knows she underestimated the power of a challenge. She starts to feel a *Quiver,* and knows she underestimated the power of the gods.

Learning Opportunities

1. The author's note indicates that Spinner researched several versions of this myth before constructing Atlanta's story. Choose another myth. Research as many versions as possible. List the constants and the variations that you find. Then using these details, explain what may have motivated the mythical character's decisions.
2. The hunting award offered to Atlanta by Meleager, the golden apples, and the quiver are central objects in the story. Explain the significance of each and what it reveals about Atlanta.

3. The title has more than one possible meaning. Discuss how you feel it relates to the story.
4. Atlanta is a modern woman in many ways, but she throws the race in order to save Hippomenes. Discuss whether you agree or disagree with her decision.
5. The gods control events, but the humans also achieve some control through their attitudes. List the events dictated by the gods. Then explain human attitudes in each event and how those attitudes affect the result. Discuss how fate and free will work together in building a happy or tragic life.

Related Works

1. Cadnum, Michael. **Starfall: Phaeton and the Chariot of the Sun.** New York: Scholastic, Inc., 2004. 128p. $16.95. ISBN 0 439 54533 1. [fiction] MJS In this retelling of the Greek myth, the main character, Phaeton, allows a critical decision in his life to be directed by bullying.
2. Logue, Mary. **Dancing with an Alien.** New York: HarperCollins, 2000. 134p. $14.95. ISBN 0 06 028318 1. [fiction] JS A large, athletic girl falls in love with an alien who admires her size and protects her from the possible consequences of living on another planet.
3. Napoli, Donna Jo. **The Great God Pan.** New York: Wendy Lamb Books, 2003. 149p. PLB $17.99. ISBN 0 385 90120 8. [fiction] JS Napoli combines the stories of Pan and Iphigenia to tell a tragic love story.
4. Napoli, Donna J. **Sirena.** New York: Scholastic, 1998. 210p. $15.95. ISBN 0 590 383 38388 4. [fiction] JS (See full Booktalk in *Booktalks Plus,* 2001, pages 91 to 93.) Like *Quiver,* the main character questions the model of heroism and discovers that within fate, each person can build personal character.
5. Smith, Sherri L. **Lucy the Giant.** (See full booktalk in "Adventure/Survival"/"Sea," pages 121 to 123.) Abused and ignored by her father, Lucy leaves home and discovers that others see her as capable and attractive.

Magical Coming of Age

෴

Dickinson, Peter. **The Ropemaker.**
New York: Delacorte, 2001. 375p. $15.95. ISBN 0 385 72921 9. [fiction] MJS

Themes/Topics: coming of age, identity, good versus evil

Summary/Description

In this coming of age fantasy adventure, Tilja, who does not possess her family's natural magic, journeys to her grandmother's home to discover why the forest's magic is failing. They join Alnor and his grandson Tahl who have also seen the water magic failing. The book tells of magic's origins, present function, and future. "Asarta" tells how magic was constructed to protect the forest people. The "Faheel" section explains the transition of the magic powers. Faheel, the magician, distinguishes natural magic, made magic, and Tilja's contribution, undoing magic. Faheel knows that Tilja is central for transferring the magic to the next generation. "Ramdatta" describes the battle for the new order after Faheel's death and Tilja's realization that her powers require her to leave the forest and contribute to a larger world. Ramdatta, the Ropemaker, will continue the powers of Asarta and Faheel.

Booktalk

Show a piece of rope. Discuss how such a common object might serve as a metaphor for time and how each strand of the rope might represent a person's life.

Tilja is common, free of the magic that touches her mother and grandmother. She cannot sing to the cedars or hear their call. Like her common aunt before her, she must find another place to live. The family home belongs to Tilja's mother and sister, blessed with forest magic. But Tilja and those she loves are tied to greater concerns. Embarking on a journey they don't fully understand, Tilja, her friends and family are pulled into a world of more powerful magic—one woven together by another common person—a *Ropemaker.* Tilja finds him, protects him, and discovers a power and mystery of her own—far from her safe and familiar home.

Learning Opportunities

1. The Ropemaker talks about changing the course of history by changing a strand of rope. Compare this character to the role of the three Fates in Greek mythology (Related Work 1).
2. Chapter 2 is the mythology of Asarta. After reading the novel, reread this chapter. Discuss its relationships to the rest of the novel.
3. Using library resources and the Internet, research creation stories in religion and mythology. Identify parallels among these stories and Asarta mythology (Related Work 4).
4. List all the magic people in the story. Then explain the function of each. Try to group them by their power or motives.
5. Draw a picture of the Ropemaker.

6. Build models of the various buildings and rooms described in the novel.
7. Discuss Tilja's power and the power's importance.
8. Asarta, Faheel, and Ramdatta have weaknesses or make a mistake. Discuss Dickinson's reasons for creating less than perfect powerful characters.
9. Reread the Epilogue. Discuss its purpose and function. Then plan the sequel.

Related Works

1. Jordon, Michael. **Encyclopedia of Gods: Over 2,500 Deities of the World.** New York: Facts on File, Inc., 1993. 337p. $40.00. ISBN 0 8160 2909 1. [reference] The entries identify and explain deities and consider how they overlap with deities in different cultures. The three fates, Antropos (p. 32), Klotho (p. 135), and Lachesis (p. 142), are described with their symbols of scales, spindle, and thread.

2. Smith, Jeff. **The First Trilogy.** Columbus, OH: Cartoon Books. [graphic] MJS/A

   Out from Boneville. 2003.142p. (Bone). $14.95. ISBN 1 4046 2251 9. Fone Bone moves his disreputable relatives out of Boneville and meets the beautiful, magical, and intelligent Thorn and her Grandma Ben. (Note: As of February, 2005, *Out from Boneville* is the first title of the new GRAPHIX imprint by Scholastic, Inc. The hardcover, 0-439-70623-8 is $18.95. The paperback edition, 0-439-70640-8, is $9.99.)
   The Great Cow Race. 1996. 143p. (Bone). $14.95. ISBN 096366095 0. Fone Bone falls in love with Thorn, and Grandma Ben wins the cow race even though Fone's disreputable relatives set up the odds against her.
   Eyes of the Storm. 1996. 180p. (Bone). $16.95. ISBN 0 9636609 9. The rat creatures, which surfaced in the first two stories, now multiply. Thorn dreams she is a princess. Grandma Ben reveals that the dream is true, and leads Fone and Thorn back to the kingdom so that they can defend it against the Rat Creatures. As a whole, this off-beat fantasy draws on comic images and focuses on Fone realizing the magical or royal powers of Thorn.

3. Pullman, Philip. **His Dark Materials Trilogy.** New York: Alfred A. Knopf. [fiction] MJS (See full booktalk in *Booktalks and More,* 2003, pages 161 to 166.)

The Golden Compass. 1995. 399p. $20.00. ISBN 0 679 87924 2. Lyra, an orphan, discovers the identity of her parents and, as the lone reader of *The Golden Compass,* finds herself in a struggle between good and evil.

The Subtle Knife. 1997. 326p. $20.00. ISBN 0 679 87925 0. Will, seeking his father, enters an alternative reality and meets Lyra. Together they find Will's father and Will's role in the universe as the keeper of *The Subtle Knife.*

The Amber Spyglass. 2000. 518p. $19.95. ISBN 0 679 87926 9. As the new Adam and Eve, Lyra and Will use their powers to keep their two worlds separate. Because they are from different worlds, they will never see each other again.

4. *What Is a Myth?* Available: www.dl.ket.org/latin1/mythology/ whatisa.htm (Accessed September, 2004). The Web site provides a clear explanation of why and how myths emerge in every culture.

The Meridian Series

ℭℨℭℨ

Kesel, Barbara. **Flying Solo.**

Oldsmar, FL: CrossGeneration Comics, 2003. 164p. (Meridian). $9.95 (Traveler Edition). ISBN 1 931484 54 6. [graphic novel] MJS

Themes/Topics: coming of age, good versus evil, post cataclysm, pollution, survival

Summary/Description

Two cosmic powers decide to promote conflict in the world because conflict is their source of energy. They decide to make sibling leaders sigil bearers. The first is the leader of Meridian. The second is the leader of Cadador. Receiving the sign, the Meridian leader dies. It passes to Sephie, his daughter. Her uncle, the leader of Cadador, takes her to Cadador. He realizes their new power and decides to appoint a regent for Sephie so he can control her government. She escapes him, but pursuing soldiers force her to Akasia where she brings new life. Knowing the uncle is pursuing Sephie, the citizens notify him that she is there and imprison her with the child laborers. Meanwhile the Meridian citizens have escaped the city and are poised to fight the uncle and help free Sephie. The uncle joins his power with Reesha Teramu of Auroud, a woman who equals his capacity for evil.

Booktalk

Sephie lives in the sky city, Meridian. Having survived a catastrophe, the citizens, led by Sephie's father, ruler of Meridian, live a life of perfect balance between available resources and their desires to possess more. Her uncle, the minister of Cadador, focuses his city on trade and riches. He wants to sell Meridian's perfect products, but his brother does not agree. A conflict ensues, and supernatural forces intervene. These forces thrive on energy generated by conflict. They place a sigil in each brother's soul. The sigil opens unbelievable supernatural powers—a heady and dangerous gift. But the leader of Meridian dies, so his sigil passes to Sephie, his teenage daughter. Now she is the sigil bearer, the one who must balance the power; but her uncle is determined to control her, her people, and their wealth. It happens so fast; Sephie doesn't really understand what she has. But with her uncle in control and her people driven away, she knows she has to learn all these sudden changes *Flying Solo*.

૮ઝૺ૨ૢ

Kesel, Barbara. **Going to Ground.**

Oldsmar, FL: CrossgenComics, 2002. 176p. (Meridian). $19.95.
ISBN 1 931484 09 0. [graphic novel] MJS

Summary/Description

Sephie escapes Akasia and the celanaugs who attack her in her flight. When she encounters a community of loggers and shipbuilders, she demonstrates her power and persuades them to help her unite the caverns, surface cities, and sky cities. Entering the caverns, she meets Deren BEQ who remembers Sehpie's mother. Deren "betrays" her to the underground city of Anheim led by Minister Geres. From these people, dedicated to saving the gardens that will prevent the decay of the world, she learns about her parents, and meets Crenner, Geres's grandson, who loves her. Sephie remains loyal to Jad, her love from Meridian, and the episode ends with Deren, Crenner, and Sephie setting out on a mission to defeat her uncle's evil and change the world. The Cadadors attack the Meridian refugees. King City helps them survive. They receive news that Sephie is dead, and move on. Jon and Mira marry. Jad and Feabie grow closer. Together they will build a new Meridian. Uncle Ilahn blows up the ships of Akasia when their leader threatens to hold him for ransom. Rho, a "merchant" from Elysia, a land outside of Demetria, proposes a merger with Ilahn. Ilahn refuses, but tricks Rho into transporting him to Elysia where Ilahn demonstrates the superiority of his universal powers while defending himself from attack.

Booktalk

Show both Flying Solo *and* Going to Ground.

In *Flying Solo,* Sephie led her country. Now, fleeing her uncle's evil powers, she runs away and plunges to her death—or so everyone thinks. The good news is that Sephie lives. The bad news is that she is a slave in the Akasian dye factories. But Sephie doesn't forget she is the minister of Meridian, and that every problem presents an opportunity. If her chains won't break, the wood that holds them will. If the other slaves won't follow her, she will find others not yet crippled by fear and pain. And if the skies are too dangerous, she will pursue her right to rule and her fate by *Going to Ground.*

Learning Opportunities

1. Describe how Meridian characterizes the forces of good and evil. Be as specific as possible.
2. Read the story of Cain and Abel (Related Work 5). What parallels do you find to this series?
3. Discuss the choice of titles and how they apply to the stories.
4. What do the stories have to say about love, self-interest, and responsibility?
5. Describe the various settings. Discuss how each supports the story.
6. List the plots that you would expect to develop in *Meridian* sequels.

Related Works

1. Constable, Kate. **The Singer of All Songs.** New York: Arthur A. Levine Books, 2004. 304p. $16.95. ISBN 0 439 55478 0. [fiction] MJS Darrow and Calwyn gather followers as they prepare to confront the evil Samos, who strives to become *The Singer of All Songs.*
2. Divakaruni, Chitra Banerjee. **The Conch Bearer.** Brookfield, CT: Roaring Brook Press/A Neal Porter Book, 2003. 263p. ISBN 0 7613 2793 2. [fiction] MJ Twelve-year-old Anand endures his abusive boss to support his splintered family, but discovers that he has been chosen to be *The Conch Bearer* who combats evil.
3. Marz, Ron. **Conflict of Conscience.** Olsmar, FL: Cross Generation Comics, 2000, 2001. 154p. (Scion). $19.95. ISBN 1 931484 02 3. [graphic novel] MJS When Heron Prince Ethan decides to participate in Avalon's ritual combat, he discovers that he has been marked with the power of the sigil and by his participation sends the two historically enemy kingdoms into war.
4. Roberts, Katherine. **Spellfall.** England: The Chicken House, 2000. New York: Scholastic, 2001. 256p. $15.95. ISBN 0 439 29653 6.

[fiction] MJ (See full booktalk in *Booktalks and More,* 2003, pages 157 to 159.) Natalie Marlins discovers her supernatural heritage directing her to defeat evil and combine the powers of nature, magic, and technology.

5. **Student Bible: New International Version.** Philip Yancey and Tim Stafford (notes). Grand Rapids, MI: Zondervan, 2002. 1440p. $32.99. ISBN 0 310 92784 6.. [Bible] MJS This text includes "Insights," "Highlights," a list of 100 important Biblical figures, "Where to Find It," and either a "Guided Tour" or a "3 track Reading Program." The story of Cain and Abel with an explanation of their characters and purpose appears on page 8.

6. Zindel, Paul. **Rats.** New York: Hyperion Books for Children, 1999. 203p. ISBN 0 7868 2820 X. [fiction] MJ Fifteen-year-old Sarah Macafee and her ten-year-old brother Michael live next to a toxic landfill breeding mutant rats able to destroy the entire community unless Sarah and Michael destroy them first.

The Circle Opens Quartet

ₒₒ

Pierce, Tamora. **Magic Steps.**

New York: Scholastic Press, 2000. 272p. (The Circle Opens.) $16.95.
ISBN 0 590 39588 2. [fiction] MJ

Themes/Topics: thread magic, responsibility of knowledge and talent, good versus evil

Summary/Description

Fourteen-year-old Sandry moves from her school, Winding Circle, to live with her uncle, Duke Vedris IV, the ruler of Emelan. First, she must foil and destroy two assassins and a decadent mage (person with magical powers) dedicated to killing an entire family. Their secret weapon, "essence of nothingness," allows them to elude the Duke's guards. Sandry's spell traps and destroys the deadly team. Second, she must train Pasco, a twelve-year-old member of the Provost guard family, who does not realize that his dances make powerful magic. Teaching him, with the help of Yazmin Hebet, a famous dancer, she unwittingly pulls him into a confrontation with the assassins and their addicted mage. Sandry realizes that she must use her magic in the real world; Pasco learns that he must control his magic or others will use it to control him; and the Duke is enamored with the alluring Yazmin.

Booktalk

If you remember *Circle of Magic,* you remember Sandry. Now she is fourteen—old enough and powerful enough to solve problems with the magical threads she weaves. And big problems are coming her way. Warring families are scattering blood and hacked up body parts all over her uncle's kingdom. Before she can figure out how to weave an action plan, she discovers Pasco, a twelve-year-old dancer who does not realize the power of his *Magic Steps.* Because she is the one who discovered him, she must be the one to train him. But everyone must learn quickly when the murderers, Pasco, her teachers, her uncle, and Sandry are woven into a mystery that changes their lives and an entire kingdom.

ℭℨℭℨ

Pierce, Tamora. **Street Magic.**

New York: Scholastic Press, 2001. 304p. (The Circle Opens.) $16.95.
ISBN 0 590 39628 5. [fiction] MJ

Themes/Topics: ecology, good versus evil,
responsibility of talent

Summary/Description

Book 2 of *The Circle Opens Quartet* tells the story of fourteen-year-old Briar Moss who uses his plant power to fight evil. Briar lives in Chammur with Dedicate Rosethorn of the Winding Circle Temple. Chammur is home to rival gangs supplied and controlled by wealthy, bored citizens. Caught in a three-way war, Briar finds Evvy, a street child who does not realize her rock magic. As he and Rosethorn try to work with the stubborn Evvy, Briar discovers that an evil gang's sponsor, Lady Zenadia doa Attaneh, wants to control Evvy so that she might find the treasures in the rocks that surround them. When the gang, the Vipers, kidnap Evvy, Briar saves her and learns that murdered gang members' bodies fertilize Lady Zenadia's gardens. The truth drives Lady Zenadia to suicide. Goodness and order return, and Evvy decides to tackle reading and magic in earnest. A glossary at the end of the novel defines Chammuran terms and geography.

Booktalk

Fourteen-year-old Briar Moss is now a mature mage—ready to fight evil and teach another young mage the pleasures and responsibilities of magic. In the middle of "fabled Chammur" he discovers Evvy who survives on the streets. Her magic lies in rocks, not the trees and plants that obey and thrive for Briar. Just as rocks resist plants, Evvy resists Briar's efforts to help her learn magic. But when the gangs of Chammur go to war, and mysterious murders multiply, rocks and plants work together and conjure up a little *Street Magic.*

ᘐᘗ

Pierce, Tamora. **Cold Fire.**

New York: Scholastic Press, 2002. 368p. (The Circle Opens.) $16.95.
ISBN 0 590 39655 2. [fiction] MJ

Themes/Topics: fire, meditation, responsibility

Summary/Description

In book 3, Daja and Frostpine plan to rest in Kugisko, but Daja becomes involved in two challenging projects. She finds herself teaching meditation to twins with magical powers, and, as a fire mage, she helps Bennat Ladradun, a local firefighter. Impressed with his intelligence, skill, and sensitivity she supports him in fighting the mysterious fires raging throughout the town—even designing special gloves for his protection. When Daja discovers that Ladradun is the arsonist, deriving a feeling of power from the fires, she accepts the court's sentence of burning at the stake, even though she realizes that his cruel, dominating mother and the loss of his own family drove him to the burnings. In sympathy, the mages intensify the fire to make his death swift and merciful. Notes at the end of the novel explain the culture's months, days, and holidays.

Booktalk

In this third book of "The Circle Opens" quartet, Daja and Frostpine visit Kugisko for a restful vacation, but find themselves embroiled in mystery and intrigue. Daja takes on the difficult task of teaching rebellious twelve-year-old twins to meditate and harness their own magical powers. More challenging, however, are the unexplained, lethal fires that rage through the town. The sensitive and intelligent Bennat Ladradun, who lost wife and children to fire, possesses only the determination, not the magic, to fight them. Daja brings her magic and skill to the struggle and fashions special gloves for his protection. But as the gloves do their work, both Ben and Daja need something more to stop this arsonist and the *Cold Fire* that threatens to destroy even those Daja loves.

ロ゚ロ

Pierce, Tamora. **Shatterglass.**

New York: Scholastic Press, 2003. 368p. (The Circle Opens.) $16.95.
ISBN 0 590 39683 8. [fiction] MJ

Themes/Topics: glass magic, lightening magic, helping others

Summary/Description

In this fourth book of the series, Trisana Chandler, a glass mage, is visiting Tharios—a city renowned for its glassmaking—with Niko, her teacher. She visits the glass blowers and encounters twenty-year-old Kethlun Warder, a frustrated glassmaker whose talent and glass magic are mixed with lightning from a freak accident. With this combination, he creates small glass balls that show the immediate past. Tris, as a lightening mage, helps Kethlun focus his magic and anger. Dema Nomasdina, an investigator mage, is looking for the killer of four dead women. All the women wear the yellow veil, the badge of licensed entertainers who work in the garden district. Kethlun frequents the district. Murder scenes and a murder victim appear in the glass balls he creates. He is accused of murder, but, with Tris's help, harnesses his powers to apprehend the real murderer, a street person abandoned by a mother who wore the yellow veil and a father who was a First Class citizen. Teaching and sleuthing, Tris discovers Glaki, a young orphan, who does not realize her own magic. Context clues and description within the text explain unfamiliar terms.

Booktalk

Trisana Chandler, a lightning glass mage, travels with her teacher to Tharios. There, they will study and observe some of the most talented glass workers and mages in the world. But Tris has little time to study and reflect. In her first walk through the city, she encounters an out-of-control lightning glass mage. Since getting hit with a lightning bolt, twenty-year-old Kethlun Warder doesn't understand why he can no longer quietly and methodically form beautiful objects from molten glass. And he certainly can't understand how he creates living glass and the mysterious glass balls that reveal evidence about the murders all around him. Maybe these glass pictures merely reflect his subconscious—the repressed thoughts of a murderer. Did he kill the mysterious women who wear the alluring yellow veil and live in the streets? No one really knows. But in the world of *Shatterglass*, only fourteen-year-old Tris can direct the lightning that frightens him, the wild talent that baffles him, and the investigation that promises to take his life.

Learning Opportunities

1. In all four books, Pierce describes the culture that the young mages encounter. Note the customs and beliefs of each culture. Then discuss what these tell about each society.
2. Draw maps or pictures that depict each society. You might include houses, characters, and clothing in your drawings.
3. Each teen mage changes because of the problems he or she confronts. Explain what each learns about living. Then discuss if the lesson applies to real life.
4. Describe the pattern that each book in this series follows. Then discuss how such a pattern affects the series. For instance, did it increase or decrease the mystery? Did it make the story easier to follow?
5. The power of magic dominates each novel. It earns each mage a great deal of respect far beyond his or her years. Discuss how a modern teenager might seek to harness his or her power and connect with the adult world.

Related Works

1. Constable, Kate. **The Singer of All Songs.** New York: Arthur A. Levine Books, 2004. 304p. $16.95. ISBN 0 439 55478 0. [fiction] MJS Sixteen-year-old Calwyn joins forces with Darrow. He helps her battle the evil Samos, who wishes to be *The Singer of All Songs*. In their journey and struggle, they discover that no one person can sing all songs.
2. Divakaruni, Chitra Banerjee. **The Conch Bearer.** Brookfield, CT: Roaring Book Press/A Neal Porter Book, 2003. 263p. ISBN 0 7613 2793 2. [fiction] MJ Twelve-year-old Anand learns that he is to be entrusted with a magical conch to heal men and animals as well as cure the land of famine and drought.
3. Nix, Garth. **Mister Monday: Book One.** New York: Scholastic Inc., 2003. 361p. (The Keys to the Kingdom.) $5.99pa. ISBN 0 439 55123 4. [fiction] MJ In this first book of the series, twelve-year-old Arthur Panhaligon receives a magical key that pulls him into a parallel universe of monsters, mythical figures, and bizarre environments where he is expected to take on a hero's role and obtain all Seven Keys of the Kingdom.
4. Roberts, Katherine. **Spellfall.** England: The Chicken House, 2000. New York: Scholastic, 2001. 256p. $15.95. ISBN 0 439 29653 6. [fiction] MJS (See full booktalk in *Booktalks and More*, 2001, pages 157 to 159.) Natalie Marlins, in a battle of good versus evil, joins the powers of nature and technology to save the world.

5.   Russell, Barbara Timberlake. **The Taker's Stone.** New York: DK
     Publishing, Inc., 1999. 231p. $16.95. ISBN 0 7894 2568 8. [fiction]
     MJS (See full booktalk in *Booktalks and More,* 2003, pages 159 to
     161.) Fourteen-year-old Fischer steals magic stones and sets in motion
     a battle between good and evil expressed through natural disasters.

ယ္သို့ဆ

Rowling, J. K., and Mary Grandpré (illus.). **Harry Potter and the Order of the Phoenix.**

New York: Arthur A. Levine, 2003. 870p. $29.99. ISBN 0 439 35806 X. [fiction] MJS

Themes/Topics: good versus evil, politics, in-group
versus out-group, friendship, love

Summary/Description

After dementors attack Harry and Dudley at the Dursleys' home, a
wizard guard escorts Harry to Order of the Phoenix headquarters,
the family home of Harry's godfather, Sirius Black. The Order is orga-
nizing for battle with Voldemort and the Ministry of Magic refusing to
acknowledge the evil wizard's return. Harry uses magic to protect himself and Dudley from the dementors, and supports the Order's claim.
Consequently, the Ministry of Magic, the press, and some of his peers
malign him. Dumbledore, the Hogwarts's headmaster, gives Harry public
support. Afraid of Dumbledore forming a takeover coalition, the Ministry
sends sadistic, sneaky, prejudiced, and tyrannical Dolores Jane Umbridge
to control the Hogwarts. Her heavy-handed methods produce revolt.
Harry spends his fifth year at Hogwarts confronting Umbridge, trying
to communicate secretly with Sirius, dealing with his crush on Cho
Chang, and preparing himself to face Voldemort. Eventually, Umbridge
is driven away, and Harry decides that his hoped-for girlfriend is too
fickle and weepy. Experiencing the feelings and thoughts of Voldemort,
Harry believes Voldemort is torturing Sirius. But Voldemort is using
Harry's vision to lure Harry and friends to the Ministry of Magic.
Voldemort wants to force Harry to retrieve the unspoken prophecy
explaining how the link between Harry and Voldemort enabled Harry
to survive Voldemort's vicious attack on Harry's parents. Order of the
Phoenix members arrive to fight Voldemort and his death eaters. Sirius
dies in battle, and the prophecy is released unheard. Dumbledore
encases Voldemort, neutralizing his power. Harry blames himself for
Sirius's death, but Dumbledore explains his own responsibility for the
tragedy, and reveals the Harry/Voldemort kill or be killed relationship

from the prophecy. The surviving wizards meet the Dursleys and put them on notice.—Harry's summers away from Hogwarts will be pleasant or else.

Booktalk

Harry Potter might not be returning to Hogwarts this year. Someone is sending dementors to kill him. When he defends himself and even his (Ugh!) cousin Dudley with his magical powers, the Ministry of Magic takes steps to get him expelled. This year, not going to Hogwarts might be a good idea. The Ministry sends Dolores Jane Umbridge to control the wizard school because, like Harry, Dumbledore claims that Voldemort is back. Umbridge and the Ministry are sure that Potter is lying and that Dumbledore is either losing his grip or plotting to take over the Ministry. She hates the faculty and most of the students—except Malfoy and his friends—the students who hate Harry Potter. And Umbridge isn't Harry's only problem. He is in love and doesn't know what to do about it. He can't talk to his godfather, Sirius Black, without revealing Sirius's hiding place. But worst of all, Harry is having visions—visions that come from Voldemort's mind, visions that burn into his scar. These evil forces seem too big for even the amazing Harry to overcome. The question is—Are they too big for *The Order of the Phoenix*?

Learning Opportunities

1. A central theme of *The Order of the Phoenix* is mind control. Voldemort and Harry are the major characters in this battle, but what other characters deal with mind control? Discuss how their conflicts parallel Harry's.
2. Ginny Weasley, Neville Longbottom, and Luna Lovegood are unlikely heroes, and yet each is strong and heroic. Describe how each character proves worthy. Discuss why Rowling might have chosen these characters to be surprisingly strong. Discuss what you think Harry may learn from each one.
3. The Forbidden Forest is a major setting in this novel. Discuss why it and its inhabitants are so important.
4. The past is still a central influence on Harry's present, even if he did not experience the events. Explain what elements of his past are important and why.
5. Dolores Jane Umbridge is a major character. Discuss how and why she is defeated. Research the development of the Third Reich in Germany. Then identify any parallels to Umbridge's organization, tactics, and beliefs.

6. Chapter 37, "The Lost Prophecy" contains a significant conversation between Harry and Dumbledore. Reread that conversation. Then discuss what each speaker reveals about his character and why those revelations are important.
7. Sirius dies. Is this the character you would have chosen? Explain your answer.

Related Works

1. Giblin, James Cross. **The Life and Death of Adolf Hitler.** (See full booktalk in "History/Period"/"Leaders and Defining Events," pages 250 to 252.) Giblin portrays a disturbed and dedicated individual who was able, with an exceptional gift for politics and speech making, to appeal to the prejudices and fears of the German people. Giblin helps the reader understand the effectiveness of hate propaganda.
2. Marshall, Joanne M. "Critically Thinking about Harry Potter: A Framework for Discussing Controversial Works in the English Classroom." *The ALAN Review.* (Winter 2003): 16–19. Marshall presents a step-by-step method for promoting critical thinking and discussion about controversial books, not just Harry Potter.
3. Radley, Gail. "Spiritual Quest in the Realm of Harry Potter." *The ALAN Review.* (Winter 2003): 20–23. Radley illustrates how Harry Potter follows the traditional hero's journey as described by Joseph Campbell.
4. Rowling, J.K. **Harry Potter and the Chamber of Secrets.** New York: Arthur A. Levine Books, 1998. 341p. $17.95. ISBN 0 439 06486 4. (See full booktalk in *Booktalks Plus,* 2001, page 182.) In Harry's second year at Hogwarts, the Malfoys plot to destroy Harry and his friends through Ginny Weasley.
5. Rowling, J.K. **Harry Potter and the Goblet of Fire.** New York: Arthur A. Levine Books, 2000. 734p. $25.95. ISBN 0 439 13959 7. (See full booktalk in *Booktalks Plus,* 2001, pages 184 and 185.) Fourth year student Harry Potter learns about his own faults as Voldemort plots his death.
6. Rowling, J.K. **Harry Potter and the Prisoner of Azkaban.** New York: Arthur A. Levine Books, 1999. 431p. $19.95. ISBN 0 439 13635 0. (See full booktalk in *Booktalks Plus,* 2001, page 183.) Third year student Harry Potter discovers that the infamous Sirius Black is his godfather.
7. Rowling, J.K. **Harry Potter and the Sorcerer's Stone.** NewYork: 1997. 509p. $17.95. ISBN 0 590 35340 3. (See full booktalk in *Booktalks Plus,* 2001, pages 181 to 182.) Harry discovers his wizard blood and confronts Voldemort.

The Unexplained

ෆ ෨

Heneghan, James. Flood.

New York: Farrar, Straus and Giroux/Frances Foster Books, 2002. 182p. $16.00.
ISBN 0 374 35057 4. [fiction] MJ

Themes/Topics: Irish folklore, loss, grief, alcoholism,
love, family, responsibility

Summary/Description

Eleven-year-old Andy Flynn loses his mother and stepfather in a flood. When his Aunt Mona comes to take him to her home, he discovers his real father is alive. Andy runs away, finds his alcoholic father, and lives with him. The father, who tells beautiful stories, provides no food, shelter, or guidance but promises to get a job and make them a home. After petty thugs break the father's leg, the father calls Mona and sends Andy back to her. Andy refuses to respond to Mona. Other family members welcome him and give insight into Mona's hopes and fears. He realizes that a solid home offering him love and responsibility is better than uncertainty with the father he loves. The Sheehogue or Little People follow Andy and add their mischief, concern, and support.

Booktalk

Andy Flynn lives in a very nice Vancouver home with his loving mother and conscientious, no nonsense stepfather. Then the rains come, and a *Flood* takes his home and his parents away. He must move all the way to Halifax and live with his uptight Aunt Mona Hogan, a woman he can't even remember. In their first meeting, she points out that he is too small for his age, calls his mother a liar, and lets him know that his father, notorious Vincent Flynn, is still alive. Andy decides he would rather take his chances with the father who loves whisky and gambling and tells wonderful Irish stories, rather than face the hard and bitter truths. The three are on a collision course. And in the course of all this, the Sheehogues, the Little People, join the mix. Andy, his aunt, and father see and say things they can't explain, have troubles they don't expect, and begin to wonder if they might eventually connect instead of collide.

Learning Opportunities

1. The Sheehogue play a significant part in the novel. Explain how they contribute to the novel beyond the plot.

2. From Chapters 17 to 21, the Little People do not directly appear. Discuss why.

3. Using your library's resources, continue to research the Irish beliefs of fantasy. Share your findings with the group in either storytelling or a visual display. You may wish to begin by reading *The Stones Are Hatching* (Related Work 5) or some of the selections from *Irish Fairy Tales* (Related Work 1).

4. On page 172, Andy sees the shape of "Janus, the two faced god of beginnings" on the ceiling. Using your library's resources, find out more about the Roman god and explain his significance to the novel (Related Work 4).

5. Uncle Hugh, Aunt Jill, Una, and Mother Costello all are minor characters, but they contribute significantly to the story. Discuss how Heneghan uses them.

6. Andy holds what any reader might characterize as unrealistic expectations. Discuss if these expectations prove to be destructive or productive.

Related Works

1. Curtin, Jeremiah. **Irish Fairy Tales.** New York: Dorset Press, 1992. 198p. $5.95. ISBN 0 880 29814 6. [nonfiction] JS/A These stories, gathered from storytellers across Ireland, illustrate the intricate relationship between reality and fantasy.

2. Ellis, Sarah. **Back of Beyond: Stories of the Supernatural.** New York: Simon & Schuster/Margaret K. McElderry Books, 1996. 136p. $15.00. ISBN 0 689 81484 4. [fiction] MJS On pages 81 and 82 of *Flood,* Vincent Flynn describes Tir Na n'Og as "in the back of beyond." All the stories in this collection deal with supernatural occurrences in that realm.

3. Heneghan, James. **The Grave.** New York: Farrar, Straus and Giroux/Frances Foster Books, 2000. 245p. $17.00. ISBN 0 374 32765 3. [fiction] MJS Time traveling between the twentieth and nineteenth centuries, Tom Mullen discovers that the coach he admires is actually the father he was separated from as a baby.

4. Jordan, Michael. **Encyclopedia of Gods: Over 2,500 Deities of the World.** New York: Facts on File, Inc., 1993. 337p. $40.00. ISBN 0 8160 2909 1. [reference] This source describes each deity and often refers to similar deities in other cultures. It explains Janus's relationship to gates, doorways, all beginnings, past, present, future, the rising and setting sun, and new seasons.

5. McCaughrean, Geraldine. **The Stones Are Hatching.** New York: Harper Collins, 1999. 230p. $15.95. ISBN 0 06 028765 9. [fiction]

MJ Based on Irish mythology, this story tells how an ordinary boy receives the task of saving the world.

6. Powell, Randy. **Run If You Dare.** New York: Farrar, Straus and Giroux, 2001. 185p. $16.00. ISBN 0 374 39981 6. [fiction] MJS (See full booktalk in *Booktalks and More,* 2003, pages 24 to 26.) A teenager who loves his father must decide to find his own path in life rather than emulating the father's destructive lifestyle.

ॐॐ

Hoffman, Alice. **Aquamarine.**

New York: Scholastic, 2001. 112p. $16.95. ISBN 0 439 09863 7. [fiction] MJ

Themes/Topics: mermaids, friendship, grief, falling in love

Summary/Description

Twelve-year-old Hailey and Claire are spending their last summer together at the deteriorating Capri Beach Club where they talk to and admire Raymond who runs the snack shop and will soon be going off to college in Miami, Florida. Having lost both parents in a recent automobile accident, Claire, now fearful and withdrawn, is moving to Florida to live with her grandparents. After a violent storm, Hailey discovers the sixteen-year-old rude mermaid, Aquamarine, living in the club's turbid and polluted pool. When Aquamarine falls in love with Raymond, Hailey and Claire arrange a blind date. Raymond loves Aquamarine though she is a mermaid. The mermaid gives the girls seashells so that they can talk with each other when they are separated. Later, Claire sees Raymond in Florida, swimming with Aquamarine. He thanks her for introducing them. Claire and Hailey plan to reunite the next summer.

Booktalk

For twelve-year-old Hailey and Claire this summer is pretty sad—the last summer they may have together. Claire, who lost her parents in an automobile accident, will move to Florida to live with her grandparents. The Capri Beach Club where Hailey and Claire hang out every summer is closing—forever. Raymond, the hunk who runs the snack shop, is going to college. Everything good is changing to something not so good. When a storm hits, it churns up the Club pool. Through all the pollution, Hailey sees something pretty unusual—a mermaid. She isn't the sweet, classic type that lives in books. In fact, she is a pretty mouthy sixteen-year-old version named *Aquamarine,* and she wants and gets things her way. That attitude sounds pretty good to Hailey and Claire. Together, the three just might make some of what they want to happen.

Learning Opportunities

1. Discuss whether or not Aquamarine is real.
2. Recall a great change in your life. Describe it through writing, drawing, or speaking.
3. Compare the change in your life to the changes expressed by others in the group. Then share the good and the difficult results that came from the changes.
4. Maury is rarely seen in the story. Discuss how you think he affects the story.
5. Describe or draw a picture of the Capri Beach Club. Discuss what you think this setting adds to the story?
6. Describe each of the characters in about five years.

Related Works

1. Coville, Bruce (comp. and ed.), and Marc Tauss (photo illus.). **Half-Human.** New York: Scholastic Press, 2001. 224p. $15.95. ISBN 0 590 95944 1. [fiction] MJS (See full booktalk in *Booktalks and More,* 2003, pages 101 to 103.) Each story in this fantasy collection describes a person "like us, but not quite" who must decide how that difference will affect his or her relationship to the human world.
2. Danziger, Paula, and Ann M. Martin. **P.S. Longer Letter Later.** New York: Scholastic, Apple Paperbacks, 1998. 234p. $4.99pa. ISBN 0 590 21311 3. [fiction] MJ (See full booktalk in *Booktalks Plus,* 2001, pages 172 to 173.) Two seventh graders, who are best friends, exchange letters about their lives and parents for an entire year when one girl's family decides to move.
3. Danziger, Paula, and Ann M. Martin. **Snail Mail No More.** New York: Scholastic, 2000. 336p. $16.95. ISBN 0 439 06335 3. [fiction] MJ (See full booktalk in *Booktalks Plus,* 2001, pages 173 to 176.) The friends from *P.S. Longer Letter Later* use e-mail to discuss their problems in their eighth grade year and discover that Snail Mail, with the advantage of pause, could be a better communication tool.
4. Napoli, Donna Jo. **Sirena.** New York: Scholastic, 1998. 210p. $15.95. ISBN 0 590 38388 4. [fiction] JS (See full booktalk in *Booktalks Plus,* 2001, pages 91 to 93.) Sirena, a siren, falls in love with the Greek hero Philoctetes and challenges the principles of human heroism.
5. November, Sharyn (ed.). **Firebirds: An Anthology of Original Fantasy and Science Fiction.** New York: Firebird/Penguin, 2003.

420p. $19.99. ISBN 0 14 250142 5. [fiction] JS. The stories empha-
size the intermingling of "real" and "fantasy" worlds.

᭦᭦

Rice, Ben. **Pobby and Dingan.**
New York: Alfred A. Knopf, 2000. 94p. $16.00. ISBN 0 375 41127 5. [fiction] JS

Themes/Topics: Australia, family, imaginary friend,
perceptions, mining, death

Summary/Description

Ashmol Williamson tells how his little sister's imaginary friends, Pobby
and Dingan, reshape the perceptions of his family and their Australian
mining town, Lightning Ridge. Kellyanne, perceived as strange and withdrawn, creates two imaginary friends. When Kellyanne's father makes
fun of them, her mother compares Kellyanne's vision to his promise that
he will discover valuable opals. As a joke, the father enters his daughter's
fantasy. One day when he returns from the mines, Kellyanne accuses him
of forgetting the friends. Everyone returns to the mines to look for them,
and the father is suspected of "ratting" or poaching. The neighbors turn
on him, and Kellyanne gets sick. Ashmol tours the country and persuades
people that his father is not a poacher, and that Kellyanne will get well if
everyone searches for the friends. The searchers encourage her, but she
grows sicker, and rejects false claims that her friends have been found.
Finally, she decides that they died, and persuades Ashmol to search the
mines. In a cave, he finds Dingan's bellybutton opal, and the bodies of
Kellyanne's imaginary friends. At his sister's direction he uses the opal to
pay for a funeral, which the entire town attends. Their father is cleared of
the poaching. The people believe he was indeed looking for the imaginary
friends. Kellyanne dies a week later and becomes Ashmol's imaginary
friend. The book explores how our belief in the unknown affects us and
implies that, in some way, each of us has an imaginary friend. The language and theme require a mature and thoughtful audience.

Booktalk

*Ask how many people in the group had an imaginary friend or know
someone who has an imaginary friend. Then ask them why they think
imaginary friends exist.*

Ashmol's sister, Kellyanne, has two imaginary friends, and he sure
wishes she would stop being such a "fruit loop." When Ashmol's father

starts to see them too, Ashmol thinks his dad is just drinking too much and spending too much time underground looking for opals. The real trouble starts when the "friends" are lost, maybe dead, and his dad is accused of poaching another miner's claim. In Lightning Ridge, Australia, poaching is "only a bit worse" than murder. And in the middle of all this, his sister gets sick. Ashmol, trying to keep his entire family together, alive, and free, decides to find Kellyanne's *Pobby and Dingan*. When he asks the entire town to help him search, they all discover some very strange and wonderful things about the friends and themselves.

Learning Opportunities

1. Is Ashmol a reliable narrator?
2. Reread Chapter 15. On the basis of the court trial, discuss whether you think Pobby and Dingan are real.
3. Reread the preacher's sermon on pages 89 and 90 aloud. Restate the sermon in your own words, and discuss whether or not you agree with the point he is trying to make. Then compare his interpretation of Pobby and Dingan with the judge's interpretation.
4. Discuss how the setting affects the story.
5. Both *Pobby and Dingan* and *The Dream Bearer* (Related Work 4) talk about the importance of dreams and a belief in the invisible. After reading the two novels, compare them in message and method.

Related Works

1. Almond, David. **Skellig.** New York: Delacorte Press, 1999. 182p. $15.95. ISBN 0 385 32653 X. [fiction] MJS (See full booktalk in *Booktalks and More*, 2003, pages 99 to 101.) Skellig appears and helps out a young boy and his family, who has moved into a new home and is struggling with the possible death of the new baby.
2. Griffin, Adele. **The Other Shepards.** New York: Hyperion Books for Children, 1998. 218p. $14.95. ISBN 0 7868 0423 8. [fiction] MJS (See full booktalk in *Booktalks and More*, pages 67 to 69.) A mysterious girl named Annie appears and changes the life of eleven-year-old Geneva and thirteen-year-old Holland Shepard, who live in the shadow of their dead brothers and sisters.
3. Hartnett, Sonya. **Thursday's Child.** (See full booktalk in "Multiple Cultures"/"World Cultures," pages 276 to 278.) Set in Australia during the Depression, the story centers on the narrator's younger brother, who tunnels under the house, becomes a feral child, and eventually delivers a large chunk of gold to the family.
4. Myers, Walter Dean. **The Dream Bearer.** New York: HarperCollins Publishers, 2003. 181p. $16.89. ISBN 0 06 029522 8. [fiction] JS

When a homeless man claims to be 303 years old and the bearer of dreams and stories, David Curry listens to him even though adults discount him.

5. Quarles, Heather. **A Door Near Here.** New York: Delacorte Press, 1998. 231p. $13.95. ISBN 0 385 32595 9. [fiction] MJS (See full booktalk in *Booktalks Plus*, 2001, pages 54 to 56.) As fifteen-year-old Katherine tries to hold together her family as her mother descends into severe alcoholism, she realizes that her little sister is escaping the stress by fantasizing about Narnia.

Schwartz, Virginia Frances. Messenger.
New York: Holiday House, 2002. 277p. $17.95. ISBN 0 8234 1716 6. [fiction] MJS

Themes/Topics: supernatural, mining life, grief, survival, blended family, Croatian immigrants, historical setting

Summary/Description

Frances Chopp's narration begins before her birth in 1923, and ends when she is seventeen years old. Born in a Canadian mining town one week after her father—a Croatian immigrant miner—dies, Frances is perceived as a mystical messenger sent to assure her mother that Phillip Chopp is safe in heaven. Frances recalls even prebirth feelings and thoughts. She describes her father's funeral, her mother's depression, the transition from their rural cabin to the city, her mother's resolve to support her three children by running a boarding house, the constant flow of aunts, uncles, and cousins, her own and her brothers' coming of age, her mother's remarriage, and the constant mystical signs that guide the family to decisions and through crises.

Booktalk

Read the definition of messenger and the poem, "Messenger" that appear on the book's opening pages.

The poem, "Messenger" is by Frances Chopp. When Frances is born in 1923, she already has the job of family *Messenger*. She has much to tell. Her father Phillip Chopp died the week before she was born. Her Croatian community believes the paths of father and daughter crossed, and Frances, being born healthy and happy, brings good news. Her father is in heaven. Just a superstition? Frances doesn't think so. She can hear her father's voice. She remembers events before her birth. But Frances's mother can't seem to hear anything. She stays in bed—mourning. She leaves Frances in the care of her two older brothers: six-year-old Phillip and two-year-old William. Frances has a message to deliver—not one of death but of life. A message so important it will change her family forever.

Learning Opportunities

1. Frances's nickname is Baby. Given Frances's role in the story, discuss how this name is both appropriate and ironic.
2. Although Frances is seen as a *Messenger* to others, she spends much of the novel discovering her own identity. Discuss how the two tasks might be related.
3. Many of the factors affecting the Chopp family are economic. Further research the boom and bust years between World War I and World War II. Explain how the information that you find relates to the story.
4. Wordsworth's poems are central to Frances's thinking. Using your library's resources, find and read as many of Wordsworth's poems as possible. Discuss each poem's spiritual perception and how that perception might affect Frances.
5. After reading the novel, describe the role of family in Frances's life. Compare it with the role that family plays in your life.
6. Angels appear several times within the story—some heavenly and some earthly. Cite instances where angels appear in the lives of the Chopp family. Discuss their significance.
7. In Chapter 32, "Who I Was," Frances discovers the magic of memorizing poetry. Select three poems that you feel define your situation or express something significant about your life. Memorize them. Share them with others who have done the same. Then explain your choices to each other.

Related Works

1. Bartoletti, Susan Campbell. **A Coal Miner's Bride: The Diary of Anetka Kaminska.** New York: Scholastic Inc., 2000. 217p. (Dear America.) $10.95. ISBN 0 439 05386 2. [fiction] MJS Set in the 1890s, the diary tells the struggles and hardships of a young Polish immigrant wedded to an American miner and after his death, permitted to choose a husband she loves.
2. Bartoletti, Susan Campbell. **Growing Up in Coal Country.** Boston, MA: Houghton Mifflin, 1996. 127p. $16.95. ISBN 0 395 77847 6. [nonfication] MJS This source explains the jobs, attitudes, and everyday details of mining life.

3. Morris, Neil, et al. (text), and Paola Ravaglia, et al. (illus.). **The Illustrated History of the World: From the Big Bang to the Third Millennium.** New York: Enchanted Lion Books, 2004. 288p. $29.95. ISBN 1 59270 019 5. [nonfication] MJS This is a global presentation of world history organized chronologically and geographically within time periods. Pages 222 to 229 deal with the years between World War I and World War II.

4. Ryan, Pam Muñoz. **Esperanza Rising.** New York: Scholastic Press, 2000. 272p. $15.95. ISBN 0 439 12041 1. [fiction] MJS (See full booktalk in *Booktalks and More,* 2003, pages 42 to 44.) Born into privilege and affluence in Mexico, Esperanza Ortega comes to the United States during the depression and confronts prejudice and backbreaking labor. She learns to judge people by their characters, stand up to those who would discriminate against and exploit her, and connect to the rhythm of the land.

5. Ylvisaker, Anne. **Dear Papa.** Cambridge, MA: Candlewick Press, 2002. 184p. $15.99. ISBN 0 7636 1618 4. [fiction] MJS After a small girl's father dies in the early 1940s, she clarifies her conflicts by writing him letters primarily over a period of seven years.

Futuristic

ᘓᘔ

Anderson, M. T. Feed.

Cambridge, MA: Candlewick Press, 2003. 235p. $16.99. ISBN 0 7636 1726 1.
[fiction] JS

Themes/Topics: commercialism, ecology,
computer control, friendship, fitting in

Summary/Description

Bored American Titus and his teenage friends party on the moon. The feed, a chip implanted in the brain by corporations, constantly gives them news, advertising, and emotional reactions. Home schooled Violet, the daughter of a college professor, tries to break into their group, which she perceives as normal. A "hacker" and "naysayer" penetrates several of the teenagers' systems and disturbs their connection to the feednet. Everyone recovers except Violet, who received her chip later in life. As Violet deteriorates, she attacks the commercial system that denies her a new implant. Titus, in love with this girl who constantly questions and criticizes the system, withdraws from her. Violet sees him as different from the others, however, and instructs her father to tell Titus when she is dead. Watching her die, Titus realizes that America is deteriorating physically, emotionally, and intellectually and that any personal dignity comes from one's ability to resist the feed. Strong language and violence requires a mature reader.

Booktalk

Titus and his friends live in the American future. In their world, a person doesn't have to sit down in front of a screen to shop the net. The net is right inside their brains—delivered by the *Feed*, a tiny implanted transmitter. One second they think about doing or wanting something. The next second, they know the best party places and shopping bargains in the world. Life should be great, but Titus notices that parties don't deliver the same kick anymore—not even the party on the moon. Violet, a very different girl, shows up and starts asking embarrassing questions. What are those big skin lesions Titus and his friend are starting to have—the ones that the feed teaches them how to decorate? Why do they buy things they don't need? Don't need?! Titus never even thinks about need. In fact, Titus and his friends don't think too much at all. Titus even starts asking questions. Now that's different! And the big question is: Can Titus, Violet, or anyone else ever "fight the feed."

Learning Opportunities

1. The feed provides a constant flow of images into each person's head. Choose one passage from the feed. List the images and the appeal of each. Then find modern advertisements that use similar images and appeals. Share your analysis and findings with the group through an oral or visual display.
2. Using your library's resources, research modern advertising techniques. Prepare a presentation in which you explain how a person may be persuaded to buy what he or she does not need.
3. List each of the parents depicted in the novel. How effective is each parent?
4. Discuss what the hacker and Violet share. Then discuss what effect, if any, each one has on the world.
5. Does Titus change? Discuss the importance of his promise to tell their story.
6. The chapter "flat hope" on pages 152 to 156 seems to be pivotal. Re-read the chapter. Discuss its significance in relation to action, images, and setting.
7. Anderson relates the narrative in standard type and the feed in italics. Discuss the placement of the two and how it impacts the story.

Be sure to include the ending of the novel and the final feed message, "Everything must go."

8. Discuss Anderson's vision for the United States. Do you agree? Why or why not? Compare his vision of the future with those of *The Last Book in the Universe* (Related Work 3), *Brave New World* (Related Work 2), and *The Time Machine* (Related Work 6). Identify what you feel to be the elements of truth in each.

Related Works

1. Haddix, Margaret Peterson. **Just Ella.** New York: Simon & Schuster Books for Young Children, 1999. 185p. $17.00. ISBN 0 689 82186 7. [fiction] MJS In this feminist retelling of the Cinderella story, fifteen-year-old Ella discovers that the court is centered on appearances and empty ceremony and decides to take charge of her own destiny instead of leaving it to tradition and the expectations of others.

2. Huxley, Aldous. **Brave New World.** New York: Perennial Classics, 1998. $11.95pa. ISBN 0 06 092987 1. [fiction] JS/A Originally published in 1932, this novel projects a society of the future built on pleasure and instant gratification.

3. Philbrick, Rodman. **The Last Book in the Universe.** New York: The Blue Sky Press, 2000. 224p. $16.95. ISBN 0 439 08758 9. [fiction] MJS Set in a future devoid of books and full of violence, the novel describes the emotional and intellectual journey of Spaz, a young Urb (city) normal (inferior breed) who, because his brain cannot tolerate the popular brain probe, remembers a world with books.

4. Shoemaker, Joel. "Hungry . . . for M. T. Anderson: An Interview with M. T. Anderson." *VOYA.* (June 2004): 98–102. Anderson talks about the relevance of *Feed,* some of the decisions he made in writing it, and his other books and short stories.

5. Skurzynski, Gloria. **Virtual War.** New York: Simon & Schuster Books for Young Readers, 1997. 152p. $16.00. ISBN 0 689 81374 0. [fiction] MJS Fourteen-year-old Corgan has been raised in a box by Mendor, a virtual figure that moves between male and female identities. He is bred to wage the next World War, a *Virtual War* that reminds the world population of war's horrors and destruction. His partners encourage him to experience life outside the box, and they negotiate to build their own lives.

6. Wells, H. G. **The Time Machine and the Invisible Man.** New York: Signet Classic, 1984. 278p. $4.95pa. ISBN 0 451 52238 9. [fiction] JS/A *The Time Machine*, written in 1895, perceives a future in which the Morlocks, prisoners in a lower world, feed on the soft, fat, indulged Eloi of the upper world.

Fire Us Trilogy

ʕ꒩ʔ꒪

Armstrong, Jennifer, and Nancy Butcher. **The Kindling: Book One.**

New York: HarperCollins, 2002. 224p. (Fire Us Trilogy.) $15.89.
ISBN 0 06 029411 6. [fiction] MJS

Themes/Topics: family, history, survival

Summary/Description

After an adult killing virus (fire us) sweeps the United States, seven orphans in Lazarus, Florida, band together as a family. Over the next five years, they take new names, which reflect their rolls in the group, and try to overcome personal traumas rooted in their pasts, which they have difficulty remembering. A knock on the door brings Anchorman into their lives, another orphan. He carries a mannequin named "Bad Guy," whom he blames for the virus and all negatives connected with it. He also carries a picture frame that he peers through when giving a "news report" about upsetting information or situations. Anchorman is going to Washington to find the President. He plans to take the two youngest and newest members of the family with him. The rest join him on a journey that forces each member, even Anchorman, to face his fears and become a responsible member of the group.

Booktalk

A mysterious virus (fire us) has killed all the adults in North America. Many children survive the virus, but die by starvation or wild animals. Seven of them, ranging in age from about eight to fourteen are still living. They are a new family that includes Mommy, Teacher, Hunter, and even an Action Figure. For five years, they have worked hard to keep each other alive, but now other children show up. Puppy and Kitty, born in the year of the fire us, can only bark and meow. The family takes them in, even though it strains the food supply. Then Anchorman comes. He has a strange look, punches a mannequin he calls "Bad Guy," and, without warning, gives some pretty wild news reports. He is going to Washington to see if somebody named President can help them solve their problems, and he's taking the whole family, whether or not they want to go. After Anchorman arrives, the house that friends built may end up as *The Kindling.*

ᚲᚱᚨᚱ

Armstrong, Jennifer, and Nancy Butcher. **The Keepers of the Flame: Book Two.**

New York: HarperCollins, 2002. 231p. (Fire Us Trilogy.) $17.89.
ISBN 0 06 029412 4. [fiction] MJS

Themes/Topics: cults, manipulation, trust, family

Summary/Description

The ten travelers from *The Kindling,* discover a cult-like community living in an abandoned mall. Each person accepted into the group takes a Bible verse as a name. One of the youngest members, Corinthians 1:19, is preparing to become a Handmaid. In her Visioning, she sees a confusing landscape, an owl, and an unreadable book that she believes reveals her future. When the survivors arrive, she realizes that the girl known as Teacher is the owl, and that the book Teacher carries is also from the vision. Corinthians 1:19 whose real name is Cory realizes that Puppy and Kitty, the five-year-old twins with the survivors, are her nieces. The cult members isolate them, but she rescues them as her dead sister tried to do. Otherwise, they will be sent away to be tested, she will be sent away to become a Handmaid, and the family will never see each other again. The survivors also decide that they will escape and take the twins. Eventually, Cory and the survivors unite against the cult members. They fight together when pursued and journey to Washington to find President.

Booktalk

Mommy, Hunter, Teacher, and Angerman are running their family of ten pretty well. Though most people in the world died, they are surviving, sometimes even thriving. They are working their way up the coast of Florida trying to discover why the terrible sickness came. Grown ups living in an abandoned mall welcome them with open arms. These Grown ups promise to give them clean clothes, plenty of food, and all kinds of loving—if the children will split up their family, if they will change their names, and if they will surrender to *The Keepers of the Flame.* That kind of love doesn't seem quite right. Angerman gets terrible vibes. The youngest ones disappear. But the Grown Ups keep smiling and giving answers—answers that seem to avoid the questions. Is there anyone who can or will tell them the truth, or will this great new home—the home with lots and lots of things the survivors forgot even existed—be the last home any of them will ever know?

〔❧〕

Armstrong, Jennifer, and Nancy Butcher. **The Kiln: Book Three.**

New York: HarperCollins, 2003. 193p. (Fire Us Trilogy.) $15.99.
ISBN 0 06 008050 7. MJS [fiction]

Themes/Topics: family, Apocalypse, biological
weapons, cults, self-sacrifice

Summary/Description

Having escaped The Keepers, the survivors and Cory journey to Washington and discover "The Woods," a senior community. Nana, a retired doctor, takes care of the residents. She believes that the deadly virus targeted only the citizens in the reproductive years. She reasons that the President, whom they seek and who had a retreat on Pisgah Island in Florida, is also dead. Cory remembers that she was being sent to Pisgah Island to be the Handmaid of the Supreme Leader. Mommy begins menstruation, and when Nana explains its significance, all realize that soon they will be susceptible to the virus. Mommy, Teacher, Cory, and Hunter decide to go to Pisgah Island. They leave emotionally deteriorating Angerman behind. On the island, they discover President J. Colin McDowell, the Supreme Leader, with Angerman. The President, Angerman's father, used the virus to purify the country. Because Cory's sister was one of his many handmaids, he fathered the twins. The group tests the presidents' babies by burning them in *The Kiln*. The surviving baby will be their next true leader. McDowell has another vial of virus to use on resisters. The Teacher, Mommy, Hunter, and Cory plan to seal the vial in the presidential bunker, which allowed The Keepers to survive the first virus. Angerman promises to help the group and plans to kill his father. As Angerman forces the President to the bunker, Cory intervenes, grabs Angerman's gun, pushes the President and virus vial into the bunker, and kills both him and herself. The Keepers flee. Nana frees the other handmaids and their babies. The "family" begins their journey, away from adults, to build a home.

Booktalk

In *The Kindling*, you met the family. In *The Keepers of the Flame* you met the cult. Now the family meets cult in the horrors of *The Kiln*. Continuing the quest to find the President, they discover The Woods, a retirement home. Like the children, these old people survived the virus. Why? The answer to that question reveals the travelers could die next. Now it is even more important to find the President, the man who can help them survive. But Cory, the girl from *The Keepers of the Flame,* fears that finding him might put them in even more danger—the danger she was trying to escape. And Angerman, the motor mouth, can't even talk about the fears and memories growing inside him. The group must move on even if the odds are against them. This time their journey, a true and shocking trial in *The Kiln,* could save or destroy what is left of the world.

Learning Opportunities

1. Each person in *The Keepers of the Flame* receives a Bible verse name. Look up each of the verses used, and discuss how the verse might apply to the character and story. You might wish to use *Student Bible* (Related Work 4).
2. Naming and renaming are very important in *The Kindling* and *The Keepers of the Flame.* Discuss why the authors focus on that issue.
3. Discuss how the mall setting influences *The Keepers of the Flame.*
4. Anchorman/Angerman is a central figure in the story. Describe his character. Be sure to discuss the relevance of his double name.
5. The trilogy begins with seven characters. Anchorman, Puppy, and Kitty join the group in *The Kindling.* Cory joins in *The Keepers of the Flame.* Discuss the dynamic each new character brings.
6. The Apocalypse is a central reference in *The Keepers of the Flame.* Using your library's resources, find as much information as you can about it. You might wish to start by reading about Armageddon in the Bible (Related Work 4). Then share the information with the group and discuss how the information supports the story.
7. Should Cory have died? Explain your answer.

Related Works

1. Hoffman, Alice. **Green Angel.** New York: Scholastic Press, 2003. 128p. $16.95. ISBN 0 439 44384 9. [fiction] JS Losing her entire family in an apocalyptic explosion, Green drinks, tattoos herself, and no longer looks to the future until she realizes that her family will always be with her and she is the ink to tell the future's story.
2. Philbrick, Rodman. **The Last Book in the Universe.** New York: The Blue Sky Press, 2000. 224p. $16.95. ISBN 0 439 08758 9. [fiction] MJ (See full booktalk in *Booktalks and More,* 2003, pages 146 to 148.) In this expansion of the short story "The Last Book," Spaz, a young Urb normal, is one of the few people who remembers books in a world devoid of books and feelings. He discovers the importance of recording events and feelings as he journeys to find his dying sister.
3. Rand, Ayn. **Anthem.** New York: Signet, 1995. 253p. $7.99pa. ISBN 0 451 19113 7. [fiction] S/A In a post-apocalyptic world where

all live for the community, one young man decides to be an individual. Inspired by Rand's view of Communism, the novel was first published in 1938. This edition includes an original text with revision markings and a Reader's Guide to the Writings and Philosophy of Ayn Rand.

4. **Student Bible: New International Version.** Philip Yancey and Tim Stafford (notes). Grand Rapids, MI: Zondervan, 2002. 1440p. $32.99. ISBN 0 310 92784 6. [Bible] JS This user-friendly Bible, a New International Version, provides commentary, a list of significant people in the Bible, an easily accessible reference section, and guided reading programs.

5. Yolen, Jane, and Bruce Coville. **Armageddon Summer.** New York: Harcourt Brace, 1998. 266p. $17.00. ISBN 0 15 201767 4. [fiction] MJS (See full booktalk in *Booktalks Plus,* 2001, pages 50 to 52.) Fourteen-year-old Marina and sixteen-year-old Jed are swept up in their parents' desire to become part of the chosen 144 when Armageddon begins.

☙❧

Farmer, Nancy. **The House of the Scorpion.**

New York: Atheneum Books for Young Readers/A Richard Jackson Book, 2002. 380p. $17.95. ISBN 0 689 85222 3. [fiction] JS

Themes/Topics: genetic engineering, identity, integrity, love, orphans, exploitation

Summary/Description

Matteo Alacrán, at 140 years old, is the El Patrón of Opium, a land, between Mexico and the United States, ruled by drug lords. His seventh clone, Matteo Alacrán, comes from a piece of his skin, and like the previous clones, is kept healthy to provide body parts for him. Matt, however, has the affection of Celia, the woman who raises him, Tam Lin, his bodyguard, and Maria, the daughter of a powerful American senator. Celia, trained in herbs and medicines, makes Matt's heart unstable enough so that it cannot be transplanted into El Patrón, who consequently dies. Tam Lin teaches Matt integrity and helps him cross the border so he can find María. Once across the border, Matt is labeled an orphan who must work for the state. Assigned first to a minor work camp and then to a plankton factory, Matt befriends three other orphans. They rebel against the corrupt guards. Esperanza, Maria's mother, a human rights activist, asks Matt to return to Opium, now in disarray, as the rightful head of the drug kingdom, and destroy it. Matt agrees, realizes the complexity of his job, and plans to ask his new friends to help him.

Booktalk

Ask someone in the group to define a clone. Briefly discuss uses for cloning.

Matteo Alacrán is El Patrón, the most powerful drug lord in Opium. He is 140 years old. A second Matteo Alacrán is the drug lord's clone, created from a patch of El Patrón's skin. Matt knows he is the most important person in El Patrón's life. El Patrón announces Matt's importance constantly. Unlike other clones, Matt has a brain. El Patrón will never allow him to belike those other clones, a brute or monster hidden away in a barn or cave. El Patrón loves Matt as much as he loves himself. He shares endless survival stories. He provides him with a beautiful apartment, books and music lessons, a loving nurse, even a terrorist bodyguard. Matt believes that someday he will rule the drug kingdom, because Matt is like El Patrón, intelligent and strong. But life in *The House of the Scorpion* is full of stings as well as pleasures. Will he replace El Patrón in power or simply body parts? This science fiction thriller has a surprise in every chapter—surprises for *The House of the Scorpion* and the clone, who dares to claim his body as his own.

Learning Opportunities

1. Using your library's resources, research the success of cloning and its possibilities. You might wish to start with *Cloning* (Related Work 5).
2. Mythical creatures and legends form a motif in the novel. List each as mentioned. Then discuss their significance in relation to the novel.
3. Much of the novel deals with the struggle between the weak and the powerful. Discuss the power that each character has and how that power is used. Discuss the weakness that each character has and how it is or is not overcome.
4. *The House of the Scorpion* and *Feed* (Related Work 1) envision a future that incorporates brain implants. After reading both, discuss how they are used in each work to accomplish the story's purpose.
5. El Viejo is a central character in the story, even though he appears only briefly. Discuss why his character and views are included.
6. Discuss if Farmer should have allowed Tam Lin to live.
7. *The House of the Scorpion* is a science fiction thriller with insights for our modern world. List the messages or themes that you find in the story. Give specifics from the story to support your choices.

Related Works

1. Anderson, M. T. **Feed.** (See full booktalk included earlier, "Fantasy/ Science Fiction/Paranormal"/"Futuristic," pages 201 to 203.) Young

Americans are controlled by chip implants constantly pushing them to buy consumer goods and seek a good time.

2. Coville, Bruce (comp. and ed.). **Half-Human.** New York: Scholastic Press, 2001. 224p. $15.95. ISBN 0 590 95944 1. [fiction] MJS (See full booktalk in *Booktalks and More,* 2003, pages 101 to 103.) The short story collection tells about people discovering that they are only half human and using their differences to make better-than-human choices.

3. Farland, David. **The Runelords: The Sum of All Men.** New York: TOR Books, 1998. 479p. $25.95. ISBN 0 312 86653 4. [fiction] S/A *The Runelords* take the wits, stamina, and even beauty of their subjects to become the best in their kingdoms, but one man wishes to become the most brilliant, powerful, and beautiful so that he can command the entire world.

4. Haddix, Margaret Peterson. **Turnabout.** New York: Simon and Schuster, 2000. 223p. $17.00. ISBN 0 689 82187 5. [fiction] JS Participating in an experiment to lengthen their lives, two women search for caregivers in a regression to infancy.

5. Nardo, Don. **Cloning.** New York: Thomson Gale/Blackbirch Press, 2003. 48p. (Science on the Edge.) $23.70. ISBN 1 56711 782 1. [nonfiction] JS Nardo discusses the history, uses, and implications of cloning. He asserts that cloning individual body parts, rather than a person from whom those can be taken, will be more practical. A bibliography of books (annotated), articles, and Web sites provide resources for additional research.

6. November, Sharyn (ed.). **Firebirds: An Anthology of Original Fantasy and Science Fiction.** New York: Firebird/Penguin, 2003. 420p. $19.99. ISBN 0 14 250142 5. [fiction] JS "Remember Me," a short story by Nancy Farmer, tells the story of another unwanted child, Flo, who realizes her soul is in the wrong body, and turns into a tree.

The Crux Series

⚘⚘

Waid, Mark. Atlantis Rising.

Oldsmar, FL: CrossGeneration Comics, 2002. 130p. (Crux) $15.95pa. ISBN 1 931484 14 7. [graphic] JS/A

Themes/Topics: Adventure, Atlantis, time travel, responsibility, cooperation

Summary/Description

In ancient Atlantis, Danik plans to lead his people to a higher level. Capricia, a shapeshifter and empath, refuses to journey to that higher plane until humanity is sufficiently directed. Danik makes the transition. Capricia's people stay in their protective chambers. A stranger wakes Capricia 100,000 years later. He asks her to choose four others to help her fend off the attack of huge insects. She chooses Tug, a telekinetic strongman; Zephyre, a hypermetabolic intellectual; Galvan and Gammid, twin commanders of the electromagnetic spectrum; and Verityn, a ten-year-old truth seer. All fight the insects, representatives of The Negation. As the citizens of Atlantis approach the entry of a new land, they encounter security troops of Terra Cognito, a land development company turning the mysteriously deserted earth into a series of museums and amusement parks. The citizens help the security guards escape The Negation. Then they meet Geromi, a Terra Cognito employee left behind. He serves as their guide and earth historian. Tug proposes finding the Earthlings, but Capricia decides that first, they must resurrect Atlantis. With much group strife, they bring back the city but not the people. Verityn, the seer, perceives that the stranger is Danik but tries unsuccessfully to penetrate the mysterious curtain around earth. At the end of this sequel, Capricia must find a way to reunite her team.

Booktalk

Ask how many people find it difficult to get up in the morning. Ask how many need time to wake up before really starting the day.

When Capricia wakes up one day after sleeping for one thousand centuries, she too is having a little trouble adjusting. Giant bugs attacking her don't help. A mysterious stranger telling her to pick a team to help fight the bugs adds to her confusion. Not a good start.

Now I'll ask you another question. (*Ask how many people have lost something that was very important to them.*) After she wakes up a little, Capricia finds out that she too has lost something pretty important—the human race. It was there when she went to sleep, but now, along with her beautiful city of Atlantis, it has disappeared. How can she get them back? Well she has that team she chose right after she woke up from her 100 century sleep—Tug, the telekinetic strongman; Zephyre, a hypermetabolic intellectual; Galvan and Gammid, commanders of the electromagnetic spectrum; and Verityn, truth seer. They might have some ideas. Time will tell how well she is thinking when she unwittingly begins the process of *Atlantis Rising*.

CʒʡC

Waid, Mark. Test of Time.

Oldsmar, FL: CrossGeneration Comics, 2002. 130p. (Crux). $15.95pa. ISBN 1 931484 36 8. [graphic] JS/A

Themes: Adventure, Atlantis, time travel,
cooperation and team dynamics

Summary/Description

The Atlanteans focus their search on Australia. They discover a group of humans judged unfit to move to a Higher Plane of Existence and Negation soldiers from another planet bent on destroying earth and the Atlanteans. Human lives are chaotic because time travelers change events in time. The humans fear acting because by mistake they could erase themselves, others, and critical equipment from existence, but they prepare for a mass evacuation. One of the twins from Atlantis will accompany the humans and help guide their destiny. Capricia discovers that the mysterious stranger who awakened the group is Danik. Tug, in questioning the Negation captives, is blinded.

An interview with Steve Epting that follows the novel explains the drawing and design process.

Booktalk

In this second *Crux* volume, the Atlanteans find themselves in a world and time gone mad. They must cooperate to control the powers against them. They don't know each other that well, but they all know the values and beliefs that bind Atlanteans. One of those values is accepting responsibility. They accept the responsibility of finding the human race. Where do they go to search? Australia. What do they find? Substandard humans and some very fierce Negation troops whose mission it is to kill everyone—especially the Atlanteans. Not everyone passes the *Test of Time*. In fact, not everyone survives. Who of this superpower team will be left standing after overwhelming powers of good and evil fight in the ever-shifting *Test of Time*?

CʒʡC

Dixon, Chuck. Strangers in Atlantis.

Olsmar, FL: CrossGeneration Comics. 2003.130p. (Crux) $15.95pa. ISBN 1 931284 63 5. [graphic] JS/A

Themes/Topics: visions, trust, battle, time travel, alliances

Summary/Description

Verity dreams about an ancient Atlantis where men fought monsters. He and Tug then discover the source of the dreams and creatures. They encounter Aristophanes, a historical legend, and Thraxis, a beast with whom Verity can communicate. Aristophanes decides to attack the Negation and bring back Galvan, lured into Negation territory by a monster posing as his brother. Aristophanes directs the group to return and awaken Atlantis. Capricia does not trust him. The Negation soldiers attack both the Atlantians and Geromi, who thought he was watching a battle long distance. He wins against them, but decides to join the Atlantians. He time travels to the Old West. Zephyr and Verityn go to meet him. Danik is setting up a questionable situation for them with a cowboy and his female sidekick.

Booktalk

Everyone is changing positions in this *Crux* volume. The mighty Tug, now temporarily blinded by a Negation prisoner, is led into a whole new world by Verity, who serves as his eyes. The mysterious Danik promises to confront Capricia with an almost impossible responsibility. Geromi decides to live with the Atlantians he has only watched. And a historical legend with a whole different mission and a very hairy monster with an entirely new language become *Strangers in Atlantis*.

Learning Opportunities

1. Capricia begins the ceremony of bonding in which each Atlantean creates part of Atlantean ancient history. Using your town, city, school, or church, form a group and ask them to complete the same exercise. Be sure to appoint a recorder. Then read back the history and discuss what the history reveals about each historian.

2. In the created history, the leader Tholan learns that people can't survive forever in a quest for an ideal unless they have a structure and provision for everyday needs and assurance for the building of a future. Read *When We Were Saints* (Related Work 2) by Han Nolan. Discuss how those principles apply to characters in this realistic setting as well as the mythology of science fiction/adventure.

3. List each character. Then discuss the qualities each character represents. Be sure to consider their physical appearance as well as their mental and emotional qualities.

4. Match the qualities listed in Learning Opportunity 3 with people or characters familiar to you. Discuss how those qualities help or hinder the person or character. Then identify and discuss other qualities that could help that person or character achieve a balanced personality.

5. Discuss what the *Crux* series suggests about time.
6. Discuss what the *Crux* series suggests about history.
7. Discuss what the *Crux* series suggests about trust.

Related Works

1. Funke, Cornelia. **Inkheart.** New York: The Chicken House, 2003. 544p. $19.95. ISBN 0 439 53164 0. [fiction] MJS A talented reader joins an author to take responsibility for the fictional characters from *Inkheart,* who have now been read into the real world.
2. Nolan, Han. **When We Were Saints.** New York: Harcourt Inc., 2003. 291p. $17.00 ISBN 0 15 216371 9. [fiction] JS Fourteen-year-old Archibald Caswell agrees to join sixteen-year-old Clare Simpson on the path to sainthood until her vision promises to end in death.
3. Pini, Wendy, and Richard Pini. **Elfquest: Wolfrider: Volume One.** New York: DC Comics, 2003. 224p. $9.95. ISBN 1 4012 0131 8. [graphic novel] S Elf and human worlds collide. Like *Test of Time,* their mythology emphasizes their values. Some of the drawings could be considered controversial and require a mature audience.
4. Pullman, Philip. **His Dark Materials Trilogy.** Throughout the novels, the characters travel among different worlds and ultimately establish a new world by becoming the new Adam and Eve. [fiction] MJS (See full booktalk in *Booktalks and More,* 2003, pages 161 to 166.)

   The Golden Compass. New York: Alfred A. Knopf, 1995. 399p. $20.00. ISBN 0 679 87924 2. Lyra, who thinks she is an orphan, discovers that her mother and father support two warring schools of thought. Lyra, her magical powers, and a group of stolen children become the focus of their battle.

   The Subtle Knife. New York: Alfred A. Knopf, 1997. 326p. $20.00. ISBN 0 679 87925 0. Will, fleeing men whom he perceives to be his father's enemies, enters an alternative universe, and becomes, with Lyra, the hope of mankind.

   The Amber Spyglass. New York: Alfred A. Knopf, 2000. 518p. $19.95. ISBN 0 679 87926 9. Lyra and Will become the new Adam and Eve, separate, and take on the responsibility of two different worlds.

History/Period

History, both peace and war, is the story of choices that make a difference. Historical novels allow the reader to "go back in time" and gain a new perspective on past events. For teen readers, these novels may also relate to topics and eras they are studying in school. "Choices in Change" involve characters who make decisions influenced by the movements and thinking of their times. "Choices in War" confront much more immediate and threatening changes brought on by national conflict. "Leaders and Defining Events" talk about the high-profile people and happenings that influence great numbers for years to come. All illustrate that although times change, the basic conflicts don't, and the choices involved are often similar to those faced by teen readers. (Note: Historical novels, nonfiction history books, and works with historical settings appear throughout the book. The Topic/Theme line includes the historical designation. The index directs the reader to works related to a particular era or idea.)

Choices in Change

Chevalier, Tracy. **Girl with a Pearl Earring.**
New York: Dutton, 2000. 233p. $21.95. ISBN 0 525 94527 X. [fiction] S/A

Themes/Topics: Vermeer, art, seventeenth-century life, love

Summary/Description

In 1664, Vermeer and his wife hire sixteen-year-old Griet to clean Vermeer's studio and complete general household chores. Griet gives her wages to her mother and blind father. Her younger sister dies from plague. Her older brother, overwhelmed by his tile apprenticeship runs away to sea after impregnating his master's wife. Over the next two years, Griet's beauty attracts the butcher's son, Vermeer, and one of Vermeer's powerful, lecherous clients. Griet manages the pressure of the three men's attentions, the jealousy of Vermeer's wife and servant girl, the hostile tricks of Vermeer's daughter Cornelia, and the business ambitions of Vermeer's mother-in-law. When Vermeer's powerful client demands that Vermeer paint a portrait of himself and Griet, Vermeer protects Griet by agreeing to sell the man a portrait of only Griet. During the sittings, which produce scandalous rumors, Vermeer and Griet control their feelings for each other as she delays responding to the marriage proposal of the butcher's son. Vermeer persuades Griet to wear his wife's pearl earrings for the portrait. Cornelia tells her mother who bursts into rage. Griet feels her only choice is to leave and marry. Ten years later, Griet and her husband have a thriving butcher business and two sons. Vermeer's wife summons her to the house and resentfully gives her the pearl earrings left to Griet by Vermeer. Griet sells them, gives her husband enough money to pay Vermeer's long overdue bill, and secretly keeps the rest. Some material might be considered objectionable and requires a mature audience.

Booktalk

At sixteen, Griet has to support her family. Her father, blinded in a work accident, can't. A fine gentleman and lady hire her to clean the man's art studio and complete a few household chores. In Holland of 1664, Griet is one of the lucky ones—or is she. As she does her job, men begin to look at her. The butcher's son smiles and talks to her. The gentleman who hired her, an artist named Vermeer, finds excuses to spend time with her. Vermeer's wealthy clients trap her in corners.

Women complicate her life more. Catherine, Vermeer's beautiful but unpredictable wife, resents her. Tanneke, the family servant, worries that she will no longer be the family's favorite. Cornelia, the Vermeer's uncontrollable daughter, plots to throw her out of the house. How could this happen to a plain, working-class girl? And how much more will happen to her when she is transformed into the *Girl with a Pearl Earring*? (*Show the picture.*)

Learning Opportunities

1. Using your library's resources, research the life and work of Vermeer. Be sure to identify the paintings mentioned in the novel. (Related Work 5)

2. Leeuwenhoek is an important figure in the novel even though he does not appear often. Using your library's resources, research his contributions to science and his relationship with Vermeer.
3. Griet makes several major decisions in the novel. Identify three of her most important ones. Explain whether you agree or disagree with them and why.
4. Identify one element of the novel's setting that you feel is particularly significant. Explain your choice.
5. Choose one other female. Describe her. Explain how her relationship with Griet affects the plot or reveals Griet's character.

Related Works

1. Duncan, Lois (ed.). **Trapped! Cages of Mind and Body.** New York: Simon & Schuster Books for Young Readers, 1998. 228p. $16.00. ISBN 0 689 81335 X. [fiction] JS Using the cage as a metaphor, the collection explores the many concrete and psychological cages that people build for themselves and how those cages can be destroyed or opened.
2. Jordan, Sherryl. **The Raging Quiet.** New York: Simon & Schuster, 1999. 266p. $17.00. ISBN 0 6899 82140 9. [fiction] JS (See full booktalk in *Booktalks and More*, 2003, pages 15 to 17.) Forced to marry an older and abusive man to save her family, sixteen-year-old Marnie suddenly becomes a widow and grows to love a deaf outcast. This romantic fantasy set in an ancient and magical time deals with how ignorance and prejudice restrict the lives of women and anyone perceived as different.
3. Morris, Neil, et al. (text), and Paola Ravaglia, et al. (illus.). **The Illustrated History of the World: From the Big Bang to the Third Millennium.** New York: Enchanted Lion Books, 2000. 288p. $29.95. ISBN 1 59270 019 5. [reference] MJS This global presentation of world history is organized chronologically and then geographically within time periods. Pages 116 and 117 briefly describe the growing affluent context in which a painter could prosper.
4. Shoup, Barbara. **Vermeer's Daughter.** Zionsville, IN: Guild Press/Emmis Publishing, 2003. 162p. $18.95. ISBN 1 57860 131 2. [fiction] MJ The story of the fictional Carelina Vermeer is aimed at a younger audience and deals with a daughter who relies on her talent rather than looks to achieve her dreams. In this story, the girl with the pearl earring is Carelina's beautiful sister Maria.
5. Smyth, Frances P. (ed.). **Johannes Vermeer.** Washington, D.C.: National Gallery of Art. The Hague: Royal Cabinet of Paintings

Mauritshuis. New Haven, CT: Yale University Press, 1996. 229p.
$42.77. ISBN 0 300 06558 2. [reference] This volume contains two-
thirds of Vermeer's works. "Girl with a Pearl Earring," with explanation, appears on page 167.

ඏ

Cushman, Karen. Rodzina.

New York: Clarion Books, 2003. 215p. $16.00. ISBN 0 618 13351 8. [fiction] MJ

Themes/Topics: nineteenth century, orphans, orphan train,
friendship, family, prejudice, women's rights

Summary/Description

Twelve-year-old Rodzina Clara Jadwiga Anastazya Brodski boards
the orphan train in Chicago. Because Rodzina is the oldest orphan
and big for her age, Doctor Wellington, the cold, stiff supervisor,
directs Rodzina to care for the other children while the doctor cares
for the babies. By Wyoming, only four orphans remain: the unruly
siblings, Sammy and Joe, who are really brother and sister; seven-year-
old Lacey, who tells any lookers that she is slow; and Rodzina, who
managed to escape two abusive adoption situations. Mr. Szprot, the
placing out agent for the Association of Aid Societies, will return these
children to a Chicago workhouse. Dr. Wellington, instead, takes them
to Utah, where her friends offer hope of placement. This decision and
the difficulties that follow illustrate Dr. Wellington's compassion. Two
families in Utah adopt Sammy, Joe, and Lacey. Dr. Wellington takes
Rodzina to a California school to train as a domestic. Rodzina learns
that Dr. Wellington took the orphan transport job because Chicago
blocks women from practicing medicine. She seeks a practice in
California. Rodzina, in spite of their personality conflicts, persuades
Dr. Wellington to adopt her. The doctor will start a practice in Berkeley
where Rodzina will attend high school. A "Pronunciation Guide" lists
the pronunciations and definitions for Polish words. The "Author's
Note" explains several "placing out" agencies including the New York
Children's Aid Society.

Booktalk

Rodzina Clara Jadwiga Anastazya Brodski isn't the most appealing
orphan in the world. She is big for twelve, she makes sour faces, she
thinks about food all the time and looks it, and she likes to give people

a hard time. Living on the streets taught her to defend herself, but now she has been caught—captured, by do gooders. They put Rodzina, with a ragged bunch of other orphans, on a train headed West. Along the way, the train stops to see who will adopt the passengers. The word on the streets is that some Westerners are looking for slave labor. Rodzina, big and strong, is a good candidate for that. She's worried, and meeting the trip supervisors doesn't ease her mind. Mr. Szprot, the placing out agent for the orphans, constantly chews his cigar and refers to her as Polish girl. Rodzina doesn't know the name of the lady doctor, but calls her "Miss Don't Touch." Who wants to be Rodzina's friend on this doubtful journey? Some seven-year-old orphan who announces to everyone "I'm slow." The world is so different from the loving Polish one that centered on her parents and brothers. Surviving in a new world forces her to discover who *Rodzina*, all alone, really is.

Learning Opportunities

1. Prejudice is a prevailing theme in the novel. List as many instances of prejudice that you can find. Discuss the causes and results.
2. On page 36, Lacey compares Rodzina to a "beautiful tree." Then she briefly explains the reason for her comparison. Choose the plant to which you might compare yourself, a friend, or a family member. Explain your comparison.
3. Throughout the novel, Rodzina reflects on her life before becoming an orphan. Explain how her background helps her.
4. *Hank's Story* also focuses on the Orphan Train. After reading both books, discuss the similarities and differences.
5. The doctor is a very important character in the novel. Explain why.
6. In the "Author's Note" Cushman elaborates on the "placing out" plans for orphans in more that just the American West. Using the list of sources at the end of the book and Cushman's citing of other placing out programs, learn more about one of the programs. Share the information with the group.

Related Works

1. Buchanan, Jane. **Hank's Story.** New York: Farrar, Straus and Giroux, 2001. 136p. $16.00. ISBN 0 374 32836 6. [fiction] MJ (See full booktalk in *Booktalks and More*, 2003, pages 148 to 150.) Twelve-year-old Hank Donohue, an orphan placed with an abusive family through the Orphan Train program, finds a good home with the most eccentric woman in the town.

2. Giff, Patricia Reilly. **All the Way Home.** New York: Dell Yearling, 2001. 169p. $5.99pa. ISBN 0 440 41182 3. [fiction] MJ Eleven-year-old Mariel, an orphan and polio victim, fantasizes about her real mother, journeys to find her, and realizes how much she loves the woman who adopted her. The story takes place in the 1940s.
3. Kirkpatrick, Katherine. **Voyage of the Continental.** (See full booktalk in "Mystery/Suspense"/"History/Period," pages 147 to 149.) Beginning in March 1865, this historical mystery traces the journey of orphaned seventeen-year-old Emeline from her mill job in Lowell, Massachusetts, to her decision to become a Mercer Girl, and eventual marriage in Seattle, Washington. After Rodzina meets a mail order bride on the train, she decides that taking her chances in marriage might be better than going into domestic service.
4. Wadsworth, Ginger. **Words West: Voices of Young Pioneers.** (See full booktalk in "Adventure/Survival"/"Land," pages 104 to 106.) Fourteen chapters use the words of children and young adults to describe the opening of the West, preparations for leaving home, the dangerous travel conditions, work, entertainment, and the fulfillment of the promise. In Chapter 6 of *Rodzina,* the main character reflects on the graves and abandoned wagons of these Western travelers.
5. Warren, Andrea. **We Rode the Orphan Trains.** Boston, MA: Houghton Mifflin Company, 2001. 132p. $18.00. ISBN 0 618 11712 1. [nonfiction] MJS These true stories of children who rode the Orphan Trains begins with information about Charles Loring Brace, the movement's founder, and Clara Comstock, one of the agents who supervised the children. The seven adults interviewed recall the good and bad experiences of their lives. Warren provides sources for additional information.

ぐを

Donnelly, Jennifer. A Northern Light.

New York: Harcourt, Inc., 2003. 389p. $17.00. ISBN 0 15 216705 6. [fiction] JS

Themes and Topics: independence,
love, family, responsibility, women's rights

Summary/Description

Two experiences of sixteen-year-old Mathilda Gokey, caring for her family and working at the Glenmore Hotel, blend into a coming of age story set in the early twentieth century. After her mother's death and her older brother's departure, an academically talented Mattie faces the drudgery of caring for her three younger sisters and helping her father maintain their farm. Her equally talented friend, Weaver, and their controversial teacher encourage her to go to college. Working at the Glenmore Hotel, Mattie can finance her dream, but a handsome local boy begins to court her, her dying mother makes her promise to care for the family, and her father discourages her further education. Her hotel job pulls her into a young woman's murder. Before drowning, the woman gives Mattie a packet of letters to destroy. Mattie reads them and realizes the young man accompanying the girl killed her. Her discovery makes her question her own suitor and promises made to the dead. She concludes that the boy wants her farmland. Knowing that the murder victim's last request will free a murderer, she sends the letters to the authorities. When Weaver's home is destroyed and his college money stolen, he decides to stay and take care of his mother. Mattie realizes how terrible wasting either his or her own talent would be. She uses her summer wages to buy a mule for her father, provide Weaver's mother with a home, and give both her and Weaver a start in New York. An "Author's Note" explains the historical background. Subject matter, language, and extensive literary allusions require a mature, experienced reader.

Booktalk

In 1906, sixteen-year-old Mattie Gorkey lives in the North Woods, a playground for rich New Yorkers. Mattie loves words. Everyday she learns a new one, but she can never seem to find just the right ones to describe her dark and muddled life. Her mother is dead. Her older brother just walked away one day. She works from morning to night taking care of her sisters. She hopes to be the first one in her family to earn a high school diploma, and her teacher talks about her even going to college. But now the handsomest boy in the county wants to marry her, a girl so plain that she never thought he knew she existed. How can words truthfully describe all these sorrows, opportunities, and conflicts?

The words come from Grace Brown, a tourist who meets Mattie one day and is dead the next. She gives Mattie letters, letters that Mattie promises to destroy. But Mattie loves words, especially such strong and mysterious ones, and as she reads the letters and slowly deciphers their meaning, she realizes they might be A Northern Light she so desperately needs in her own life.

Learning Opportunities

1. For one week, learn and apply one new word per day. Keep a word diary in which you define each word, record how you use it,

and how others react. At the end of the week, create a word that describes your feelings or situation. Explain the word's construction and application.

2. Like Mattie and Weaver, set up a series of word duels with a friend. Keep a running score.

3. Donnelly uses time in an unusual way. After reading the book, describe her use of time and how it affected her story.

4. Each character contributes to Mattie's final decision. List each character and his or her influence. Share your reactions with other readers.

5. Do you agree with Mattie's decision to leave? Consider her promise to her dying mother.

6. If you are unfamiliar with the Adirondacks, research their history and geography. Share your information with others who have read *A Northern Light* or who are interested in reading it. Discuss how the setting affects the story.

7. Mattie wonders about how she can combine her literary and personal lives. She mentions several women authors. Using your library's resources, research the personal and professional lives of one of these women. Share your information with the group.

8. Choose one event from the novel. Describe it from the point of view of one of the male characters. Share your description with others in the group. Discuss the perceptions and questions that your description generates.

Related Works

1. Fradin, Dennis Brindell, and Judith Bloom Fradin. **Ida B. Wells: Mother of the Civil Rights Movement.** New York: Clarion Books, 2000. 178p $18.00. ISBN 0 395 89898 6. [nonfiction]. MJS (See full booktalk in *Booktalks and More,* 2003, pages 249 and 252.) Born a slave, Ida B. Wells maintained her status as a political activist for African-Americans and women all of her life and campaigned extensively against lynching.

2. Holt, Kimberly Willis. **Keeper of the Night.** (See full booktalk in "Multiple Cultures"/"World Cultures," pages 278 to 280.) A young girl feels responsible for her family after her mother's suicide and her distant father's reaction to the family.

3. Holubitsky, Katherine. **Alone at Ninety Foot.** Victoria, BC: Orca Book Publishers, 1999. 169p. $5.95pa. ISBN 1 55143 129 7. [fiction] MJ (See full booktalk in *Booktalks and More,* 2003, pages 201 to 203.) A young girl struggles to move on with her life after her mother's suicide.

4. Rinaldi, Ann. **Mine Eyes Have Seen.** New York: Scholastic Press, 1998. 275p. $16.95. ISBN 0 590 54318 0. [fiction] MJS (See full booktalk in *Booktalks Plus*, 2001, pages 243 to 245.) Annie Brown, John Brown's scholarly and reflective fifteen-year-old daughter, finds herself relegated to the housework and telling the story of her father's raid on Harper's Ferry. Ironically, John Brown the abolitionist never fully valued or accurately perceived any of his daughters.
5. Wharton, Edith. **Summer.** New York: Signet Classic, 1993. 196p. $4.95pa. ISBN 0 451 52566 3. [fiction] S/A Eighteen-year-old Charity Royall wants to leave the small town of North Dormer. She never improves herself but pours her hopes into a romantic relationship with a visiting architect who leaves her for a woman of his own social class.

Griffin, Adele. Hannah, Divided.
New York: Hyperion/Disney Press, 2002. 208p. $15.99.
ISBN 0 7868 0879 9. [fiction] MJ

Themes/Topics: The Great Depression, learning disability, education, city versus country life, friendship

Summary/Description

When social climber, Mrs. Sweet, comes to thirteen-year-old, illiterate Hannah Bennett's one-room school, she discovers Hannah's unusual math talent and offers her a chance to compete for a scholarship to an elite Philadelphia school. Against most of her family's wishes but with her grandfather's support, Hannah goes to Philadelphia and bonds with other scholarship students sponsored and shown off by Mrs. Sweet. Joe Elway, gifted with dramatic talent and a photographic memory, helps her learn to read by using newspaper accounts of Baby Face Nelson and teaches her how to make her way in the city. Hannah returns home when her grandfather dies. Doubting that she will ever fit with the snobbish students in her school, she tries to stay home, but misses the academic challenge. Her brother, an itinerant worker, encourages her to follow her own dream. She goes back to school, decides to take the scholarship test, realizes that she cannot pass it, and resolves to overcome her learning problems so that she can try again. Set in the Depression, the story emphasizes how people dealing with tough personal problems in tough times still reach out to help others.

Booktalk

Thirteen-year-old Hannah Bennett loves numbers. She can add them, divide them, count them, and come up with answers faster than anybody, even her teacher. But what most people know about Hannah is that she can't read, sit still, or think before she opens her mouth. So when Mrs. Sweet drives up to Hannah's one-room schoolhouse in a "banana yellow Packard" and has a big pile of money to give away, nobody antici-pates that the entire sum will go to Hannah, or that Hannah will go to a fancy school in Philadelphia. Mom and Dad don't want her to go. Her older brother doesn't think it's fair. But it happens, and suddenly Hannah is in a world that she never knew existed—fancy parties with written invitations, too much meat to eat, private tutors, and snobs. And if all that isn't confusing enough, she has to live across the hall from some tough talking kid named Joe Elway who is determined to beat her out of the scholarship. Should she go back to the farm and the people she loves, or take on a city where contacts replace friends and where agencies instead of neighbors take care of people? Hannah, confused—*Hannah, Divided* is trying to figure it all out.

Learning Opportunities

1. Hannah mentions several film stars. Research these stars and the movies they made. Share your information and any pictures that you find with the group. Then discuss what these idols tell about Hannah and her dreams.
2. Baby Face Nelson and other Robin Hood type gangsters of the time period fascinate Joe Elway. Research the crime waves of the thirties and the public's attitudes toward them. Share the information with the group.
3. Technology plays a big part in the story. Note all the technology mentioned, its place in the story, and the change it invites.
4. Choose one technological advance in the novel. Research its devel-opment and its effect on society.
5. Hannah's grandfather and Hepp, her oldest brother, play important roles in the novel although they appear briefly. Discuss the function of each.
6. The opening chapter presents a detailed picture of Mrs. Sweet. Examine the techniques Griffin uses to build the picture. Using the chapter as a model, choose a person and write a character sketch.
7. *Hannah, Divided* presents a picture of the Depression in the city and country. Research the period. Share the information with the group. Discuss how the time period affects the story.

Related Works

1. Denenberg, Barry. **Mirror, Mirror on the Wall: The Diary of Bess Brennan.** New York: Scholastic Inc., 2002. 144p. (Dear America.) $10.95. ISBN 0 439 19446 6. [fiction] MJ Blinded in a sledding accident, a mirror twin attends the Perkins School for the Blind. Like *Hannah, Divided* she faces this problem in the Depression.
2. Hesse, Karen. **Out of the Dust.** New York: Scholastic, 1997. 227p. $4.99. ISBN 0 590 37125 8. [fiction] MJS (See full booktalk in *Booktalks Plus*, 2001 on pages 30 to 32.) In a series of poems, fourteen-year-old Billie Joe tells about her personal struggle within the context of the Oklahoma Dust Bowl.
3. Hunt, Irene. **No Promises in the Wind.** New York: Berkley Publishing Group, 1986. 224p. $4.99pa. ISBN 0 425 09969 5. [fiction] MJS A brother and friend leave home to find work during the Depression. Their travels bring graphic and somber experiences.
4. Janke, Katelan, **Survival in the Storm: The Dust Bowl Diary of Grace Edwards.** New York: Scholastic Inc., 2002. 192p. (Dear America.) ISBN 0 439 21599 4. [fiction] MJ Written by the fifteen-year-old winner of the 1998 Arrow Book Club/Dear America Student Writing Contest, this diary records the struggles of a Depression family in the Texas panhandle.
5. Ryan, Pam Muñoz. **Esperanza Rising.** New York: Scholastic Press, 2000. 272p. $15.95. ISBN 0 439 12041 1. [fiction] MJS (See full booktalk in *Booktalks and More*, 2003 pages 42 to 44.) Uprooted from an elite and privileged life during the Depression, a young Mexican girl discovers that love and loyalty are more important than status.

ꗨꗠ

Lowry, Lois. The Silent Boy.
Boston, MA: Walter Lorraine Books/Houghton Mifflin Company,
2003. 178p. $15.00. ISBN 0 618 28231 9. [fiction] MJS

Themes/Topics: attitudes toward mentally challenged, early twentieth-century life, family history

Summary/Description

In 1987, a great grandmother and retired doctor recalls her childhood relationship with a mentally challenged farm boy. When Katy

Thatcher is eight, Peggy Stoltz, the new hired girl comes to live with the family. Her thirteen-year-old brother, Jacob Stoltz, is considered "touched" because he is slow to learn and mute. Peggy's sister Nell, is the hired girl for the Bishops, the Thatcher's next-door neighbors. Katy accompanies her doctor father on his rounds, and through Peggy's stories, becomes acquainted with Jacob. Jacob trusts her and comes to the barn to be near the family horses and Katy. After Katy's baby sister is born, Nell has a baby she doesn't want by the oldest Bishop boy. Jacob brings it to the Thatcher nursery, but the baby dies from exposure on the trip. The townspeople think that Jacob killed the infant, but Katy knows that Jacob saw the baby as a lamb rejected by its natural mother and wanted to put it with Mrs. Thatcher, a good mother. Jacob is placed in the local asylum. Old pictures introduce and set the tone for each chapter.

Booktalk

In 1987, Katy Thatcher is a great grandmother, and there is a story in her life that she must tell. When she was eight years old, a hired girl came to stay with the Thatchers. The hired girl had a brother named Jacob. Everyone in town thought he was "touched." He wouldn't speak, kept his head down, and wore the same old heavy dark cap no matter what the weather. Some people made fun of him and blamed him for bad things that happened in the town. But Katy liked him. She thought he understood her even though he wouldn't answer her. She was sure that she understood him. But she never anticipated the wrong that could come from something she thought was so good, or why so many lives might depend on her very strange friendship with *The Silent Boy.*

Learning Opportunities

1. Lowry introduces each chapter with pictures that represent the characters and settings of the story. Find an old picture of an interesting person or place. Make up a brief story about it. Share it with the group.
2. At the end of the story, many small details come together. List the details that anticipate the conclusion.
3. Using your library's resources, find pictures, advertisements, music, dances, and theatrical presentations that give a sense of the time period. Share them with the group in either a presentation or in a bulletin board display.

4. In Chapter 7, Katy talks about the devastating fire at the Triangle Shirtwaist Company. Using your library's resources, research the fire and its place in the larger picture of labor conditions at the time. You may wish to start with *Kids on Strike* (Related Work 1).
5. The words "imbecile" and "asylum" reveal some of the attitudes of the time toward mentally and emotionally challenged people. Using your library's resources, research some specific mental health methods or treatments used during the period.

Related Works

1. Bartoletti, Susan Campbell. **Kids on Strike.** Boston, MA: Houghton Mifflin, 1999. 208p. $20.00. ISBN 0 395 88892 1. [nonfiction] MJS In several examples from the early nineteenth to the early twentieth centuries, Bartoletti shows the abuses of child labor and the victims' determination to succeed.
2. Hesse, Karen. **Witness.** New York: Scholastic Press, 2001. 176p. $16.95. ISBN 0 439 27199 1. [fiction] JS (See full booktalk in *Booktalks and More,* 2003, pages 180 to 183.) Acts of kindness defeat the Ku Klux Klan invasion of a small Vermont town.
3. Jordan, Sherryl. **The Raging Quiet.** New York: Simon & Schuster, 1999. 266p. $17.00. ISBN 0 689 82140 9. [fiction] JS (See full booktalk in *Booktalks and More,* 2003, pages 15 to 17.) In this romantic fantasy set in an ancient and magical time, sixteen-year-old Marnie falls in love with Raven, a deaf boy persecuted by the villagers, and faces charges of witchcraft.
4. Lawlor, Laurie. **Helen Keller: Rebellious Spirit.** (See full booktalk in "Issues"/"Social Challenges," pages 40 to 42.) Lawlor describes the Keller household, its post-Reconstruction Southern context, and the period's prevailing prejudice against "defectives." She details Helen Keller's commitment to social causes such as child welfare and fair labor practices.
5. Mikaelsen, Ben. **Petey.** New York: Hyperion Books, 1998. 280p. $15.95. ISBN 0 7868 0426 2. [fiction] MJS (See full booktalk in *Booktalks Plus,* 2001, pages 6 to 8.) A man born with cerebral palsy in 1920 is labeled an idiot and raised in a mental institution, but he still inspires and supports people who walk into his life.
6. Trueman, Terry. **Stuck in Neutral.** New York: HarperCollins, 2000. 114p. $14.95. ISBN 0 06 028519 2. [fiction] JS Severely handicapped Shawn McDaniel, processing information he cannot communicate, realizes that his father may kill him.

Choices in War

✿✿

Bolognese, Don. **The Warhorse.**

New York: Simon & Schuster Books for Young Readers,
2003. 165p. $16.95. ISBN 0 689 85458 7. [fiction] MJ

Themes/Topics: Renaissance, warfare,
armor, leprosy, art, love

Summary/Description

Against his father's wishes, fifteen-year-old Lorenzo Arrighi from the house of master armorers joins his duke in a war against a treacherous count and a mercenary army. A talented artist, Lorenzo draws the plans and pictures of weapons and armor. Delivering weapons to the duke, Lorenzo saves the duke's life. When Lorenzo's father forbids his son from going to war, Lorenzo gives the duke Scoppio, a warhorse Lorenzo raised from a colt. Lorenzo delivers weapons a second time and finds himself in the middle of defeat. He fears that the duke is dead and tries to rescue Scoppio. Driven away from the horse and field, Lorenzo takes shelter in the woods where he discovers a leper family who ask him to save their daughter, Beatrice, from mercenaries. Lorenzo saves her and falls in love with her. Beatrice helps Lorenzo rescue his horse, but refuses his love. She believes that her gift from God is being free of the disease, and that his gift is his art. Both must share their talents with others. The duke decides to adopt Lorenzo as his heir. Seeing Lorenzo's drawings of war's horrors, the duke releases Lorenzo from battlefield obligations. Lorenzo becomes a monk who paints pictures of the Virgin Mary with Beatrice's face. They reunite just before Beatrice dies. The "Author's Note" explains the story's relationship to history. "About the Art" explains the book's many weapon and character illustrations.

Booktalk

Ask members of the group what they know about the Renaissance. Briefly explain the system of city-states and the development of art at the time.

Fifteen-year-old Lorenzo Arrighi lives in Renaissance Italy. He is the son of the master armorer, and like his father, designs and makes weapons for the duke. Lorenzo's profession is valuable and respected, but he wants to be the knight in the thick of battle, not just the craftsman preparing for it. His father says no. Lorenzo cannot join the soldiers.

But Lorenzo is determined to find a way. After all, he knows about the power of swords and the protection of armor. Even more important, he has Scoppio, the strong and beautiful warhorse he raised from a colt. Together, they can help the duke defeat any enemy. When war suddenly comes, Lorenzo and Scoppio are part of it. What he and the beautiful Scoppio contribute is much different than Lorenzo ever dreamed when he saw himself so clearly riding *The Warhorse*.

Learning Opportunities

1. Chapter 4 depicts the work of the armorer. Read it again. Then write a modern day job description for someone applying for the job.
2. Discuss why the author used *The Warhorse* as a title for this book?
3. Discuss how the war changes Lorenzo.
4. After reading the epilogue, discuss whether or not you agree with it. If you disagree, write an epilogue of your own.
5. The armorer, like the novel, dealt with the balance between creation and destruction. Discuss how those seemingly conflicting elements worked together.
6. Using your library' research materials, continue to research either a particular weapon or artist of that period. Share your information with the group. Be sure to explain how your specifics support the novel's events.
7. Keep your own sketchbook.

Related Works

1. Barrett, Tracy. **Anna of Byzantium.** New York: Delacorte Press, 1999. 209p. $14.95. ISBN 0 385 32626 2. [fiction] JS (See full book-talk in *Booktalks and More*, 2003, pages 196 to 199.) Once thinking that she would be queen, Anna Comnena, confined to a convent by her brother, becomes a writer and healer.
2. Eastwood, Kay. **The Life of a Knight.** New York: Crabtree Publishing Company, 2004. 32p. (Medieval World.) $8.95pa. ISBN 0 7787 1374 1. [nonfiction] MJ In describing the life of a knight, Eastwood includes brief descriptions of the Middle Ages, the process of becoming a knight, construction of a knight's armor, weapons, heraldry, battle, the crusades, military orders, Samurai of Japan, tournaments, chivalry, home life, famous warriors within the period, and the end of the age.
3. Hilliam, Paul. **Medieval Weapons and Warfare: Armies and Combat in Medieval Times.** New York: Rosen Central, 2004. 64p.

(The Library of the Middle Ages.) $29.95. ISBN 0 8239 3995 2. [nonfiction] MJ With many illustrations, this book tells about knights, the social structure, weapons and armor, going to war, famous wars, and castles.

4. Hunter, Mollie. **The King's Swift Rider.** New York: HarperCollins, 1998. 241p. $16.95. ISBN 0 06 027186 8. [fiction] MJ (See full booktalk in *Booktalks Plus,* 2001, pages 119 to 121.) Sixteen-year-old Martin Crawford uses his wits and skill to rescue a man he discovers to be Robert the Bruce and serves him as a spy.

5. Morris, Neil, et al. (text), and Paola Ravaglia, et al. (illus.). **The Illustrated History of the World: From the Big Bang to the Third Millennium.** New York: Enchanted Lion Books, 2004. 288p. $29.95. ISBN 1 59270 019 5. [nonfiction] MJS This is a global presentation of world history organized chronologically and then geographically within time periods. Explanations and illustrations relevant to the Renaissance appear on pages 106 and 107.

ᘓᘔ

Hobbs, Valerie. **Sonny's War.**
New York: Farrar, Straus and Giroux/Frances Foster Books,
2002. 215p. $16.00. ISBN 0 374 37136 9. [fiction] JS

Themes/Topics: Vietnam War, women's liberation,
grief, drug addiction, family, love

Summary/Description

Fourteen-year-old Cory lives in a small California town in 1967. Her father dies. Her older brother Sonny goes to Vietnam, and she falls in love with her pacifist social studies teacher. Cory tries to help her mother keep their restaurant, stay loyal to her brother and the war he fights, and join the debate team as well as the peace protest to get her social studies teacher's attention. At a weekend peace rally, she witnesses the teacher destroying a recruiting office, and discovers that he comes from a wealthy protective family. He lies to Cory about his involvement.

A bitter Sony returns from Vietnam with a leg wound, and a drug habit. Challenged by the town celebrity who builds his "hero" reputation on reckless car races, Sonny causes an accident that hospitalizes the other teenager with multiple injuries. Cory's mother learns to cook, keeps the restaurant alive, and attracts a boyfriend. The family's world completely changes. Cory cannot distinguish good and evil. Sonny sells his car and goes to Canada, and their mother remains independent and unmarried in spite of the boyfriend's constant attention.

Booktalk

Fourteen-year-old Cory lives with her mother, dad, and brother in a small California town where street racing is the central event. They've lived there for about a year and run a restaurant. It's 1967, and things are changing—Big Time.

Cory's dad goes to the hospital with a lingering cold and dies.

Sonny, Cory's older brother, goes to Vietnam. His army money will pay for his dad's funeral if the army doesn't pay for his first.

Cory's mother decides to run the restaurant, but she can't cook. She gets a new boyfriend, but doesn't think marriage is such a great idea anymore.

And Cory is left alone—with a whole lot of grief and no one to share it.

Then a new social studies teacher shows up—Lawrence. He is magic. Cory is in love, but Lawrence is against the war—the war Cory's brother is fighting. Should she listen to this wonderful, sympathetic man who tells her that American soldiers kill innocent people everyday? With his help she feels different—strong and determined. With him she thinks she could build a whole new life. But then she learns what *Sonny's War* is really all about.

Learning Opportunities

1. The title *Sonny's War* can mean several things. Two major ones are the Vietnam War and Sonny's belief that his father is not proud of him. Discuss how those two themes are developed as well as additional interpretations of the title.
2. After discussing the title in Learning Opportunity 1, write a poem with the title *Sonny's War.*
3. Jason is an important character in the novel. Discuss why.
4. The changing role of women is central in the story. Discuss what the changes in Cory and Cory's mother reveal about the time period. Be sure to include the scene in which Cory and her mother discover they have dressed alike and the scene in which Cory's mother is applying make up to go away for the weekend.
5. The margin notes in the cookbook reveal the father's deep care and love for his family. Discuss the role that the cookbook plays in the novel. Be sure to include its disappearance and mysterious appearance.

6.   Write an essay about a recipe or food occasion that you associate with another person's care for you.

7.   On pages 126 and 127, Cory listens to the mockingbird and asks, "Did it matter if you didn't have your own song?" How is that question central to the novel? How is it connected to the mother's remark on page 148—"If you went through life wearing somebody else's glasses, she said, you were bound to get a "distorted view of things"?

8.   The sixties saw rapid and radical social change. Choose an aspect of the period such as women's rights, war protest, civil rights, drug use, spiritual belief, or appearance. Using your library's resources, research the topic. Then share and discuss with others in the group who have also chosen topics, the changes that took place, what motivated the changes, and how those changes affected the rest of the century.

Related Works

1.   Crist Evans, Craig. **Amaryliss.** Cambridge, MA: Candlewick Press, 2003. 184p. $15.99. ISBN 0 7636 1863 2. [fiction] MJS With letters from his brother and a narrative describing his own feelings, fifteen-year-old Jimmy tells about his dysfunctional family's home life and about his brother, Frank, fighting in Vietnam and eventually being reported Missing in Action. Some language and situations may be considered controversial.

2.   Johnson, Angela. **Songs of Faith.** New York: Alfred A. Knopf, 1998. 103p. $4.99. ISBN 0 679 89488 8. [fiction] MJ This journey of two dysfunctional families involves Vietnam Veterans' posttraumatic stress.

3.   Murphy, Claire Rudolf. **Free Radical.** (See full booktalk in "Contemporary Life"/"Sports," pages 66 to 68.) As fifteen-year-old Luke concentrates on qualifying for baseball All Stars, his mother declares that she will make restitution for her crimes during the Vietnam War.

4.   White, Ellen Emerson. **The Journal of Patrick Seamus Flaherty.** New York: Scholastic, Inc., 2002. 192p. (Dear America Book/My Name is America.) $10.95. ISBN 0 439 14890 1. [fiction] MJ Patrick gives up football scholarships and enlists in the Marines on his eighteenth birthday. He records horrific war conditions and a series of pointless deaths that change his attitudes about war and life.

5.   White, Ellen Emerson. **Where Have All the Flowers Gone? The Diary of Molly MacKenzie Flaherty.** New York: Scholastic Inc., 2002. 176p. (Dear America.) $10.95. ISBN 0 439 14889 8. [fiction] MJ Molly, questioning and intelligent, is in conflict over the rules

and attitudes of school and church. Her diary starts the day Patrick lands in Vietnam and records her reaction to protestors, politicians, leaders, women's rights, and wounded soldiers.

ҐӠҗ

Kerr, M. E. **Slap Your Sides.**

New York: HarperCollins, 2001. 198p. $15.95. ISBN 0 06 029481 7. [fiction] MJS

Themes/Topics: World War II, Quakers, conscientious objection, propaganda, prejudice

Summary/Description

Beginning in 1942, fourteen-year-old Jubal Shoemaker, who lives in Sweet Creek, Pennsylvania, tells about his Quaker family confronting conscientious objection during World War II. Radio Dan, his lovely daughter Daria, Jubal's Aunt Lizzie, and her Jewish husband see war as the only way to stop Hitler. Popular, dapper, and athletic, Tommy Shoemaker—the seventeen-year-old brother—tries to avoid moral issues. Twenty-year-old Bud Shoemaker—the devout, self-righteous brother—chooses the "conchie" classification of 4E over 1AO that allows noncombatant military service. Jubal watches his parents grow more estranged as his mother supports Bud, and his father sees longtime customers refusing to buy in his store.

Jubal loves Daria. Their relationship is fraught with conflict over Bud's decision. It ends when Daria calls Jubal for help. Jubal, thinking she is being attacked, kills the intruder. The intruder and victim is Abel Hart, who refused to register for the draft, went to prison, suffered excessive abuse, escaped, and was hiding. Jubal—the Quaker Killer—receives a suspended sentence forbidding any contact with Daria. By 1945, Tommy is a pampered and indulged husband; Bud is a ragged, emaciated, worker for the poor; Mr. Shoemaker is dead of a heart attack; Jubal knows that he is free because his victim refused to fight in the war; and Daria and her father take their shallow sentiments to a radio station in Auburn, New York.

Booktalk

Read the poem on page 3 that begins "If you want to win . . ." and ends "Clap your hands!"

That poem comes from Radio Dan's radio show. His lovely daughter Daria sings it. In World War II, everyone in Sweet Creek, Pennsylvania, is cheering for the war effort. But on April 9, 1942, the war becomes much more serious. Seventy-five thousand United States soldiers at Bataan surrender to the Japanese. Radio Dan decides that *Slap Your Sides* is more appropriate now. He'll save "clap you hands" for when the soldiers, sailors, and marines return safe and triumphant.

Some people in Sweet Creek aren't clapping hands or slapping sides. Fourteen-year-old Jubal Shoemaker and his family are Quakers. They don't believe in war—period. When Jubal's older brother Bud decides to be a conscientious objector, signs like "Your Son is Yellow" and "Bud Yellowbelly" appear on the family store windows. Customers disappear. Friends become enemies. Should the Shoemakers join the effort to destroy the monster Hitler—a man already responsible for millions of deaths? Or should they follow their hearts and "Mind the Light" according to their Quaker heritage? Jubal doesn't know. He may never know, but the world isn't waiting for him to decide. It is going to force him to make up his mind—one confrontation at a time.

Learning Opportunities

1. Using your library's resources, research the draft and the fighting classifications used in World War II. Share the information with the group.
2. Research the definition of a conscientious objector. Distinguish a conscientious objector from someone who flees a compulsory draft.
3. Find examples of World War II propaganda that glorified and drew sympathy for the American soldier. Share the example with the group.
4. Cite the instances of prejudice in the novel. Discuss how they are shocking and ironic.
5. Why does Kerr create Abel Hart? What does he represent?
6. Radio Dan's importance is related to his radio program. Read each radio broadcast aloud. Discuss what it reveals about Dan, Daria, the audience, and the time period.
7. Jubal sees two very different role models in his brothers Bud and Tommy. Discuss the qualities of each brother and how each deals with the consequences of his decisions.
8. Each male character is connected to a female character. Discuss each relationship and the woman's role in the relationship.
9. By the end of the novel, how has Jubal changed?

Related Works

1. Hughes, Dean. **Soldier Boys.** New York: Atheneum Publishers, 2001. 162p. $16.00. ISBN 0 689 81748 7. [fiction] MJS (See full

booktalk in *Booktalks and More,* 2003, pages 51 to 54.) In World War II, teenagers Dieter Hedrick, a decorated member of Hitler's Youth, and Spencer Morgan, an American Mormon, want to prove their manhood by fighting.

2. Philip, Neil (ed.), and Michael McCurdy (illus.). **War and the Pity of War.** New York: Clarion Books, 1998. 96p. $20.00. ISBN 0 395 84982 9. [poetry] JS (See full booktalk in *Booktalks Plus,* 2001, pages 44 to 46.) The universal problem of war is presented through the eyes of poets.

3. Remarque, Erich Maria. **All Quiet on the Western Front.** New York: Fawcett Crest, 1975. 296p. $4.95pa. ISBN 0 449 21394 3. [fiction] S/A A young German soldier, pressured to go to war and disillusioned by what he sees, tells this anti-war story, set in World War I and first published in 1928.

4. Tunnell, Michael O. **Brothers in Valor: A Story of Resistance.** New York: Holiday House, 2001. 260p. $16.95. ISBN 0 8234 1541 4. [fiction] JS Based on fact, this novel describes the efforts of a resistance group organized by Mormon teenagers within Germany.

5. Williams, Jean Kinney. **The Quakers.** Danbury, CT: Franklin Watts, 1998. 110p. $22.00. ISBN 0 531 11377 9. [nonfiction] MJS (See full booktalk in *Booktalks Plus,* 2001, pages 248 to 249.) This explanation of The Children of the Light includes their origins, development, service, relationship to U.S. history, and modern form.

🐏🐏

Park, Linda Sue. **When My Name Was Keoko: A Novel of Korea in World War II.**

New York: Clarion Books, 2002. 199p. $16.00. ISBN 0 618 13335 6. [fiction] JS

Themes/Topics: Korea, World War II, Japanese occupation, family, Kamikaze, war resistance, national identity

Summary/Description

Told through the eyes of Sun hee and her older brother Tae yul, the story, spanning five years, recounts the Korean experience of Japanese occupation during World War II. Sun hee's opening chapter sets the Japanese agenda, in operation since 1910, for wiping out all Korean culture—language, customs, leadership, and now names. Sun hee is close to her father, a teacher and scholar who resents the Japanese but does little against them. Tae yul identifies with his uncle, a local printer who works for the resistance. As the war escalates, the uncle flees, and

Tae yul escapes interrogation by joining the Japanese army. To prove Korean bravery, he volunteers for the Kamikaze. By the end of the novel, Sun hee learns that her father and her old, feeble neighbor worked for the resistance, that bad weather prevented her brother from identifying his target and saved his life, and that her uncle is safe but stranded in North Korea. The book ends with brother and sister dedicated to restoring the Korean culture.

Booktalk

Sun hee lives in Korea, but this is 1940, and she is living a Japanese life. Japan began to set the rules for her country in 1910. They told the Koreans how to dress, talk, and act. Now they want everything to have Japanese names—even the people. She will no longer be Su hee, "girl of brightness" to her family, but the Japanese Keoko. Soon the Japanese will conquer America. If they are powerful enough to take over such a big country, how can one small girl or one small family refuse to make one more small concession? Her father doesn't think they can refuse. Her uncle and brother do. They say that if small steps can conquer the Koreans then small steps can conquer the Japanese as well. Should Sun hee take these revolutionary steps? How will she know the right ones? While she ponders, her family moves in directions Sun hee does not understand. Anger, secrecy, and fear surround her. Their small steps build to running away and battle. She must be brave, and she must think Korean, even though her name is Keoko.

Learning Opportunities

1. *When My Name Was Keoko* deals with only five years of Korean history. Continue to research Korean history in the twentieth century. In your research, try to explain why Korea is so important to other countries. You may wish to begin with the "Bibliography" provided at the end of the novel, the entries concerning Korea in *The Illustrated History of the World: From the Big Bang to the Third Millennium* (Related Work 3), or with *I Remember Korea: Veterans Tell Their Stories of the Korean War, 1950–53* (Related Work 2).

2. Research Japanese and Korean customs. Construct a visual display that illustrates the differences between Japanese and Korean customs.

3. Sun hee and Tae yul see the same events quite differently. Choose an event either one describes. React to it from the point of view of the uncle, the father, or the mother.

4. Describe an event in your own family from your point of view and the point of view of another family member.
5. Continue to research the Kamikaze effort in World War II. Compare it to suicide missions used in war or terrorism.

Related Works

1. Cain, Timothy. **The Book of Rule: How the World is Governed.** New York: DK Publishing, 2004. 320p. $30.00. ISBN 0 7894 9354 3. [reference] MJS Including 193 countries, this source explains how the world is governed in both theory and practice. The entries include some historical background. North Korea appears on page 302. South Korea appears on 233. Japan appears on pages 66 and 67.
2. Granfield, Linda. **I Remember Korea: Veterans Tell Their Stories of the Korean War, 1950–53.** New York: Clarion Books, 2003. 136p. $16.00. ISBN 0 618 17740 X. [nonfiction] JS Through the collected stories of thirty-two men and women who were part of the U.S. and Canadian forces in Korea, Granfield communicates the personal conflicts and tragedies in historical and geographical contexts. The essay, "The Kids of the Korean War," pages 87 to 90, alludes to the resilience and self-discipline of Korean children who have experienced strife and occupation all of their lives.
3. Morris, Neil et al.(text), and Paola Ravaglia et al. (illus.). **The Illustrated History of the World: From the Big Bang to the Third Millennium.** New York: Enchanted Lion Books, 2000. 288p. $29.95. ISBN 1 59270 019 5. [reference] MJS Organized chronologically and then geographically, this user-friendly reference highlights events of one country in relation to the events occurring at the same time in other parts of the world.
4. Nam, Vickie. **Yell-Oh Girls!** New York: HarperCollins/Quill, 2001. 294p. $13.00pa. ISBN 0 06 095944 4. [nonfiction] JS (See full booktalk in *Booktalks and More,* 2003, pages 262 to 264.) Asian American girls talk about their struggle to find their identities while balancing two very different cultures.
5. Talarigo, Jeff. **The Pearl Diver.** New York: Doubleday, 2004. 240p. $18.95. ISBN 0 385 51051 9. [fiction] S/A Shortly after Hiroshima, a young Japanese pearl diver discovers that she has leprosy, a disease that was perceived during the war as a block to expansionism. She is sent to an island for lepers, declared dead to her family, and given a new name. One of the other island citizens is a Korean, who came to Japan as a war slave. The content requires mature readers.

cᵌ ꞔᵌ

Patneaude, David. **Thin Wood Walls.**

Boston, MA: Houghton Mifflin, 2004. 240p. $16.00. ISBN 0 618 34290 7. [fiction]
MJS

Themes/Topics: World War II, Japanese Internment, prejudice, family, friendship, coming of age

Summary/Description

In three parts, Joe Hanada describes how World War II and the Japanese Internment impact his family. Part 1 describes the stable Hanada family and their community life shattered by Pearl Harbor. Anti-Japanese prejudice surfaces, the FBI arrests Mr. Hanada, and Roosevelt signs the relocation order. Part 2 tells about the fatherless Hanada family adjusting to Tule Lake: the difficult living conditions, small kindnesses, prejudices, the loyalty oath requirement, and the growing desire of young Japanese men to prove their allegiance to the United States. Mike, Joe's older brother, enlists. Part 3 details the growing discontent in the camp, the father's return, Mike's heroic death, and the Hanada family's decision that life in Canada will be easier than in the United States.

Booktalk

Ask how many people heard about the Japanese evacuation and relocation in World War II. Allow anyone who knows about it to share what they know.

Joe Hanada is eleven years old. He lives with his older brother, mother, father, and grandmother in California. The Hanadas like America even though their parents and grandparents can never be citizens here, even though they can never own land. When the Japanese attack Pearl Harbor, some of their neighbors begin to fear them, yell insults, spit on them. But the Hanadas are strong. They know that their patience will help them weather this storm. The government isn't so patient. The FBI arrests Joe's father. President Roosevelt signs an order that will take the rest of the family from their homes and place them in camps, concentration camps located in the desert. Like all other Japanese Americans, they must sell all they own, for almost nothing. They must leave friends, schools, and churches and build a whole new world wherever they land. They do, and in the years spent there, they discover

Behind thin wood walls,
Freedoms die, pasts dim, but dreams—
Dreams still ramble free! (See the opening of Part 3.)

Learning Opportunities

1. Using your library's resources research the Japanese Relocation. Share your information with the group. You might wish to start by reading *Japanese American Internment* (Related Work 4).

2. Using your library's resources, research the 442nd Regiment. Share your information with the group. You might wish to start by reading *Fighting for Honor: Japanese Americans and World War II.* (Related Work 2).

3. Discuss the qualities that allowed the Hanada family to endure their treatment and life in the camps. Be sure to consider the role of patience.

4. Two pieces of advice play central roles in the novel: "To lose is to win." and "Fear and ignorance give birth to absurdity." Discuss how these apply to the novel and the political situation. In your discussion be sure to consider why German Americans were not placed in camps.

5. Discuss the character of the grandmother and what she adds to the novel.

6. Compare the Japanese camps and the German concentration camps. You might wish to read *The Holocaust Camps* (Related Work 1).

7. After reading the definition of Haiku on page 100 of *How to Write Poetry* (Related Work 6), read the poems written by Joe and Mike. Discuss the role the poems played in relationships throughout the novel. Then attempt to write a haiku of your own.

Related Works

1. Byers, Ann. **The Holocaust Camps.** Berkeley Heights, NJ: Enslow Publishers, Inc., 1998. 128p. (The Holocaust Remembered Series.) $20.95. ISBN 0 89490 995 9. [nonfiction] MJS Beyers explains how the German camps, which began as prison and labor camps with torture and high death rates, ended as extermination camps.

2. Cooper, Michael L. **Fighting for Honor: Japanese Americans and World War II.** New York: Clarion Books, 2000. 118p. $16.00. ISBN 0 395 91375 6. [nonfiction] MJS Cooper explains the history of discrimination and war hysteria that created the camps, the horrific battles in which Japanese-American soldiers proved their bravery and patriotism, and the problems in leaving the relocation camps and rebuilding lives in post-war America.

3. Denenberg, Barry. **The Journal of Ben Uchida: Citizen 13559, Mirror Lake Internment Camp, California, 1942.** New York: Scholastic, Inc., 1999. 157p. (A Dear America Book/My Name is

America.) $10.95. 157p. ISBN 0 590 48531 8. [fiction] MJ Twelve-year-old Ben Uchida, in a very American voice, records his World War II experiences as a Japanese-American living in Mirror Lake, an Internment Camp. The journal novel includes photographs by Toyo Miyatake, who also experienced internment.

4. Fremon. David K. **Japanese-American Internment in American History.** Berkeley Heights, NJ: Enslow Publishers, Inc., 1996. 128p. (In American History.) $20.95. ISBN 0 89490 767 0. [nonfiction] MJS This account stresses the internment camps but mentions the 442nd Regiment.

5. Glasgow, Jacqueline N. "Reconciling Memories of Internment Camp Experiences During WWII in Children's and Young Adult Literature." *The ALAN Review.* (Fall 2002): 41–45. The author illustrates through children's and young adult's literature that knowing personal history and working through memories clarifies one's identity and expands humanitarian sentiment for those with whom the stories are shared.

6. Janeczko, Paul B. **How to Write Poetry.** New York: Scholastic, 1999. 117p. (Scholastic Guides). $12.95. ISBN 0 590 10077 7. [nonfiction] MJS This guide provides step-by- step advice about the poetry writing process, from gathering ideas and words to sharing finished poems.

ॐ॰ॐ

Spinelli, Jerry. Milkweed.
New York: Alfred A. Knopf, 2003. 208p. $15.95. ISBN 0 375 81374 8. [fiction] JS

Themes/Topics: Holocaust, labels, friendship, family, physical and emotional survival

Summary/Description

The approximately eight-year-old narrator, who steals to survive on the streets of Poland, thinks his name is Stopthief. Uri, an older boy, who brings him into a group of street boys, identifies him as a gypsy and eventually names him Misha Pilsudski. When the Germans march into Poland, Uri teaches Misha to be invisible. But Misha befriends Janina, a wealthy Jewish girl about two years younger than he. As her family suffers discrimination and moves to the ghetto, he spends more time with them, steals food for them, and eventually becomes part of their family. Janina begins to steal with Misha. When the "Resettlement" begins, Janina's father tells Misha to take her, leave the ghetto, and hide. Janina refuses and joins her father in the cattle cars, but Uri who is now a jackboot, pulls Misha away from the trains and pretends to kill him by shooting off his ear. Waking up delirious, Misha finds the trains gone. He walks the tracks to join Janina in the ovens, but a farmer enslaves him until the end of the War. Misha returns to street life, eventually travels to the United States, and feels compelled to tell his story everyday. He marries one of his listeners, but, unable to tolerate his emotionally charged behavior, she leaves him within five months. Twenty-five years later, his daughter finds him, introduces him to his granddaughter, and invites him to live with her.

Booktalk

Ask how many people know what a milkweed is. You might want to show a picture or bring in an actual sample.

Most people just kill milkweed or ignore it, but not one man who used to live in Warsaw, Poland. He knows that milkweed carries the angels to heaven.

When this man was a boy, people yelled "Stopthief" at him so many times, he thought that it was his name. He would rather have been something else—a Jew maybe, or one of the German Jackboots who march so proudly into Warsaw's streets. Then he found a friend—Uri. Uri showed him how to get lots of food and how to stay warm at night, but best of all he gave Stopthief a real name, Misha Pilsudski, and a life story. Now he had parents, grandparents, great grandparents, and brothers and sisters. A boy with such a large family would never be alone. Life was good. It got even better when he met Janina, a very rich and lovely Jewish girl who invited him to her sixth birthday party. He saved her beautiful birthday cake from burning up, and when she was not so rich anymore, he began to bring her the food he was so good at stealing. But one day, there was a magnificent parade. The German Jackboots marched proudly into Warsaw. Misha wanted to become one of them. The world had wonderful opportunities and even angels to help him take advantage of them—beautiful angels riding to heaven on the white, gentle *Milkweed*.

Learning Opportunities

1. Read aloud the passage on page 7 that begins "Answer the runt . . ." and ends "A Jew is that." Discuss what it reveals about Warsaw and the speaker. Compare it to the passage from *The Merchant of Venice*, (3.1.47–61) by William Shakespeare that begins "I am a Jew" (Related Work 5).

2. On page 32, Uri makes up a life story for Misha Pilsudski. Why does the story make Misha so happy? Make up a life story for yourself. Then explain why that is the story you would choose.

3.   Spinelli uses several parades in the story. List them. Discuss what each reveals.
4.   In Chapter 24, Misha decides he will not be a Jackboot. Discuss his reason and what it reveals about prejudice and supremacy.
5.   Chapter 13 focuses on the merry-go-round in front of the orphanage. Read the chapter aloud. Then discuss Spinelli's reasons for making it a central image in the book. Compare his use of the merry-go-round with that in "Merry-Go-Round: Colored Child at Carnival" by Langston Hughes (Related Work 1). Discuss how the illustration used in *I, Too, Sing America: Three Centuries of African American Poetry* might apply to both works.
6.   What makes Misha a survivor?
7.   Using your library's resources, research the invasion and occupation of Poland by the Germans during World War II. Share your information with the group.

Related Works

1.   Clinton, Catherine (prose text), and Stephen Alcorn (illus.). **I, Too, Sing America: Three Centuries of African American Poetry.** Boston: Houghton Mifflin, 1998. 128p. $20.00. ISBN 0 395 89599 5. [poetry] MJS (See full booktalk in *Booktalks Plus*, 2001, pages 219 to 221.) This collection includes thirty-six poems by twenty-five African-American poets, and spans three centuries. The poem "Merry Go Round: Colored Child at Carnival" appears on page 82. Like Spinelli, Hughes uses the merry go round as a central image in revealing the cruelties of prejudice.
2.   Morris, Neil et al. (text), and Paola Ravaglia et al. (illus.). **The Illustrated History of the World: From the Big Bang to the Third Millennium.** New York: Enchanted Lion Books, 2004. 288p. $29.95. ISBN 1 59270 019 5. [nonfiction] JS Organized chronologically and then geographically within time periods, this illustrated global history of the world contains informative and motivating sections focused on Hitler: "The Growth of Fascism," pages 226 to 227; "The Build up to War," pages 228 to 229; and "The War in Europe," pages 230 to 231.
3.   Nir, Yehuda. **The Lost Childhood.** New York: Scholastic Press, 2002. 288p. $16.95. ISBN 0 439 16389 7. [fiction] JS After his father is shot dead in a mass execution of Jewish men in Poland, Yehuda, his mother, and sister hide in the open, as Catholics.
4.   Opdyke, Irene Gut, with Jennifer Armstrong. **In My Hands: Memories of a Holocaust Rescuer.** New York: Alfred A. Knopf,

1999. 276p. $18.00. ISBN 0 679 89181 1. [nonfiction] JS (See full booktalk in *Booktalks and More*, 2003, pages 255 to 258.) Opdyke's family life and personal beliefs led her to help and hide Jews persecuted during the German occupation of Poland.

5.   Shakespeare, William, and John Crowther (ed.). **Merchant of Venice.** New York: Spark Notes, 2003. 231p. (No Fear Shakespeare.) $4.95pa. ISBN 1 58663 850 5. [drama] JS In this famous play centering on Shylock, the hated moneylender, Shakespeare, in this passage (*The Merchant of Venice*, 3.1.47–61), poses the question of Shylock's humanity.

Leaders and Defining Events

ය්බ

Adler, David A. **B. Franklin, Printer.**
New York: Holiday House, 2001. 126p. $19.95. ISBN 0 8234 1675 5. [nonfiction] MJS

Themes/Topics: pre-revolutionary and revolutionary times, industry, practical application, founding fathers

Summary/Description

In fifteen chapters, Adler describes Benjamin Franklin's background, education, family, accomplishments, and death. With working-class roots and a desire for religious freedom, Josiah Franklin comes to America. Although he intends for his son to be a minister, Benjamin leaves school at ten and eventually apprentices to his older and abusive brother as a printer. Running away, he secures work and makes his way to England but finds himself alone and jobless after opening his own print shop. Through hard work and ingenuity, he recovers, returns to America, opens a shop in a partnership, marries, and becomes a "First Citizen of Philadelphia." He publishes a flourishing newspaper and *Poor Richard's Almanac,* pursues scientific experiments, shares his inventions, becomes a major voice in the American Revolution and the development of a new government, and serves as an ambassador to France.

A map, "Franklin's Travels," introduces the text. Extensive illustrations, documents, and sample writings give a sense of the times. Chronologies, "Benjamin Franklin, 1706–1790," and "The New World, 1706–1790," put Franklin's life in perspective with his times. Extensive source notes expand on the text. "Recommended Web Sites" and "Selected Bibliography" suggest further sources of information. The index gives easy access to information.

Booktalk

If you have a pocketful of Benjamins, you are probably in good shape financially. Do you know why? Benjamin Franklin is the man on the hundred-dollar bill. But if you have a Benjamin head, a Benjamin Franklin head, you are probably even better off. Why?

Franklin left school when he was ten, apprenticed to his abusive older brother in a print shop, working twelve to fourteen hours a day. Then, he was swindled, lied to, and laughed at. Was he discouraged? If he was, he didn't show it. He managed to own a business, survive some risky electrical experiments (Have you heard the kite story?), invent the Franklin stove and bifocals, organize the first American subscription library, postal system, fire and police departments, and—oh yes—help found the United States. How? By being a man who saw every problem as an opportunity. No matter how popular, rich, and famous he became, Benjamin Franklin remembered where he came from—always proudest to be known as *B. Franklin, Printer.*

Learning Opportunities

1. "About the Title" appears on page v. Read Franklin's epitaph aloud. Discuss how and why he compared himself to a book. Imitating Franklin's style, write a possible epitaph of a worker in another job or profession.
2. Read the first chapter aloud. Discuss the importance and irony of the closing statement by newspaperman Horace Greeley.
3. Adler offers a list of "Recommended Web Sites" and a "Selected Bibliography" for more information. Choose one of the sources. Investigate it and report your findings to the group.
4. On page 47, in the paragraph beginning with the words, "He made a list …" are the thirteen virtues, Franklin attempted to develop. Using the method described in the paragraph, make a list of the virtues that you wish to develop and then record your progress. At the end of three months, write as essay about your progress.
5. In the last source note on page 117, Adler notes that Franklin wanted to revisit earth a hundred years after his death, to see the "improvements and discoveries." Using your library's resources, investigate an improvement or discovery that you feel would have interested or impressed Franklin the most. Explain the discovery and your choice based on what you learned about Franklin.

Related Works

1. Cox, Clinton. **Come All You Brave Soldiers.** New York: Scholastic, 1999. 182p. $15.95. ISBN 0 590 47576 2. [nonfiction] JS (See full booktalk in *Booktalks Plus,* 2001, pages 155 to 157.) Cox describes the contribution that black soldiers made to both sides during the Revolutionary War. Franklin was against slavery, but was unable to bring enough people to his point of view.

2. Fradin, Dennis. **Samuel Adams: The Father of American Independence.** New York: Clarion Books, 1998. 182p. $18.00. ISBN 0 395 82510 5. [nonfiction] MJS (See full booktalk in *Booktalks Plus,* 2001, pages 234 to 236.) This founding father, very different from Franklin, purposely twisted facts and made alliances so that he could justify the break with England.

3. Freedman, Russell. **Give Me Liberty! The Story of the Declaration of Independence.** New York: Holiday House, 2000. 90p. $12.95. ISBN 0 8234 1753 0. [nonfiction] MJS. Freedman includes the thinking, the politics, and the battles that lead to The Declaration of Independence as well as the document's influence on future generations.

4. Meyer, Carolyn. **Mary, Bloody Mary.** New York: Gulliver Books, 1999. 227p. $16.00. ISBN 0 15 201906 5. [fiction] MJ In this historical novel, Mary, daughter of Henry VIII and Catherine of Aragon, recalls the childhood and early adulthood that sealed her loyalty to her mother and the Catholic Church. On page 6 of *B. Franklin, Printer,* Adler alludes to Mary's reign so that he can establish the long, strong Protestant line of the Franklins.

5. Severance, John B. **Thomas Jefferson: Architect of Democracy.** New York: Clarion Books, 1998. 192p. $18.00. ISBN 0 395 84513 0. [nonfiction] MJS (See full booktalk in *Booktalks Plus,* 2001, pages 245 to 247.) In this biography of the founding father thought to be a man of great contradiction, Severance discusses Jefferson's role in the American Revolution and the great trial of writing and revising The Declaration of Independence.

❧

Aronson, Marc. John Winthrop, Oliver Cromwell, and the Land of Promise.

New York: Clarion Books, 2004. 205p. $20.00. ISBN 0 618 18177 6. [nonfiction] JS

Themes/Topics: John Winthrop, Oliver Cromwell, religious tolerance, social equality, political democracy, British and early American history, Puritans, Early Stuarts

Summary/Description

Setting the stage for the clash between the worldly, Catholic tolerant court of Charles I and religious extremists fueled by the Book of Revelations, *The Land of Promise* explains the seventeenth-century social context that produced John Winthrop and Oliver Cromwell. Each man sought an idyllic government. Winthrop wanted to build a New World. Cromwell wanted to reform the old. Each man confronted the issues of conscience versus community, exclusiveness versus social equality. Both faced extreme positions within their groups. Their decisions changed them and the world. Aronson discusses each man's integrity and flaws, emphasizes the difficulty of combining government and religion, and shows how the struggles of Winthrop and Cromwell apply today. "Why This Book" explains the men and the period in world history. "Cast of Characters" groups the significant figures in each group. "Endnotes and Bibliography" presents and explains Aronson's sources. "Timeline" lists relevant events in "England, Scotland, Ireland," "The New World," and "Europe, Asia, India" from 1600 to 1776.

Booktalk

In seventeenth century England, Wm. Prynne, a Protestant lawyer, had his ears cut off by the order of Charles I. Why? Because the Charles's Catholic queen liked to dance. It doesn't make much sense does it? But sense was not a big issue at that time—religion was. Charles and his court were the devil. Men like John Winthrop and Oliver Cromwell were the righteous warriors, gathering their followers and waiting for the second Coming of Christ. They would create perfect kingdoms or kill everyone and everything in the attempt. Armageddon was upon them, and only a holy war could save the true believers. Sound familiar? Read today's headlines. The names and dates are different, but the thinking is much the same. For a whole new view of history, take some time to look through the eyes of *John Winthrop, Oliver Cromwell, and The Land of Promise.*

Learning Opportunities

1. Aronson's "Endnotes and Bibliography" provides extensive explanation of his sources and suggestions for further research. Choose one of the suggested topics. Using the suggested resources and additional resources available in your library, research it and present the information that you find to the group.
2. Re-read "Why This Book" after reading the main text. Also read the first section of the dedication. Then try to state, in your own words, the purpose of Aronson's book.

3. Compare the missions of John Winthrop and William Bradford. You might wish to start by reading *William Bradford: Plymouth's Faithful Pilgrim* (Related Work 6).

4. Compare the missions of John Winthrop, Oliver Cromwell, and Sir Walter Ralegh. You might want to start by reading *Sir Walter Ralegh and the Quest for El Dorado* (Related Work 1).

5. Re-read the "Epilogue." Explain Aronson's ideas in your own words. Then discuss whether or not you agree with what he is saying.

Related Works

1. Aronson, Marc. **Sir Walter Ralegh and the Quest for El Dorado.** New York: Clarion Books, 2000. 222p. $20.00. ISBN 0 395 84827 X. [nonfiction] JS (See full booktalk in *Booktalks and More,* 2003, pages 232 to 235.) Well integrated into the Elizabethan world of drama, materialism, and intrigue, Ralegh, also a supporter of scholarship, focused on gain and glory. He is referred to several times in *John Winthrop, Oliver Cromwell, and The Land of Promise.*

2. Cain, Timothy (ed.). **The Book of Rule: How the World Is Governed.** New York: DK Publishing, Inc., 2004. 320p. $30.00. ISBN 0 7894 9354 3. [reference] MJS. The text examines the governments of the world's 193 countries. Pages 86 to 95 explain the evolution of the United Kingdom into a parliamentary democracy. Pages 204 to 215 explain the system of presidential democracy used in the United States of America.

3. Carmi, Daniella. **Samir and Yonatan.** New York: Arthur A. Levine Books, 2000. 192p. $15.95. ISBN 0 439 13504 4. [fiction] MJ Samir, a Palestinian, and Yonatan, a Jew, bond while in a Jewish hospital. Only in an imaginary world created by Yonatan, do they feel that they can live in peace.

4. Cox, Clinton. **Come All You Brave Soldiers.** New York: Scholastic, 1999. 182p. $15.95. ISBN 0 590 47576 2. [nonfiction] JS (See full booktalk in *Booktalks Plus,* 2001, pages 155 to 157.) This description of the role of slaves in the Revolutionary War illustrates, like Cromwell's fighting force, that those supporting a revolution are sometimes blocked from its benefits.

5. Provost, Anne, and John Nieuwenhuizen (trans.). **In the Shadow of the Ark.** New York: Arthur A. Levine Books, 2004. 368p. $17.95. ISBN 0 439 44234 6. [fiction] S/A In this retelling of Noah and the Ark, Rrattika, Ham's concubine, and her father help to build the Ark and realize they will be left to die. Controversial topics like ethnic cleansing, mercy killing, and homosexuality require a mature

and sophisticated audience also familiar with sustained allusion. It speaks directly to the conflict in the Middle East and the problems of imperfect men directed to build a perfect world.

6. Schmidt, Gary D. **William Bradford: Plymouth's Faithful Pilgrim.** Grand Rapids, MI: Eerdmans Books for Young Readers, 1999. 200p. $18.00. ISBN 0 8028 5151 7. [nonfiction] JS (See full booktalk in *Booktalks and More*, 2003, pages 244 to 246.) William Bradford, with his fellow Separatists, signed the Mayflower Compact and established the basis for democracy in the New World. This is the story of his beliefs and their community.

ᘓᘔ

Freedman, Russell. **The Voice That Challenged a Nation: Marian Anderson and the Struggle for Equal Rights.**
New York: Clarion Books, 2004. 114p. $18.00. ISBN 0 618 15976 2. [nonfiction] MJS

Themes/Topics: civil rights, entertainment, contraltos, African-Americans

Summary/Description

Opening with Anderson's Lincoln Memorial concert on Easter Sunday, April 9, 1939, this autobiography traces the life and talent of a self-effacing artist and champion for civil rights. Growing up in South Philadelphia, Anderson learned about tacit segregation in an integrated community. When her father died suddenly, Marian, her mother and two sisters moved in with Marian's grandparents. Marian left school after eighth grade to earn money through singing and domestic work. The Union Baptist Church financially supported her talent. Rejected by a local music school, Marian received private voice lessons and eventually enrolled in the South Philadelphia High School for Girls where she focused on music. In concert tours, she encountered Jim Crow laws. She eventually won a contest sponsored by the National Music League and studied in Europe to expand her language skills. On her return, she found "a capacity audience," extensive tour requests, and an invitation to the Roosevelt White House. Her talent, skill, and fame, however, did not admit her to Constitution Hall owned by the Daughters of the American Revolution. Eleanor Roosevelt resigned her DAR membership in protest and helped arrange the Lincoln Memorial concert, a defining moment for Anderson's career and civil rights.

The biography includes excellent photographs, relevant documents, extensive "Chapter Notes," an annotated bibliography, a "Selected Discography" of Marian Anderson's recent releases, and an index of significant names and places.

Booktalk

Ask how many people in the audience have ever heard of Marian Anderson? Ask how many people have ever seen the Lincoln Memorial, or pictures of the Lincoln Memorial?

On Easter Sunday, April 9, 1939, an exceptionally talented singer named Marian Anderson and a monument that stands for freedom and equal rights came together. Let me read you an account of that performance.

Read Chapter 1 aloud.

That day, thousands heard *The Voice That Challenged a Nation.* Here is the story behind that voice and its moment in history.

Learning Opportunities

1. The "Selected Discography" lists "Recent Marian Anderson Releases." Listen to the selections from one of those releases. Then write about how those selections affect you. Compare your reaction with that of others in the group.
2. The "Selected Bibliography" provides an extensive list of resources. Choose one of them. Examine it and share the information with the group.
3. Marian Anderson did not intend to be an equal rights activist, but her talent produced situations that demanded social action. Choose one of the women listed in Related Works 2–5. Explain how that woman found her path to equal rights. Share the information that you find with the group.
4. Using your library's resources, continue to research the history of spirituals. You might wish to start with *Slave Spirituals and the Jubilee Singers* (Related Work 1).
5. On page 68, Freedman notes that in her rendition of "America," Marian Anderson uses "To thee we sing" instead of "Of thee I sing." Discuss some of the implications of that choice.

Related Works

1. Cooper, Michael L. **Slave Spirituals and the Jubilee Singers.** New York: Clarion Books, 2001. 86p. $16.00. ISBN 0 395 97829 7.

[nonfiction]MJS Cooper relates the roots and importance of the spirituals as well as the history of the Fisk University Julibee Singers, who helped to save the spiritual tradition.

2. Fradin, Dennis Brindell, and Judith Bloom Fradin. **Fight On! Mary Church Terrell's Battle for Integration.** New York: Clarion Books, 2003. 181p. $17.00. ISBN 0 618 13349 6. [nonfiction] MJS A lifelong friend of Ida B. Wells, Terrell was born in the middle of the Civil War, experienced the pain of her parents' divorce, excellent educational opportunities, and the stings of discrimination.

3. Fradin, Dennis Brindell, and Judith Bloom Fradin. **Ida B. Wells: Mother of the Civil Rights Movement.** New York: Clarion Books, 2000. 178p. $18.00. ISBN 0 395 89898 6. [nonfiction] MJS (See full booktalk in *Booktalks and More*, 2003, pages 249 to 252.) Born a slave in 1862, Ida B. Wells became one of the first African-American investigative reporter and was a lifelong civil rights activist.

4. Freedman, Russell. **Eleanor Roosevelt: A Life of Discovery.** New York: Clarion Books, 1993. $17.95. ISBN 0 89919 862 7. [nonfiction] MJS In this biography, Freedman relates the difficult challenges and victories in Eleanor Roosevelt's personal and professional lives.

5. Lawlor, Laurie. **Helen Keller: Rebellious Spirit.** (See full booktalk in "Issues"/"Social Challenges," pages 40 to 42.) Lawlor emphasizes that Keller is a driving force supporting herself, those around her, and social movements such as child welfare, equal rights, and socialism.

ᏻᏺ

Giblin, James Cross.
The Life and Death of Adolf Hitler.
New York: Clarion Books, 2002. 246p. $21.00. ISBN 0 395 90371. [nonfiction] MJS

Topics/Themes: Post-World War I Germany, World War II, leadership, prejudice, propaganda

Summary/Description

Giblin portrays a disturbed and dedicated individual who, with an exceptional gift for politics and speech making, appealed to the prejudices and fears of the German people after World War I. The book describes Hitler's early life, military service, and involvement in the National Socialist German Worker's Party, prison sentence, and the personal friends who supported him before and during his reign of power. It explains the Reich's successful propaganda machine, the domination of Europe, the reasons Hitler believed he could rule the world, the Final Solution, and his destruction. In the last chapter, Giblin points out that the neo-Nazi movement racism continues Hitler's racism.

Booktalk

Thinking he was too artistically talented to do ordinary work, he persuaded a nation to work for his dream. Isolating himself from fellow soldiers, he inspired soldiers to march to their destruction. Compassionate enough to care for a small dog, he ruthlessly killed millions of his people.

As a detached and rather odd young man, Adolf Hitler was not a candidate for the greeting "Heil, Mein Führer!" but he focused his hate with the right words and surrounded himself with others who relentlessly shared his vision. He became one of the most powerful and destructive men in history. In *The Life and Death of Adolf Hitler,* James Giblin portrays a charismatic and twisted man who dedicates a people to blind superiority and destruction. And Giblin warns us that, in any time, a Hitler can come again.

Learning Opportunities

1. At the end of Chapter 1, "The Most Dangerous Dictator," Giblin lists the questions his book explores. After reading the book, answer them. With the help of your librarian, as well as Giblin's "Source Notes and Bibliography," continue to research one question and present your conclusions to the group.
2. Identify other dictators of the twentieth century who used ethnic cleansing. Research their early lives and rise to power. Compare them to Hitler. You might wish to read *Forgotten Fire* (Related Work 1) and *First They Killed My Father: A Daughter of Cambodia Remembers* (Related Work 6).
3. Using the facts from *The Life and Death of Adolf Hitler,* construct a timeline of Hitler's life.
4. On page 29, in the paragraph beginning "Hitler also sought an emblem ..." Giblin recounts the history of the swastika. Choose one other symbol. Research its history. Create a display to communicate that history.

5. Propaganda had a central role in Hitler's success. Research the propaganda techniques used in his regime. Identify those same techniques in present day commercial and political messages.

Related Works

1. Bagdasarian, Adam. **Forgotten Fire.** New York: DK Publishing, Inc., 2000. 273p. $17.95. ISBN 0 7894 2627 7. [fiction] MJS (See full booktalk in *Booktalks and More,* 2003, pages 49 to 51.) Twelve-year-old Vahan Kenderian recounts his terrible physical and emotional journey between 1915 and 1918 as the youngest son in a well-respected and prosperous Armenian family during the Armenian holocaust.

2. Bennett, Cherie, and Jeff Gottesfeld. **Anne Frank & Me.** New York: G. P. Putnam's Sons, 2001. 288p. $18.99. ISBN 0 399 23329 6. [fiction] MJS (See full booktalk in *Booktalks and More,* 2003, pages 192 to 194.) A young girl time travels to Nazi occupied France and contributes to the resistance by distributing anti-German flyers. See the explanation of the White Rose student group in Chapter 22 of *The Life and Death of Adolf Hitler.*

3. Hughes, Dean. **Soldier Boys.** New York: Atheneum/Simon and Schuster, 2001. 162p. $16.00. ISBN 0 689 81748 7. [fiction] MJS (See full booktalk in *Booktalks and More,* 2003, pages 51 to 54.) An American boy's heroism makes a young German soldier question his indoctrination.

4. Müller, Melissa. **Anne Frank: The Biography,** translated by Rita and Robert Kimber. New York: Henry Holt and Co., 1998. 330p. $14.00pa. ISBN 0 8050 5997 0. [nonfiction] JS Müller explains the political, sociological, and psychological environment that allowed Hitler to rise to power.

5. Tunnell, Michael O. **Brothers in Valor: A Story of Resistance.** New York: Holiday House, 2001. 260p. $16.95. ISBN 0 8234 1541 4. [fiction] JS Based on the story of the Helmuth Hübener Group, the novel explains how young Mormons resisted Hitler's claim that he was above God.

6. Ung, Loung. **First They Killed My Father: A Daughter of Cambodia Remembers.** New York: HarperCollins Publishers, 2000. 239p. $23.00. ISBN 0 06 019332 8. [nonfiction] JS (See full booktalk in *Booktalks and More,* pages 54 to 56.) Loung Ung begins to witness ethnic cleansing when she is five years old, and her family is driven from their comfortable city life and sent to government camps.

ᘒᘓ

Murphy, Jim. An American Plague: The True and Terrifying Story of the Yellow Fever Epidemic of 1793.

New York: Clarion Books, 2003. 165p. $17.00.
ISBN 0 395 77608 2. [nonfiction] JS

Themes/Topics: Yellow Fever, Pennsylvania, Philadelphia, eighteenth century, perceptions

Summary/Description

Murphy explores one of the worst plagues of post-revolutionary America. Eminent physicians argue over cause and treatment. Prominent citizens join President Washington in an evacuation that robs the city of necessary services. Then heroes emerge. The Free African Society, the first organization created by blacks for blacks, provides help and nursing. A committee of twelve citizens decides to run the city and accept complete liability for their decisions. They provide homes for orphans, inspect burials, harvest grain, distribute supplies, and soothe disgruntled citizens. Two members manage Bush Hill, the city's hastily formed emergency hospital. A volunteer doctor, against the wishes of his opinionated colleagues, makes the "hospital" a safe, healing place. Their efforts help control but not eliminate the disease. They fight the greedy, powerful, and cowardly as well as the disease. After the crisis passes, some of the heroes are vilified, but the disease effects radical change in personal lives, public policy, city maintenance, water supplies, and even the residence policy of future presidents. Murphy suggests that successful management of future epidemics will depend on the disease being approached as a scientific problem, a political challenge, or a punishment from God.

Extensive pictures and sample documents provide a historical context. Thirteen pages of "Sources" offer opportunities for additional information. The index, with bolded pages numbers indicating relevant pictures, affords easy access to information.

Booktalk

Ask how many people in the group have heard of Yellow Fever. If no one knows the symptoms, read the description on page 13 to 14, beginning with "The sickness began ... and ending with "delirious."

Most of the time, the victim died. Today, those symptoms would bring fast action from health authorities. In 1793, Philadelphia, they caused panic. Almost everyone, who could, left the city—including George Washington, the first president of the United States. So many people died that the bodies were picked up in wheelbarrows and dumped in mass graves—if they were buried at all. And so the problem grew.

Who stayed? The mayor who was sixty years old, had a wife and nine children, and almost no real power; eleven men who believed in Philadelphia; a prominent doctor convinced he had the answer; and The Free African Society, who nursed the sick at the risk of their own lives.

Who lived? Who died? What good and terrible change came about? Read *An American Plague: The True and Terrifying Story of the Yellow Fever Epidemic of 1793* and find out.

Learning Opportunities

1. Murphy provides thirteen pages of his sources. Select one available to you. Read it, and share the information with the group.
2. Discuss the human flaws that you feel worsened the epidemic.
3. List the flaws cited in Learning Opportunity 2. Note how they intensified an emergency in which you have been involved.
4. Using your library's resources, research the origins and goals of other African-American organizations in the United States. Share your findings with the group.
5. Using your library's resources, find the agencies and officials in your community who are responsible in an epidemic crisis.

Related Works

1. Altman, Linda Jacobs. **Plague and Pestilence: A History of Infectious Disease.** Springfield, NJ: Enslow Publishers, Inc., 1998. 128p. (Issues in Focus.) $17.95. ISBN: 0 89490 957 6. [nonfiction] JS (See full booktalk in *Booktalks and More,* 2003, pages 166 to 169.) Altman traces the history of disease outbreaks and the detections of their sources from the Bronze Age to the present and asks if disease should be treated scientifically, spiritually, or morally.
2. Anderson, Laurie Halse. **Fever, 1793.** New York: Simon & Schuster, 2000. 251p. $16.00. ISBN 0 689 83858 1. [fiction] MJS (See full booktalk in *Booktalks and More,* 2003, pages 178 to 180.) This account of fourteen-year-old Mattie Cook's encounter with the epidemic includes many of the aspects mentioned in Murphy's narrative.
3. Cefey, Holly. **Yellow Fever.** New York: Rosen Publishing Group, 2002. 64p. (Epidemics: Deadly Diseases Throughout History.) $19.95. ISBN 0 8239 3489 6. [nonfiction] MJS. Opening with a description of

a yellow fever victim, *Yellow Fever* explains the disease, its history, and its control.

4. Cox, Clinton. **Come All You Brave Soldiers.** New York: Scholastic, 1999. 182p. $15.95. ISBN 0 590 47576 2. [nonfiction] JS (See full booktalk in *Booktalks Plus*, 2001, pages 155 to 157.) *Come All You Brave Soldiers* describes the contribution that black soldiers made to both armies in the Revolutionary War. The new government then refused to acknowledge their contribution.

5. Farrell, Jeanette. **Invisible Enemies.** New York: Farrar, Straus and Giroux, 1998. 224p. $17.00. ISBN 0 374 33637 7. [nonfiction] MJS (See full booktalk in *Booktalks Plus*, 2001, pages 146 to 148.) Telling the stories of seven diseases, Farrell emphasizes that prejudice, fear, and misconception are the most effective allies of disease.

Multiple Cultures

The titles in this chapter explore how diversification affects culture. Teens are curious about other cultures, and these stories appeal to that curiosity. In the many ways to be multiple, "Mixed Cultures" explores the conflicts, adjustments, and learning experiences that occur when two different ways of life try to blend. "World Cultures" highlights different worlds that make up this earth, even, in *Clan Apis*, the world of the honeybee. "Multi-Cultural America" talks about the unique American experience of diverse cultures building one country with many shared values. The selections remind readers how much we share with the worlds around us and give hope for getting along.

Mixed Cultures

Cooney, Caroline B. **The Ransom of Mercy Carter.**
New York: Laurel Leaf Books, 2001. 249p. $5.50pa. ISBN 0 440 22775 5. [fiction] MJ

Themes/Topics: Indian captives, life in eighteenth-century North America, historical novel

Summary/Description

Eleven-year-old Mercy Carter and her brothers and sisters are kidnapped by Mohawks in a raid on Deerfield, Massachusetts, 1704. As the Mohawks march their captives to Canada, Mercy sees the weak and uncooperative killed. The Mohawk Tannhahorens, who captured Mercy, honors her by claiming her as his property. All captives are isolated from each other so that they might assimilate into the Mohawk culture. By the time the group arrives at Kahnawake, Tannhahoren's

257

Indian/French community, all adult hostages have disappeared, and the children are indicating how they will or will not grow into their new lives. Mercy, although beginning to have affection for Tannhahorens and his wife, still remembers the savagery directed to her family and friends. She hopes to be ransomed by the English, and when she is permitted to visit Montreal, attempts to run away. Her Mohawk family realizes her feelings. Instead of restraining her, they keep her from danger. About a year after Tannhahorens dies in a hunting expedition, Englishmen appear with a ransom offer. Persuaded by her Mohawk mother, Mercy decides to stay in a community that loves her.

In the chapter titled "The Endings," Cooney explains what happens to each of the characters. The "Author's Note" explains how Cooney came to write the story.

Booktalk

In 1704, eleven-year-old Mercy Carter is a woman. She has full care of her brothers and sister because her sick and confused stepmother is struggling to save her own baby's life. Soon, Mercy will be expected to marry. She worries about that day because her isolated English settlement, Deerfield, Massachusetts, doesn't have many men to choose from. But there are bigger worries—Indian attacks and freezing weather. It's ten degrees below zero. Snow drifts against the fort. Everyone bundles up in anything they can find, and suddenly in the night there is a terrible sound. Hundreds of Indians run up the drifts and pour over the walls of the fort. They smash doors and burn homes. Ignoring the cold, they carry and drag the settlers and their possessions out of the fort and into the wilderness. Mercy is one of them. She will have to survive a sub-zero walk to Canada. Even if she braves the elements, her captors will decide if she lives or dies. She will have new names—one Mohawk and one French. She will have new family—the people who killed her old one. Can they kill her memories and feelings? Can she become a new person in the enemy's world? How will she survive until *The Ransom of Mercy Carter* comes?

Learning Opportunities

1. Each young person captured by the Indians reacts differently. Discuss how the choices each makes reveals the person's character.
2. Reverend Williams is related to Cotton and Increase Mather, significant figures in early America. Research their lives and beliefs. Discuss how their relationship might have influenced the attitude

of Reverend Williams. You may with to begin by investigating *John Winthrop, Oliver Cromwell, and The Land of Promise* (Related Work 1).

3. Using your library's resources, research the French and Indian War. Explain the issues and the alliances involved.

4. On pages 116 and 117, Cooney describes Kahnawake. From that description, draw a plan or a sketch of the community. Then describe another community or area. Ask someone else to draw a sketch based on your description.

5. Discuss Mercy's decision to stay. Do you think she made the right choice?

Related Works

1. Aronson, Marc. **John Winthrop, Oliver Cromwell, and The Land of Promise.** (See full booktalk in "History/Period"/ "Leaders and Defining Events," pages 245 to 248.) Aronson explains the social context that produced both Winthrop and Cromwell. Chapter 3 touches on the influence of Cotton and Increase Mather.

2. Durrant, Lynda. **Echohawk.** New York: Clarion Books, 1996. 181p. $14.95. ISBN 0 395 74430 X. [fiction] MJ Echohawk discovers that he is really Jonathan Starr and that his Mohican father killed his white parents, then found and adopted him.

3. Durrant, Lynda. **The Turtle Clan Journey.** New York: Clarion Books, 1999. 180p. $15.00. ISBN 0 395 90369 6. [fiction] MJ (See full booktalk in *Booktalks and More,* 2003, pages 194 to 196.) Echohawk and his family must flee both white and Indian groups who wish to turn them in to the government for ransom.

4. Osborne, Mary Pope. **Standing in the Light: The Captive Diary of Catharine Carey Logan.** New York: Scholastic Incorporated, 1998. 184p. (Dear America.) $10.95. ISBN 0 590 13462 0. [fiction] MJ Catherine Carey Logan tells about being captured by the Lenape. While living with the tribe, she learns to admire their culture and falls in love with Snow Hunter who was captured at about the age of four.

5. Philip, Neil (ed.). **In a Sacred Manner I Live: Native American Wisdom.** New York: Clarion Books, 1997. 93p. $20.00. ISBN 0 395 84981 0. [nonfiction] JS (See full booktalk in *Booktalks and More,* 2003, pages 44 to 46.) This collection of Native American pictures, poems, songs, and speeches from 1609 to 1995 demonstrates the great cultural clash bound to occur between Native Americans and white settlers.

Cℛℰ

Lynch, Chris. **Gold Dust.**

New York: HarperCollins, 2000. 196p. $15.95. ISBN 0 06 028174 X. [fiction] MJ

Themes/Topics: Integration of the 1970s, friendship, baseball, prejudice, historic setting

Summary/Description

Set during the Boston bussing of the 1970s, *Gold Dust* tells about the friendship of seventh graders Napoleon Charlie Ellis and Richard Riley Moncrief. The boys come from drastically different social, cultural, and racial backgrounds. Napoleon, whose father is a professor, recently moved to Boston from the island of Dominica and loves the arts, especially music. Richard, whose father installs mufflers, has lived in Boston all his life and obsesses about baseball. Richard befriends Napoleon, and fantasizes about their becoming like the Gold Dust twins—Fred Lynn and Jim Rice, Red Sox rookies. Redheaded Beverly, Richard's friend who loves music, is their mutual friend. Her friendship disturbs Richard and the rest of the white boys in the class. Bigoted toward Napoleon and intimidated by his talent, the boys gang up on him. Napoleon demands that Richard defend him. But Richard avoids conflict. Napoleon constantly cites instances of prejudice in the school, sports, and the city. Richard would rather talk about baseball plays and statistics. He pushes the athletically talented Napoleon to practice in even the coldest weather. They both improve. Then Napoleon, also a talented singer, receives an invitation to attend the prestigious choir school. Richard's denial, frustration, and anger about Napoleon's leaving and rejecting the dream of a baseball career place the two at odds. Later, a more thoughtful Richard sends his best wishes to Napoleon via Beverly, and although he keeps his passion for baseball, realizes that Napoleon has made him a better player and person.

Booktalk

Richard Riley Moncrief's world is a baseball diamond. Anything worth talking about happens there. Why should he clutter up his seventh grade mind with the court ordered bussing for racial integration in Boston, when he knows that 1975 might be the year that the Red Sox win the pennant?

Then he meets Napoleon Charlie Ellis, a new student from the island of Dominica. For Napoleon, who is black, bussing is very important. He plays cricket, not baseball, and he loves Symphony Hall a lot more than Fenway Park.

But Richard Riley Moncrief has a dream—a dream that will make him and Napoleon baseball stars—just like those hot shot rookies, Fred Lynn and Jim Rice, the Boston fans dubbed the Gold Dust twins. He is sure that Napoleon, will see things his way—all the way and all the time, especially if Napoleon stops thinking about that *blackness* thing. Does Richard really have a twenty-two carat idea or is he just blinded by a little *Gold Dust*?

Learning Opportunities

1. Richard is Napoleon's friend even though he knows very little about him. Discuss the friendship between the two and discuss how prejudice influences it.
2. In the chapter "Snap Crackle Pop," Richard explains what the sounds of the bat mean to him. Those sounds also reveal a great deal about him as a person. Discuss his description and how it connects with the rest of the novel.
3. On page 27, Richard tells Napoleon, "Remember, if you put your mind to it, you can do better than reality." Discuss how his advice applies to the rest of the novel.
4. Richard begins the chapter "Girl 17" with the words "As a rule, I don't like exceptions. I like rules" even though he goes against rules in his friendships. List the "rules" of Richard's world. Then discuss how he follows them or breaks them and why.
5. The chapter "Gold Dust" illustrates the great differences that exist between Richard and Napoleon. List those differences. Then list their similarities. Discuss their chances of continuing a friendship.
6. Describe the sequel that you feel would be most appropriate for *Gold Dust*.
7. In both *Gold Dust* and *Starplace* (Related Work 4) political events are central. Read each novel. Research the political events affecting the characters' actions and attitudes. Share with the group what you learn about those events.
8. In "I Swear," Richard hits Napoleon twice with the ball. Describe the incident from Napoleon's point of view.

Related Works

1. Budhos, Marina. **Remix: Conversations with Immigrant Teenagers.** New York: Henry Holt and Company, 1999. 145p. $16.95. ISBN 0 8050 5113 9. [nonfiction] MJS Teenagers moving to the United States describe the difficulties of their adjustment as they try to blend the two cultures.

2.   Cain, Timothy. **The Book of Rule: How the World Is Governed.** New York: DK Publishing, 2004. 320p. $30.00. ISBN 0 7894 9354 3. [reference] MJS Including 193 countries, Cain explains how the world is governed in both theory and practice. The island of Dominica, Napoleon's relatively impoverished homeland, appears on page 154.

3.   Carter, Alden R. **Bull Catcher.** New York: Scholastic, 1997. 279p. $15.95. ISBN 0 590 50959 6. [fiction] JS (See full booktalk in *Booktalks Plus,* 2001, pages 96 to 98.) A winning baseball team becomes less important as the team members mature. Some controversial language may require a more mature audience.

4.   Grove, Vicki. **The Starplace.** New York: G. P. Putnam's Sons, 1999. 214p. $17.99. ISBN 0 399 23207 9. [fiction] MJ (See full booktalk in *Booktalks Plus,* 2001, pages 4 to 6.) This story about two friends— Francine Driscoll, a Quiver, Oklahoma, native and Celeste Chisholm, an African-American girl who moves there with her professor father—takes place in 1961 when the Berlin Wall is new, and prejudice manifests itself through segregation and the Ku Klux Klan.

5.   Martin, Ann M. **Belle Teal.** New York: Scholastic Press, 2001. 224p. $15.95. ISBN 0 439 09823 8. [fiction] MJ As fifth grader Belle Teal tries to help the first black student in her school, she faces a web of prejudice, child abuse, and lies.

6.   Robinson, Sharon. **Jackie's Nine: Jackie Robinson's Values to Live By.** New York: Scholastic Incorporated, 2001. 192p. $15.95. ISBN 0 439 23764 5. [nonfiction] MJS (See full booktalk *Booktalks and More,* 2003, pages 123 to 125.) Jackie Robinson's daughter outlines the values that allowed Robinson to break into a very prejudiced sport.

Cᗑ Ꮙᗛ

Mosher, Richard. Zazoo.

New York: Clarion, 2001. 248p. $16.00. ISBN 0 618 13534 0. [fiction] MJS

Themes/Topics: World War II, French/Vietnamese war orphan, friendship, love, loss and regret, discovery, reconciliation, dreams and rebirth, conflict, prejudice, risk

Summary/Description

Zazoo, a Vietnamese orphan, lives in an old mill house with her failing seventy-eight-year-old adopted French grandfather. As she struggles with puberty, friendship, and first love, she discovers that her grandfather, a French resistance fighter in World War II loved a Jewish girl whom the Germans killed in retaliation for his attacks. The town pharmacist, the Jewish girl's younger brother, befriends Zazoo even though he and the grandfather have not spoken since the war. The grandfather saved the pharmacist's life by hiding him with a Huguenot family who refused to allow the pharmacist to marry their daughter. This daughter's grandson arrives in the town, becomes close to Zazoo, and together they reunite the grandfather, the pharmacist, and the Huguenot daughter.

Booktalk

Zazoo rows through the canal in her purple boat. Most days she talks only to her adopted French grandfather and to the "sad gray cat" that others can't see. Her heart tells her that she is French, but her eyes, her skin, and her hair tell the world she is Vietnamese. Each day her grandfather becomes quieter and does less. She worries that soon she will be all alone. Then a stranger appears—a boy with a bike and binoculars. With him she travels deep into history and sees into the heart. She learns about the war that brought her here, the war that brought her grandfather here, and how love and hate shaped all their lives. She realizes that events of long ago continue to change the already very different life of the orphan called *Zazoo*.

Learning Opportunities

1. Chapter 2, "The Mill of a Thousand Years," is an elaborate explanation of names—the mill's and the grandfather's. After reading the entire novel, re-read this chapter. Then discuss how it supports the rest of the story.
2. On page 41, Zazoo describes the gray cat to Juliette. Zazoo says, "His business was to move gracefully. And, well, to keep searching." Discuss the function of this cat in the story.
3. On pages 52 to 54, Zazoo shares the poem that her grandfather wrote about her with Marius. Using the poem as a model, choose a defining event about a person you know. Write a poem about that person (Related Work 3).
4. Plan with a friend or family member to exchange a poem or a picture at least once a week.
5. *Zazoo* deals with love, conflict, regrets, dreams, loss, prejudice, risk, and reconciliation. Ask eight people to trace one of those themes throughout the novel. Then, discuss the book together from eight perspectives. How do those themes overlap?

Related Works

1. Armstrong, Jennifer (ed.). **Shattered: Stories of Children and War.** New York: Alfred A. Knopf, 2002. 166p. $15.95. ISBN 0 375 91112 X. [fiction] MJS The stories include the Middle East, Vietnam, World War II, Mexico, Cold War, Afghanistan, American Civil War, and Bosnia.

2. Chambers, Aidan. **Postcards from No Man's Land.** New York: Dutton Books, 1999. 320p. $19.99. ISBN 0 525 46863 3. [fiction] JS When seventeen-year-old Jacob Todd travels to Amsterdam to honor his grandfather who died in World War II, he finds the secrets of his grandfather's life blending with his own coming of age story.

3. Janeczko, Paul B. **How to Write Poetry.** New York: Scholastic, 1999. 117p. (Scholastic Guides). $12.95. ISBN 0 590 10077 7. [nonfiction] MJS (See full booktalk in *Booktalks Plus*, 2001, pages 215 to 217.) Janeczko takes the writer step-by-step through the writing process.

4. Kustanowitz, Esther. **The Hidden Children of the Holocaust: Teens Who Hid from the Nazis.** The Rosen Publishing Group, 1999. 63p. (Teen Witnesses to the Holocaust.) $17.95. ISBN 0 8239 2562 5. [nonfiction] MJS (See full booktalk in *Booktalks Plus: Motivating Teens to Read,* 2001, pages 158 to160.) Hidden children of the Holocaust explain how they survived in hideouts and under false identities.

5. Metzger, Lois. **Missing Girls.** New York: Viking, 1999. 176p. $15.99. ISBN 0 670 87777 8. [fiction] MJ The daughter of an Austrian war bride now living with her immigrant grandmother discovers her deceased mother's past when her family renews their ties to a man who hid her mother during World War II.

CฝD

Shea, Pegi Deitz. **Tangled Threads: A Hmong Girl's Story.**

New York: Clarion Books, 2003. 236p. $15.00. ISBN 0 618 24748 3. [fiction] JS

Themes/Topics: Hmong culture, refugees, family, mixed cultures

Summary/Description

Chronically ill, thirteen-year-old Mai Yang lives in a Thailand refugee camp with her grandmother. When the refugees are told that they must leave the camp, Mai Yang and her grandmother brave brutal soldiers and cultural misunderstanding to travel to America. They arrive in

Providence, Rhode Island, to live with the family of Mai Yang's uncle. Mai Yang rediscovers her Americanized cousins, Heather and Lisa, and a culture she likes but can't understand. Heather and Lisa are in constant conflict with their parents over drugs, clothes, and boys. Mai Yang's grandmother helps Mai Yang keep her balance between the two cultures. They sew to earn money, and Mai Yang buys seeds for the grandmother to plant. Western medicine rids Mai Yang of the parasite that causes her illness, but it cannot cure the grandmother's bad heart. On her deathbed, she admits that she and Mai Yang stayed in the camp so long because the grandmother feared the United States. After the grandmother's dies, Mai Yang moves in with the aunt and uncle. Heather runs away with a Latino boy. Lisa marries a Hmong boy and will probably drop out of school. The story ends at a New Year's party. Lisa attends and announces she is pregnant. Heather refuses to return until her father accepts her for the person she is. Mai, dressed in the traditional clothing her late grandmother stitched for her, plans for a future of school and a boyfriend.

Booktalk

Thirteen-year-old Mai Yang is sometimes so sick that her grandmother tells her it is time for her to die. They live in a crowded refugee camp in Thailand. Mai Yang dreams of going to beautiful America, a country with so much space and healthy, happy people. They watch many leave the camp, but she and her grandmother stay. When the authorities tell them that the camp is closing, they must decide. Will they return to Laos or go live with Mai Yang's uncle in America? America it is. Mai Yang cannot believe their good luck. But her grandmother sees many omens against traveling to a country they don't know. And the grandmother is right. Brutal soldiers and American customs are so unexpected, so dangerous. Grandmother and granddaughter have each other, the family they remember from years ago, and the precious story cloths that record their travels and heritage. Will these be enough? Or will the many threads of life and living become merely *Tangled Threads* that can never be smoothed out again?

Learning Opportunities

1. Using your library's resources, research the Hmong people and their way of life. You may wish to start with books listed for further reading, pages 231 to 233.
2. Roger Williams is mentioned several times in the novel. Using your library's resources, find out who he is and why he is significant. Share your information with the group. You might wish to start

with *John Winthrop, Oliver Cromwell, and The Land of Promise* (Related Work 1).

3. Did the grandmother make the right decision in bringing Mai Yang to the United States? Did she make the right decision in waiting so long? In your discussion, consider Pa Nhia, Lisa, and Heather.

4. Compare the relationship between the grandmother and Mai Yang with the relationship between Mai Yang's uncle and his daughters.

5. Discuss why the author ends the novel with a New Year's celebration. Describe the New Year's celebration that might take place in ten years.

Related Works

1. Aronson, Marc. **John Winthrop, Oliver Cromwell, and The Land of Promise.** (See full booktalk in "History/Period"/"Leaders and Defining Events," pages 245 to 248.) Aronson explains how the visions of John Winthrop and Oliver Cromwell changed as they confronted practical obstacles. Roger Williams was considered a radical who resisted their vision.

2. Atkin, Beth S. **Voices from the Streets: Young Former Gang Members Tell Their Stories.** Boston: Little, Brown and Company, 1996. 131p. $17.95. ISBN 0 316 05634 0. [nonfiction] JS Former gang members tell why they joined a gang. On pages 18 to 31 in the article "Surviving in Between," a young Cambodian man explains how the gang substitutes for family in a new culture.

3. Brown, Jackie. **Little Cricket.** New York: Hyperion Books for Children, 2004. 224p. $15.99. ISBN 0 7868 1852 2. [fiction] MJ Twelve-year-old Kia Vang comes to Minnesota with her fourteen-year-old brother and grandfather. Each discovers how difficult adjusting to a new country can be. Like *Tangled Threads*, this story deals with Hmong adjustment to the United States, but it omits the more adult details.

4. Budhos, Marina. **Remix: Conversations with Immigrant Teenagers.** New York: Henry Holt, 1999. 145p. $16.95. ISBN 0 8050 5113 9. [nonfiction] JS Budhos interviews teenagers about their journeys and reactions to America. On pages 95 to 102, an eighteen-year-old Laotion girl of the Hmong tribe tells about her life on the border during the war and why she is studying math and science to get a better, discrimination-free job.

5. Nam, Vickie, ed. **Yell-Oh Girls!** New York: HarperCollins/Quill, 2001. 294p. $13.00pa. ISBN 0 06 095944 4. [nonfiction] JS (See full booktalk in *Booktalks and More,* 2003 pages 262 to 264.) In this essay

and poetry collection, Asian-American females express joy, frustration, and determination in relation to their ancestry, their integration into America, and their personal identity.

6. Ung, Loung. **First They Killed My Father: A Daughter of Cambodia Remembers.** New York: HarperCollins Publishers, 2000. 239p. $23.00. ISBN 0 06 019332 8. [nonfiction] JS (See full booktalk in *Booktalks and More,* 2003, pages 54 to 56.) Loung Ung's nonfiction narrative begins when the Khmer Rouge take over Loung Ung's city and ends when her family relocate to refugee camps and other countries.

ญ๚

Taylor, Mildred D. **The Land: Prequel to Roll of Thunder, Hear My Cry.**
New York: Phyllis Fogelman Books, 2001. 275p. $17.99.
ISBN 0 8037 1950 7. [fiction] JS

Themes/Topics: biracial family, slavery, post-war discrimination, historical novel

Summary/Description

Paul Logan's mother is half African and half Native-American. His father is white, a former plantation owner for whom Paul's mother, Paul, and his sister Cassie were slaves. The story begins when Paul is nine and ends when he is starting his own family. Called a "white nigger," Paul suffers bullying from both the white and black races. Mitchell Thomas, an older and bigger black boy, picks on him. Paul promises to teach him to read if Mitchell will teach Paul to fight. Their truce grows into friendship. Paul's father raises Paul with his three white brothers, but as Paul grows older the inevitable division occurs. Paul apprentices to a carpenter, but his brother Robert receives private, academic schooling. Robert makes white friends who hate blacks. His betrayal destroys their relationship. After racing a horse Paul's father forbids him to ride, Paul runs away with Mitchell. They try various jobs and contend with dishonest businessmen who know that black men have little or no recourse in the courts. Finally Paul and Mitchell clear lumber from land in exchange for its ownership. Mitchell marries the girl both men love. When a jealous white man kills Mitchell, Paul marries Mitchell's widow, and with his family's help, buys the land.

The epilogue is Paul's letter telling what happened in his adult life. The author's note explains how closely the story relates to the author's family.

Booktalk

Paul Logan's mother is African and Native-American. His father is white. Before the Civil War, Paul's father owned Paul's mother, sister, and Paul. But Paul has always lived just like his three white brothers—almost. He has good clothes, fine food, and an education. He just doesn't belong anywhere. He can't sit at his father's table when company comes. The black children hate him because he is white. And soon his brothers will be the family landowners and his bosses. So Paul Logan carves a new world. He makes friends out of enemies, leaves some family behind, watches loved ones die, and forms a world of hard work, skill, and love—not skin color or bloodlines, on—*The Land*.

Learning Opportunities

1. On page 90, in the paragraph beginning "My mama turned to face me again ..." Paul's mother explains why she is glad that Paul's father whipped him. After reading the paragraph, explain what you think she means when she uses the word "glad."
2. Mitchell and Caroline have significant roles in the novel. Discuss Mitchell's marriage to Caroline and his death in terms of the novel's purpose.
3. *Cast Two Shadows* (Related Work 4) and *The Land* both tell stories about slave children raised in the home of the slaveholder. After reading the two novels, compare the characters' revelations and their reactions to them.
4. After reading *The Land* and *Roll of Thunder, Hear My Cry* (Related Work 5) discuss the family traits and story elements consistent in both.
5. During Reconstruction, some former slaves achieved wealth and status. Research some of these success stories. You might start with the story of Bob Church, Mary Church Terrell's father, in *Fight On! Mary Church Terrell's Battle for Integration* (Related Work 2).

Related Works

1. Fradin, Dennis Brindell. **Bound for the North Star: True Stories of Fugitive Slaves.** (See full booktalk in "Issues"/"Social Challenges," pages 30 to 33.) Fradin uses first person accounts to explain the conditions of slavery and the cooperation that broke the

system. Chapter 9 tells the story of John Anderson. His story illustrates the tenuous position of any slave being considered part of the white family.

2. Fradin, Dennis Brindell, and Judith Bloom Fradin. **Fight On! Mary Church Terrell's Battle for Integration.** New York: Clarion Books, 2003. 181p. $17.00. ISBN 0 618 13349 6. [nonfiction] MJS Bob Church was the son of a slave owner, who escaped the Yankees, opened a saloon, acquired land, and became the South's first black millionaire. Bob Church's Daughter, Mary Church Terrell, was isolated from discrimination until much later in her life.

3. Paulsen, Gary. **Sarny: A Life Remembered.** New York: Bantam Doubleday Dell Books for Young Readers, 1997. 180p. $4.99pa. ISBN 0 440 21973 6. [fiction] JS (See full booktalk in *Booktalks and More,* 2003, pages 183 to 185.) This composite character, in telling her own story from slavery through Reconstruction, explores the situations of black women during slavery and post-emancipation—the slave girl, the free black woman in the South, the free black woman in the North, and the black female entrepreneur who is successful because of her ability to pass as white.

4. Rinaldi, Ann. **Cast Two Shadows.** New York: Gulliver Books, 1998. 276p. $16.00. ISBN 0 15 200881 0. [fiction] MJS (See full booktalk in *Booktalks Plus,* 2001, pages 46 to 48.) Caroline Whitaker, raised in her white father's household, learns that her biological slave mother was sold. Set in the Revolutionary War, the historical novel shows a conscientious and loving girl torn between two worlds.

5. Taylor, Mildred. D. **Roll of Thunder, Hear My Cry.** New York: Dial Books, 1976. 276p. $14.95. ISBN 0 8037 7473 7. [fiction] MJS The descendents of Paul Logan fight to hold onto their land and keep their families safe in the prejudiced South during the Depression.

World Cultures

ɔʃʕɔ

Cameron, Ann. **Colibrí.**

New York: Farrar, Straus and Giroux/Frances Foster Books, 2003. 240p. $17.00. ISBN 0 374 31519 1. [fiction] MJS

Themes/Topics: Guatemala, kidnapping, abuse, mind control

Summary/Description

Twelve-year-old Tzunún, nicknamed Colibrí and traveling under the name Rosa, was kidnapped when she was four. Her kidnapper, whom she calls Uncle, believes she will give him treasure. Uncle, an ex-soldier and petty thief, tells her that he found her wandering in Guatemala City and that he searches for her parents who don't really want her. She believes she owes him loyalty and obedience. When Uncle visits a Day-Keeper (a person with magical powers) to check on the status of his luck and fortune, the Day-Keeper counsels Tzunún to leave the obviously dominating and abusive Uncle, but recognizes that part of Tzunún is attached to him. Tzunún moves with him to the next city where she becomes part of a plan to rob a local church. Tzunún reports the plan to the priest and makes her way back to the Day-Keeper who shelters her and helps her find her parents. Uncle escapes, follows Tzunún, forces her to find real treasure, and tries to kill her, but dies in the attempt. Tzunún finds her parents and maintains her close friendship with the Day-Keeper.

Booktalk

Rosa travels all over Guatemala with Uncle. They stay alive by begging. She remembers that her real name is Tzunún Chumil, and that her nickname is Colibrí, or hummingbird. She thinks she might be twelve or thirteen years old, almost a woman. Uncle tells her that he found her wandering the streets of Guatemala when she was four. He says her parents abandoned her. He saved her, and for his good deed, fortunetellers say she will bring him treasure—enough to last a lifetime. All this news seems strange to Rosa.

She remembers how her parents loved her and taught her to do good. Why would such people abandon her?

Begging with Uncle, Rosa has never even learned to read. How can she be smart enough to bring this man a treasure?

But Uncle works hard on luck. He goes to see a Day-Keeper, a woman who knows magic. He asks her many questions, and she assures him that his treasure is coming. When Rosa asks questions, the Day-Keeper seems to answer her with more questions. Rosa doesn't know if she is smart enough or tough enough to answer them, but she does know that if she, a small *Colibrí*, can find the answers and live, many lives will change forever.

Learning Opportunities

1. Using your library's resources, research the geography and history of Guatemala. Then explain how the information enhances your understanding of the story.

2. Uncle continually tells Colibrí that she is free to leave but manages to keep her under his control. Using the library's sources, research psychological techniques that keep a person emotionally dependent. Then identify the techniques Uncle uses in the novel.
3. Discuss the appropriateness of the book's title.
4. How is the end of the book determined by the personal choices and friends that Colibrí and Uncle make?
5. In Chapter 25, Colibrí concludes that, "There's more to life than being safe. There's being happy." Discuss her statement in relation to the novel and to life decisions in general.

Related Works

1. Banks, Lynne Reid. **The Dungeon.** New York: HarperCollins Publishers, 2002. 279p. $17.89. ISBN 0 06 623783 1. [fiction] JS A Scottish laird, focusing on revenge after his wife is captured and his children are killed, rejects his feelings for his slave girl and is eventually responsible for her death as well as his own.
2. Cameron, Sara in conjunction with UNICEF. **Out of War: True Stories from the Front Lines of the Children's Movement for Peace in Colombia.** New York: Scholastic Press, 2001. 224p. $15.95. ISBN 0 439 29721 4. [nonfiction] JS Nine teenagers, members of the Movement for Peace in Colombia, discuss their encounters with violence and abuse as well as their belief that any permanent change in their country's status begins with their personal decisions.
3. Mikaelsen, Ben. **Tree Girl.** (See full booktalk in "Adventure/ Survival"/"Land," pages 94 to 96.) Seeing her family wiped out by government soldiers, fifteen-year-old Gabriela Flores escapes two raids and flees to Mexico where she builds a new family in the refugee camp.
4. Ryan, Pam Muñoz. **Becoming Naomi León.** New York: Scholastic Press, 2004. 256p. $16.95. ISBN 0 439 26969 5. [fiction] MJ When Naomi's mother appears after seven years, Naomi, who has been raised by her great-grandmother, begins to recall her abuse and abandonment and realizes she must live up to her lion name if she is to prevent it all from happening again.
5. Wynne Jones, Tim. **Stephen Fair.** New York: DK Ink, 1998. 218p. $15.95. ISBN 0 7894 2495 9. [fiction] MJ (See full booktalk in *Booktalks Plus*, 2001, pages 56 to 59.) Plagued with nightmares and a disintegrating family, Stephen discovers, with the help of an alternative health care practitioner, that his troubled mother stole him from his birth parents, whose neglect threatened his life.

The Breadwinner Trilogy

ርን ჭე

Maps of Afghanistan and Pakistan in relation to the
world map introduce each book. An "Author's Note"
gives the historical background. A "Glossary" explains
possibly unfamiliar terms.
Ellis, Deborah. **The Breadwinner.**

Toronto: Groundwood Books, 2000. 170p. $5.95pa. ISBN 0 88899 416 8. [fiction] MJ

Themes/Topics: Taliban, Afghanistan, family, survival,
historic setting

Summary/Description

When the Taliban take eleven-year-old Parvana's father away,
Parvana masquerades as a boy so that she can work to support
her family. She discovers Shauzia, a classmate doing the same, and they
learn to cooperate. Parvana's older sister Nooria is betrothed, so the rest
of the family takes her to Mazar for the wedding. Parvana stays behind
with a family friend, Mrs. Weera. They learn that the Taliban captured
Mazar and massacred many of the residents. Parvana's father returns
from jail. Sick and beaten, he decides to set out with Parvana to find the
rest of the family. Shauzia discovers that her own family plans to sell her
as a bride. She decides to leave and work her way to France where she
envisions herself in a peaceful and beautiful life.

Booktalk

*Ask the group what they know about Afghanistan and women's lives
under the Taliban.*

Parvana is eleven years old. She lives in Afghanistan. The Taliban
forbid her to go to school. Instead, she accompanies her father to the
marketplace each day where he reads and writes letters for people and
sells a few possessions left from many years of war. He even sold his
artificial leg. Parvana's job is to help him walk. Then one day, the Taliban
break into the house and take her father away. Women are forbidden
to leave the house without a man. The family, all women, will starve.
Parvana has known for a long time that she can do her father's job. She
uses her dead brother's clothes for the masquerade. No one will know.
But Parvana has no idea how her life will change when she agrees to
become *The Breadwinner.*

Cℱℒ

Ellis, Deborah. Parvana's Journey.

Toronto: Groundwood Books, 2002. 199p. $5.95pa. ISBN 0 88899 519 9. [fiction] MJ

Themes/Topics: Taliban, war, orphans, survival, family, refugee camp, historic setting

Summary/Description

As the story opens, Parvana, still disguised as a boy, is thirteen. Her father just died, and she leaves the village when she discovers the villagers plan to sell her to the Taliban. She continues her journey to find her family and finds an orphaned baby, a hostile nine-year-old boy with a missing leg, and an eight-year-old girl. Parvana keeps a journal, which she writes as a letter to Shauzia, her street friend from home. The four form a new family and eventually arrive at a camp for Internally Displaced Persons. Parvana hopes to find her birth family. When the eight-year-old girl attempts to retrieve a food package dropped by Americans in a minefield, she is blown up. People gather around the grieving Parvana who holds the body. One person is Parvana's mother. The surviving members of Parvana's birth and blended families form a new family.

Booktalk

Thirteen-year-old Parvana lives in Afghanistan. She has a large family. She doesn't know where most of them are right now. She does know where her father is. He is dead. But she continues to search for her mother, sisters, and brother. Parvana lives as a boy. That way, the Taliban are less likely to stop her, ask questions, or hurt her. Realizing the Taliban will pay a big price for such a strong boy, she keeps moving into new territory. She looks for help, but instead finds others without family and hope. Can any of them survive? Or can they help each other survive, in *Parvana's Journey*?

Cℱℒ

Ellis, Deborah. Mud City.

Toronto: Groundwood/Douglas&McIntyre, 2003. 164p. $5.95pa.
ISBN 0 88899 542 3. [fiction] MJ

Themes/Topics: social responsibility, family, historic setting

Summary/Description

Shauzia, Parvana's friend who wished to escape Afghanistan's devastation, now lives in a Pakistani refugee camp dominated by the socially conscious Mrs. Weera from *The Breadwinner*. Constantly doing volunteer jobs for other camp residents, Shauzia decides to leave the camp and work in Pheshawar so she can earn enough money to make her way to France. She takes odd jobs, collects junk, and begs, but the police eventually arrest her and take her earnings. An American family, working in Pakistan, gets her out of jail and invites her to live with them. Left alone in the house, Shauzia lets other beggars in. Shocked, the family returns her to the refugee camp. She begins to realize her responsibility to help her people, initiates programs in the camp, and returns to Afghanistan with Mrs. Weera.

Booktalk

Shauzia is thirteen or fourteen years old. She was born in Afghanistan, but decides that Afghanistan will never be a safe place to live, so she leaves. Now in Pakistan, she lives in a camp for displaced persons. Shauzia wants to live in France, but it takes money to get there. Mrs. Weera is always finding jobs for Shauzia to do in the camp, but has no money to pay her. So Shauzia is going to go to Peshawar. She supported herself and her family in Afghanistan; surely, she can earn enough for one small ticket. Will she be successful in the new and dangerous streets of Peshawar? Will she find her way to France? Or will she be stuck in the *Mud City* the rest of her life?

Learning Opportunities

1. Research the origins and development of the Taliban. Share your information with the group, and explain how it relates to the stories.
2. Trace the events that diminish and reconstruct Parvana's family in *The Breadwinner* and *Parvana's Journey*. Then explain what each event demonstrates about Parvana and the other characters involved.
3. Women are central in all three novels. Using your library's resources, research women's rights issues in one country other than the United States or Canada. Share your information with the rest of the group.
4. Both Parvana and Shauzia make decisions about their lives in relation to a larger community. Identify the decisions that they make. Discuss whether you agree or disagree with those decisions.
5. Assume that Parvana and Shauzia are able to meet each other at the top of the Eiffel Tower in twenty years as they plan. Describe the scene that you feel will take place.

6. Contact one of the Web sites listed in the author's note. Share the information that you find with the group.

Related Works

1. Banting, Erinn. **Afghanistan: The Culture.** New York: Crabtree Publishing Company, 2003. 32p. (The Lands, Peoples, and Cultures Series.) $16.95. ISBN 0 7787 9337 0. [nonfiction] MJ This volume describes the art, festivals, and literature of the country and how the Taliban occupation affected them.
2. Banting, Erinn. **Afghanistan: The Land.** New York: Crabtree Publishing Company, 2003. 32p. (The Lands, Peoples, and Cultures Series.) $16.95. ISBN 0 7787 9335 4. [nonfiction] MJ This volume explains the landscape and how it affects livelihood, cultural groups, and invaders.
3. Banting, Erinn. **Afghanistan: The People.** New York: Crabtree Publishing Company, 2003. 32p. (The Lands, Peoples, and Cultures Series.) $16.95. ISBN 0 7787 9336 2.[nonfiction] MJ This volume explains the many tribes and lifestyles blending in the country. Pages 22 and 23 explain the special problems the women faced during the Taliban occupation.
4. Cain, Timothy. **The Book of Rule: How the World Is Governed.** New York: DK Publishing, Inc., 2004. 320p. $30.00. ISBN 0 7894 9354 3. [reference] MJS This source explains 193 governments and the challenging situations that they face. Afghanistan is on page 310.
5. Mankell, Henning, and Anne Connie Stuksrud (trans.). **Secrets in the Fire.** Toronto, ON: Annick Press LTD, 2003. 166p. $17.95. ISBN 1 55037 801 5. [fiction] MJS Sophia, a young refugee from war-torn Mozambique, builds a new life after losing her sister and her legs in a land mine explosion.
6. Mikaelsen, Ben. **Tree Girl.** (See full booktalk in "Adventure/ Survival"/"Land," pages 94 to 96.) A young girl driven from her home by war, finds herself in a refugee camp where she decides how much she is willing to help those around her.
7. Murdico, Suzanne J. **Osama Bin Laden.** New York: The Rosen Publishing Group, Inc., 2004. 112p. (Middle East Leaders). $31.95. ISBN 0 8239 4467 0. [nonfiction] MJS Murdico explains Bin Laden's early life and his rise to power.
8. Romano, Amy. **A Historical Atlas of Afghanistan.** New York: The Rosen Publishing Group, Inc., 2003. 64p. (Historical Atlases of South Asia, Central Asia, and the Middle East.) $30.95.

ISBN 0 8239 3863 8. [nonfiction] MJS This combination of maps, illustrations, pictures, and diagrams explains the history of the tumultuous area now called Afghanistan.

ᘓᘔ

Hartnett, Sonya. **Thursday's Child.**
Cambridge, MA: Candlewick Press, 2000. 261p. $15.99. ISBN 0 7636 1620 6. [fiction] JS

Themes: Australia, Depression, feral child, alcoholism, dysfunctional family, historic setting

Summary/Description

Harper Flute lives through the Depression in Australia with her father, mother, sister, and three brothers. The story begins when Harper is seven and ends when she is twenty-one. Tin, Harper's younger brother, seeks refuge under the homestead's porch when his baby brother is born. He digs a series of tunnels under the house. His parents do little to bring him back. Years later the house collapses into the tunnels. The father, an alcoholic, gives up hope. The neighbors help the family rebuild on rock, but with the father's ineptitude, his bad attitude, and the bleak Depression, the family cannot prosper. When two traveling salesmen steal the Flute's livestock, the father pressures Harper's older sister to become the housekeeper to a much older, prosperous farmer. Burdened with guilt over a baby brother's death, she agrees. Harper's older brother, disgusted by his father's meanness, leaves. The farmer attacks Harper's sister. The father sets out to confront him and Harper follows. At the farm, they discover that Tin killed him. Harper and her father hide the evidence. The neighbors think that the man ran away rather than face the father's rage, and Harper's father becomes a local hero. Tin eventually reappears looking like a wild, mythical figure. He delivers a large chunk of gold to the family and returns to the tunnels. Harper and her sister move to a house on the ocean. The mother and father stay to mine for gold. Although she enjoys security and comfort, Harper still wishes for her days of innocence. Subject matter requires a mature reader.

Booktalk

Twenty-one-year-old Harper Flute lives in a beautiful seacoast home in Australia. But during the Great Depression, she, her sister, and three brothers lived on their parents' homestead. When she was seven years old, her four-year-old brother Tin was buried alive. He liked it. He liked it so much he started digging holes and caves to live in. Soon no one could coax him out. He honeycombed the countryside with tunnels that only he could follow—tunnels that held secrets of love, and crime, and horrible death. Tin is *Thursday's Child*—wandering far from his family, but tangling his life in theirs with a wildness that mystifies them and their community. Harper is just his messenger, someone to tell the bizarre combination of events that destroy her innocence.

Learning Opportunities

1. On page 213 of *Thursday's Child*, Harper describes her life as a cage. Read it aloud. The novels *Girl in a Cage* (Related Work 5) and *In the Shadow of the Pali: A Story of the Hawaiian Leper Colony* (Related Work 1) as well as the short story collection *Trapped! Cages of Mind and Body* (Related Work 2) explore the cage theme as well. Ask four people in the group to choose one of the works. Then ask each person to share his or her interpretation of how the theme is treated.

2. Describe a situation in which you see yourself or someone else enclosed in a cage.

3. A great deal of information explores the Depression in the United States in the 1930s. Using the Internet, or your library's resources, research how the Depression affected Australia. Share your information with the rest of the group.

4. Draw a picture of Tin on the night that he delivers the gold to the family.

5. Ask everyone in the group who has read *Thursday's Child* to identify three judgments important to the novel. In a group, share the judgments and their significance.

Related Works

1. Cindrich, Lisa. **In the Shadow of the Pali: A Story of the Hawaiian Leper Colony.** (See full booktalk in "Adventure/ Survival"/"Land," pages 90 to 94.) A twelve-year-old leper must create a new home when she is sent to a lawless leper colony.

2. Duncan, Lois (ed.). **Trapped! Cages of Mind and Body.** New York: Simon & Schuster Books for Young Readers, 1998. 228p. $16.00. ISBN 0 689 81335 X. [fiction] JS This collection of short stories involves physical and psychological prisons within which people must escape or learn to survive.

3.   Hesse, Karen. **Out of the Dust.** New York: Scholastic, 1997. 227p. $4.99. ISBN 0 590 37125 8. [fiction] MJS (See full booktalk in *Booktalks Plus,* 2001, pages 30 to 32.) In a series of poems, fourteen-year-old Billie Joe tells her story of survival within the context of the Oklahoma Dust Bowl and the Great Depression.

4.   Ryan, Pam Muñoz. **Esperanza Rising.** New York: Scholastic Press, 2000. 272p. $15.95. ISBN 0 439 12041 1. [fiction] MJS (See full book-talk in *Booktalks and More,* 2003, pages 42 to 44.) Esperanza Ortega, born into wealth and privilege, immigrates to the United States, and, working as a migrant farmer, learns to appreciate people and the rhythms of nature more than things.

5.   Yolen, Jane, and Robert J. Harris. **Girl in a Cage.** New York: Philomel Books, 2002. 234p. $18.99. ISBN 0 399 23627 9. [fiction] MJ In 1306, Edward Longshanks, the King of England, tries to stop Robert Bruce's rebellion by imprisoning his daughter in a public cage.

ɕʒ ʡɔ

Holt, Kimberly Willis. **Keeper of the Night.**
New York: Henry, Holt and Co., 2003. 308p. $16.95.
ISBN 0 8050 6361 7. [fiction] MJS

Themes/Topics: grief, family, individuality, communication

Summary/Description

One morning, thirteen-year-old Isabel, who lives in Guam, finds her mother dead in a kneeling position. The mother committed suicide. The father sends the children to live with his stingy, compulsive, and overly religious sister. After six months they return to their home in Malesso where Isabel tries to protect the family from their grief. The father remains distant and sleeps every night on the floor where his wife died. Isabel's little sister Olivia wets the bed and wakes with nightmares. Frank starts to carve the bedroom wall and his body. Isabel worries but does not ask for help. Frank attempts suicide. Isabel blames herself for not telling, but Frank's actions pull the family into counseling. The counselor, Ed, helps Isabel realize that she carried too many family responsibilities before and after her mother's death. He encourages her to pursue outside interests. Having a great love for the water, she begins to demonstrate her diving talent. Her father realizes she needs him, supports her, and helps free her time so that she can compete with a team.

Booktalk

Thirteen-year-old Isabel lives in Guam. Each day, the beauty of water and the love of family surround her. Her father is a successful fisherman. Her mother is beautiful. Her younger brother is so smart that he can finish her math homework for her, and her little sister adores her. Then Isabel's life changes. (*Read "A Dutiful Daughter" aloud.*) By day, she is the keeper of the house cooking, cleaning, washing. She is strong. She can do it. Night a different story. Her father sleeps on the floor where her mother died. Her brother Frank carves strange messages on his bedroom wall and sometimes even on himself. Her little sister wets the bed or battles haunting nightmares. Isabel sees it all, tries to help them, and wonders what happened to that beautiful life. But strange memories start coming back to her, bits and pieces that aren't so pretty. She begins to wonder what is truth and what is dream. And she begins to wonder if she can do this second job, the job of *Keeper of the Night*.

Learning Opportunities

1. Isabel tells her story in very short narratives, essays, poems, and even lists. How does this combination support the purpose of the novel?
2. The novel involves the relationships in many different families, not just Isabel's. Discuss the reason for including these different families.
3. Blood and water play important roles in the story. Find where each is mentioned. Then discuss how each supports the story's purpose.
4. Auntie Bernadette is a paradox—a healer who takes Tylenol and has a withered hand. She cannot heal herself. Discuss how this character functions in the novel. Consider the fact that she is the mother's sister. Contrast her to Auntie Minerva, the father's sister.
5. Discuss the function of the fiesta in the story.
6. Using your library's resources, learn the cha cha. Teach the dance to other members of the group.
7. Discuss the importance of the setting to the story.
8. Using your library's resources, research the signs of depression and its treatment. You may wish to start by reading *Depression* (Related Work 5).

Related Works

1. Donnelly, Jennifer. **A Northern Light.** (See full booktalk in "History/ Period"/"Choices in Change," pages 220 to 223.) Sixteen-year-old Mathilda, overwhelmed by her family's expectations after

her mother's death and the attention of a handsome local boy, eventually decides to leave home and establish her own life as a writer.

2. Holubitsky, Katherine. **Alone at Ninety Foot.** Victoria, BC: Orca Book Publishers, 1999. 169p. $5.95pa. ISBN 1 55143 129 7. [fiction] MJS (See full booktalk in *Booktalks and More,* 2003, pages 201 to 203.) Fourteen-year-old Pamela Mary Collins isolates herself at Ninety Foot, the site of her mother's suicide, until her father's new girlfriend helps her build some new perspectives and stronger self-esteem.

3. Nolan, Han. **Dancing on the Edge.** New York: Puffin Books, 1997. 244p. $4.99pa. ISBN 0 14 130203 8. [fiction] JS (See full booktalk in *Booktalks and More,* 2003, pages 26 to 28.) Sixteen-year-old Miracle McCloy becomes withdrawn and self-destructive in reaction to the lies her grandmother tells her about her mother and father.

4. McCormick, Patricia. **Cut.** Asheville, NC: Front Street, 2000. 168p. $16.95. ISBN 1 886910 61 8. [fiction] JS (See full booktalk in *Booktalks and More,* 2003, pages 169 to 171.) Fifteen-year-old Callie cuts herself in reaction to her parents' neglect and accepts therapy after her father admits his own responsibility for problems in the household.

5. Silverstein, Alvin, Virginia Silverstein, and Laura Silverstein Nunn. **Depression** Springfield, NJ: Enslow Publishers, 1997. 128p. (Diseases and People.) $18.95. ISBN 0 89490 713 1. [nonfiction] MJS The book explains the disease, relates its history, provides guidelines for recognizing it, and suggests sources of treatment for it.

ɕʃɕʃ

Hosler, Jay. Clan Apis.

Columbus, OH: Active Synapse, 2000. 158p. $15.00.
ISBN 1 4046 1367 6. [graphic] JS/A

Themes/Topics: life cycle of the honeybee

Summary/Description

In five chapters, Hosler describes the life cycle of the honeybee through the life journey of Nyuki, a worker bee. Chapter 1: "Transitions," starts with the "Big Bloom" theory and describes the larvae stage. In Chapter 2: "Swarm," Nyuki leaves the hive with the queen and finds a new home. In Chapter 3: "Hide and Seek," Nyuki learns to cope with her natural predators. Although, she resolves never to leave the hive again, she is reminded that no one gets out of life alive and that risk is an inherent part of living. Chapter 4: "Homefront" depicts the many threats to the hive, its defenses, construction, and interaction. Chapter 5: "The Plan" is Nyuki's attempt to live on through the knowledge she gives others and the new flower growth as her dead body fertilizes.

"Bee Lines," which follows the story, includes bee trivia, a bibliography, and contact information for educators (www.jayhosler.com/clanapis. html or ActiveSynapse@hotmail.com). "Killer Bee," a "promotional mini comic" follows "Bee Lines."

Booktalk

Most people think honeybees are pretty cute. They paint them on greeting cards and hang their pictures on the wall. It's a compliment for someone to say that a person is "as busy as a bee." The real life details, though, are a little grimmer. The bee's sisters bury them alive. Bee larvae build their cocoons with their own waste. Bees from competitive hives kill each other to get more honey. In fact, another bee is a bee's own worst enemy. And speaking of the honey that we all like to eat—Well that's bee vomit. *Clan Apis* follows Nyuki, a worker bee, from listening to her first stories about the "Big Bloom" theory, the way life for all bees began, to her death. Bees face the fact that nobody gets out of life alive. The eyes of Nyuki have a whole different way of looking at the world.

Learning Opportunities

1. Throughout the book, Nyuki introduces us to other insects. Using your library's resources, research their lives. Share the information that you find with the group. You may wish to begin your research with *Insects: Spiders and Other Terrestrial Arthropods* or *Insect* (Related Works 4 and 5).

2. Copying Hosler's style, tell the story of an insect selected in Learning Opportunity 1.

3. List the most interesting thing that Hosler's book taught you about a bee's life. Share, with the group, the information and why you thought it was interesting.

4. List the most important insight that Nyuki's story gave you about your own life. Share that insight with the group.

5. Read both *A Hive for the Honeybee* (Related Work 3) and *Clan Apis*. Both works give the bee human characteristics. Compare the human qualities each author develops. Then discuss how humanizing the bee helps each author achieve very different purposes.

Related Works

1. Clement-Davies, David. **Fire Bringer.** New York: Firebird, 1999. 498p. $6.99pa. ISBN 0 14 230060 8. [fiction] JS In this animal fantasy based on the real facts of deer life, Rannoch becomes the leader of the deer and decides to direct them away from a life of violence.
2. Johnson, Spencer, M. D. **Who Moved My Cheese?** New York: G. P. Putnam's Sons, 1998. 94p. $19.95. ISBN 0 399 14446 3. [fiction] JS/A This allegory about mice teaches people how to deal with change in their lives.
3. Lally, Soinbhe. **A Hive for the Honeybee.** New York: Arthur A. Levine Books, 1996. 226p. $16.95. ISBN 0 590 51038 X. [fiction] MJS (See full booktalk in *Booktalks Plus*, 2001, pages 179 to 181.) The hive allegory portrays the lives of honeybees as they develop as much individualism as possible within the constraints of fate.
4. McGavin, George C. (text), and Steve Gorton (photography). **Insects Spiders and Other Terrestrial Arthropods.** New York: Dorling Kindersley, Inc., 2000. 255p. (Dorling Kindersley Handbooks.) $18.95. ISBN 0 7894 5337 1. [reference] MJS Divided into 41 main sections, each explaining a separate order of terrestrial arthropods, the book also divides the sections into entries that describe the characteristics of each family with photographs of representative species.
5. Mound, Laurence. **Insect.** New York: Alfred A. Knopf, 1990. 63p. (Eyewitness Books.) $19.00. ISBN 0 679 80441 2. [nonfiction] MJS This book describes insects in general and moves to characteristics that distinguish one group from another. It also cites movies and books that have humanized insects to carry out particular themes or fantasies.

꺄꺼

Park, Linda Sue. **A Single Shard.**

New York: Clarion Books, 2001. 152p. $15.00. ISBN 0 395 97827 0. [fiction] MJS

Themes/Topics: Korea, family, craftsmanship, faithfulness, historical novel

Summary/Description

In a small village, on the west coast of Korea, in the middle to late twelfth century, a young boy named Tree-ear lives with the old, crippled Crane-man under a bridge. Tree-ear, scavenging even for a little food, is fascinated by the work of Min the potter. Inspecting the pottery too closely, he breaks a piece, and agrees to work nine days in reparation. He chops wood for the kilns, a most menial and physically demanding job. At the end of his obligation, he asks if he might work for the potter. He hopes that someday the potter will give him lessons. The potter cannot pay him but must feed him. Min's kind wife provides food and clothes, which Tree-ear shares with Crane-man. Now Tree-ear cuts and drains the clay. Word comes that a royal commission is imminent. Kang, another potter, wins a limited commission with his new, flashy technique, but the royal representative asks Min to send additional work to Songdo, the capital, to gain a permanent commission. Tree-ear volunteers to carry Min's prize vases to the commissioner, even though Min refuses to teach him how to throw pots. On the road, bandits destroy the vases. Tree-ear rescues one small shard and carries it to the representative, who awards Min a permanent commission. Tree-ear returns to find that Crane-man died in an accident, that Min and his wife want him to live in their home, and that Min has seen molding work that Tree-ear secretly completed. Min offers him a pottery wheel. The "Author's Note" explains necessary background about Korean culture, geography, history, and pottery.

Booktalk

Ask if anyone in the group knows what shard means. Ask a volunteer to explain or explain it yourself.

Tree-ear is an orphan. You might say that he is just a shard of his family. He was named after the mushroom that grows on tree trunks. Like that mushroom, he has no parents, only the crippled, old Crane-man. Together, they comb the rubbish dumps and fields for food and live under a bridge. Sometimes they can catch a fish. Tree-ear has nothing, and yet he dreams. Again and again, he approaches the workplace of Min, the great potter. First he just looks. (*Read page 15 in Chapter 2, beginning with "For the first time ..." and ending with "... the lid of the jug."*) Then he sees a box. It is very uninteresting on the outside, but Tree-ear knows the inside must be a treasure. He opens the box to see, hears an angry shout, feels the rapid blows, and drops it. The box indeed holds a treasure. Tree-ear must repay what he has destroyed. That repayment, often brutal and hard, begins Tree-ear's life journey— a journey that helps form not only many beautiful works of art, but also Tree-ear's heart and soul—all from *A Single Shard*.

Learning Opportunities

1. Tree-ear is a talented artist, but he has many other talents and abilities as well. List the qualities that make him a successful person. Then give specifics from the book to support your opinion.

2. Using your library's resources, find pictures and more information about celadon pottery. Share the information that you find with the group.
3. On page 93, begin reading with the words "I am going to ..." and end with the words "my friend." Discuss how Crane-man's advice applies to more than just a physical journey.
4. On page 97, Crane-man observes, "... the same wind that blows one door shut often blows another open...." Discuss how these words apply to other situations in the novel and in life.
5. On page 115, Tree-ear reflects, "We are afraid of the things we do not know—just because we do not know them." Do you agree?
6. List each adult in the novel. Decide what that character contributes to revealing Tree-ear's character and the novel's purpose.
7. Discuss how the novel deals with the balance of sad and happy events.

Related Works

1. Alsup, Janet. "The Artistic Identity: Art as a Catalyst for 'Self Actualization' in Lois Lowry's *Gathering Blue* and Linda Sue Park's *A Single Shard.*" *The ALAN Review.* (Fall 2003) 13–16. This discussion asserts that the pursuit of talent leads each person from an ego-centered perception to responsibility in a greater community.
2. McCaughrean, Geraldine. **The Kite Rider.** New York: HarperCollins, 2001. 272p. $15.95. $23.95. ISBN 0 06 623874 9. [fiction] MJS With a remarkable ability to construct kites and much perseverance, twelve-year-old Haoyou supports his family after his father's death and finds an extended family to which he can belong.
3. Morris, Neil, et al. (text), and Paola Ravaglia et al. (illus.). **The History of the World: From the Big Bang to the Third Millennium.** New York: Enchanted Lion Books, 2000. 288p. $29.95. ISBN 1 59270 019 5. [nonfiction] JS With short explanations and many pictures, this volume helps place historical events in relation to each other. Pages 98 and 99 deal with "Medieval Japan and Korea." A picture of a ceramic piece appears on page 99.
4. Ryan, Pam Muñoz. **Becoming Naomi León.** New York: Scholastic Press, 2004. 256p. $16.95. ISBN 0 439 26969 5. [fiction] MJ A ten-year-old girl finds her home and identity through her Mexican heritage and her carving talent.
5. Whelan, Gloria. **Homeless Bird.** New York: HarperCollins Publishers, 2000. 216p. $15.95. ISBN 0 06 028454 4. [fiction] MJS (See full booktalk in *Booktalks and More,* 2003, pages 215 to 217.)

Thirteen-year-old Koly marries to free her family of the burden of supporting her. Suffering the abuse and abandonment of her mother-in-law after her husband dies, she rebuilds her life through her embroidery talent.

6.   Wilson, Diane Lee. **I Rode a Horse of Milk White Jade.** New York: Orchard Books, 1998. 232p. $17.95. ISBN 0 531 330024 2. [fiction] MJ (See full booktalk in *Booktalks Plus,* 2001, pages 8 to 10.) A handicapped twelve-year-old Chinese girl living in the time of Kublai Khan rejects the idea that she is a jinx, undertakes a dangerous physical journey to carry a message to the great Khan, and discovers her own talents and love.

Multi-Cultural America

ඏ෬

Flake, Sharon G. **Money Hungry.**
New York: Hyperion Books for Children/Jump at the Sun, 2001. 187p. $15.99.
ISBN 0 786 80548 X. [fiction] MJS

Themes/Topics: homelessness, responsibility, family, friendship, biracial conflicts

Summary/Description

Thirteen-year-old Raspberry Hill, living in the projects with her mother, constantly tries to make money because she fears living, as she and her mother used to, on the streets. She hides over $600.00 in her room. Ja'nae, her friend, borrows $200.00 to finance an unsuccessful meeting with the mother who deserted her. She promises to pay back Raspberry by helping her in a cleaning venture, but keeps the money. When Raspberry takes and then returns it, Ja'nae reacts in her diary. Her grandfather misreads the entry and accuses Raspberry of stealing. Angry and upset, Raspberry's mother throws Raspberry's money out the window and marks the house. Local thieves strip it. With the help of the mother's boyfriend and the man who works at their corner, Raspberry and her mother, homeless again, get shelter and the promise of a more permanent home.

Booktalk

What will *you* do for money? Raspberry Hill will do just about anything legal. She will sell stale candy, wash cars, skip lunch, or clean houses.

And she is willing to get her friends to help her, even if they don't want to. Nobody is as hungry for money as Raspberry. And if she stays so obsessed, her only friends may be Washington, Lincoln, and Jackson. Raspberry lives in the projects. Her friends don't. She wants to move out, but not to the street—where she and her mother survived before. For Raspberry, money can make good things happen and stop the bad. Raspberry is going to do what it takes to get it—even if everyone thinks she's just *Money Hungry*.

Learning Opportunities

1. Money and people's attitudes toward it are major issues in the novel. Identify incidents in the story that involve money. What does each reveal about the character?
2. In the story, is "Money the root of all evil"?
3. Several adults in the story make critical mistakes. Identify some of those mistakes. Discuss the harmful effects those mistakes have on the teenagers.
4. Several adults in the story make strong decisions that help them and the young people around them. Identify these decisions, why they are important, and how others perceive them.
5. Discuss the many ways the title might apply to the story.
6. Using the Internet and other library resources, research the homeless population in this country. Find out the percentage of children who are homeless and the services offered to them.

ርያ ቀነ

Flake, Sharon G. **Begging for Change.**
New York: Hyperion Books for Children/Jump at the Sun, 2003. 235p. $15.99.
ISBN 0 786 80601 X. [fiction] MJS

Themes/Topics: poverty, family, responsibility, identity, trust

Summary/Description

When Raspberry Hill's mother is "whacked over the head" by a neighbor, Raspberry's father, a crack addict who begs for change, comes to the hospital. Raspberry, embarrassed by her father, fears that her mother will die, leaving her alone. She steals money from Zora, the daughter of Dr. Mitchell, whom her mother dates. As the story develops, Raspberry wonders if, resembling her father physically, she will also find excuses to take from others. While dealing with that possibility, she falls in love with Sato, a boy from her neighborhood, becomes more estranged from Zora, and helps her friend, Mai, deal with her racial identity. Raspberry's father steals from her, and Raspberry begins to understand how stealing destroys trust. With guilt and the pressure of friends and family, she and her mother start over in a new neighborhood. She pays back the money, tries to mend her relationship with Zora, becomes a couple with Sato, and hopes that her father will conquer his drug habit and become self-supporting.

Booktalk

Hold up a copy of Money Hungry *and* Begging for Change *as you speak.*

Money Hungry Raspberry Hill is at it again. Her mother gets "whacked over the head" by mouthy and tough Shikita Nixon, their neighbor. Raspberry worries that she will be on the streets once more, penniless and friendless. She can't depend on her father, who uses all his money and everyone else's to stay drunk or high. When her good friend Zora leaves her purse unguarded, Raspberry steals money from it. Zora has plenty, and neither her doctor father nor Zora will ever wind up living on the streets. But Raspberry forgets that her mother and Zora's father are pretty close now. Someday, she and Zora might live in the same house—like sisters. She knows that sisters who steal don't stay close. And suddenly she wonders if she shares more with her father than just looks. She, too, might find herself hanging out on the corners of life and just—*Begging for Change*.

Learning Opportunities

1. Fathers are a central issue in *Begging for Change*. Identify each character who is a father or takes a father's role. Then discuss how each carries out that fatherhood role.
2. The title *Begging for Change* can carry several meanings. Discuss each way it might be interpreted.
3. Discuss what Raspberry might learn from each of her friends.
4. In *Begging for Change*, Raspberry's mother writes letters to Shiketa Nixon. Discuss the letters and what they reveal about the mother.
5. Miracle and Miz Evelyn appear only a few times in *Begging for Change*, but have a great impact. Discuss their roles.
6. Responsibility is a central theme in the novel. Cite one situation or character focusing on that theme.
7. Distinguish among forgiving, helping, and enabling. Then illustrate each with examples from life or the books.

8. In *Begging for Change,* Raspberry and her mother move out of the neighborhood. Discuss the good and bad aspects of that decision.

9. Discuss the following statement by Dr. Mitchell, "A thousand locks won't keep you safe if you let the boogeyman make your bed."

Related Works

1. Angelou, Maya. **I Know Why the Caged Bird Sings.** New York: Bantam Books, 1993. 389p. $5.99pa. ISBN 0 553 27937 8. [nonfiction] S/A Maya Angelou describes her coming-of-age that includes family conflict and homelessness.

2. Crutcher, Chris. **Whale Talk.** New York: Greenwillow Books, 2001. 220p. $15.89. ISBN 0 06 029369. [fiction] JS The Tao Jones born from Caucasian, Japanese, and African-American ancestry recalls his senior year, during which he formed a successful swim team of student misfits and saw his father killed by a bigot.

3. McDonald, Janet. **Chill Wind.** New York: Farrar, Straus and Giroux/Frances Foster Books, 2002. 134p. $16.00. ISBN 0 374 39958 1. [fiction] MJS In this sequel to *Spellbound,* nineteen-year-old Aisha, mother of two, realizes that her welfare will be terminated in sixty days while her friend Raven is reaping the positive benefits of hard work and honesty.

4. McDonald, Janet. **Spellbound.** New York: Farrar, Straus and Giroux/Frances Foster Books, 2001. 138p. $16.00. ISBN 0 374 37140 7. [fiction] MJS Raven Jefferson faces the responsibility of her pregnancy and vows to finish high school, go to college, and be self-supporting in contrast to Aisha Ingram, her friend, who plans to lie and play the welfare system.

5. McDonald, Janet. **Twists and Turns.** New York: Farrar, Straus and Giroux/Frances Foster Books, 2003. 135p. $16.00. ISBN 0 374 39955 7. [fiction] MJS Keeba and Teesha, friends of Raven (Related Work 4) and Aisha (Related Work 3) find success in the hair business after overcoming jealous friends, scheming politicians, and greedy landlords.

6. Myers, Walter Dean. **145th Street: Short Stories.** New York: Delacorte Press, 2000. 151p. $15.95. ISBN 0 385 32137 6. [fiction] MJS (See full booktalk in *Booktalks and More,* 2003, pages 91 to 93.) In ten short stories about residents of Harlem's 145th Street, Myers portrays tragedy, frustration, achievement, and compassion.

7. Meyers, William Dean. **The Dream Bearer.** New York: HarperCollins Publishers, 2003. 181p. $16.89. ISBN 0 06 029522 8. [fiction] JS In

the midst of family strife, old Moses Littlejohn, a stranger gifted with bearing dreams, explores the borders between anger and insanity as people cope with the limits imposed by poverty.

☙❧

Hidier, Tanuja Desai. **Born Confused.**
New York: Scholastic Press, 2002. 432p. $16.95. ISBN 0 439 35762 4. [fiction] S

Themes/Topics: arranged marriage, lesbian lifestyle, transvestites, generational relations, ethnic and personal identity, friendship

Summary/Description

Seventeen-year-old Dimple rebels against her parents' traditions by trying to be more like her "supertwin" and best friend—blond, model-thin Gwyn. After Dimple comes home drunk and sick on her seventeenth birthday, her parents decide to help arrange her marriage. They introduce her to Kasha, the son of a rediscovered old friend. Dimple's resistance, attraction, and finally love for this young man as well as Gwyn's attraction to him forces Dimple to examine her feelings about her parents, culture, friendships, and self.

Dimple confronts Gwyn's drinking, drug use, and jealousy; her cousin's lesbian lifestyle; the dreams her parents ignored; and her culture's beliefs and rituals. Using a camera, a gift from her grandfather, she overcomes their language barrier and learns to release frustrations and communicate feelings. With pictures focusing on the transformation of a transvestite from a man to a woman, Dimple explains her own summer transformation, expresses her feelings to Kasha, and receives respect and recognition as a photographer.

The content requires a mature audience.

Booktalk

Dimple Lala wants to be "USA all the way" even if her parents are from India. She even tries to look like her blond, model-thin friend Gwyn. Her parents think Dimple is already beautiful and will be even more beautiful if she respects them and their beliefs. When Dimple comes home drunk from an American date, she puts herself on a collision course with Mom and Dad. They decide it's time to be matchmakers, and the match is a good Indian boy—well a good American boy from a good Indian family. Dimple decides to show him how much she dislikes dressing up in a sari and making nice with someone who prefers to talk about old phono-graph records with her father. So much for first impressions. When this "suitable boy" turns out to be the DJ at the cutting-edge Indian Club, Gwyn decides to do Dimple a favor and take him off her hands. Now Dimple has second thoughts. Will she get a second chance? Or will she end up the way she started—*Born Confused*?

Learning Opportunities

1. In Chapter 24, Dimple relates the folk tale of the five blind men who were asked to describe the elephant. Read the story that appears at the end of the chapter. Explain why it is so important to understand.
2. The number of English words that come from Indian words sur-prises Dimple. Research the number of words that come from your own ethnic heritage. Share your list in a display or compare it with other lists researched by members of the group.
3. In Chapter 8, Kavita reveals some of the conflicts of Indian/American life and shares two versions of an Indian/American alpha-bet. Make up a similar alphabet that identifies you and the situa-tions and conflicts that you face.
4. As Dimple learns about her parents' early life, she begins to respect and enjoy them as people. Interview an adult whom you know well. After the interview, tell them or write a letter in which you explain what surprised you and why.
5. At the end of Chapter 33, Kavita talks about finding one's iden-tity. In Chapter 38, Dimple and Kavita talk about exploring new beginnings, concentrating on the outside instead of the inside, and pursuing individual strengths. The conversations focus on the Indian/American experience. How could they apply it to a world beyond that experience?
6. In Chapter 40, Dimple moves her photography from a black and white to a color world. Discuss the significance of that decision.
7. Many of Dimple's realizations come from observing the love of older, heterosexual, and homosexual couples. Discuss what Dimple learns about love, family, and friendship in her observations.
8. Discuss the many ways that Hidier unifies the story.

Related Works

1. Glenn, Mel. **Split Image: A Story in Poems.** New York: HarperCollins, 2000. 159p. $15.95. ISBN 0 688 16249 5. [poetry] S The poems that structure the novel present Laura Li's life and

death through the eyes of Laura Li, her parents, the school staff, and her fellow students. No one, not even Laura Li, sees herself clearly. Overwhelmed by trying to live up to the expectations of two cultures, she commits suicide.

2. Na, Ah. **A Step from Heaven.** Asheville, NC: Front Street, 2001. 156p. $15.95. ISBN 1 886910 58 8. [fiction] S (See full booktalk in *Booktalks and More,* 2003, pages 33 to 35.) In short reflections, a young girl records her journey through family and cultural conflict. Photographs are central to the story.

3. Nam, Vickie (ed.). **Yell-Oh Girls!** New York: HarperCollins/Quill, 2001. 294p. $13.00pa. ISBN 0 06 095944 4. [nonfiction] JS (See full booktalk in *Booktalks and More,* 2003, pages 262 to 264.) Through poems and essays, young girls express the problems of being Asian in the United States.

4. Staples, Suzanne Fisher. **Shiva's Fire.** New York: Farrar, Straus and Giroux/Frances Foster Books, 2000. 276p. $17.00. ISBN 0 374 36824 4. [fiction] JS Parvati, a gifted dancer, pursues her talent instead of romance. Her journey to this decision highlights the importance of dance in the Indian culture, and contrasts the decision that Dimple's mother makes.

5. Whelan, Gloria. **Homeless Bird.** New York: HarperCollins, 2000. 216p. $15.95. ISBN 0 06 028454 4. [fiction] MJS (See full booktalk in *Booktalks and More,* 2003, pages 215 to 217.). Thirteen-year-old Koly is betrothed to a terminally ill boy. After his death, she begins her journey to independence.

ᘓᘓ

Mochizuki, Ken. Beacon Hill Boys.

New York: Scholastic, 2002. 208p. $16.95. ISBN 0 439 26749 8. [fiction] JS

Themes/Topics: seventies, minority rights, stereotypes, Japanese American history, family, peer pressure, historical setting

Summary/Description

Sixteen-year-old Dan and his friends are Asian students in the Beacon Hill area of Seattle during the early 1970s. At Herbert Hoover High, whose population is one-third white, one-third African-American, and one-third Asian, they resist the pressure of parents and community to excel academically and fit in socially. They experiment with drugs, imitate other races, and focus on popular music. Dan, joined by other minorities, pressures the school to institute a Comparative American Cultures class, where he can learn about the Japanese camps and war service that his family refuses to talk about. His rebellion and persistence create family conflict but also understanding. By the end of the story, he questions his friend's decisions, bonds with his family, and accepts responsibility for his actions.

Booktalk

Dan Inagaki is sixteen and part of a 1970s Asian family. His older brother Brad, superathlete and student, is the school and family star. His mother is always working—even when she is talking. His father sets tough rules and high standards. His little brother Steve supplies the smart remarks. His grandmother just loves to see him walk in the door. And Dan? Well, Dan is the quitter, the rabble-rouser, the guy who wants to make new rules for life. He wants to know why dating white girls is such a status thing, why Asian kids always have to make the highest grades, and why Japanese adults mention camps but won't tell their children anything about them. Asking questions all the time, Dan isn't too popular at home or at school. That's why he fits in with the *Beacon Hill Boys*, his loser rebel friends. But maybe Dan and friends aren't such losers after all. Maybe they just have a different definition of winning.

Learning Opportunities

1. Dan wants to understand the Japanese experience in World War II. Research both the military and civilian experiences in World War II. Share your information with the group. You may wish to start by reading Related Works 1, 2, and 4.
2. Using the "Discography," a musical bibliography, included at the end of *Beacon Hill Boys*, listen and react to the music of the time period.
3. Dan and each of his friends have a different way of rebelling. Describe the method that each uses and discuss which is constructive and which is destructive.
4. Women and girls play interesting roles in the novel. List each female and explain the impact she has on the story.
5. African-American students are an important part of the story. List the African-American characters and explain the role of each.
6. Interview a parent or someone who is at least thirty years older than you are. Ask them about a defining event of their lives that involved their country. Then ask them how that experience separated them from or joined them to the preceding and subsequent generations.
7. How does Mochizuki unify his story? Why do you think he uses this method?

Related Works

1. Cooper, Michael L. **Fighting for Honor: Japanese Americans and World War II.** New York: Clarion Books, 2000. 118p. $16.00. ISBN 0 395 91375 6. [nonfiction] MJS This description of the camps and the outstanding war record of the Japanese-Americans illustrates why Japanese parents are reluctant to discuss the details with their children. It also reveals the outstanding family values that they wish to pass on to them.

2. Cooper, Michael. **Remembering Manzanar: Life in a Japanese Relocation Camp.** New York: Clarion Books, 2002. 68p. $15.00. ISBN 0 618 06778 7. [nonfiction] MJS With photographs and text, Cooper describes the origin of the camp, life in the camp, and the Manzanar Pilgrimage that began in 1969 to educate young Japanese about the hardships their parents and grandparents faced.

3. Denenberg, Barry. **The Journal of Ben Uchida: Citizen 13559 Mirror Lake Internment Camp, California, 1942.** New York: Scholastic, Inc., 1999. 157p. (A Dear America Book: My Name is America.) $10.95. ISBN 0 590 48531 8. [fiction] MJ Twelve-year-old Ben Uchida, in a very American voice, records his World War II experiences as a Japanese-American living in Mirror Lake, an Internment Camp.

4. Fremon, David K. **Japanese American Internment in American History.** Berkeley Heights, NJ: Enslow Publishers, Inc., 1996. 128p. (In American History.) $20.95. ISBN 0 89490 767 0. [nonfiction] MJS This account of the Internment camps includes the outstanding record of the 442nd Regiment.

5. Glasgow, Jacqueline N. "Reconciling Memories of Internment Camp Experiences during WWII in Children's and Young Adult Literature." *The ALAN Review.* (Fall, 2002): 41–45. This article emphasizes the importance of accurate historical memory and provides a bibliography and discussion that will help librarians and teachers achieve that end.

6. Meyers, Walter Dean. **The Greatest: Muhammad Ali.** New York: Scholastic Press, 2000. 192p. $16.95. ISBN 0 590 54342 3. [nonfiction] MJS In this biography, Meyers includes Ali's declaration of Black Pride and the punishment he received for refusing to fight in Vietnam.

7. Otsuka, Julie. **When the Emperor Was Divine.** New York: Alfred A. Knopf, 2002. 144p. $18.00. ISBN 0 375 41429 0. [fiction] S/A Otsuka describes the banishment, internment in the grim desert camp, and the return to a ransacked house and an unwelcoming community. All these experiences teach the children not to stand out.

8. Yamaguchi, Yoji. **A Student's Guide to Japanese American Genealogy.** Phoenix, AZ: Oryx Press, 1996. 168p. (Oryx American Family Tree Series.) $24.95. ISBN 0 89774 979 0. [nonfiction] MJS This source explains how to use family, outside sources, oral history and basic knowledge of kinship protocol to research Japanese genealogy. Chapter 4, "Oral History," would be useful in completing Learning Opportunity 6, even though the activity does not specify that the person interviewed should be Japanese.

ᘓᘔ

Soto, Gary. **The Afterlife.**
New York: Harcourt, Inc., 2003. 161p. $16.00. ISBN 0 15 204774 3. [fiction] JS

Themes/Topics: Mexican Americans, murder, suicide, grief, life after death, revenge, personal choices

Summary/Description

Stabbed to death in a restroom when he comments on a man's yellow shoes, eighteen-year-old Jesús, having grown up in a Mexican/ Hmong Fresno neighborhood, moves from life to the afterlife, and sees how much his family loves him and wants to protect him, and how much he meant to his friends. Learning he has some worldly power left, Jesús finds "yellow shoes" scheming with a fellow thug. Jesús opens up their warehouse of stolen goods, and with the ghost of a homeless man, continues to harass the killer. He briefly touches those who miss him, and, with much satisfaction, sees his cousin refuse to avenge his death. He falls in love with Crystal, beautiful and pampered, whom he remembers from picking grapes on her parents' farm. Crystal, an outstanding student and school leader, rejected from Harvard and Stanford, thought she could never make it big and committed suicide. She realizes her family's pain and now misses simple joys. As the two fade, they move into the afterlife. Jesús describes them as "long distance runners who didn't get very far." "Selected Spanish Works and Phrases" and their translations appear at the end of the novel.

Booktalk

(*Read from the opening of Chapter 1 to the sentence, "When I opened them a minute later, I was dead," on page 4.*)

This is the way eighteen-year-old Jesús ended his earthly life. At East Fresno High School, they called him Chuy. He was pretty popular.

And that girl in the back row of his English class, Rachel, really did want to meet him. But now all those plans are finished. It's a new life now, *The Afterlife,* with all the surprises and newly released souls that happen in the journey between.

Learning Opportunities

1. *Buried Onions* (Related Work 5) is the companion book to *The Afterlife.* After reading both books, discuss Eddie's decision not to seek revenge.
2. Discuss why Soto may have decided to write this companion book to *Buried Onions.*
3. Jesús describes Crystal and himself as "long distance runners who didn't get very far." Discuss how many ways "long distance runners" can apply to Jesús and Crystal. How might the phrase apply to Eddie?
4. Discuss the character of Robert Montgomery. Why do you think Soto includes him?
5. In describing the book, the publisher uses the words "Oftentimes hilarious." If you disagree explain why. If you agree, point to passages and events that you perceive as humorous and discuss why Soto would include humor in the novel, especially in relation to *Buried Onions* (Related Work 5).

Related Works

1. Cadnum, Michael. **Starfall: Phaeton and the Chariot of the Sun.** New York: Scholastic, Inc., 2004. 128p. $16.95. ISBN 0 439 54533 1. [fiction] JS In this retelling of the Greek myth, Phaeton never sees how much people love and respect him for himself.
2. Helbig, Alethea K., and Agnes Regan Perkins. **Dictionary of American Young Adult Fiction, 1997–2001: Books of Recognized Merit.** Westport, CT: Greenwood Press, 2004. 558p. $75.00. ISBN 0 313 32430 1. [professional reference] This dictionary provides author information, book summaries, and character descriptions concerning literature for young adults. The *Buried Onions* entry appears on pages 45 and 46. The Gary Soto entry appears on pages 330 and 331.
3. Johnston, Tony. **Any Small Goodness: A Novel of the Barrio.** New York: Blue Sky Press, 2001. 128p. $15.95. ISBN 0 439 18936 5. [fiction] MJ When Arturo is eleven, he moves from Mexico to the barrio of East Los Angeles. His teacher tries to Americanize him

by changing his name to Arthur, but Arturo and his friends finally decide to take their names back and live in the best traditions of their culture.

4. Rylant, Cynthia. **The Heavenly Village.** New York: The Blue Sky Press, 1999. 95p. $15.95. ISBN 0 439 04096 5. [fiction] MJS (See full booktalk in *Booktalks Plus,* 2001, pages 52 to 54.) In this village, between heaven and earth, souls who still have business on earth complete their tasks before moving on.

5. Soto, Gary. **Buried Onions.** New York: Harcourt Brace, 1997. 149p. $17.00. ISBN 0 15 201333 4. [fiction] JS (See full booktalk in *Booktalks Plus,* 2001, pages 124 to 126.) Nineteen-year-old Eddie goes through the process of deciding whether or not to avenge Jesús's death and finally decides to leave the neighborhood.

6. Woodson, Jacqueline. **Behind You.** New York: G. P. Putnam's Sons, 2004. 128p. $15.99. ISBN 0 399 23988 X. [fiction] JS In this series of first-person essays, Jeremiah Roselind, the African-American young man mistakenly killed in *If You Come Softly,* and the people who love him, work through their losses and transitions and eventually move on.

7. Woodson, Jacqueline. **If You Come Softly.** New York: G. P. Putnam's Sons, 1998. 181p. $15.99. ISBN 0 399 23112 9. [fiction] JS Jeremiah, the young man who speaks from the afterlife in *If You Come Softly,* and Ellie decide to date even when they know they will encounter resistance and condemnation for being an interracial couple. At the end of the novel, Jeremiah is shot and killed.

Index

About the Author

LUCY SCHALL a retired middle school English teacher, is a reviewer for VOYA, and author of two other acclaimed booktalking guides, *Booktalks Plus* and *Booktalks and More,* both published with Libraries Unlimited.